D1685206

Becker Professional Education, a global leader in professional education, has been d
for ACCA for more than 20 years, and thousands of candidates studying for the ACC
succeeded in their professional examinations through its Platinum and Gold ALP training centers in Central and Eastern Europe and Central Asia.*

Becker Professional Education has also been awarded ACCA Approved Content Provider Status for materials for the Diploma in International Financial Reporting (DipIFR).

Nearly half a million professionals have advanced their careers through Becker Professional Education's courses. Throughout its more than 50-year history, Becker has earned a strong track record of student success through world-class teaching, curriculum and learning tools.

We provide a single destination for individuals and companies in need of global accounting certifications and continuing professional education.

*Platinum – Moscow, Russia and Kiev, Ukraine. Gold – Almaty, Kazakhstan

Becker Professional Education's ACCA Study Materials

All of Becker's materials are authored by experienced ACCA lecturers and are used in the delivery of classroom courses.

Study Text: Gives complete coverage of the syllabus with a focus on learning outcomes. It is designed to be used both as a reference text and as part of integrated study. It also includes the ACCA Syllabus and Study Guide, exam advice and commentaries and a Study Question Bank containing practice questions relating to each topic covered.

Revision Question Bank: Exam style and standard questions together with comprehensive answers to support and prepare students for their exams. The Revision Question Bank also includes past examination questions (updated where relevant), model answers and alternative solutions and tutorial notes.

Revision Essentials Handbook*: A condensed, easy-to-use aid to revision containing essential technical content and exam guidance.

*Revision Essentials are substantially derived from content reviewed by ACCA's examining team.

Becker Professional Education
is an ACCA approved content provider

BECKER
PROFESSIONAL EDUCATION®

ACCA

PAPER F8

AUDIT AND ASSURANCE

REVISION QUESTION BANK

For Examinations to June 2017

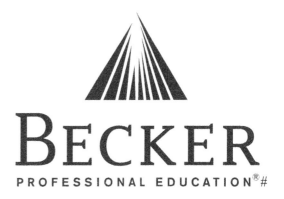

BECKER

PROFESSIONAL EDUCATION®#

No responsibility for loss occasioned to any person acting or refraining from action as a result of any material in this publication can be accepted by the author, editor or publisher.

This training material has been prepared and published by Becker Professional Development International Limited:

Parkshot House
5 Kew Road
Richmond
Surrey
TW9 2PR
United Kingdom

ISSBN: 978-1-78566-317-8

Acknowledgement

Past ACCA examination questions are the copyright of the Association of Chartered Certified Accountants and have been reproduced by kind permission.

CONTENTS

As shown by the Specimen Examination provided, Section A will include three "objective test case" questions of 10 marks each and Section B will include one 30 mark and two 20 mark constructed response ("long") questions. Questions indicated * are not current exam style but provided for further revision of areas of the syllabus.

COMPUTER BASED EXAM SUPPLEMENT

This supplement includes OT question types that will appear **only** in a computer-based exam, but provides valuable practice for all students whichever version of the exam they are sitting.

Question 1 NON-AUDIT ENGAGEMENTS AND TRUE AND FAIR *(non-exam style)*

(a)   Auditors are frequently required to provide assurance for a range of non-audit engagements.

    Required:

    List and explain the elements of an assurance engagement.   (5 marks)

(b)   **Explain the concept of TRUE and FAIR presentation.**   (5 marks)

                                                                           (10 marks)

Question 2 SERENA** [1]

The following scenario relates to questions 1–5

Serena Co has been trading for over 20 years and obtained a listing on a stock exchange five years ago. It provides specialist training in accounting and finance. The directors recently received an email from a significant shareholder who is concerned that Serena Co does not comply with corporate governance principles.

Serena Co's board is comprised of six directors: four executives who originally set up the company and two non-executive directors who joined Serena Co just prior to the listing. The board has not established an audit committee and no internal audit function has been set up to monitor internal controls.

The chief executive officer, Daniel Brown, has recently taken on the role of chairman of the board. The finance director and the chairman make decisions on the appointment and remuneration of the external auditors. The executive directors' remuneration is proposed by the finance director and approved by the chairman. They are paid an annual salary and share options. Since the company listed, the directors have remained unchanged continuing the practice of automatic annual reappointment.

1   **Which of the following describes the benefits to Serena of forming an audit committee?**

    (1)   The audit committee will provide a formal link between the auditors, the non-executive directors and the shareholders

    (2)   The audit committee will assume responsibility for making decisions regarding the appointment and remuneration of the external auditors and executive directors

    (3)   The audit committee will assume responsibility for the company's financial statements and budgets

    (4)   An audit committee can monitor and review the company's internal controls

    A   1 and 2
    B   2 and 3
    C   3 and 4
    D   1 and 4

---

[1] Questions highlighted ** are also presented in the supplement at the end of this Revision Question Bank with OT types applicable only to computer based exams.

2   **Which of the following individuals should be included on the audit committee?**

(1)   The CEO, Daniel Brown
(2)   The two non-executive directors
(3)   The finance director
(4)   Three of the executive directors

A   2 only
B   1 and 2
C   3 and 4 only
D   1, 3 and 4

3   The board has compiled the following responses to the email from the shareholder:

(1)   The composition of our board, with four executive directors and two non-executive directors, allows for strong governance because the executive directors understand the company's decision making and operations

(2)   Our CEO, Daniel Brown, is a strong chairman of the board because of the perspective he brings as the day-to-day leader of Serena

(3)   The inclusion of share options in the directors' remuneration package helps to keep them focused on the long-term results of Serena

(4)   One of the strengths of our board is the many years we continue to serve as directors, which gives us a deep understanding of the company's history

Which of these responses reflects a correct understanding of the principles of corporate governance?

A   3 only
B   1 and 2 only
C   3 and 4
D   1, 2 and 4

4   In a recent board meeting, Daniel Brown suggested that an internal audit department be created that reports directly to the board.

Which of the following functions could internal audit perform and be considered independent of management?

(1)   Examination of financial and operational information for management
(2)   Authorisation of transactions in excess of limits set by management
(3)   Review of accounting systems and related controls
(4)   Advising management on cost effective controls for systems and activities
(5)   Routinely preparing bank reconciliations

A   1, 3 and 5
B   2, 4 and 5
C   3, 4 and 5
D   1, 3 and 4

5 In response to Daniel Brown's suggestion, the finance director suggested that they hire Serena's external auditors to carry out the internal audit function, rather than create an internal audit department.

Under what circumstances could an internal audit function be carried out by the entity's external auditor?

A When any threats to the external auditor's objectivity have been reduced to an acceptable level

B When requested to do so by those charged with governance

C When combining the two functions would result in lower costs

D When the internal audit functions have no direct impact on the financial statements

(10 marks)

Question 3 BLUEBIRD ENTERPRISES

The following scenario relates to questions 1–5

Bluebird Enterprises Co (Bluebird) is a retail company planning to list on a stock exchange within the next six months. Management has been advised by the company's auditors about the need for compliance with corporate governance provisions. In particular, the finance director is looking to recruit non-executive directors, as he understands that Bluebird will need to establish an audit committee.

1 Which of the following best describes a benefit to Bluebird of establishing an audit committee?

A It enables executive directors to contribute independent judgement to matters of critical importance

B It offers the internal auditors a direct, formal link with the executive directors

C It enables management to delegate a thorough and detailed review of audit matters

D It provides effective and informed oversight to help ensure confidence in high-quality financial reporting

2 The finance director has two potential non-executive directors whom he is considering approaching to join the board of Bluebird. The first, Antony Goldfinch, is currently an executive sales director of a listed multi-national banking company; he sits on an audit committee of another company as a non-executive director and is agreeable to being paid a fixed fee that is not related to profits.

Which of the following is a disadvantage of appointing Anthony Goldfinch as a non-executive director?

A He works at a banking company
B He is a non-executive director of another company
C He has audit committee experience
D He is agreeable to being paid a flat fee

3   The second potential director is Jacob Mallard. Mallard is currently a finance director of a small retail company, which does not compete with Bluebird. He has expressed an interest in a fixed seven-year contract, is willing to be paid a fee only when the Bluebird's share price increases and he is the brother of Bluebird's chief executive.

Which of the following is an advantage of appointing Anthony Goldfinch as a non-executive director?

A   He is the brother of the chief executive
B   He willing to contract as a non-executive director for seven years
C   He is currently a finance director for another company
D   He is agreeable to being paid only when the share price increases

4   The following are statements that could be made about corporate governance:

(1)   It is the system by which business corporations are directed and controlled
(2)   It involves entrepreneurism, innovation, development and exploration
(3)   It aims to achieve a long-term increase in shareholder value
(4)   It narrows the expectation gap
(5)   It only applies to entities that are listed on a stock exchange

Which combination of these statements best describes the meaning of corporate governance?

A   1, 4 and 5
B   1, 2 and 5
C   1, 2 and 3
D   2, 3 and 5

5   In establishing an audit committee, the board of Bluebird should be conscious of the disadvantages of giving too much of its financial assurance responsibility to the audit committee.

Which of the following are examples of such disadvantages?

(1)   The audit committee is only empowered to make recommendations to the board not to make decisions in its own right

(2)   Directors who are not audit committee members may not fully grasp major accounting or risk issues

(3)   The full board may abdicate its responsibilities to the audit committee

(4)   There is increased risk that controls will be circumvented by collusion or inappropriate management override

A   1 and 3 only
B   2 and 3 only
C   1, 3 and 4
D   2, 3 and 4

(10 marks)

Question 4 STARK**

The following scenario relates to questions 1–5

You are a manager in the audit firm of Ali & Co, and this is the first time you have been assigned the audit of one of the firm's established clients, Stark Co (Stark). The main activity of Stark is providing investment advice to individuals on retirement planning, purchase of shares and securities and investing in tax-efficient savings schemes. Stark is regulated by the relevant financial services authority and is considered to be a public interest entity.

Mr Son has been the audit engagement partner for Stark for the previous nine years and so has excellent knowledge of the client. Mr Son has informed you that he would like his daughter Zoe to be part of the audit team this year; Zoe is currently studying for her first set of fundamentals papers for her ACCA qualification. Mr Son also informs you that Mr Far, an audit junior, received investment advice as a regular client of Stark during the year and intends to do the same next year.

In an initial meeting with Stark's finance director, you learn that the audit team will not be entertained on Stark's yacht this year. Instead, he has arranged a balloon flight costing less than one-tenth of the expense of using the yacht and hopes this will be acceptable. The director also states that the fee for tax advisory services this year should be based on a percentage of tax saved.

1   From a review of the information above, your audit assistant has highlighted some of the potential risks to independence in respect of the audit of Stark.

        (1)   Engagement partner has been in the position for nine years
        (2)   The audit junior receives investment advice
        (3)   The audit team has been offered a balloon flight
        (4)   The fee for tax advisory services will be based on a percentage of tax saved

        Which of the following options correctly identifies the valid threats to independence and allocates the threat to the appropriate category?

	Familiarity	*Self-interest*	*Self-review*
A	1 only	3 only	4 only
B	1 and 2	4 only	3 only
C	1 and 3	3 and 4	4 only
D	3 only	1 and 4	1 and 2

2   **In relation to Mr Son holding the role for nine years and his request that his daughter be part of the audit team, which of the following safeguards should be implemented in order to comply with ACCA's *Code of Ethics and Conduct*?**

        A   Ali & Co should resign from the audit
        B   An independent review partner should be appointed
        C   The audit partner should be removed from the audit team
        D   The audit partner should be removed if his daughter is part of the team

3   **In line with ACCA's *Code of Ethics and Conduct*, which of the following factors must be considered before the tax advisory services engagement can be accepted?**

        (1)   The level of tax expertise in the audit engagement team
        (2)   The period of time over which the advice is expected to be provided
        (3)   The extent to which the advice will be supported by tax law or regulation
        (4)   The extent to which the outcome of the tax advice will have a material effect on the financial statements

A	1 and 4 only	
B	1, 2 and 3	
C	1, 2 and 4	
D	3 and 4 only	

4   **What safeguards, if any, are required in relation to the basis for the fees for taxation services and the external audit assignment?**

A   As long as the total fee received from Stark is less than 15% of Ali & Co's total fee income, no safeguards are required

B   Stark Co should be informed that the taxation services must be based on time spent and experience of staff involved

C   As long as the audit fee is based on time spent and experience of staff involved, no safeguards are required

D   Taxation services cannot be accepted as there are no safeguards to reduce the threat to objectivity in the conduct of the external audit

5   The finance director further suggests that Ali & Co be paid a fixed fee for representing Stark in a dispute regarding the amount of sales tax payable to the taxation authorities.

In line with ACCA's *Code of Ethics and Conduct*, which of the following factors must be considered by Ali & Co?

A   Fixed fees are prohibited
B   The audit firm cannot perform this service
C   The fee may be contingent depending on the outcome of the dispute
D   The client's management must provide written representation that the basis of the dispute is not unlawful

(10 marks)

Question 5 LV FONES**

The following scenario relates to questions 1–5

You are the audit manager of Jones & Co and you are planning the audit of LV Fones Co, which has been an audit client for four years and specialises in manufacturing luxury mobile phones.

During the planning of the audit you have ascertained the following:

The employees of LV Fones Co are entitled to purchase mobile phones at a discount of 10%. The audit team has in previous years been offered the same level of staff discount.

During the year the financial controller of LV Fones was ill and unable to work. The company had no spare staff able to fulfil the role and a qualified audit senior of Jones & Co was seconded to the client for three months. The audit partner has recommended that the audit senior work on the audit as he has good knowledge of the client. The fee income from LV Fones was boosted by this engagement and, along with the audit and tax fee, now accounts for 16% of the firm's total fees.

From a review of the correspondence files you note that the audit partner and finance director have known each other socially for many years and took a family holiday together last summer. As a result of this friendship the partner has not yet spoken to the client about the fee for last year's audit, 20% of which is still outstanding.

1 From a review of the information above, your audit assistant has highlighted some of the potential risks to independence in respect of the audit of LV Fones.

  (1) The audit team in previous years was offered a staff discount of 10% on luxury mobile phones

  (2) An audit senior of Jones & Co has been on secondment as the financial controller of LV Fones and is part of the current audit team

  (3) Total fee income from LV Fones is 16% of the total fees for the audit firm

  (4) The partner and finance director know each other socially and have holidayed together

Which of the following options correctly identifies the valid threats to independence and allocates the threat to the appropriate category?

	Familiarity	*Self-interest*	*Self-review*
A	1 and 2	3 only	4 only
B	1, 2 and 4	1, 3 and 4	2 only
C	1 and 3	1, 3 and 4	4 only
D	4 only	1 and 3	2 and 4

2 **In relation to the audit senior's work on secondment and his current position as an audit senior, which of the following safeguards should be implemented in order to comply with ACCA's *Code of Ethics and Conduct*?**

  A Jones & Co should determine what areas the audit senior assisted the client on and make sure that the senior does not audit those areas

  B An independent review partner should be appointed to oversee the work of the audit senior

  C The audit senior should be removed from the engagement

  D No safeguards are necessary as the audit senior was only on secondment to LV Fones for three months

3 **In relation to the unpaid fee still outstanding for last year's audit, what safeguard should Jones & Co implement in order to comply with ACCA's *Code of Ethics and Conduct*?**

  A Resign from the current year audit

  B Regard the outstanding fee to be a loan to the client and continue with the current year audit

  C Cease work on the current year audit until the fee is paid in full

  D Agree a payment schedule with LV Fones that results in the fees being paid before much more work is done on the current year audit

4   The finance director of LV Fones has asked the partner if Jones & Co can take on a consultancy project to evaluate several possible new sales systems, advise on which system should be selected, and oversee the installation of the new system.

Which of the following threats would arise, if the consultancy project is accepted by Jones & Co?

     A   Advocacy
     B   Familiarity
     C   Self-review
     D   Intimidation

5   Jones & Co has been asked to consider taking on two new statutory audits:

     (1)   Titania Co, a listed company, will also require Jones & Co to prepare the financial statements

     (2)   The finance director of Puck Co, an unlisted company, is the brother of one of the partners of Jones & Co

In line with ACCA's *Code of Ethics and Conduct*, which companies should be accepted as audit clients?

     A   Both companies
     B   Neither company
     C   With safeguards, Titania Co only
     D   With safeguards, Puck Co only

                                                                    (10 marks)

Question 6   GOOFY *(non-exam style)*

You are an audit manager in NAB & Co, a large audit firm which specialises in the audit of retailers. The firm currently audits Goofy Co, a food retailer, but Goofy Co's main competitor, Mickey Co, has approached the audit firm to act as auditors. Both companies are highly competitive and Goofy Co is concerned that if NAB & Co audits both companies then confidential information could pass across to Mickey Co.

Required:

(a)   **Explain the safeguards that your firm should implement to ensure that this conflict of interest is properly managed.**   (4 marks)

(b)   Goofy Co's year end is 31 December, which is traditionally a busy time for NAB & Co. Goofy Co currently has an internal audit department of five employees but they have struggled to undertake the variety and extent of work required by the company, hence Goofy Co is considering whether to recruit to expand the department or to outsource the internal audit department. If outsourced, Goofy Co would require a team to undertake monthly visits to test controls at the various shops across the country, and to perform ad hoc operational reviews at shops and head office.

         Goofy Co is considering using NAB & Co to provide the internal audit services as well as remain as external auditors.

Required:

Discuss the advantages and disadvantages to both Goofy Co and NAB & Co of outsourcing their internal audit department. (10 marks)

(c) The audit engagement partner for Goofy Co has been in place for approximately six years and her son has just accepted a job offer from Goofy Co as a sales manager; this role would entitle him to shares in Goofy Co as part of his remuneration package. If NAB & Co is appointed as internal as well as external auditors, then Goofy Co has suggested that the external audit fee should be renegotiated with at least 20% of the fee being based on the profit after tax of the company as they feel that this will align the interests of NAB & Co and Goofy Co.

Required:

Explain the ethical threats which may affect the independence of NAB & Co in respect of the audit of Goofy Co, and for each threat explain how it may be reduced. (6 marks)

(20 marks)

Question 7 ORANGE FINANCIALS *(non-exam style)*

(a) **Explain the external auditors' responsibilities in relation to the prevention and detection of fraud and error.** (4 marks)

(b) You are the audit manager of Currant & Co and you are planning the audit of Orange Financials Co (Orange), who specialise in the provision of loans and financial advice to individuals and companies. Currant & Co has audited Orange for many years.

The directors are planning to list Orange on a stock exchange within the next few months and have asked if the engagement partner can attend the meetings with potential investors. In addition, as the finance director of Orange is likely to be quite busy with the listing, he has asked if Currant & Co can produce the financial statements for the current year.

During the year, the assistant finance director of Orange left and joined Currant & Co as a partner. It has been suggested that due to his familiarity with Orange, he should be appointed to provide an independent partner review for the audit.

Once Orange obtains its stock exchange listing it will require several assignments to be undertaken, for example, obtaining advice about corporate governance best practice. Currant & Co is very keen to be appointed to these engagements; however, Orange has implied that in order to gain this work Currant & Co needs to complete the external audit quickly and with minimal questions/issues.

The finance director has informed you that once the stock exchange listing has been completed, he would like the engagement team to attend a weekend away at a luxury hotel with his team, as a thank you for all their hard work. In addition, he has offered a senior member of the engagement team a short-term loan at a significantly reduced interest rate.

Required:

(i) **Explain SIX ethical threats which may affect the independence of Currant & Co's audit of Orange Financials Co; and**

(ii) **For each threat explain how it might be reduced to an acceptable level.**

(12 marks)

(c)   Orange is aware that subsequent to the stock exchange listing it will need to establish an audit committee and has asked for some advice in relation to this.

Required:

Explain the benefits to Orange of establishing an audit committee.   (4 marks)

(20 marks)

Question 8 WILLOW WANDS**

The following scenario relates to questions 1–5

You are an audit senior of Beech & Co and have been allocated to the audit of Willow Wands Co (Willow), a listed company which has been an audit client for eight years and specialises in manufacturing musical instruments.

Having completed seven years as the audit engagement partner for Willow, Bethan Oak has recently been rotated off the audit engagement. The current audit partner, Sandeep Pine, has suggested that in order to maintain a close relationship with Willow, Bethan should be the independent review partner this year. In addition, Willow has requested that Bethan assists them by attending their audit committee meetings, as a non-executive director has recently left the company.

Willow has also asked Sandeep and the other partners at Beech & Co to help them in recruiting a new non-executive director.

The total fees received by Beech & Co for last year equated to 16% of the firm's total fee income. This year's fees could be greater.

1   From a review of the information above, you have determined that the following are potential threats to independence in respect of the audit of Willow:

  (1)   The proposal that the former engagement partner be independent review partner
  (2)   The request that the former engagement partner attends audit committee meetings
  (3)   The request for help in recruiting a new non-executive director
  (4)   Total fees for the year could be greater than 16%

  Which of these represent self-interest threats?

  A   1 and 4 only
  B   2 and 3 only
  C   1, 2 and 4
  D   2, 3 and 4

2   Sandeep has been informed that the father of a new trainee assigned to the Willow audit team owns a 10% interest in Willow.

  Which of the following safeguards are appropriate in this situation?

  (1)   Beech & Co should resign from the current period audit engagement
  (2)   Disposal of the interest by the team member's father
  (3)   Independent reviews of the audit work performed by the team member
  (4)   Removal of the team member from the willow engagement

A   1, 2 and 4
B   2, 3 and 4
C   1, 2 and 3
D   1, 3 and 4

3   The audit manager for Willow has just announced that he is leaving Beech & Co to join Willow as the financial controller. He will leave Beech before the commencement of the current period audit of Willow.

Which of the following procedures should be implemented to ensure quality control over engagement performance?

(1)   A new audit manager should be appointed
(2)   Beech & Co should resign from the current period audit engagement
(3)   Any work performed by the former audit manager should be independently reviewed
(4)   The audit plan should be modified so that the former manager is not overly familiar with the audit approach

A   2 only
B   1 and 3 only
C   1 and 4 only
D   1, 3 and 4

4   **Which of the following is NOT a principle of the UK Corporate Governance Code?**

A   There should be a rigorous and transparent procedure for the appointment of new directors to the board

B   The board should use the annual general meeting (AGM) to communicate with investors

C   The non-executive chairman should decide on the remuneration of all directors

D   All directors should receive induction training on joining the board

5   **Which of the following statements best expresses Beech & Co's duty of confidentiality to Willow and its other clients in respect of information acquired in the course of professional work?**

A   The auditor should only reveal confidential client data after having received consent from the client's board of directors to do so

B   The auditor must supply any client data requested of him by a shareholder at the annual general meeting

C   The auditor should never reveal client confidential data unless it is essential to the understanding of a modified auditor's report

D   The auditor should reveal certain client confidential data if there is a legal right or duty to do so

(10 marks)

Question 9 ZIRCON, RIVET AND PLUSHY

You are employed as the quality control reviewer in your firm. You have identified the following issues during your recent visit to one of your firm's offices:

Zircon Co

In your review of the audit documentation of Zircon, you noted a copy of a letter from the audit manager to Zircon's finance director advising on the investment of surplus cash. The letter makes recommendations on specific shares in the electrical industry. Some of the recommended shares are in companies which are audit clients of other offices of your firm.

Rivet Manufacturing Co

You had requested the audit working paper files for Rivet as the financial statements are to be issued next week. The audit manager informs you that all the audit files for inventory were only on a laptop in the audit senior's car which has been stolen. The files had not been back-up and the police have been unable to trace the vehicle or its contents.

Plushy Electrical Co

The major audit client of the office, Plushy, has demanded that the financial statements be published a month earlier than originally planned. This is because a minority shareholder needs them urgently to negotiate the sale of his shares. The audit partner has advised you that the revised audit timetable means there will be no time for you to review audit documentation or the financial statements before the auditor's report must be signed.

Required:

(a)   **Explain engagement quality control review.**   (5 marks)

(b)   **In respect of each of the issues:**

       (i)   **Identify the significant risks arising;**
       (ii)   **Explain the steps you or the firm should now take; and**
       (iii)   **Recommend a quality control procedure to address each risk.**   (15 marks)

(20 marks)

Question 10 BONDI

You are a partner with a firm of Chartered Certified Accountants that has been invited, by the board of directors, to accept nomination as external auditors to Bondi. Bondi operates a number of car dealerships and has grown rapidly over the past two years through an aggressive take-over strategy.

You are aware that the company's existing auditors, a much smaller firm, modified their last auditor's report. Over lunch with a number of your firm's partners, the company's finance director maintained that their existing auditors could not cope with the audit of a company their size and, in particular, were not equipped to audit the recently installed sophisticated computer accounting program. He also suggests that they need a firm of your reputation in order to reassure the market as they intend to seek a public listing within two years.

The existing auditors, in response to your enquiry, advise against accepting the audit on the following grounds:

(i)   Insufficient consideration has been devoted by management to developing the accounting system in line with the expanding business. In particular, there is a lack of concern as to control. The auditors detected a number of petty employee frauds as a result of control weaknesses. No action was taken against the employees identified as engaged in fraud. The attitude seems to be to encourage risk taking employees who, if they make money on the side whilst securing good deals for the company, that is seen as a legitimate bonus.

(ii)   The newly installed computer accounting system is unreasonably complicated. Bondi claims this is necessary because of the need to maintain records to justify the company's claims for volume rebates, and bonuses under the complex incentive schemes by which car manufacturers reward dealers.

(iii)   The auditors have no evidence of deliberate misrepresentation by the directors but audit staff were hindered in their audit work by a less than helpful attitude by senior management who adopted an aggressive stance whenever a query was raised.

Further, the existing auditor mentioned that the finance director was constantly phoning the partner claiming the audit staff were incompetent and accusing them of wasting his time asking unnecessary questions.

At a partner's meeting a majority of partners accepted the story that the existing auditors were out of their depth and that their complaints were merely an attempt to cover up their own shortcomings. Your firm accepted nomination and was duly appointed as auditors.

Required:

(a)   State factors the partners should have considered for and against accepting nomination.
(7 marks)

(b)   Detail the matters to which you should pay particular attention in obtaining the required knowledge of the business and in developing your audit plan.   (7 marks)

(c) During the first audit, your firm discovers that the reason for the complexity of the computer system is to falsify records in order to reduce the amount of tax payable to the government.

Describe the action you should take on discovery of the fraud.   (6 marks)

(20 marks)

Question 11 AGNESAL

You are the manager responsible for the quality of the audits of new clients of Signet & Co. You are visiting the audit team at the head office of Agnesal Co. The audit team comprises Artur (audit supervisor), Carla (audit senior) and Errol and Gavin (trainees). The company provides food hygiene services which include the evaluation of risks of contamination and providing advice on health regulations and waste disposal.

Agnesal's principal customers include food processing companies and wholesale fresh food markets (meat, fish and dairy products). The draft financial statements for the year ended 31 December 2016 show revenue $19.8 million (2015 $13.8 million) and total assets $6.1 million (2015 $4.2 million).

You have summarised the findings of your monitoring visit and your review of the current year's audit working papers as follows:

(1) Against the analytical procedures section of the audit planning checklist, Carla has written "not applicable – new client". The audit planning checklist has not been signed off as having been reviewed by Artur.

(2) Artur is currently assigned to three other jobs and is working from Signet's office. He last visited Agnesal's office when the final audit commenced two weeks ago. In the meantime, Carla has completed the audit of tangible non-current assets (including property and service equipment) which amount to $1.1 million as at 31 December 2016 (2015 $1.1 million).

(3) Errol has only just now finished sending out the requests for confirmation of accounts receivable balances as at 31 December 2016 when trade receivables amounted to $3.5 million (2015 $1.6 million).

(4) Errol has been assigned to the audit of inventory (comprising consumable supplies) which amounts to $150,000 (2015 $90,000). Signet was not appointed as auditor until after the year-end physical count. Errol has therefore carried out tests of controls over purchases and issues to confirm the "roll-back" of a sample of current quantities to quantities as at the year-end count.

Required:

(a) **Explain the quality control procedures that should be in place over engagement performance.** (4 marks)

(b) **Identify and explain the weaknesses in Signet's quality control procedures over engagement performance.** (16 marks)

(20 marks)

Question 12 SALT & PEPPER *(non-exam style)*

Salt & Pepper & Co (Salt & Pepper) is a firm of Chartered Certified Accountants which has seen its revenue decline steadily over the past few years. The firm is looking to increase its revenue and client base and so has developed a new advertising strategy where it has guaranteed that its audits will minimise disruption to companies, as they will not last longer than two weeks. In addition, Salt & Pepper has offered all new audit clients a free accounts preparation service for the first year of the engagement, as it is believed that time spent on the audit will be reduced if the firm has produced the financial statements.

The firm is seeking to reduce audit costs and has therefore decided not to update the engagement letters of existing clients, on the basis that these letters do not tend to change much on a yearly basis. One of Salt & Pepper's existing clients has proposed that this year's audit fee should be based on a percentage of their final pre-tax profit. The partners are excited about this option as they believe it will increase the overall audit fee.

Salt & Pepper has recently obtained a new audit client, Cinnamon Brothers Co (Cinnamon), whose year end is 31 December. Cinnamon requires their audit to be completed by the end of February; however, this is a very busy time for Salt & Pepper and so it is intended to use more junior staff as they are available. Additionally, in order to save time and cost, Salt & Pepper have not contacted Cinnamon's previous auditors.

Required:

(a) Describe the steps that Salt & Pepper should take in relation to Cinnamon:

    (i)   Prior to accepting the audit; and   (5 marks)

    (ii)   To confirm whether the preconditions for the audit are in place.   (3 marks)

(b) State FOUR matters that should be included within an audit engagement letter.

     (2 marks)

(c)   **(i)**   Identify and explain FIVE ethical risks which arise from the above actions of Salt & Pepper & Co; and

     (ii)   For each ethical risk explain the steps which Salt & Pepper & Co should adopt to reduce the risks arising.   (10 marks)

Note: The total marks will be split equally between each part.

(20 marks)

Question 13 SPECS4YOU

(a) ISA 230 *Audit Documentation* establishes standards and provides guidance regarding documentation in the context of the audit of financial statements.

Required:

List the purposes of audit working papers.   (3 marks)

(b) You have recently been promoted to audit manager in the audit firm of Trums & Co. As part of your new responsibilities, you have been placed in charge of the audit of Specs4You Co, a long-established audit client of Trums & Co. Specs4You Co sells spectacles; the company owns 42 stores where customers can have their eyes tested and choose from a range of frames.

Required:

List the documentation that should be of assistance to you in familiarising yourself with Specs4You Co. Describe the information you should expect to obtain from each document.   (8 marks)

(c) The time is now towards the end of the audit and you are reviewing working papers produced by the audit team. An example of a working paper you have just reviewed is shown below:

Client Name **Specs4You Co**   Year end **30 April**   Page **xxxxxxx**
Working paper **Payables transaction testing**

         Prepared by   Date
         Reviewed by **CW**   Date **12 June**

Audit assertion: To make sure that the purchases day book is correct.

Method: Select a sample of 15 purchase orders recorded in the purchase order system. Trace details to the goods received note (GRN), purchase invoice (PI) and the purchase day book (PDB) ensuring that the quantities and prices recorded on the purchase order match those on the GRN, PI and PDB.

Test details: In accordance with audit risk, a sample of purchase orders were selected from a numerically sequenced purchase order system and details traced as stated in the method. Details of items tested can be found on another working paper.

Results: Details of purchase orders were normally correctly recorded through the system. Five purchase orders did not have any associated GRN, PI and were not recorded in the PDB. Further investigation showed that these orders had been cancelled due to a change in spectacle specification. However, this does not appear to be a system weakness as the internal controls do not allow for changes in specification.

Conclusion: Purchase orders are completely recorded in the purchase day book.

Required:

Explain why the working paper shown above does not meet the standards normally expected of a working paper. (9 marks)

Note: You are not required to reproduce the working paper.

(20 marks)

Question 14 DASH

Your firm has recently been appointed as auditor of Dash Ltd ("Dash"), a sports and leisure company. Your audit manager, David, has arranged a meeting with the company's finance director early next week and asked you to assist him, in advance of this meeting, with the audit planning for the year ending 30 June 2017. David has also asked you to carry out some preliminary analytical procedures on the year-end financial statements of Dash when these become available.

Dash's business can be split into the following three divisions

(i)   Sports equipment retail: 35 outlets located in "out of town" retail parks;
(ii)   Fitness clubs: 15 centres each offer gym facilities and fitness classes;
(iii)   Machine manufacture: a unit which assembles treadmills and rowing machines.

Further information

Each retail outlet holds a standard range of products which are supplied from a central warehouse operated by Dash. The salaries of full-time staff are paid from Dash's head office by direct bank transfer. Each outlet has an operational manager who is responsible for hiring casual staff to cover busy periods. Casual staff are generally paid using cash from the till.

Dash received some bad publicity during the year following a television documentary which revealed that one of its overseas suppliers of sports footwear makes its employees work long hours for very low wages. Dash has now had to source these products from alternative national suppliers.

The fitness clubs are all located directly above a Dash retail outlet. Each club has an on-site manager and is operated independently of the retail outlet. Club members can pay by one of three methods: over-the-counter on a "pay-as-you-go"; by monthly direct debit paid into Dash's head office bank account; or by annual subscription to head office.

Dash offers a bonus incentive scheme to all managers linked to the profitability of their individual operation.

During the year Dash started to manufacture its own treadmills and rowing machines. Machines are assembled from components purchased from overseas and sold to Dash's retail outlets under the "Dash" brand and to independent retailers under the "Champion" brand. The latter accounts for approximately 80% of Dash's total manufacture of machines. Sales to independent retailers achieve a gross profit margin of 50%, whereas sales to Dash's own shops are made at cost plus 10%.

Components are heavy and sent by sea, which means that the typical lead time from placing an order to receipt is three months. Dash is required to pay the suppliers 50% on ordering and 50% on receipt of the components.

Required:

(a)   **Explain the information you should require in order to carry out analytical procedures on the draft financial statements of Dash for the year ending 30 June 2017.** (4 marks)

(b)   **Identify FOUR limitations of using analytical procedures at the planning stage of an audit.** (4 marks)

(c)   **Identify and describe EIGHT audit risks, and explain the auditor's response to each risk, in planning the audit of Dash.** (16 marks)

(d)   In line with your firm's system of quality control, procedures were followed before accepting Dash as an audit client, to ensure that it was appropriate to accept the engagement. David has asked you to consider the objective and elements of a system of quality control and why they may be particularly relevant to Dash.

      (i)   **State the objective of a system of quality control for an audit firm.** (2 marks)

      (ii)   **Identify and explain TWO elements of your firm's system of quality control that may be particularly relevant to the audit of Dash.** (4 marks)

(30 marks)

Question 15 URBAN ROCK

Urban Rock Co (Urban) is a music events company. It has a head office and organises and stages seven live events held in the same seven locations across the country each year. Your firm, Diaz & Co, has five offices throughout the country and specialises in audit and advisory services to clients in the entertainment industry. The finance director, Sam Smith, has recently approached Diaz & Co to accept appointment as external auditor for the year ended 31 December 2016. Urban's previous auditors have not been reappointed.

Live music events are performed on open-air stages. The musical acts vary between locations and from year to year. Each event is held over a weekend in the summer, between June and August.

Tickets can be purchased in advance online from Urban's website or on the day of the event at the entrance gate. Online tickets are available for the next year's event the week after the current year's event has finished and paid for by credit card. Tickets bought at the entrance can be paid for by credit card or by cash. Cash received at the entrance is periodically transferred to the on-site cash office during the day.

Customers with tickets bought online are required to exchange their booking confirmation for a wristband. Wristbands are colour-coded for each day of the event. Customers who buy tickets on the day receive a wristband at the entrance. Entry is not permitted without the correct wristband.

Urban arranges performances through the musicians' agents. Fees to major musicians are usually agreed and paid in advance. Some musicians ask for a portion of their fee in cash on the day of their performance. Less well-known musicians are fully paid in cash at the end of their performance. Cash fees are collected by musicians, or their agents, from the on-site cash office.

Urban recruits a number of stewards for each event to provide information and direct customers. Other casual staff work at the entrance or in the wristband exchange. Stewards and casual staff are paid in cash at the on-site cash office at the end of the event.

Permission to hold each event has to be obtained each year from the local police authority and municipal authority. The municipal authority determines the maximum number of tickets that may be sold for each day of an event.

Sam Smith has provided you with the following information:

(1)   At one event in August 2016 a customer was seriously injured after attempting to climb floodlights for a better view of the stage. He has been unable to work since his fall. Urban is currently being sued for damages after a national newspaper started a campaign on behalf of the injured customer. There were no warning signs against climbing the floodlights and there were no stewards nearby at the time of the accident.

(2)   The weaker economic climate and unpredictable summer weather resulted in a decline in ticket sales in 2016. This, together with increasing costs from suppliers, has led Urban to investigate expansion overseas. Urban is currently negotiating to purchase the right to stage an event in Eastern Europe. The purchase would be funded by a loan from Urban's bank. As part of the loan negotiation the bank will require a copy of the audited financial statements.

Sam Smith has asked that the audit be completed and auditor's report signed by 3 April 2017 so that the bank loan can be agreed quickly and the purchase finalised by 10 April 2017.

As well as carrying out the statutory audit Sam Smith has requested that you carry out a review of the controls at each event, in particular the controls over cash and the wristband exchange. Controls at two events would be reviewed in the coming year, two in 2018, two in 2019 and the final event in 2020. After each review you would be expected to attend a board meeting to discuss your firm's findings and present your recommendations.

Required:

(a)   Explain the factors Diaz & Co should consider to decide whether to accept:

     (i)   appointment as external auditor of Urban; and

     (ii)   the additional work on controls proposed by the finance director.   (8 marks)

(b)   Using the information provided, identify and describe SEVEN audit risks, and explain the auditor's response to each risk, in planning the audit of Urban Rock Co.   (14 marks)

(c)   Identify the internal controls that you would expect to be in operation during each event in respect of:

     (i)   cash; and

     (ii)   the wristband exchange.   (8 marks)

(30 marks)

Question 16 BRIDGFORD PRODUCTS

Your firm has been the auditor of Bridgford Products, a listed company, for a number of years. The engagement partner has asked you to describe the matters you should consider when planning the audit for the year ended 30 June 2016.

During a recent visit to the company you obtained the following information:

(i) The management accounts for the 10 months to 30 April 2016 show sales of $130 million and profit before tax of $4 million. Sales and profits are assumed to accrue evenly throughout the year. In the year ended 30 June 2015, Bridgford Products had sales of $110 million and profit before tax of $8 million.

(ii) The company installed a new computerised inventory control system which has operated from 1 November 2015. As the inventory control system records inventory movements and current inventory quantities, the company is proposing:

   – to use the inventory quantities on the computer to value the inventory at the year end; and
   – not to carry out an inventory count at the year end.

(iii) You are aware there have been reliability problems with the company's products, which have resulted in legal claims being brought against the company by customers, and customers refusing to pay for the products

(iv) The sales increase in the 10 months to 30 April 2016 over the previous year has been achieved by attracting new customers and by offering extended credit. The new credit arrangements allow customers three months credit before their debt becomes overdue, rather than the one-month credit period allowed previously. As a result of this change, receivables age has increased from 1·6 to 4·1 months

(v) The chief financial officer and purchasing manager were dismissed on 15 January. A replacement purchasing manager has been appointed but it is not expected that a new chief financial officer will be appointed before the year end of 30 June 2016. The chief accountant will be responsible for preparing the financial statements for audit.

Required:

(a)   Describe the reasons why it is important that auditors should plan their audit work.

(6 marks)

(b)   Describe SEVEN audit risks and explain the auditor's response to each risk in planning the audit of Bridgford.

(14 marks)

(20 marks)

Question 17 EUKARE CHARITY

(a)   Explain the term "audit risk" and the three elements of risk that contribute to total audit risk.

(4 marks)

The EuKaRe charity was established in 1960. The charity's aim is to provide support to children from disadvantaged backgrounds who wish to take part in sports such as tennis, badminton and football.

EuKaRe has a detailed constitution which explains how the charity's income can be spent. The constitution also notes that administration expenditure cannot exceed 10% of income in any year.

The charity's income is derived wholly from voluntary donations. Sources of donations include:

(i)   Cash collected by volunteers asking the public for donations in shopping areas;

(ii)   Cheques sent to the charity's head office;

(iii)   Donations from generous individuals. Some of these donations have specific clauses attached to them indicating that the initial amount donated (capital) cannot be spent and that the income (interest) from the donation must be spent on specific activities, for example, provision of sports equipment.

The rules regarding the taxation of charities in the country EuKaRe is based are complicated, with only certain expenditure being allowable for taxation purposes and donations of capital being treated as income in some situations.

Required:

(b)   Identify areas of inherent risk in the EuKaRe charity and explain the effect of each of these risks on the audit approach.   (12 marks)

(c)   Explain why the control environment may be weak at the charity EuKaRe.   (4 marks)

(20 marks)

Question 18 ABRAHAMS

Abrahams Co develops, manufactures and sells a range of pharmaceuticals and has a wide customer base across Europe and Asia. You are the audit manager of Nate & Co and you are planning the audit of Abrahams Co whose financial year end is in two months' time, on 31 January. You attended a planning meeting with the finance director and engagement partner and are now reviewing the meeting notes in order to produce the audit strategy and plan. Revenue for the year is forecast at $25 million.

During the year the company has spent $2·2 million on developing several new products. Some of these are in the early stages of development whilst others are nearing completion. The finance director has confirmed that all projects are likely to be successful and so he is intending to capitalise the full $2·2 million.

Once products have completed the development stage, Abrahams begins manufacturing them. At the year end it is anticipated that there will be significant levels of work in progress. In addition the company uses a standard costing method to value inventory; the standard costs are set when a product is first manufactured and are not usually updated. In order to fulfil customer orders promptly, Abrahams Co has warehouses for finished goods located across Europe and Asia; approximately one third of these are third party warehouses where Abrahams just rents space.

In September a new accounting package was introduced. This is a bespoke system developed by the information technology (IT) manager. The old and new packages were not run in parallel as it was felt that this would be too onerous for the accounting team. Two months after the system changeover the IT manager left the company; a new manager has been recruited but is not due to start work until January.

In order to fund the development of new products, Abrahams has restructured its finance and raised $1 million through issuing shares at a premium and $2·5 million through a long-term loan. There are bank covenants attached to the loan, the main one relating to a minimum level of total assets. If these covenants are breached then the loan becomes immediately repayable. The company has a policy of revaluing land and buildings, and the finance director has announced that all land and buildings will be revalued as at the year end.

The reporting timetable for audit completion of Abrahams Co is quite short, and the finance director would like to report results even earlier this year.

Required:

(a)   **Explain the components of audit risk and, for each component, state an example of a factor which can result in increased audit risk.**   (6 marks)

(b)   **Using the information provided, identify and describe FIVE audit risks and explain the auditor's response to each risk in planning the audit of Abrahams Co.**   (10 marks)

(c)   **Describe substantive procedures you should perform to obtain sufficient appropriate evidence in relation to:**

        (i)   **Inventory held at the third party warehouses; and**
        (ii)   **Use of standard costs for inventory valuation.**   (4 marks)

(20 marks)

Question 19 SUNFLOWER STORES

Sunflower Stores Co (Sunflower) operates 25 food supermarkets. The company's year end is 31 December 2016. The audit manager and partner recently attended a planning meeting with the finance director and have provided you with the planning notes below.

You are the audit senior, and this is your first year on this audit. In order to familiarise yourself with Sunflower, the audit manager has asked you to undertake some research in order to gain an understanding of Sunflower, so that you are able to assist in the planning process. He has then asked that you identify relevant audit risks from the notes below and also consider how the team should respond to these risks.

Sunflower has spent $1·6 million in refurbishing all of its supermarkets; as part of this refurbishment programme their central warehouse has been extended and a smaller warehouse, which was only occasionally used, has been disposed of at a profit. In order to finance this refurbishment, a sum of $1·5 million was borrowed from the bank. This is due to be repaid over five years.

The company will be performing a year-end inventory count at the central warehouse as well as at all 25 supermarkets on 31 December. Inventory is valued at selling price less an average profit margin as the finance director believes that this is a close approximation to cost.

Prior to 2016, each of the supermarkets maintained their own financial records and submitted returns monthly to head office. During 2016 all accounting records have been centralised within head office. Therefore at the beginning of the year, each supermarket's opening balances were transferred into head office's accounting records. The increased workload at head office has led to some changes in the finance department and in November 2016 the financial controller left. His replacement will start in late December.

Required:

(a)   **List FIVE sources of information that would be of use in gaining an understanding of Sunflower Stores Co, and for each source describe what you would expect to obtain.**   (5 marks)

(b)   **Using the information provided, describe FIVE audit risks and explain the auditor's response to each risk in planning the audit of Sunflower Stores Co.**   (10 marks)

(c)   The finance director of Sunflower Stores Co is considering establishing an internal audit department.

Required:

Describe the factors the finance director should consider before establishing an internal audit department. (5 marks)

(20 marks)

Question 20 RECORDER COMMUNICATIONS

Recorder Communications Co (Recorder) is a large mobile phone company which operates a network of stores in countries across Europe. The company's year end is 30 June 2016. You are the audit senior of Piano & Co. Recorder is a new client and you are currently planning the audit with the audit manager. You have been provided with the following planning notes from the audit partner following his meeting with the finance director.

Recorder purchases goods from a supplier in South Asia and these goods are shipped to the company's central warehouse. The goods are usually in transit for two weeks and the company correctly records the goods when received. Recorder does not undertake a year-end inventory count, but carries out monthly continuous (perpetual) inventory counts and any errors identified are adjusted in the inventory system for that month.

During the year the company introduced a bonus based on sales for its sales persons. The bonus target was based on increasing the number of customers signing up for 24-month phone line contracts. This has been successful and revenue has increased by 15%, especially in the last few months of the year. The level of receivables is considerably higher than last year and there are concerns about the creditworthiness of some customers.

Recorder has a policy of revaluing its land and buildings and this year has updated the valuations of all land and buildings.

During the year the directors have each been paid a significant bonus, and they have included this within wages and salaries. Separate disclosure of the bonus is required by local legislation.

Required:

(a)   **Describe FIVE audit risks, and explain the auditor's response to each risk, in planning the audit of Recorder Communications Co.** (10 marks)

(b)   **Explain the audit procedures you should perform in order to place reliance on the continuous (perpetual) counts for year-end inventory.** (3 marks)

(c)   **Describe substantive procedures you should perform to confirm the directors' bonus payments included in the financial statements.** (3 marks)

The finance director of Recorder informed the audit partner that the reason for appointing Piano & Co as auditors was because they audit other mobile phone companies, including Recorder's main competitor. The finance director has asked how Piano & Co keeps information obtained during the audit confidential.

Required:

(d)   **Explain the safeguards which your firm should implement to ensure that this conflict of interest is properly managed.** (4 marks)

(20 marks)

Question 21 WALTERS

You are the audit senior of Holtby & Co and are planning the audit of Walters Co (Walters) for the year ended 31 December 2016. The company produces printers and has been a client of your firm for two years; your audit manager has already had a planning meeting with the finance director. He has provided you with the following notes of his meeting and financial statement extracts.

Walters's management were disappointed with the 2015 results and so in 2016 undertook a number of strategies to improve the trading results. This included the introduction of a generous sales-related bonus scheme for their salesmen and a high profile advertising campaign. In addition, as market conditions are difficult for their customers, they have extended the credit period given to them.

The finance director of Walters has reviewed the inventory valuation policy and has included additional overheads incurred this year as he considers them to be production related.

The finance director has calculated a few key ratios for Walters; the gross profit margin has increased from 44·4% to 52·2% and receivables days have increased from 61 days to 71 days. He is happy with the 2016 results and feels that they are a good reflection of the improved trading levels.

Financial statement extracts for year ended 31 December

	DRAFT 2016 $m	ACTUAL 2015 $m
Revenue	23·0	18·0
Cost of sales	(11·0)	(10·0)
Gross profit	12·0	8·0
Operating expenses	(7·5)	(4·0)
Profit before interest and taxation	4·5	4·0
Inventory	2·1	1·6
Receivables	4·5	3·0
Cash –	2·3	
Trade payables	1·6	1·2
Overdraft	0·9	–

Required:

(a)   **Using the information above:**

   (i)   **Calculate an additional THREE ratios, for BOTH years, which would assist the audit senior in planning the audit; and**   (3 marks)

   (ii)   **From a review of the above information and the ratios calculated, describe SIX audit risks and explain the auditor's response to each risk in planning the audit of Walters Co.**   (12 marks)

(b)   **Describe the procedures that the auditor of Walters Co should perform in assessing whether or not the company is a going concern.**   (5 marks)

                                                                                           (20 marks)

Question 22 EAGLE HEATING

The following scenario relates to questions 1–5

You are the audit supervisor of Seagull & Co and are currently planning the audit Eagle Heating Co (Eagle) for the year ending 31 December 2016. Eagle manufactures and sells heating and plumbing equipment to a number of home improvement stores across the country.

Eagle has experienced increased competition over the past 12 months. In order to maintain its current levels of sales, it has decreased the selling price of its products significantly since September 2016. The finance director has informed your audit manager that he expects increased inventory levels at the year end, which you plan to verify when you attend Eagle's year-end inventory count. He also notified your manager that one of Eagle's key customers has been experiencing financial difficulties. Therefore, Eagle has agreed that the customer can take a six-month payment break, after which payments will continue as normal. The finance director does not believe that any allowance is required against this receivable.

You have undertaken a preliminary analytical review of the draft year to date statement of profit or loss, and you are surprised to see a significant fall in administration expenses.

1   Based on this information, your audit assistant has suggested the following as areas of increased audit risk that should be considered in planning the audit of Eagle:

       (1)   The risk that inventory is undervalued
       (2)   The risk that receivables are overvalued
       (3)   The risk that Eagle is facing going concern difficulties
       (4)   The risk that administrative expenses are understated

       Which areas of increased audit risk have been correctly identified by your assistant?

       A   1 and 4 only
       B   2, 3 and 4
       C   1, 2 and 3
       D   1, 2, 3 and 4

2   In October 2016 the financial controller of Eagle was dismissed. He had been employed by the company for over 20 years and has threatened to sue the company for unfair dismissal. The role of financial controller has not yet been filled and so his tasks have been shared between the existing finance department team.

       Which of the following would be appropriate auditor responses to the audit risks arising from the controller's dismissal?

       (1)   Visit the company's lawyers and enquire of the existence and likelihood of success of any claim from the former controller

       (2)   Offer to assist Eagle in recruiting a new financial controller

       (3)   Discuss with the finance director whether he will be able to provide the team with assistance for any audit issues as there is no financial controller available

       (4)   Remain alert throughout the audit for errors

       A   1 and 2
       B   2 and 3
       C   3 and 4
       D   1 and 4

3   **Which of the following procedures are TESTS OF CONTROL that you should perform in testing the inventory cycle of Eagle whilst attending the inventory count?**

(1)   Observe whether the client's staff are following the inventory count instructions

(2)   Review inventory present in the warehouse for evidence of damage or obsolescence

(3)   Obtain a sample of the last goods received notes and goods despatched notes and follow through to ensure inclusion in the correct accounting period

(4)   Inspect and review management's inventory count instructions

A   2 and 3
B   1 and 4
C   1 and 2
D   3 and 4

4   **Which of the following substantive procedures are you likely to perform when auditing Eagle to provide evidence over the EXISTENCE of trade receivables?**

(1)   Agreeing a sample of goods despatched notes to sales invoices and to the sales ledger

(2)   Undertaking a direct confirmation of trade receivables

(3)   Review of post year-end cash receipts, if these relate to year-end receivables follow through to the sales ledger

(4)   Recalculating the allowance for uncollectible accounts

A   1 and 3
B   2 and 4
C   2 and 3
D   1 and 4

5   **Which of the following statements regarding the use of analytical procedures during the PLANNING stage of the audit are correct?**

(1)   They are useful when forming an overall conclusion on whether the financial statements are consistent with the auditor's understanding of the company

(2)   They can be used to obtain relevant and reliable audit evidence

(3)   They can assist in identifying the risks of material misstatement

(4)   They can assist in identifying unusual transactions and events

A   1 and 2
B   2 and 3
C   3 and 4
D   2 and 4

(10 marks)

Question 23 KANGAROO CONSTRUCTION

(a) **Explain the concepts of materiality and performance materiality in accordance with ISA 320 *Materiality in Planning and Performing an Audit*.** (5 marks)

(b) You are the audit senior of Rhino & Co and you are planning the audit of Kangaroo Construction Co (Kangaroo) for the year ended 31 March 2017. Kangaroo specialises in building houses and provides a five-year building warranty to its customers. Your audit manager has held a planning meeting with the finance director. He has provided you with the following notes of his meeting and financial statement extracts:

Kangaroo has had a difficult year; house prices have fallen and, as a result, revenue has dropped. In order to address this, management has offered significantly extended credit terms to their customers. However, demand has fallen such that there are still some completed houses in inventory where the selling price may be below cost. During the year, whilst calculating depreciation, the directors extended the useful lives of plant and machinery from three years to five years. This reduced the annual depreciation charge.

The directors need to meet a target profit before interest and taxation of $0·5 million in order to be paid their annual bonus. In addition, to try and improve profits, Kangaroo changed their main material supplier to a cheaper alternative. This has resulted in some customers claiming on their building warranties for extensive repairs. To help with operating cash flow, the directors borrowed $1 million from the bank during the year. This is due for repayment at the end of 2017.

Financial statement extracts for year ended 31 March

	DRAFT 2017 $m	ACTUAL 2016 $m
Revenue	12·5	15·0
Cost of sales	(7·0)	(8·0)
Gross profit	5·5	7·0
Operating expenses	(5·0)	(5·1)
Profit before interest and taxation	0·5	1·9
Inventory	1·9	1·4
Receivables	3·1	2·0
Cash	0.8	1·9
Trade payables	1·6	1·2
Loan	1·0	–

Required:

Using the information above:

(i) **Calculate FIVE ratios, for BOTH years, which would assist the audit senior in planning the audit; and** (5 marks)

(ii) **Using the information provided and the ratios calculated, identify and describe FIVE audit risks and explain the auditor's response to each risk in planning the audit of Kangaroo Construction Co.** (10 marks)

(20 marks)

Question 24 BESTWOOD ENGINEERING

Bestwood Engineering, a privately owned incorporated business, manufactures components for motor vehicles and sells them to motor vehicle manufacturers and wholesalers. It has sales of $10 million and a profit before tax of $400,000.

The company has a new chief executive (CEO) who inherited this role from his father. He has not worked in the company before, has little financial background and has therefore asked your advice on controls in the company's purchases and accounts payable system.

Bestwood Engineering has separate accounts, purchasing and goods received departments. Most purchases are required by the production department, but other departments are able to raise requisitions for goods and services. The purchasing department is responsible for obtaining goods and services for the company at the lowest price which is consistent with the required delivery date and quality, and for ensuring their prompt delivery.

The accounts department is responsible for obtaining authorisation of purchase invoices before they are input into the computer which posts them to the accounts payable ledger and the general ledger. The accounting records are kept on a microcomputer and the standard accounting software was obtained from an independent supplier. The accounting software maintains the accounts payable ledger, accounts receivable ledger, general ledger and payroll. The company does not maintain inventory records, as it believes the costs of maintaining these records outweigh the benefits.

Required:

(a)   **Describe the procedures which should be in operation in the purchasing department to control the purchase and receipt of goods.**   (8 marks)

(b)   **Describe the controls the accounts department should exercise over obtaining authorisation of purchase invoices before posting them to the accounts payable ledger.**
                                                                                         (6 marks)

(c)   **Explain how controls over the purchase of services might differ from the controls over the purchase of goods, as described in your answers to parts (a) and (b) above.** (6 marks)

(20 marks)

Question 25 PEAR INTERNATIONAL

Pear International Co (Pear) is a manufacturer of electrical equipment. It has factories across the country and its customer base includes retailers as well as individuals, to whom direct sales are made through their website. The company's year end is 30 September 2016. You are an audit supervisor of Apple & Co and are currently reviewing documentation of Pear's internal control in preparation for the interim audit.

Pear's website allows individuals to order goods directly, and full payment is taken in advance. Currently the website is not integrated into the inventory system and inventory levels are not checked at the time when orders are placed.

Goods are despatched via local couriers; however, they do not always record customer signatures as proof that the customer has received the goods. Over the past 12 months there have been customer complaints about the delay between sales orders and receipt of goods. Pear has investigated these and found that, in each case, the sales order had been entered into the sales system correctly but was not forwarded to the despatch department for fulfilling.

Pear's retail customers undergo credit checks prior to being accepted and credit limits are set accordingly by sales ledger clerks. These customers place their orders through one of the sales team, who decides on sales discount levels.

Raw materials used in the manufacturing process are purchased from a wide range of suppliers. As a result of staff changes in the purchase ledger department, supplier statement reconciliations are no longer performed. Additionally, changes to supplier details in the purchase ledger master file can be undertaken by purchase ledger clerks as well as supervisors.

In the past six months Pear has changed part of its manufacturing process and as a result some new equipment has been purchased, however, there are considerable levels of plant and equipment which are now surplus to requirement. Purchase requisitions for all new equipment have been authorised by production supervisors and little has been done to reduce the surplus of old equipment.

Required:

(a)   **In respect of the internal control of Pear International Co:**

          (i)   **Identify and explain SEVEN deficiencies;**
          (ii)   **Recommend a control to address each of these deficiencies; and**
          (iii)   **Describe a test of control Apple & Co would perform to assess if each of these controls is operating effectively.**   (21 marks)

(b)   Pear's directors are considering establishing an internal audit department next year. The finance director has asked about the differences between internal audit and external audit and what impact, if any, establishing an internal audit department would have on future external audits performed by Apple & Co.

       Required:

          (i)   **Distinguish between internal audit and external audit.**   (4 marks)

          (ii)   **Explain the potential impact on the work performed by Apple & Co during the interim and final audits, if Pear International Co was to establish an internal audit department.**   (5 marks)

(30 marks)

Question 26 OREGANO

You are a member of the recently formed internal audit department of Oregano Co (Oregano). The company manufactures tinned fruit and vegetables which are supplied to large and small food retailers. Management and those charged with governance of Oregano have concerns about the effectiveness of their sales and despatch system and have asked internal audit to document and review the system.

Sales and despatch system

Sales orders are mainly placed through Oregano's website but some are made via telephone. Online orders are automatically checked against inventory records for availability; telephone orders, however, are checked manually by order clerks after the call. A follow-up call is usually made to customers if there is insufficient inventory. When taking telephone orders, clerks note down the details on plain paper and afterwards they complete a three part pre-printed order form. These order forms are not sequentially numbered and are sent manually to both despatch and the accounts department.

As the company is expanding, customers are able to place online orders which will exceed their agreed credit limit by 10%. Online orders are automatically forwarded to the despatch and accounts departments.

A daily pick list is printed by the despatch department and this is used by the warehouse team to despatch goods. The goods are accompanied by a despatch note and all customers are required to sign a copy of this. On return, the signed despatch notes are given to the warehouse team to file.

The sales quantities are entered from the despatch notes and the authorised sales prices are generated by the invoicing system. If a discount has been given, this has to be manually entered by the sales clerk onto the invoice.

Due to the expansion of the company, and as there is a large number of sale invoices, extra accounts staff have been asked to help temporarily with producing the sales invoices. Normally it is only two sales clerks who produce the sales invoices.

Required:

(a)   **Describe TWO methods for documenting the sales and despatch system; and for each explain an advantage and a disadvantage of using this method.**   (6 marks)

(b)   **List TWO control objectives of Oregano Co's sales and despatch system.**   (2 marks)

(c)   **Identify and explain SIX deficiencies in Oregano Co's sales and despatch system and provide a recommendation to address each of these deficiencies.**   (12 marks)

(20 marks)

Question 27   CHERRY BLOSSOM

The following scenario relates to questions 1–5

Cherry Blossom Co (Cherry) manufactures custom made furniture and its year end is 30 April. The company purchases its raw materials from a wide range of suppliers. Below is a description of Cherry's purchasing system.

When production supervisors require raw materials, they complete a requisition form and submit it to the purchase ordering department. Requisition forms do not require authorisation and no reference is made to the current inventory levels of the materials being requested. Staff in the purchase ordering department use the requisitions to raise sequentially-numbered purchase orders based on the approved suppliers list, which was last updated 24 months ago. The purchasing director authorises the orders before they are sent to the suppliers.

When goods are received, the warehouse department verifies the quantity to the supplier's despatch note and checks that the quality of the goods received. If satisfactory, a sequentially-numbered goods received note (GRN) is completed and a copy sent to the finance department.

Purchase invoices are sent directly to the purchase ledger clerk. At the end of each week he gives each invoice a unique number based on the supplier code and inputs them to the purchase ledger using batch controls. Invoices are reviewed and authorised for payment by the finance director. All invoices are paid 60 days after input.

1   **Which of the following is NOT an internal control deficiency in Cherry Blossom's purchasing system?**

        A   Production supervisors complete a requisition form and submit it to the purchase ordering department

        B   The warehouse department verifies the quantity of goods received to the supplier's despatch note and checks the quality of goods received

        C   The purchase ledger clerk gives each invoice a unique number based on the supplier code

        D   Payment is made 60 days after the invoice is input into the system

2 **Which of the following controls should be used to address Cherry's control deficiencies in the purchase ordering department?**

(1)   Requiring authorisation on requisition forms
(2)   The finance director authorises the orders before they are sent to suppliers
(3)   Management sets minimum authorised reorder levels for inventory
(4)   The approved supplier list is updated on at least an annual basis

A   2 only
B   1 and 4 only
C   2 and 3 only
D   1, 3 and 4

3 Cherry Blossom's controls over cash include:

(1)   the financial accountant signing the monthly bank reconciliation prepared by the cash accountant

(2)   the finance director comparing monthly cash expenditure to budgeted expenditure

These controls are examples of which of the following control activities?

	Control 1	Control 2
A	Authorisation	Segregation of duties
B	Authorisation	Performance reviews
C	Performance reviews	Physical controls
D	Segregation of duties	Physical controls

4 An effective system of internal control requires segregation of basic functions (segregation of duties).

Which of the following functions should ideally be segregated?

(1)   Authorisation of transactions
(2)   Preparation of financial statements
(3)   Custody or handling of assets
(4)   Budgetary control
(5)   Recording of transactions

A   1, 3 and 5
B   1, 2 and 3
C   1, 2 and 5
D   3, 4 and 5

5 The finance director has recently discovered that Cherry has been paying suppliers' invoices in respect of raw materials which had been returned due to poor quality.

Which of the following controls would have prevented this from occurring?

A   Comparison of supplier statements with payables ledger accounts
B   Date stamping purchase invoices on receipt
C   Matching of purchase invoices with goods received notes
D   Matching of purchase invoices with purchase orders

(10 marks)

Question 28 DOCUMENTATION AND MATERIALITY *(non-exam style)*

(a)   ISA 230 Audit Documentation deals with the auditor's responsibility to prepare audit documentation for an audit of financial statements.

Required:

State FOUR benefits of documenting audit work.   (4 marks)

(b)   ISA 320 Materiality in Planning and Performing an Audit provides guidance on the concept of materiality in planning and performing an audit.

Required:

Define materiality and determine how the level of materiality is assessed.   (6 marks)

(10 marks)

Question 29 TYE *(non-exam style)*

One of your audit clients, Tye Co, provides petrol, aviation fuel and similar oil-based products to the government of the country it is based in. Although the company is not listed on any stock exchange, it does follow best practice regarding corporate governance regulations. The audit work for this year is complete, apart from the matter referred to below.

As part of Tye Co's service contract with the government, it is required to hold an emergency inventory reserve of 6,000 barrels of aviation fuel. The inventory is to be used if the supply of aviation fuel is interrupted due to unforeseen events such as natural disaster or terrorist activity.

This fuel has, in the past, been valued at its cost price of $15 a barrel. The current value of aviation fuel is $120 a barrel. Although the audit work is complete, as noted above, the directors of Tye Co have now decided to show the "real" value of this closing inventory in the financial statements by valuing closing inventory of fuel at market value, which does not comply with relevant accounting standards. The draft financial statements of Tye Co currently show a profit of approximately $500,000 with net assets of $170 million.

Required:

(a)   **List the audit procedures and actions that you should now take in respect of the above matter.**   (6 marks)

(b)   *For the purposes of this section assume from part (a) that the directors have agreed to value inventory at $15 per barrel.*

Having investigated the matter in part (a) above, the directors present you with an amended set of financial statements showing the emergency reserve stated not at 6,000 barrels, but reported as 60,000 barrels. The final financial statements now show a profit following the inclusion of another 54,000 barrels of oil in inventory. When queried about the change from 6,000 to 60,000 barrels of inventory, the finance director stated that this change was made to meet expected amendments to emergency reserve requirements to be published in about six months' time. The inventory will be purchased this year, and no liability will be shown in the financial statements for this future purchase. The finance director also pointed out that part of Tye Co's contract with the government requires Tye Co to disclose an annual profit and that a review of bank loans is due in three months. Finally the finance director stated that if your audit firm issues a modified opinion on the financial statements in respect of the increase in inventory, they will not be recommended for re-appointment at the annual general meeting.

The finance director refuses to amend the financial statements to remove this "fictitious" inventory.

Required:

(i)   State the external auditor's responsibilities regarding the detection of fraud;

(4 marks)

(ii)   Discuss to which groups the auditors of Tye Co could report the "fictitious" aviation fuel inventory;   (6 marks)

(iii)   Discuss the safeguards that the auditors of Tye Co can use in an attempt to overcome the intimidation threat from the directors of Tye Co.   (4 marks)

(20 marks)

Question 30 BESTWOOD TRADING

The following scenario relates to questions 1–5

Your firm is the auditor of Bestwood Trading Co. The working papers which recorded the audit work on the bank reconciliation at 30 April 2016 noted cash receipts of $7,000 recorded in the cash book before the end of the reporting period which were not credited to the bank statement until a week or more after the year end. No further work was carried out as the amount was not considered material, and this conclusion was noted in the audit working papers. Two months after the financial statements had been issued the company investigated delays in banking cash receipts and discovered a fraud of $18,000. The fraud was carried out by the cashier who was responsible for banking all receipts and preparing the bank reconciliation.

1   The Senior Partner has asked you to explain the importance of audit working papers to unqualified audit staff who have recently joined your audit firm.

Which of the following are reasons why auditors use working papers to record their work?

(1)   To enhance the efficiency of future audits
(2)   To evidence that the audit was carried out in accordance with audit regulations
(3)   To assist managers and partners in reviewing the audit work
(4)   To enable the auditor to escape liability in a subsequent lawsuit

A   1, 2 and 4
B   2, 3 and 4
C   1, 3 and 4
D   1, 2 and 3

2   Standardised working papers may improve the efficiency with which the audit file is prepared and reviewed. However, the extent to which a standardised approach is desirable will vary from audit to audit and will be more appropriate for some forms of documentation than others.

For which document would a standardised approach be particularly appropriate?

A   An engagement letter
B   An annual bank confirmation letter
C   An audit programme
D   Written representations from management

3 **To whom did your firm have a primary duty to report the late banking of the cash receipts?**

    A   Management and those charged with governance

    B   Legal authorities

    C   The company's shareholders

    D   It was not necessary to report the delay because the amount was immaterial

4 **Which of the following items of information noted during the audit of Bestwood Trading would most likely suggest non-compliance with laws and regulations?**

    A   Bestwood's failure to develop adequate segregation of duties related to cash

    B   The presence of several complex transactions affecting expense accounts

    C   An exchange of property for similar property

    D   The discovery of unexplained payments made to government employees

5 Your firm is facing a legal claim for negligence in relation to the audit of Woodferns Agencies Co. It is alleged that a fraud was perpetrated by the manager of one of the smallest of the company's 80 branches. Your firm had not visited that branch for three years as it visits branches on a rotational basis. As a result the fraud went undetected for two years.

Which of the following could be used by the firm as defence against the claim?

    (1)   Audit documentation showing that the audit was carried out in accordance with International Standards on Auditing

    (2)   An up-to-date letter of engagement stating that the directors should not rely on the audit to detect all frauds which may exist

    (3)   Written representations from management acknowledging their primary responsibility for the prevention and detection of fraud

    (4)   Case law judgements indicating that an auditor should not be held responsible for ingeniously laid frauds

    A   2 and 3 only

    B   1, 2, and 3 only

    C   2, 3 and 4 only

    D   1, 2, 3 and 4

(10 marks)

Question 31 SYCAMORE SCIENCE

You are the audit supervisor of Maple & Co and are currently planning the audit of an existing client, Sycamore Science Co (Sycamore), whose year end was 30 April 2016. Sycamore is a pharmaceutical company, which manufactures and supplies a wide range of medical supplies. The draft financial statements show revenue of $35·6 million and profit before tax of $5·9 million.

Sycamore's previous finance director left the company in December 2015 after it was discovered that he had been claiming fraudulent expenses from the company for a significant period of time. A new finance director was appointed in January 2016 who was previously a financial controller of a bank, and she has expressed surprise that Maple & Co had not uncovered the fraud during last year's audit.

During the year Sycamore has spent $1·8 million on developing several new products. These projects are at different stages of development and the draft financial statements show the full amount of $1·8 million within intangible assets. In order to fund this development, $2·0 million was borrowed from the bank and is due for repayment over a ten-year period. The bank has attached minimum profit targets as part of the loan covenants.

The new finance director has informed the audit partner that since the year end there has been an increased number of sales returns and that in the month of May over $0·5 million of goods sold in April were returned.

Maple & Co attended the year-end inventory count at Sycamore's warehouse. The auditor present raised concerns that during the count there were movements of goods in and out the warehouse and this process did not seem well controlled.

During the year, a review of plant and equipment in the factory was undertaken and surplus plant was sold, resulting in a profit on disposal of $210,000.

Required:

(a) **State Maples & Co's responsibilities in relation to the prevention and detection of fraud and error.** (4 marks)

(b) **Describe SIX audit risks, and explain the auditor's response to each risk, in planning the audit of Sycamore Science Co.** (12 marks)

(c) Sycamore's new finance director has read about review engagements and is interested in the possibility of Maple & Co undertaking these in the future. However, she is unsure how these engagements differ from an external audit and how much assurance would be gained from this type of engagement.

Required:

(i) **Explain the purpose of review engagements and how these differ from external audits; and** (2 marks)

(ii) **Describe the level of assurance provided by external audits and review engagements.** (2 marks)

(20 marks)

Question 32 TINKERBELL

Introduction

Tinkerbell Toys Co (Tinkerbell) is a manufacturer of children's building block toys; they have been trading for over 35 years and they sell to a wide variety of customers including large and small toy retailers across the country. The company's year end is 31 May.

The company has a large manufacturing plant, four large warehouses and a head office. Upon manufacture, the toys are stored in one of the warehouses until they are despatched to customers. The company does not have an internal audit department.

Sales ordering, goods despatched and invoicing

Each customer has a unique customer account number and this is used to enter sales orders when they are received in writing from customers. The orders are entered by an order clerk and the system automatically checks that the goods are available and that the order will not take the customer over their credit limit. For new customers, a sales manager completes a credit application; this is checked through a credit agency and a credit limit entered into the system by the credit controller. The company has a price list, which is updated twice a year. Larger customers are entitled to a discount; this is agreed by the sales director and set up within the customer master file.

Once the order is entered an acceptance is automatically sent to the customer by mail/email confirming the goods ordered and a likely despatch date. The order is then sorted by address of customer. The warehouse closest to the customer receives the order electronically and a despatch list and sequentially numbered goods despatch notes (GDNs) are automatically generated. The warehouse team pack the goods from the despatch list and, before they are sent out, a second member of the team double checks the despatch list to the GDN, which accompanies the goods.

Once despatched, a copy of the GDN is sent to the accounts team at head office and a sequentially numbered sales invoice is raised and checked to the GDN. Periodically a computer sequence check is performed for any missing sales invoice numbers.

Fraud

During the year a material fraud was uncovered. It involved cash/cheque receipts from customers being diverted into employees' personal accounts. In order to cover up the fraud, receipts from subsequent unrelated customers would then be recorded against the earlier outstanding receivable balances and this cycle of fraud would continue.

The fraud occurred because two members of staff "who were related" colluded. One processed cash receipts and prepared the weekly bank reconciliation; the other employee recorded customer receipts in the sales ledger. An unrelated sales ledger clerk was supposed to send out monthly customer statements but this was not performed. The bank reconciliations each had a small unreconciled amount but no-one reviewed the reconciliations after they were prepared. The fraud was only uncovered when the two employees went on holiday at the same time and it was discovered that cash receipts from different customers were being applied to older receivable balances to hide the earlier sums stolen.

Required:

(a) Recommend SIX tests of controls the auditor would normally carry out on the sales system of Tinkerbell, and explain the objective of each test. (12 marks)

(b) Describe substantive procedures the auditor should perform to confirm Tinkerbell's year-end receivables balance. (8 marks)

(c) Identify and explain controls Tinkerbell should implement to reduce the risk of fraud occurring again and, for each control, describe how it would mitigate the risk. (6 marks)

(d) Describe substantive procedures the auditor should perform to confirm Tinkerbell's revenue. (4 marks)

(30 marks)

Question 33 BONSAI TRADING

The following scenario relates to questions 1–5

Bonsai Trading Co (Bonsai) manufactures electrical equipment. Its year end is 30 September 2016. As audit supervisor of Poplar & Co you are developing the audit programmes for the forthcoming interim audit.

The company's internal audit department has provided you with documentation relating to the non-current assets cycle including the related controls listed below:

■ All purchase orders for capital items are required to be authorised by the capital expenditure committee.

■ On receipt, each asset is assigned a unique serial number that is recorded on the asset and in the non-current assets register.

■ When the asset arrives, a goods received note (GRN) is completed and the GRN classification is reviewed and initialled by a responsible official

■ Periodically, internal audit undertakes a review of assets in the register and compares them to assets on site, using the serial number to confirm existence of the asset.

1 **In relation to the above controls, which of the following are tests of control that that should be performed during the interim audit?**

(1) Review a sample of capital expenditure purchase orders for evidence of authorisation by the capital expenditure committee

(2) From a list of serial numbers extracted from the non-current asset register, select a sample of assets purchased and verify their physical existence

(3) Select a sample of GRNs and confirm whether each GRN is initialled as reviewed by a responsible official

(4) Accompany internal audit on its next review of the asset ledger, select a sample of the serial numbers confirmed by internal audit and verify the existence of the assets

A	1 and 2
B	1 and 3
C	3 and 4
D	2 and 4

2   As you develop the audit programme for Bonsai, you identify the financial controller's review of the bank reconciliation as another control to test. In connection with this test, you:

   (1)   interview the financial controller to understand the specific data reviewed on the reconciliation

   (2)   verify that the bank reconciliation is properly prepared by the accountant and reviewed by the financial controller as evidenced by their respective signatures.

These actions are examples of which of the following types of audit procedure?

	Action 1	Action 2
A	Inquiry	Inspection of records
B	Confirmation	Reperformance
C	Analytical procedures	Reperformance
D	Observation and	Inspection of records

3   **Under what circumstances would you be most likely to perform substantive procedures during the interim audit?**

A	The account being tested fluctuates based on management's discretion
B	The account being tested has very little activity from year to year
C	The account being tested has a high level of inherent risk and control risk
D	The account being tested is not reasonably predictable in terms of its relative significance to the financial statements

4   During the interim audit of Bonsai you are informed by your audit manager that during the year a fraud occurred at the client. A payroll clerk set up fictitious employees and the wages were paid into the clerk's own bank account. This clerk has subsequently left the company, but the audit manager is concerned that additional frauds have taken place in the wages department.

Which of the following procedures should you undertake as a result of the increased risk arising from the payroll fraud?

   (1)   Review board minutes for evidence of management's discussion of the materiality of the payroll fraud

   (2)   Review the supporting documentation to confirm the total of the fraudulent payments and assess the materiality of the misstatement

   (3)   Recommend and assist Bonsai in implementing better internal controls over payroll

   (4)   Inform local law enforcement authorities of the fraud and give them the name of the payroll clerk

A	1 and 2
B	1 and 3
C	2 and 4
D	3 and 4

5   Another material fraud was discovered at Bonsai shortly after Poplar & Co presented an unmodified auditor's report to the annual general meeting. Your standard letter of engagement indicated that Poplar & Co "would plan the audit to have reasonable expectation of detecting material misstatements in the financial statements resulting from errors or fraud", but also stated that the primary responsibility for the prevention and detection of fraud lay with management.

Which of the following statements most accurately reflects the likelihood that Poplar & Co being held liable for the failure to find the fraud?

A   Poplar is likely to be liable because the engagement letter accepted specific responsibility to find material misstatements

B   Poplar is likely to be found liable if you found indications of a possible fraud but dismissed them as immaterial having failed to investigate them adequately

C   Poplar is likely to be held liable if you have not designed specific tests to look for fraud in all areas of the accounting records

D   Poplar is unlikely to be held liable because the engagement letter specifically stated that management were responsible for the prevention and detection of fraud

(10 marks)

Question 34 BLAKE

Introduction

Blake Co assembles specialist motor vehicles such as lorries, buses and trucks. The company owns four assembly plants to which parts are delivered and assembled into the motor vehicles.

The motor vehicles are assembled using a mix of robot and manual production lines. The "human" workers normally work a standard eight hour day, although this is supplemented by overtime on a regular basis as Blake has a full order book. There is one shift per day; mass production and around the clock working are not possible due to the specialist nature of the motor vehicles being assembled.

Wages system – shift workers

Shift-workers arrive for work at about 7.00 am and "clock in" using an electronic identification card. The card is scanned by the time recording system and each production shift-worker's identification number is read from their card by the scanner. The worker is then logged in as being at work. Shift-workers are paid from the time of logging in. The logging in process is not monitored as it is assumed that shift-workers would not work without first logging in on the time recording system.

Shift-workers are split into groups of about 25 employees, with each group under the supervision of a shift foreman. Each day, each group of shift-workers is allocated a specific vehicle to manufacture. At least 400 vehicles have to be manufactured each day by each work group. If necessary, overtime is worked to complete the day's quota of vehicles. The shift foreman is not required to monitor the extent of any overtime working although the foreman does ensure workers are not taking unnecessary or prolonged breaks which would automatically increase the amount of overtime worked. Shift-workers log off at the end of each shift by re-scanning their identification card.

Payment of wages

Details of hours worked each week are sent electronically to the payroll department, where hours worked are allocated by the computerised wages system to each employee's wages records. Staff in the payroll department compare hours worked from the time recording system to the computerised wages system, and enter a code word to confirm the accuracy of transfer. The code word also acts as authorisation to calculate net wages. The code word is the name of a domestic cat belonging to the department head and is therefore generally known around the department.

Each week the computerised wages system calculates:

(i) gross wages, using the standard rate and overtime rates per hour for each employee;
(ii) statutory deductions from wages; and
(iii) net pay.

The list of net pay for each employee is sent over Blake's internal network to the accounts department. In the accounts department, an accounts clerk ensures that employee bank details are on file. The clerk then authorises and makes payment to those employees using Blake's online banking systems. Every few weeks the financial accountant reviews the total amount of wages made to ensure that the management accounts are accurate.

Termination of employees

Occasionally, employees leave Blake. When this happens, the personnel department sends an e-mail to the payroll department detailing the employee's termination date and any unclaimed holiday pay. The receipt of the e-mail by the payroll department is not monitored by the personnel department.

Salaries system – shift managers

All shift managers are paid an annual salary; there are no overtime payments. Salaries were increased in July by 3% and an annual bonus of 5% of salary was paid in November.

Required:

(a) **List FOUR control objectives of a wages system.** (2 marks)

(b) **As the external auditors of Blake Co, write a report to management in respect of the shift-workers' wages recording and payment systems which:**

(i) **Identifies and explains FIVE weaknesses in that system;**
(ii) **Explains the possible effect of each weakness;**
(iii) **Provides a recommendation to alleviate each weakness.**

Note: Up to two marks will be awarded within this requirement for presentation. (16 marks)

(c) **List THREE substantive analytical procedures you should perform on the shift managers' salary system. For each procedure, state your expectation of the result of that procedure.** (6 marks)

(d) Audit evidence can be obtained using various audit procedures, such as inspection.

APART FROM THIS PROCEDURE, in respect of testing the accuracy of the time recording system at Blake Co, explain THREE procedures used in collecting audit evidence and discuss whether the auditor will benefit from using each procedure.

(6 marks)

(30 marks)

Question 35 GREYSTONE

(a) Auditors have a responsibility under ISA 265 *Communicating Deficiencies in Internal Control to those Charged with Governance and Management*, to communicate deficiencies in internal controls. In particular SIGNIFICANT deficiencies in internal controls must be communicated in writing to those charged with governance.

Required:

Explain examples of matters the auditor should consider in determining whether a deficiency in internal controls is significant. (5 marks)

(b) Greystone Co is a retailer of ladies clothing and accessories. It operates in many countries around the world and has expanded steadily from its base in Europe. Its main market is aimed at 15 to 35 year olds and its prices are mid to low range. The company's year end was 30 September 2016.

In the past the company has bulk ordered its clothing and accessories twice a year. However, if their goods failed to meet the key fashion trends then this resulted in significant inventory write-downs. As a result of this the company has recently introduced a just in time ordering system. The fashion buyers make an assessment nine months in advance as to what the key trends are likely to be, these goods are sourced from their suppliers but only limited numbers are initially ordered.

Greystone Co has an internal audit department but at present their only role is to perform regular inventory counts at the stores.

Ordering process

Each country has a purchasing manager who decides on the initial inventory levels for each store, this is not done in conjunction with store or sales managers. These quantities are communicated to the central buying department at the head office in Europe. An ordering clerk amalgamates all country orders by specified regions of countries, such as Central Europe and North America, and passes them to the purchasing director to review and authorise.

As the goods are sold, it is the store manager's responsibility to re-order the goods through the purchasing manager; they are prompted weekly to review inventory levels as although the goods are just in time, it can still take up to four weeks for goods to be received in store.

It is not possible to order goods from other branches of stores as all ordering must be undertaken through the purchasing manager. If a customer requests an item of clothing, which is unavailable in a particular store, then the customer is provided with other branch telephone numbers or recommended to try the company website.

Goods received and invoicing

To speed up the ordering to receipt of goods cycle, the goods are delivered directly from the suppliers to the individual stores. On receipt of goods the quantities received are checked by a sales assistant against the supplier's delivery note, and then the assistant produces a goods received note (GRN). This is done at quiet times of the day to maximise sales. The checked GRNs are sent to head office for matching with purchase invoices.

As purchase invoices are received they are manually matched to GRNs from the stores, this can be a very time consuming process as some suppliers may have delivered to over 500 stores. Once the invoice has been agreed then it is sent to the purchasing director for authorisation. It is at this stage that the invoice is entered onto the purchase ledger.

Required:

As the external auditors of Greystone Co, write a report to management in respect of the purchasing system which:

(i)	**Identifies and explains FOUR deficiencies in that system;**
(ii)	**Explains the possible implication of each deficiency;**
(iii)	**Provides a recommendation to address each deficiency.**

A covering letter is required.

Note: Up to two marks will be awarded within this requirement for presentation.   (14 marks)

(c)   **Describe substantive procedures the auditor should perform on the year-end trade payables of Greystone Co.**   (5 marks)

(d)   **Describe additional assignments that the internal audit department of Greystone Co could be asked to perform by those charged with governance.**   (6 marks)

(30 marks)

Question 36 FOX INDUSTRIES

(a)   ISA 260 *Communication with Those Charged with Governance* provides guidance to auditors in relation to communicating with those charged with governance on matters arising from the audit of an entity's financial statements.

Required:

(i)	**Explain why it is important that auditors communicate throughout the audit with those charged with governance; and** (2 marks)
(ii)	**Describe THREE examples of matters that the auditors may communicate to those charged with governance.** (3 marks)

Introduction

Fox Industries Co (Fox) manufactures engineering parts. It has one operating site and a customer base spread across Europe. The company's year end was 30 April 2016. Below is a description of the purchasing and payments system.

Purchasing system

Whenever production materials are required, the relevant department sends a requisition form to the ordering department. An order clerk raises a purchase order and contacts a number of suppliers to see which can despatch the goods first. This supplier is then chosen. The order clerk sends out the purchase order. This is not sequentially numbered and only orders above $5,000 require authorisation.

Purchase invoices are input daily by the purchase ledger clerk, who has been in the role for many years and, as an experienced team member, he does not apply any application controls over the input process. Every week the purchase day book automatically updates the purchase ledger, the purchase ledger is then posted manually to the general ledger by the purchase ledger clerk.

Payments system

Fox maintains a current account and a number of saving (deposit) accounts. The current account is reconciled weekly but the saving (deposit) accounts are only reconciled every two months.

In order to maximise their cash and bank balance, Fox has a policy of delaying payments to all suppliers for as long as possible. Suppliers are paid by a bank transfer. The finance director is given the total amount of the payments list, which he authorises and then processes the bank payments.

Required:

(b)   As the external auditors of Fox Industries Co, write a report to management in respect of the purchasing and payments system described above which:

        (i)   Identifies and explains FOUR deficiencies in the system; and
        (ii)   Explains the possible implication of each deficiency; and
        (iii)   Provides a recommendation to address each deficiency.

        Note: A covering letter IS REQUIRED.

        Note: Up to two marks will be awarded within this requirement for presentation and the remaining marks will be split equally between each part.   (14 marks)

(c)   Identify and explain FOUR application controls that should be adopted by Fox Industries Co to ensure the completeness and accuracy of the input of purchase invoices.
                                                                                                                         (4 marks)

(d)   Describe substantive procedures the auditor should perform to confirm the bank and cash balance of Fox Industries Co at the year end.   (7 marks)

(30 marks)

Question 37 TROMBONE

Trombone Co (Trombone) operates a chain of hotels across the country. Trombone employs in excess of 250 permanent employees and its year end is 31 August 2016. You are the audit supervisor of Viola & Co and are currently reviewing the documentation of Trombone's payroll system, detailed below, in preparation for the interim audit.

Trombone's payroll system

Permanent employees work a standard number of hours per week as specified in their employment contract. However, when the hotels are busy, staff can be requested by management to work additional shifts as overtime. This can either be paid on a monthly basis or taken as days off.

Employees record any overtime worked and days taken off on weekly overtime sheets which are sent to the payroll department. The standard hours per employee are automatically set up in the system and the overtime sheets are entered by clerks into the payroll package, which automatically calculates the gross and net pay along with relevant deductions. These calculations are not checked at all. Wages are increased by the rate of inflation each year and the clerks are responsible for updating the standing data in the payroll system.

Employees are paid on a monthly basis by bank transfer for their contracted weekly hours and for any overtime worked in the previous month. If employees choose to be paid for overtime, authorisation is required by department heads of any overtime in excess of 30% of standard hours. If employees choose instead to take days off, the payroll clerks should check back to the "overtime worked" report; however, this report is not always checked.

The "overtime worked" report, which details any overtime recorded by employees, is run by the payroll department weekly and emailed to department heads for authorisation. The payroll department asks department heads to only report if there are any errors recorded. Department heads are required to arrange for overtime sheets to be authorised by an alternative responsible official if they are away on annual leave; however, there are instances where this arrangement has not occurred.

The payroll package produces a list of payments per employee; this links into the bank system to produce a list of automatic payments. The finance director reviews the total list of bank transfers and compares this to the total amount to be paid per the payroll records; if any issues arise then the automatic bank transfer can be manually changed by the finance director.

Required:

(a)   **In respect of the payroll system of Trombone Co:**

     (i)   **Identify and explain FIVE deficiencies;**
     (ii)   **Recommend a control to address each of these deficiencies; and**
     (iii)   **Describe a test of control Viola & Co should perform to assess if each of these controls is operating effectively.**

     Note: The total marks will be split equally between each part.   (15 marks)

(b)   **Explain the difference between an interim and a final audit.**   (5 marks)

(c)   **Describe substantive procedures you should perform at the final audit to confirm the completeness and accuracy of Trombone Co's payroll expense.**   (6 marks)

(d)   Trombone deducts employment taxes from its employees' wages on a monthly basis and pays these to the local taxation authorities in the following month. At the year end the financial statements will contain an accrual for income tax payable on employment income. You will be in charge of auditing this accrual.

     Required:

     Describe the audit procedures required in respect of the year end accrual for tax payable on employment income.   (4 marks)

     (30 marks)

Question 38 GARCIA INTERNATIONAL

Garcia International Co (Garcia) is a manufacturer of electrical equipment. It has factories across the country and its customer base includes retailers as well as individuals, to whom direct sales are made through their website. The company's year end is 30 September 2016. You are an audit supervisor of Suarez & Co and are currently reviewing documentation of Garcia's internal control in preparation for the interim audit.

Garcia's website allows individuals to order goods directly, and full payment is taken in advance. Currently the website is not integrated into the inventory system and inventory levels are not checked at the time when orders are placed. Inventory is valued at the lower of cost and net realisable value.

Goods are despatched via local couriers; however, they do not always record customer signatures as proof that the customer has received the goods. Over the past 12 months there have been customer complaints about the delay between sales orders and receipt of goods. Garcia has investigated these and found that, in each case, the sales order had been entered into the sales system correctly but was not forwarded to the despatch department for fulfilling.

Garcia's retail customers undergo credit checks prior to being accepted and credit limits are set accordingly by sales ledger clerks. These customers place their orders through one of the sales team, who decides on sales discount levels.

Raw materials used in the manufacturing process are purchased from a wide range of suppliers. As a result of staff changes in the purchase ledger department, supplier statement reconciliations are no longer performed. Additionally, changes to supplier details in the purchase ledger master file can be undertaken by purchase ledger clerks as well as supervisors.

In the past six months Garcia has changed part of its manufacturing process and as a result some new equipment has been purchased, however, there are considerable levels of plant and equipment which are now surplus to requirement. Purchase requisitions for all new equipment have been authorised by production supervisors and little has been done to reduce the surplus of old equipment.

Required:

(a)   **In respect of the internal control of Garcia International Co:**

      (i)   **Identify and explain SIX deficiencies;**

      (ii)   **Recommend a control to address each of these deficiencies; and**

      (iii)   **Describe a test of control Suarez & Co would perform to assess if each of these controls is operating effectively.**

      Note: The total marks will be split equally between each part   (18 marks)

(b)   **Describe substantive procedures Suarez & Co should perform at the year end to confirm plant and equipment additions.**   (2 marks)

                                           (20 marks)

Question 39 HUMMINGBIRD SCENTS

Hummingbird Scents Co (Hummingbird) manufactures and sells luxury toiletries; they have been trading for over 20 years and the company's year end is 30 September 2016. Hummingbird sells products to trade customers via its own website; this represents 60% of revenue. Remaining revenue is generated by contracts to supply toiletries to hotels. Below is a description of the sales system.

Hotel revenue

The hotel revenue is made up of four key customers. Hummingbird has one sales clerk, Brenda, who maintains all aspects of this revenue stream; Brenda receives customer orders, raises sales invoices and processes payments. In raising invoices, the sales system automatically inserts the online trade customer prices for products. However, each hotel customer has contracted prices which are lower than the online prices and hence Brenda manually edits the invoices prior to despatch.

Online revenue

New trade customers are set up in the sales ledger master file upon passing suitable credit checks, and a credit limit is set at this stage by the finance director. Customers place online orders up to their pre-set credit limit; they receive an email confirmation and the sales order interfaces into the despatch system. The order number is linked to the customer account number. Goods are despatched daily with a goods despatched note which is referenced to the sales order number but are not sequentially numbered. Hummingbird used to despatch goods via a reliable national courier company. However, to reduce costs they have changed to a cheaper local courier and some orders have been delivered to customers late.

Trade customers' sales invoices are automatically generated by the system on the day the online order is placed. The prices are inserted in accordance with the website rates. Occasionally Hummingbird makes special offers or discounts sales; when this occurs the master file data has to be amended to ensure that the correct prices are used on invoices. This task is usually performed by a senior sales ledger clerk.

Revenue and receivables records

On a monthly basis statements are sent to the hotel customers; a number of trade customers have been requesting monthly statements and Hummingbird is considering this request. The company only reconciles the sales ledger control account at the end of September in order to verify the year-end balance.

Required:

(a)   **As the external auditor of Hummingbird Co, write a report to management in respect of the sales system described above which:**

     (i)   **Identifies and explains SEVEN deficiencies in the sales system; and**
     (ii)   **Provides a recommendation to address each of these deficiencies.**

     A covering letter IS required.

     Note: Up to two marks will be awarded within this requirement for presentation and the remaining marks will be split equally between each part.   (16 marks)

(b)   **Describe substantive procedures the auditor should perform to confirm Hummingbird Co's revenue.**   (4 marks)

(20 marks)

Question 40 BOULDER

ISA 315 *Identifying and Assessing the Risks of Material Misstatement through Understanding the Entity and its Environment* states that management implicitly or explicitly makes assertions relating to the various elements of financial statements including related disclosures. Auditors may use two categories of assertions to form a basis for risk assessments and the design and performance of further audit procedures. The categories suggested by ISA 315 relate to (i) classes of transactions and related disclosures and (ii) account balances and related disclosures.

One assertion applicable to both categories is *completeness*: that all transactions, events, assets, liabilities, equity interests that should have been recorded have been recorded, and all related disclosures that should have been included in the financial statements have been included.

Required:

(a)   **List and describe SIX financial statement assertions, other than completeness, used by auditors in the audit of financial statements.**   (6 marks)

(b)   Boulder is a small company that manufactures hosiery products. It employs approximately 150 staff, all of whom are paid by bank transfer.

Temporary factory staff are hired through an agency and are paid on piece rates (i.e. for the number of items that they produce or process) on a weekly basis. Supervisors at Boulder authorise documentation indicating the number of items produced or processed by agency staff. The agency is paid by bank transfer and it, not Boulder, is responsible for the deduction of tax and social insurance.

Permanent factory staff are paid on a weekly basis on the basis of hours worked as evidenced by clock cards. Administration and sales staff are paid a monthly salary. The two directors of the company are also paid a monthly salary.

Sales staff are paid a quarterly bonus calculated on the basis of sales. Directors are paid an annual bonus based on profits.

You will be performing the audit of the financial statements for the year ending 31 December and you will be responsible for the figures in the financial statements relating to payroll.

Required:

Describe the substantive audit procedures you will perform on:

(i)   **the payroll balances in the statement of financial position of Boulder;** (10 marks)
(ii)   **the payroll transactions in the statement of profit or loss of Boulder.**
                                                                                            (4 marks)

                                                                                    (20 marks)

Question 41 DONALD

(a)   The auditor has a responsibility to design audit procedures to obtain sufficient and appropriate evidence. There are various audit procedures for obtaining evidence, such as external confirmation.

Required:

Apart from external confirmation:

(i)   State and explain FOUR procedures for obtaining evidence; and

(ii)   For each procedure, describe an example relevant to the audit of purchases and other expenses.   (8 marks)

(b)   Donald Co operates an airline business. The company's year end is 31 July.

You are the audit senior and you have started planning the audit. Your manager has asked you to have a meeting with the client and to identify any relevant audit risks so that the audit plan can be completed. From your meeting you ascertain the following:

In order to expand their flight network, Donald Co will need to acquire more airplanes; they have placed orders for another six planes at an estimated total cost of $20 million and the company is not sure whether these planes will be received by the year end. In addition the company has spent an estimated $15 million on refurbishing their existing planes. In order to fund the expansion Donald Co has applied for a loan of $25 million. It has yet to hear from the bank as to whether it will lend them the money.

The company receives bookings from travel agents as well as directly via their website. The travel agents are given a 90-day credit period to pay Donald Co, however, due to difficult trading conditions a number of the receivables are struggling to pay. The website was launched last year and has consistently encountered difficulties with customer complaints that tickets have been booked and paid for online but Donald Co has no record of them and hence has sold the seat to another customer.

Donald Co used to sell tickets via a large call centre located near to their head office. However, in May they closed it down and made the large workforce redundant.

Required:

Using the information provided, describe SIX audit risks and explain the auditor's response to each risk in planning the audit of Donald Co.   (12 marks)

(20 marks)

Question 42 ANALYTICAL PROCEDURES *(non-exam style)*

(a)   ISA 500 Audit Evidence requires audit evidence to be reliable.

Required:

List FIVE factors that influence the reliability of audit evidence.   (5 marks)

(b)   ISA 520 Analytical Procedures requires that the auditor uses analytical procedures as part of performing risk assessment procedures and to design and perform analytical procedures near the end of the audit to assist in forming an overall conclusion as to whether the financial statements are consistent with their understanding of the entity. In addition, substantive analytical procedures may be used to obtain audit evidence, provided such evidence can be considered as sufficient, relevant and reliable.

Required:

Explain the nature and purpose of analytical procedures.   (5 marks)

(10 marks)

Question 43 NEWTHORPE ENGINEERING

The following scenario relates to questions 1–5

You are auditing the financial statements of Newthorpe Engineering (Newthorpe) for the year ended 30 April 2016.

In March 2016 the Board decided to close one of the company's factories on 30 April 2016. This is the first time that the company has closed a factory. All items of plant and equipment and inventory will be sold. The employees will either be transferred to another factory or made redundant.

At the time of your audit in June 2016, you are aware that:

(i)   some of the plant and equipment has been sold;
(ii)   most of the inventory has been sold;
(iii)   all employees have either been made redundant or transferred to another factory.

The company has provided you with a schedule of the closure costs, the recoverable amounts of the plant and machinery, the net realisable value of inventory and the redundancy cost.

Details of the plant and machinery are maintained in a non-current asset register.

1   Which of the following audit procedures are appropriate to verify the company's estimate of the recoverable amounts of the plant and equipment?

(1)   Inspect the unsold plant and equipment at the factory

(2)   Recalculate the recoverable amount using a schedule of the non-current asset carrying amounts and estimated disposal proceeds

(3)   For plant and equipment sold, agree proceeds to sales invoices and cash book receipts

(4)   Examine purchase invoices for evidence of ownership of material items of plant and equipment

A   1 and 4 only
B   2 and 3 only
C   1, 2 and 4
D   2, 3 and 4

2   A full physical inventory count was carried out at 30 April 2016. Audit tests have confirmed that the counts are accurate and there are no purchases or sales cut-off errors.

Which of the following audit procedures are appropriate to verify the company's estimate of the realisable value of inventory?

(1)   Trace a sample of goods received notes and goods despatch notes from before and after the year end to accounting records

(2)   Inspect the inventory records for evidence of obsolete or slow-moving inventory

(3)   For inventory that has been sold, agree sale proceeds to sales invoices and cash book receipts

(4)   Confirm the reasonableness of advertising and delivery costs and other estimated costs of sales

A 1 and 2 only
B 3 and 4 only
C 1, 2 and 4
D 2, 3 and 4

3   The redundancy payments were based on the number of years' service and annual salary of each employee. Most employees received one week's pay for each year's service. The few employees with service contracts were paid the amount stated in their service contract, which was more than the redundancy pay offered to other employees. Employees transferred to another factory were not paid any redundancy.

Which of the following audit procedures are appropriate for testing the estimate of the redundancy costs?

(1) Develop an independent estimate and compare with management's estimate

(2) Compare management's estimate with redundancy payments made in prior periods

(3) Review the redundancy payments after the year end and compare to management's estimate

(4) Evaluate the reasonableness of the assumptions used by management to calculate the estimate

A 1, 2 and 3
B 1, 2 and 4
C 1, 3 and 4
D 2, 3 and 4

4   **Which of the following procedures would assist an auditor in determining whether management has identified all accounting estimates that could be material to the financial statements?**

(1) Inquire about the existence of any subsequent events
(2) Review communications with lawyers for information about litigation
(3) Confirm inventory held by third parties
(4) Determine whether accounting estimates deviate from historical patterns

A 1 and 2
B 2 and 3
C 1 and 3
D 2 and 4

5   **Which of the following are factors that may influence estimation uncertainty?**

(1) Management judgement
(2) Observable or unobservable inputs
(3) The length of any forecast period
(4) The auditor's professional judgement

A 1, 2 and 3
B 1, 2 and 4
C 1, 3 and 4
D 2, 3 and 4

(10 marks)

Question 44 TAM

Tam Co is owned and managed by two brothers with equal shareholdings. The company specialises in the sale of expensive motor vehicles. Annual revenue is in the region of $70,000,000 and the company requires an audit under local legislation. About 500 cars are sold each year, with an average value of $140,000, although the range of values is from $130,000 to $160,000. Invoices are completed manually with one director signing all invoices to confirm the sales value is correct. All accounting and financial statement preparation is carried out by the directors. A recent expansion of the company's showroom was financed by a bank loan, repayable over the next five years.

The audit manager is starting to plan the audit of Tam Co. The audit senior and audit junior assigned to the audit are helping the manager as a training exercise.

Comments are being made about how to select a sample of sales invoices for testing. Audit procedures are needed to ensure that the managing director has signed them and then to trace details into the sales day book and sales ledger.

"We should check all invoices" suggests the audit manager.

"How about selecting a sample using statistical sampling techniques" adds the audit senior.

"Why waste time obtaining a sample?" asks the audit junior. He adds "taking a random sample of invoices by reviewing the invoice file and manually choosing a few important invoices will be much quicker".

Required:

Explain each of the sample selection methods suggested by the audit manager, audit senior and audit junior, and discuss whether or not they are appropriate for obtaining a representative sample of sales invoices.

(10 marks)

Question 45 CRIGHTON-WARD

The following scenario relates to questions 1–5

You are the manager in charge of the audit of Crighton-Ward, a company which manufactures specialist cars for use in films. Audited turnover is $140 million with profit before tax of $7.5 million.

All audit work up to, but not including, obtaining written representations from management has been completed. A review of the audit file has disclosed two outstanding points:

Legal claim

The company is facing a legal claim from Lion's Roar in respect of the supply of a defective car. Lion's Roar maintains that the car was not built strongly enough while the directors of Crighton-Ward argue that the specification was not sufficiently detailed. Lion's Roar is seeking to claim $4 million for the cost of a replacement car and lost production time. Crighton-Ward's solicitors are unable to determine liability at the present time.

Depreciation

Depreciation of specialist production equipment has been included in the financial statements at the amount of 10% annually based on reducing balance. The treatment is consistent with prior accounting periods (which received an unmodified auditor's report) and other companies in the same industry and sales of old equipment show negligible profit or loss on sale. The audit senior, who is new to the audit, feels that depreciation is being undercharged in the financial statements.

1   An objective of the written representations from management is to reduce which of the following?

A   Management's responsibility for preventing and detecting fraud

B   The possibility of a misunderstanding concerning management's responsibility for the financial statements

C   The auditor's responsibility to detect misstatements

D   The risk that uncorrected misstatements could be material

2   Which of these matters should be included in the written representations from management?

A   Legal claim only
B   Depreciation only
C   Both legal claim and depreciation
D   Neither legal claim nor depreciation

3   Which of the following additional matters should be included in Crighton-Ward's written representations from management?

(1)   There were no irregularities involving management or employees that could have a material effect on the financial statements

(2)   All books of account and supporting documentation have been made available to the auditors

(3)   The financial statements are free from immaterial misstatements including omissions

(4)   Adjustments and disclosures of events subsequent to the date of the financial statements have been made

(5)   Significant deficiencies in internal control have been corrected

A   1, 2 and 3
B   3, 4 and 5
C   1, 2 and 4
D   2, 3 and 5

4   In the course of auditing Crighton-Ward, you received verbal representations from management for which independent evidence is not available.

For what reason should written confirmation of these representations from the directors be sought?

A   To ensure that the directors formally accept their responsibility for providing such information to the auditor

B   To enable the auditor to escape legal liability for any misstatement in the accounts

C   To provide evidence that the directors have kept proper accounting records

D   To reduce the extent of the alternative procedures which the auditor would otherwise have to undertake

5   The management and directors of Crighton-Ward refuse to provide you with a written management representation that you consider essential in relation to the impairment of a material asset.

Which of the following best describes this refusal?

A   It provides prima facie evidence that the financial statements are not presented fairly
B   It is an illegal act by management and the directors
C   It is grounds for an opinion modified on the basis of material misstatement
D   It is grounds for an opinion modified on the basis of insufficient audit evidence

(10 marks)

Question 46 RIGHTS AND REPRESENTATIONS *(non-exam style)*

(a)   Auditors have various duties to perform in their role as auditors, for example, to assess the truth and fairness of the financial statements.

Required:

Explain FOUR rights that enable auditors to carry out their duties.   (4 marks)

(b)   ISA 580 *Management Representations* provides guidance on the use of management representations as audit evidence.

Required:

List SIX items that could be included in the written representations from management.
(3 marks)

(c)   After performing tests of controls, the auditor is of the opinion that audit evidence is not sufficient to support the audit opinion; in other words many control errors were found.

Required:

Explain THREE actions that the auditor may now take in response to this problem.
(3 marks)

(10 marks)

Question 47 GREENFIELDS

Greenfields Co specialises in manufacturing equipment which can help to reduce toxic emissions in the production of chemicals. The company has grown rapidly over the past eight years and this is due partly to the warranties that the company gives to its customers. It guarantees its products for five years and if problems arise in this period it undertakes to fix them, or provide a replacement product.

You are the manager responsible for the audit of Greenfields and you are performing the final review stage of the audit and have come across the following two issues.

Receivable balance owing from Yellowmix Co

Greenfields has a material receivable balance owing from its customer, Yellowmix Co. During the year-end audit, your team reviewed the ageing of this balance and found that no payments had been received from Yellowmix for over six months, and Greenfields would not allow this balance to be included in the direct confirmation request. Instead, management has assured your team that they will provide a written representation confirming that the balance is recoverable.

Warranty provision

The warranty provision included within the statement of financial position is material. The audit team has performed testing over the calculations and assumptions which are consistent with prior years. The team has requested a written representation from management confirming the basis and amount of the provision are reasonable. Management has yet to confirm acceptance of this representation.

Required:

(a)   **Describe the audit procedures required in respect of accounting estimates.**   (5 marks)

(b)   **For each of the two issues above:**

  (i)   **Discuss the appropriateness of written representations as a form of audit evidence; and**   (4 marks)

  (ii)   **Describe additional procedures the auditor should now perform in order to reach a conclusion on the balance to be included in the financial statements.**   (6 marks)

  Note: The total marks will be split equally between each issue.

(c)   The directors of Greenfields have decided not to provide the audit firm with the written representation for the warranty provision as they feel that it is unnecessary.

  Required:

  Explain the steps the auditor of Greenfields Co should now take and the impact on the auditor's report in relation to the refusal to provide the written representation. (5 marks)

  (20 marks)

Question 48 WALSH

Walsh Co sells motor vehicle fuel, accessories and spares to retail customers. The company owns 25 shops.

The company has recently implemented a new computerised wages system. Employees work a standard eight hour day. Hours are recorded using a magnetic card system; when each employee arrives for work, they hold their card close to the card reader; the reader recognises the magnetic information on the card identifying the employee as being "at work". When the employee leaves work at the end of the day the process is reversed showing that the employee has left work.

Hours worked are calculated each week by the computer system using the magnetic card information. Overtime is calculated as any excess over the standard hours worked. Any overtime over 10% of standard hours is sent on a computer generated report by e-mail to the financial accountant. If necessary, the accountant overrides overtime payments if the hours worked are incorrect.

Statutory deductions and net pay are also computer calculated with payments being made directly into the employee's bank account. The only other manual check is the financial accountant authorising the net pay from Walsh's bank account, having reviewed the list of wages to be paid.

Required:

(a)   Using examples from Walsh Co, explain the benefits of using Computer-Assisted Audit Techniques to help the auditor to obtain sufficient appropriate audit evidence to be able to draw reasonable conclusions on which to base the audit opinion.   (8 marks)

(b)   List SIX examples of audit tests on Walsh Co's wages system using audit software.

(6 marks)

(c)   Explain how using test data should help in the audit of Walsh Co's wages system, noting any problems with this audit technique.   (6 marks)

(20 marks)

Question 49 DELPHIC *(non-exam style)*

Delphic Co is a wholesaler of furniture (such as chairs, tables and cupboards). Delphic buys the furniture from six major manufacturers and sells them to over 600 different customers ranging from large retail chain stores to smaller owner-controlled businesses. The receivables balance therefore includes customers owing up to $125,000 to smaller balances of about $5,000, all with many different due dates for payments and credit limits. All information is stored on Delphic's computer systems.

You are the audit senior in charge of the audit of the receivables balance. For the first time at this client, you have decided to use audit software to assist with the audit of the receivables balance. Computer staff at Delphic are happy to help the auditor, although they cannot confirm completeness of systems documentation, and warn that the systems have very old operating systems in place, limiting file compatibility with more modern programs.

The change in audit approach has been taken mainly to fully understand Delphic's computer systems prior to new internet modules being added next year. To limit the possibility of damage to Delphic's computer files, copy files will be provided by Delphic's computer staff for the auditor to use with their own audit software.

Required:

(a)   Explain the audit procedures that should be carried out using audit software on the receivables balance at Delphic Co. For each procedure, state the reason for that procedure.   (9 marks)

(b)   Explain the potential problems of using audit software at Delphic Co. For each problem, explain how it can be resolved.   (8 marks)

(17 marks)

Question 50 WEAR WRAITH

Wear Wraith (WW) Co's main activity is the extraction and supply of building materials including sand, gravel, cement and similar aggregates. The company's year end is 31 May and your firm has audited WW for a number of years. The main asset on the statement of financial position relates to non-current assets. A junior member of staff has attempted to prepare the non-current asset note for the financial statements. The note has not been reviewed by the senior accountant and so may contain errors.

	Land and buildings $	Plant and machinery $	Motor vehicles $	Railway trucks $	Total $
Cost					
1 June 2015	100,000	875,000	1,500,000	–	2,475,000
Additions	10,000	125,000	525,000	995,000	1,655,000
Disposals	–	(100,000)	(325,000)	–	(425,000)
31 May 2016	110,000	900,000	1,700,000	995,000	3,705,000
Depreciation					
1 June 2015	60,000	550,000	750,000	–	1,360,000
Charge	2,200	180,000	425,000	199,000	806,200
Disposals	–	(120,000)	(325,000)	–	(445,000)
31 May 2016	62,200	610,000	850,000	199,000	1,721,200
Carrying amount					
31 May 2016	47,800	290,000	850,000	796,000	1,983,800
Carrying amount					
31 May 2015	40,000	325,000	750,000	–	1,115,000

■ Land and buildings relate to company offices and land for those offices.

■ Plant and machinery includes extraction equipment such as diggers and dumper trucks used to extract sand and gravel, etc.

■ Motor vehicles include large trucks to transport the sand and gravel, etc.

■ Railway trucks relate to containers used to transport sand and gravel over long distances on the railway network.

Depreciation rates stated in the financial statements are all based on cost and calculated using the straight line basis. The rates are:

Land and buildings	2%
Plant and machinery	20%
Motor vehicles	33%
Railway trucks	20%

Disposals in the motor vehicles category relates to vehicles which were five years old.

Required:

(a)   **List and explain the audit work you should perform on railway trucks.**   (10 marks)

(b)   You have just completed your analytical procedures of the non-current assets note.

   Required:

   (i)   **Excluding railway trucks, identify and explain any issues with the non-current asset note to raise with management.**

   (ii)   **Explain how each issue could be resolved.**   (10 marks)

   Note: You are not required to re-cast the schedule.   **(20 marks)**

Question 51 GALARTHA

The following scenario relates to questions 1–5

You are the audit manager in JonArc & Co. A new client, Galartha Co, has net assets of $15 million. During the audit you noted that the directors have decided not to charge depreciation on buildings in the financial statements although this is required under International Financial Reporting Standards (IFRS).

1   **Which of the following additional audit procedures and actions should now be taken?**

   (1)   Meet with the directors to discuss their reasons for not depreciating buildings
   (2)   Explain to the directors that all buildings must be depreciated in accordance with IFRS
   (3)   Determine the effect of the disagreement on the auditor's report
   (4)   Adjust the financial statements to include the correct depreciation charge

   A   1 and 2 only
   B   3 and 4 only
   C   1, 2 and 3
   D   2, 3 and 4

2   You are currently planning the audit approach to the containers in which goods are delivered by Galartha to customers. Customers are not charged for the containers, which remain the property of Galartha and must be returned within 30 days after receipt of the goods. Container records identify each container separately and record their current location.

   Which of the following audit procedures would provide evidence of the existence of the containers?

   (1)   Inspect a sample of containers held by customers

   (2)   Inspect a sample of containers on hand during the year-end inventory count

   (3)   Trace a sample of containers held by customers at the year end to container records showing that the containers were returned after the year end

   (4)   Trace a sample of invoices for new containers purchased during the year to the container records

   A   1 and 2
   B   2 and 3
   C   3 and 4
   D   1 and 4

3   During the year Galartha made a significant investment in an unquoted company. Audit procedures will include inspecting the share certificate, contract note and statutory records of the company.

For which of the following assertions will these procedures provide evidence?

(1)   Existence
(2)   Rights and obligations
(3)   Completeness
(4)   Accuracy, valuation and allocation

A   1 only
B   1 and 2 only
C   1, 2 and 3 only
D   1, 2, 3 and 4

4   Galartha's directors have identified three major applied research projects whose results they hope will be developed into viable products. They have therefore capitalised the expenditure on these projects and will amortise it over three years. The financial statements fully disclose the accounting policy adopted.

Based on this information only, what form should the auditor's report take?

A   Unmodified with no reference to the accounting policy

B   Unmodified with reference to the inherent uncertainty drawing attention to the relevant disclosure note

C   Modified with a disclaimer arising from uncertainty about the viability of the products

D   Modified except for capitalisation of the expenditure

5   JonArc & Co was appointed after the end of Galartha Co's financial year. Consequently, the auditors could not attend the year-end inventory count. Inventory is material to the financial statements. You have not been able to apply alternative procedures to verify the existence of the inventory.

Based on this information only, what form should the auditor's report take?

A   Unmodified

B   Unmodified, with an emphasis of matter paragraph describing why the inventory count was not attended

C   Modified, except for the inability to gather the necessary evidence related to inventory

D   Modified, disclaimer due to the pervasive lack of evidence

(10 marks)

Question 52 TRENT TEXTILES

Your firm is the auditor of Trent Textiles which is a privately owned incorporated business. You are planning your audit work on the physical inventory count, which will be carried out at the firm's year end in one months' time.

Trent Textiles manufactures knitted garments, including sweaters. The production process comprises:

(a)   knitting the individual components (e.g. body and arms)
(b)   sewing the components together to form the finished garment
(c)   cleaning, finishing, pressing and folding the garments
(d)   packing the garments, ready for dispatch to the customer

Trent Textiles does not have a perpetual inventory system, so the value of the inventory in the financial statements is found from the physical count of the inventory at the end of the reporting period. For management purposes, Trent Textiles carries out a full inventory count every three months.

Your permanent file of the company confirms that it has a single factory and no internal audit department:

You have been asked by the manager in charge of the audit to suggest the work you will perform in relation to the inventory count at the stages listed below.

Required:

(a)   Describe the work you will carry out prior to the start of the inventory count.   (5 marks)

(b)   Explain the procedures you will check during the inventory count to ensure the company's staff have accurately recorded the inventory.   (8 marks)

(c)   Describe the work you will carry out and the matters you will record during the inventory count.   (7 marks)

(20 marks)

Question 53 SMOOTHBRUSH *(non-exam style)*

Introduction and client background

You are an audit senior in Staple & Co and you are commencing the planning of the audit of Smoothbrush Paints Co (Smoothbrush) for the year ending 31 August 2016.

Smoothbrush, a paint manufacturer, has been trading for over 50 years and operates from one central site which includes the production facility, warehouse and administration offices.

Smoothbrush sells all of its goods to large home improvement stores, with 60% being to one large chain store Homewares. The company has a one year contract to be the sole supplier of paint to Homewares. It secured the contract through significantly reducing prices and offering a four-month credit period, the company's normal credit period is one month.

Goods in/purchases

In recent years, Smoothbrush has reduced the level of goods directly manufactured and instead started to import paint from South Asia. Approximately 60% is imported and 40% manufactured. Within the production facility is a large amount of old plant and equipment that is now redundant and has minimal scrap value. Purchase orders for overseas paint are made six months in advance and goods can be in transit for up to two months. Smoothbrush accounts for the inventory when it receives the goods.

To avoid the disruption of a year-end inventory count, Smoothbrush has this year introduced a continuous/perpetual inventory counting system. The warehouse has been divided into 12 areas and these are each to be counted once over the year. The counting team includes a member of the internal audit department and a warehouse staff member. The following procedures have been adopted:

(1)   The team prints the inventory quantities and descriptions from the system and these records are then compared to the inventory physically present.

(2)   Any discrepancies in relation to quantities are noted on the inventory sheets, including any items not listed on the sheets but present in the warehouse area.

(3)   Any damaged or old items are noted and they are removed from the inventory sheets.

(4)   The sheets are then passed to the finance department for adjustments to be made to the records when the count has finished.

(5)   During the counts there will continue to be inventory movements with goods arriving and leaving the warehouse.

At the year end it is proposed that the inventory will be based on the underlying records. Traditionally Smoothbrush has maintained an allowance for slow-moving inventory based on 1% of the inventory value, but management feels that as inventory is being reviewed more regularly this allowance is no longer required.

Finance Director

In May 2016 Smoothbrush had a dispute with its finance director (FD) and he immediately left the company. The company has temporarily asked the financial controller to take over the role while they recruit a permanent replacement. The former FD has notified Smoothbrush that he intends to sue for unfair dismissal. The company is not proposing to make any provision or disclosures for this, as they are confident the claim has no merit.

Required:

(a)   **Identify and explain the audit risks identified at the planning stage of the audit of Smoothbrush Paints Co.**   (10 marks)

(b)   **Discuss the importance of assessing risks at the planning stage of an audit.**   (4 marks)

(c)   **List and explain suitable controls that should operate over the continuous/perpetual inventory counting system, to ensure the completeness and accuracy of the existing inventory records at Smoothbrush Paints Co.**   (10 marks)

(d)   **Describe THREE substantive procedures the auditor of Smoothbrush Paints Co should perform at the year end in confirming each of the following:**

      (i)   **the valuation of inventory;**   **(3 marks)**
      (ii)   **the completeness of provisions or contingent liabilities.**   (3 marks)

(30 marks)

Question 54 MISTIREAD

You are an audit manager in Ron & Co. One of your audit clients, MistiRead Co, is a specialist supplier of crime fiction with over 120,000 customers. The company owns one large warehouse, which contains at any one time about 1 million books of up to 80,000 different titles. Customers place orders for books either over the Internet or by mail order. Books are dispatched on the day of receipt of the order. Returns are allowed up to 30 days from the dispatch date provided the books look new and unread.

Due to the high inventory turnover, MistiRead maintains a perpetual inventory system using standard "off the shelf" software. Ron & Co has audited the system for the last five years and has found no errors within the software. Continuous inventory checking is carried out by MistiRead's internal audit department.

You are currently reviewing the continuous inventory checking system with an audit junior. The junior needs experience in auditing continuous inventory checking systems.

Required:

(a)   **Explain the advantages of using a perpetual inventory system.**   (4 marks)

(b)   **List the audit procedures you should perform to confirm the accuracy of the continuous inventory checking at MistiRead Co. For each procedure, explain the reason for carrying out that procedure.**   (12 marks)

(c)   During your preliminary audit planning you note that the engagement letter has been returned un-signed by the directors of MistiRead. When asked to explain their action, the directors indicate that they cannot allow you access to information on the company's new website development as this contains various trade secrets. You will not, therefore, be able to perform audit procedures on the research and development expenditure incurred on the website and included in non-current assets.

        Briefly explain the actions you should take as a result of the directors not signing the engagement letter.   (4 marks)

                                                                                (20 marks)

Question 55 PINEAPPLE BEACH HOTEL

(a)   (i)   **Identify and explain FOUR financial statement assertions relevant to account balances at the year end; and**

        (ii)   **For each identified assertion, describe a substantive procedure relevant to the audit of year-end inventory.**   (8 marks)

(b) Pineapple Beach Hotel Co (Pineapple) operates a hotel providing accommodation, leisure facilities and restaurants. Its year end was 30 April. You are the audit senior of Berry & Co and are currently preparing the audit programmes for the year end audit of Pineapple. You are reviewing the notes of last week's meeting between the audit manager and finance director where two material issues were discussed.

Depreciation

Pineapple incurred significant capital expenditure during the year on updating the leisure facilities for the hotel. The finance director has proposed that the new leisure equipment should be depreciated over 10 years using the straight-line method.

Food poisoning

Pineapple's directors received correspondence in March from a group of customers who attended a wedding at the hotel. They have alleged that they suffered severe food poisoning from food eaten at the hotel and are claiming substantial damages. Pineapple's lawyers have received the claim and believe that the lawsuit against the company is unlikely to be successful.

Required:

Describe substantive procedures to obtain sufficient and appropriate audit evidence in relation to the above two issues.

Note: The total marks will be split equally between each issue. (8 marks)

(c) **List and explain the purpose of FOUR items that should be included on every working paper prepared by the audit team.** (4 marks)

(20 marks)

Question 56 LILY WINDOW GLASS

Lily Window Glass Co (Lily) is a glass manufacturer, which operates from a large production facility, where it undertakes continuous production 24 hours a day, seven days a week. Also on this site are two warehouses, where the company's raw materials and finished goods are stored. Lily's year end is 31 December.

Lily is finalising the arrangements for the year-end inventory count, which is to be undertaken on 31 December 2016. The finished windows are stored within 20 aisles of the first warehouse. The second warehouse is for large piles of raw materials, such as sand, used in the manufacture of glass. The following arrangements have been made for the inventory count:

The warehouse manager will supervise the count as he is most familiar with the inventory. There will be ten teams of counters and each team will contain two members of staff, one from the finance and one from the manufacturing department. None of the warehouse staff, other than the manager, will be involved in the count.

Each team will count an aisle of finished goods by counting up and then down each aisle. As this process is systematic, it is not felt that the team will need to flag areas once counted. Once the team has finished counting an aisle, they will hand in their sheets and be given a set for another aisle of the warehouse. In addition to the above, to assist with the inventory counting, there will be two teams of counters from the internal audit department and they will perform inventory counts.

The count sheets are sequentially numbered, and the product codes and descriptions are printed on them but no quantities. If the counters identify any inventory which is not on their sheets, then they are to enter the item on a separate sheet, which is not numbered. Once all counting is complete, the sequence of the sheets is checked and any additional sheets are also handed in at this stage. All sheets are completed in ink.

Any damaged goods identified by the counters will be too heavy to move to a central location, hence they are to be left where they are but the counter is to make a note on the inventory sheets detailing the level of damage.

As Lily undertakes continuous production, there will continue to be movements of raw materials and finished goods in and out of the warehouse during the count. These will be kept to a minimum where possible.

The level of work-in-progress in the manufacturing plant is to be assessed by the warehouse manager. It is likely that this will be an immaterial balance. In addition, the raw materials quantities are to be approximated by measuring the height and width of the raw material piles. In the past this task has been undertaken by a specialist; however, the warehouse manager feels confident that he can perform this task.

Required:

(a) For the inventory count arrangements of Lily Window Glass Co:

(i) Identify and explain SIX deficiencies; and
(ii) Provide a recommendation to address each deficiency.

The total marks will be split equally between each part   (12 marks)

You are the audit senior of Daffodil & Co and are responsible for the audit of inventory for Lily. You will be attending the year-end inventory count on 31 December 2016.

In addition, your manager wishes to utilise computer-assisted audit techniques for the first time for controls and substantive testing in auditing Lily Window Glass Co's inventory.

(b) Describe the procedures to be undertaken by the auditor DURING the inventory count of Lily Window Glass Co in order to gain sufficient appropriate audit evidence.

           (6 marks)

(c) For the audit of the inventory cycle and year-end inventory balance of Lily Window Glass Co:

(i) Describe FOUR audit procedures that could be carried out using computer-assisted audit techniques (CAATS);

(ii) Explain the potential advantages of using CAATs; and

(iii) Explain the potential disadvantages of using CAATs.

The total marks will be split equally between each part.   (12 marks)

        (30 marks)

Question 57 WESTERN INDUSTRIES

You are the audit senior for the audit of Western Industries Co (Western), a manufacturing company whose year end was 31 December 2016. During the audit of Western's trade receivables balance you sent positive confirmation requests to a sample of Western's customers. You received the following confirmation responses in which the customers did not agree with the account balances that they were being asked to confirm:

Customer name	Amount	Customer response
Ames	$25,000	We ordered $25,000 worth of merchandise from Western in November. However, we mailed a $25,000 cheque to Western on 22 December 2016.
Brown	$50,000	We received goods with a cost of $30,000 and a retail value of $50,000 on consignment from Western on 15 December 2016. These goods have not been sold yet.
Copper	$35,000	We ordered $35,000 of merchandise on 30 October 2016 but Western was out of stock. They back-ordered the goods and we received them on 4 January 2017.
Devon	$60,000	Our records show that a courier attempted to deliver the goods from Western on 31 December 2016 but our premises were closed. We accepted the redelivery on 3 January.
Epoch	$15,000	Western promised these goods in 15 days on 5 December 2016. When we didn't receive them, I cancelled the order on 20 December 2016.
Fynes	$40,000	Western sent a duplicate shipment. We only ordered $20,000 of goods. The duplicate shipment was returned to Western on 3 January 2017.

Required:

(a)   **Identify and explain the management assertions that are relevant to the audit of accounts receivable.**   (4 marks)

(b)   **For each confirmation response:**

    (i)   **Explain the audit procedure the auditor should perform to confirm the response;**

    (ii) **Conclude what amount should be included in year-end trade receivables if the audit evidence gathered supports the customer's response.**   (12 marks)

(c)   **Describe the procedures the auditor should perform to obtain sufficient and appropriate audit evidence in relation to the valuation of Western's trade receivables.**   (4 marks)

(20 marks)

Question 58 SHERWOOD MACHINES

The following scenario relates to questions 1–5

Sherwood Machines Co (Sherwood) is a manufacturing company whose year end was 30 June. You are the audit supervisor and currently planning the audit of Sherwood's accounts receivable. At 30 June, Sherwood's accounts receivable balance was $2,600,000. Sherwood has 300 customers, including 10 customers with balances owed of more than $100,000 each. Tests of control have shown that there are weaknesses in Sherwood's internal control over sales and accounts receivable. In prior year audits, confirmations revealed misstatements in several customer accounts.

1   **Which of the following best describes the type of confirmation that should be sent to Sherwood's customers and the reason for that type of confirmation?**

A   Negative confirmation because misstatements were revealed in the prior year
B   Negative confirmations because there is a large number of small balance accounts
C   Positive confirmations because the risk of material misstatement is high
D   Positive confirmations because Sherwood's customers are expected to ignore the confirmation requests

2   After sending confirmations to Sherwood's customers, you received a statement from a customer which shows that the balance is not agreed.

Which of the following best describes an audit procedure that should be carried out following this response?

A   Send a second confirmation request asking the customer to recheck their records

B   Check whether invoices not included in the customer's statement agree to despatch notes raised before the year end

C   Check that payments included in the customer's statement agree to cash received by Sherwood before year end

D   Require Sherwood to adjust the customer's receivable balance to the amount owed according to the customer

3   One of Sherwood's customers responds that it cannot confirm the amount owed due to the form in which it keeps its accounting records.

Which of the following best describe the audit procedures that should be carried out in respect of this response?

(1)   Examine cash receipts received from the customer shortly before the year end
(2)   Examine supporting documentation such as the invoice and despatch note
(3)   Examine cash receipts received from the customer after the year end
(4)   Send a second confirmation request asking the customer to have their auditor check their records

A   1 and 2
B   2 and 3
C   3 and 4
D   1 and 4

4   Tests of control revealed that there is often a delay between Sherwood's delivery of goods to customers and the subsequent raising of a sales invoice.

Which test is most likely to establish the extent of any understatement of receivables at the year end?

A   Comparing goods despatch notes issued shortly after the year end with sales records

B   Comparing goods despatch notes issued shortly before the year end with sales records

C   Comparing sales invoices issued shortly before the year end with goods despatched notes

D   A receivables confirmation with a detailed investigation of all reconciling items

5   The managing director of Sherwood has refused to allow inclusion of a major customer, whose account has been selected, in the direct confirmation request. He asserts that the customer is a close personal friend who may be offended by the request.

Which of the following should be the auditor's next step?

A   Indicate that his refusal constitutes a restriction of scope which will lead to a modification of the audit opinion

B   Perform the confirmation procedures as planned since the auditor's responsibility is to the members and not the directors

C   Perform the confirmation procedures substituting another receivable with similar characteristics to preserve the integrity of the sample

D   Perform the confirmation procedures on the other receivable balances selected and search for alternative audit evidence to confirm the balance of that customer

(10 marks)

Question 59 ALTERNATIVE PROCEDURES *(non-exam style)*

Auditors obtain several different confirmations from various sources during the course of their audit.

Required:

Describe the audit evidence provided by each of the confirmations listed below, the practical difficulties in obtaining them and the alternative procedures that should be performed when they are not provided:

(a)   **Direct confirmation of receivables; and**   (5 marks)
(b)   **Confirmation of inventory held by third parties.**   (5 marks)

(10 marks)

Question 60 TORRES LEISURE CLUB **

The following scenario relates to questions 1–5

Torres Leisure Club Co (Torres) operates a chain of health and fitness clubs. Its year end was 31 October 2016. You are the audit manager and the year-end audit is due to commence shortly. The following matter has been brought to your attention:

Torres's trade receivables have historically been low as most members pay monthly subscriptions in advance. However during the year a number of companies have taken up group memberships at Torres and hence the receivables balance is now material. The audit senior has undertaken a direct confirmation of accounts receivable balances at the year end; however, a number of customers have not responded and a number of responses show differences.

Your preliminary evaluation of Torres' internal controls over sales and accounts receivable is that they are effective in ensuring the completeness and accuracy of the accounting records because the company has implemented multiple controls, including good segregation of duties. However, the auditor is aware that the effectiveness of the company's internal controls is limited by the possibility of collusion.

1   What level of reliance on internal controls and what types and extent of testing would you most likely plan to carry out during the audit of Torres sales and receivables?

	Level of reliance on controls	*Extent of tests of control*	*Extent of substantive procedures*
A	low	nil	extensive
B	moderate	reduced	reduced
C	high	extensive	reduced
D	low	extensive	extensive

2   Which of the following financial statement assertions are relevant to subscription income?

(1)   Existence

(2)   Occurrence

(3)   Classification

(4)   Presentation

(5)   Rights and obligations

A	1, 2 and 3
B	2, 3 and 4
C	2, 3 and 5
D	1, 4 and 5

3   Which the following audit procedures and actions are appropriate to obtain sufficient and appropriate audit evidence in relation to Torres's trade receivables?

(1)   For non-responses, the team should arrange to send a follow-up circularisation

(2)   If the customer does not respond to the follow up, the senior should telephone the customer and obtain verbal confirmation of the receivable balance

(3)   For each response with differences, the senior should propose adjustments for the errors in Torres's accounting records

(4)   Any balances that have been flagged as disputed should be discussed with management to determine whether a loss allowance is necessary

A	1 and 3
B	2 and 4
C	2 and 3
D	1 and 4

4   Another audit client, Blackmoore Co, sells around 30 units of product each year. The majority of sales are made in the first nine months of the year. Annual sales have not changed significantly in the past five years.

Which of the following approaches to the audit of revenue would be most effective in the audit of Blackmoore?

A   Perform all audit procedures after the year end because the volume of transactions is low

B   Perform tests of details at the end of nine months followed by analytical procedures from that interim date to the year end

C   Perform analytical procedures at the end of nine months and additional analytical procedures after the year end

D   Perform tests of controls at the end of nine months and tests of details at the year end

5   **In order to detect an understatement of sales, which of the following procedures would be most effective?**

A   Select sales delivery notes and check the details with the related sales invoices
B   Select sales invoices and check the details with the related sales orders
C   Select sales invoices and check the details with the related sales delivery notes
D   Select sales orders and check the details with the related sales invoices

(10 marks)

Question 61 CHESTNUT & CO

The following scenario relates to questions 1–5

You are the audit manager of Chestnut & Co and are reviewing the key issues identified in the files of two audit clients, Palm Industries Co (Palm) and Ash Trading Co (Ash).

Palm's year end was 31 March 2017. The fieldwork stage for this audit has been completed.

A customer of Palm owed an amount of $350,000 at the year end. Testing of receivables in April highlighted that no amounts had been paid to Palm from this customer as they were disputing the quality of certain goods received from Palm. The finance director is confident the issue will be resolved and no credit loss allowance for receivables was made with regards to this balance.

Ash is a new client of Chestnut & Co, its year end was 31 January 2016 and the firm was only appointed auditors in February 2016. The fieldwork stage for this audit is currently ongoing.

At the commencement of the audit, Chestnut ascertained that Ash has its own flowcharts and detailed systems manual, which had been prepared by the internal audit department. The internal audit department also observed the inventory count at Ash's warehouse on 31 January. Neither Chestnut & Co nor the previous auditors attended the count. Detailed inventory records were maintained.

1 **Which of the following audit procedures should be performed related to Palm's disputed receivable?**

(1)   Make an adjusting entry to correct the $350,000 misstatement of the loss allowance

(2)   Discuss with management whether the issue of quality of goods sold to the customer has been resolved

(3)   Review the latest customer correspondence with regards to an assessment of the likelihood of the customer making payment

(4)   Review whether any payments have subsequently been made by this customer since the audit fieldwork was completed

A   1 only
B   1 and 4 only
C   2 and 3 only
D   2, 3 and 4

2   A percentage is often applied to a chosen benchmark in determining whether an item is material to the financial statements as a whole. Examples of benchmarks include:

(1)   Revenue
(2)   Profit before tax
(3)   Total assets
(4)   Total liabilities

Which of these benchmarks are relevant to determining the materiality of the disputed amount receivable by Palm?

A   1 and 2 only
B   2 and 3 only
C   1, 2 and 3
D   1, 2 and 4

3   **Assuming that $350,000 is material, what is the most likely impact on the auditor's report on the financial statements of Palm for the year ended 31 March 2017 if the dispute with the customer is not resolved?**

A   Emphasis of matter
B   Qualified opinion
C   Adverse opinion
D   Disclaimer of opinion

4   **Which of the following audit procedures would provide Chestnut with audit evidence regarding the completeness and existence of Ash's inventory?**

(1)   Perform an analytical review to assess inventory turnover

(2)   Recalculate a sample of inventory value calculations and count-sheet castings from the inventory count

(3)   Compare quantities of items in the warehouse to inventory records and from inventory records to the warehouse on a sample basis

(4)   Review internal audit's report on the inventory count to identify the level of adjustments made to the records to assess their reliability

A	3 only
B	1 and 2 only
C	3 and 4 only
D	2, 3 and 4

5 **How should the auditors proceed with obtaining a understanding of Ash's internal controls given the flowcharts and detailed systems manual prepared by Ash's internal audit department ?**

A	Ascertain and record the systems independently to confirm the accuracy of the company's systems documentation
B	Accept the company's systems documentation and evaluate the controls by means of an internal control questionnaire
C	Design and carry out compliance tests on controls shown by the company's systems documentation
D	Carry out "walk-through" checks based on the company's own systems documentation to confirm its accuracy

(10 marks)

Question 62 HAWTHORN ENTERPRISES

(a) **(i)** **Identify and explain FOUR financial statement assertions relevant to classes of transactions and events for the year under audit; and**

(ii) **For each identified assertion, describe a substantive procedure relevant to the audit of REVENUE.** (8 marks)

(b) Hawthorn Enterprises Co (Hawthorn) manufactures and distributes fashion clothing to retail stores. Its year end was 31 March 2017. You are the audit manager and the year-end audit is due to commence shortly. The following three matters have been brought to your attention.

(i) *Supplier statement reconciliations*

Hawthorn receives monthly statements from its main suppliers and although these have been retained, none have been reconciled to the payables ledger as at 31 March 2017. The engagement partner has asked the audit senior to recommend the procedures to be performed on supplier statements. (3 marks)

(ii) *Bank reconciliation*

During last year's audit of Hawthorn's bank and cash, significant cut off errors were discovered with a number of post year-end cheques being processed prior to the year end to reduce payables. The finance director has assured the audit engagement partner that this error has not occurred again this year and that the bank reconciliation has been carefully prepared. The audit engagement partner has asked that the bank reconciliation is comprehensively audited. (4 marks) *(iii)*   *Receivables*

Hawthorn's receivables ledger has increased considerably during the year, and the year-end balance is $2·3 million compared to $1·4 million last year. The finance director of Hawthorn has requested that a receivables circularisation is not carried out as a number of their customers complained last year about the inconvenience involved in responding. The engagement partner has agreed to this request, and tasked you with identifying alternative procedures to confirm the existence and valuation of receivables.   (5 marks)

Required:

Describe substantive procedures you would perform to obtain sufficient and appropriate audit evidence in relation to the above three matters.

Note: The mark allocation is shown against each of the three matters above.

(20 marks)

Question 63 BANK AND CASH

(a)   Internal control systems are designed, amongst other things, to prevent error and misappropriation.

Required:

Describe the errors and misappropriations that may occur if the following are not properly controlled:

(i)	**receipts paid into bank accounts;**	(4 marks)
(ii)	**payments made out of bank accounts;**	(4 marks)

(b)   A book-selling company has a head office and 25 shops, each of which holds cash (banknotes, coins, and credit card vouchers) at the end of the reporting period. There are no receivables. Accounting records are held at shops. Shops make returns to head office and head office holds its own accounting records. Your firm has been the external auditor to the company for many years and has offices near to the location of some but not all of the shops.

Required:

List FOUR audit objectives for the audit of cash and state how you should gain the audit evidence in relation to those objectives at the year end.   (8 marks)

(c)   The external auditors of companies often write to companies' bankers asking for details of bank balances and other matters at the year end.

Required:

Explain why auditors write to companies' bankers and list the matters you would expect banks to confirm.   (4 marks)

(20 marks)

Question 64 NEWTHORPE, TOUREX AND PUDCO

The following scenario relates to questions 1–5

Your firm is the external auditor to three companies with potential provisions, contingent liabilities and contingent assets.

Newthorpe Engineering

In February 2016 the directors suspended the Managing Director. He was dismissed, without compensation, for gross misconduct on 17 March at a disciplinary hearing held by the company.

The Managing Director has claimed unfair dismissal and is taking legal action to obtain compensation for loss of employment on the bases that his service contract entitles him to two years' salary from the date of dismissal.

Tourex and Pudco

Tourex is a hotel and Pudco is a food wholesaler that supplies Tourex. Just before the year end, which is the same for both companies, a large number of guests became ill at a wedding reception at the hotel, possibly as a result of food poisoning.

The guests have taken legal action against Tourex and Tourex has taken action against Pudco. Tourex is negotiating out-of court settlements with the guests; Pudco is negotiating an out-of-court settlement with Tourex.

Pudco has disclosed a contingent liability in the notes to the financial statements. Tourex has made no provision and argues that disclosure is not necessary because a settlement has not been reached.

Pudco's lawyers have said that negotiations are "going well" but refuse to confirm this or comment on an estimated settlement amount in writing. Tourex's lawyers have confirmed, in writing, the status of the negotiations. The amounts involved are material to the financial statements of both companies.

Neither company has objection to your firm also being the auditor to the other company.

1   **Which of the following procedures should be performed to determine the likelihood that the Managing Director of Newthorpe is successful in his claim?**

    (1)   Obtain a copy of the service contract
    (2)   Review correspondence between the company and the Managing Director
    (3)   Ask your firm's legal advisor to provide guidance on the likely outcome of the case
    (4)   Review Newthorpe's insurance policies for cover against such claims

    A   1, 2 and 3
    B   2, 3 and 4
    C   1, 2 and 4
    D   1, 3 and 4

2   **How should the audit firm manage the conflict that has arisen between Tourex and Pudco?**

    A   Resign as the auditor of one or both of the companies
    B   Require that the audit of each client be performed by different offices
    C   Assign different audit teams and different engagement partners to each audit
    D   Facilitate meetings between Tourex and Pudco to ensure that the disputes are resolved as quickly as possible

3   **Which form of audit opinion is most likely to be issued on the financial statements of Pudco?**

     A   Unmodified with emphasis of matter paragraph
     B   Qualified
     C   Adverse
     D   Disclaimer

4   **Which form of audit opinion is most likely to be issued on the financial statements of Tourex?**

     A   Unmodified with emphasis of matter paragraph
     B   Qualified
     C   Adverse
     D   Disclaimer

5   **Which of the following procedures provide evidence concerning contingent liabilities?**

     (1)   Review of replies received from customers in response to a direct confirmation
     (2)   Review of board minutes
     (3)   Discussion with the company's legal representatives
     (4)   Discussion with management

     A   3 only
     B   1 and 2
     C   1 and 4
     D   2, 3 and 4

(10 marks)

Question 65 METCALF

ISA 500 *Audit Evidence* requires that auditors "should obtain sufficient appropriate audit evidence to be able to draw reasonable conclusions on which to base the audit opinion".

Required:

(a)   **List and explain the factors which will influence the auditor's judgement concerning the sufficiency of audit evidence obtained.**   (4 marks)

(b)   You are the audit senior in charge of the final audit of Metcalf Co, a company that has been trading for over 50 years. Metcalf Co manufactures and sells tables and chairs directly to the public.

Current liabilities are shown on Metcalf Co's statement of financial position as follows:

	Current Year $	Prior year $
Trade payables	884,824	816,817
Accruals	56,903	51,551
Provision for legal action	60,000	–
	1,001,727	868,368

The provision for legal action relates to a claim from a customer who suffered an injury while assembling a chair supplied by Metcalf Co. The directors of Metcalf Co dispute the claim, although they are recommending an out of court settlement to avoid damaging publicity against Metcalf Co.

Required:

List the substantive audit procedures that you should undertake in the audit of current liabilities of Metcalf Co for the current year end. For each procedure, explain the purpose of that procedure.

Marks are allocated as follows:

(i)	**Trade payables;**	(9 marks)
(ii)	**Accruals;**	(3 marks)
(iii)	**Provision for legal action.**	(4 marks)

(20 marks)

Question 66 ROSE LEISURE CLUB

(a) **Identify and explain each of the FIVE fundamental principles contained within ACCA's Code of Ethics and Conduct.** (5 marks)

(b) Rose Leisure Club Co (Rose) operates a chain of health and fitness clubs. Its year end was 31 October 2016. You are the audit manager and the year-end audit is due to commence shortly. The following three matters have been brought to your attention.

(i)   Trade payables and accruals

Rose's finance director has notified you that an error occurred in the closing of the purchase ledger at the year end. Rather than closing it on 1 November, it was accidentally closed one week earlier on 25 October. All purchase invoices received between 25 October and the year end have been posted to the 2017 year-end purchase ledger. (6 marks)

(ii)   Receivables

Rose's trade receivables have historically been low as most members pay monthly in advance. However, during the year a number of companies have taken up group memberships at Rose and hence the receivables balance is now material. The audit senior has undertaken a receivables circularisation for the balances at the year end; however, there are a number who have not responded and a number of responses with differences. (5 marks)

(iii)   Reorganisation

The company recently announced its plans to reorganise its health and fitness clubs. This will involve closing some clubs for refurbishment, retraining some existing staff and disposing of some surplus assets. These plans were agreed at a board meeting in October and announced to their shareholders on 29 October. Rose is proposing to make a reorganisation provision in the financial statements. (4 marks)

Required:

Describe substantive procedures you would perform to obtain sufficient and appropriate audit evidence in relation to the above three matters.

Note: The mark allocation is shown against each of the three matters above.

(20 marks)

Question 67 FIREFLY TENNIS CLUB

The FireFly Tennis Club owns 12 tennis courts. The club uses "all weather" tarmac tennis courts, which have floodlights for night-time use. The club's year end is 31 December 2016.

Members pay an annual fee to use the courts and participate in club championships. The club had 430 members as at 1 January 2017.

Income is derived from two main sources:

(1)   Membership fees. Each member pays a fee of $200 per annum. Fees for the new financial year are payable within one month of the club year end. Approximately 10% of members do not renew their membership. New members joining during the year pay 50% of the total fees that would have been payable had they been members for a full year. During 2016, 50 new members joined the club. No members pay their fees before they are due.

(2)   Court hire fees: Non-members pay $5 per hour to hire a court. Non-members have to sign a list in the club house showing courts hired. Money is placed in a cash box in the club house for collection by the club secretary.

All fees (membership and court hire) are paid in cash. They are collected by the club secretary and banked on a regular basis. The paying-in slip shows the analysis between fees and court hire income. The secretary provides the treasurer with a list of bankings showing member's names (for membership fees) and the amount banked. Details of all bankings are entered into the cash book by the treasurer.

Main items of expenditure are:

(1)   Court maintenance including repainting lines on a regular basis.
(2)   Power costs for floodlights.
(3)   Tennis balls for club championships. Each match in the championship uses 12 tennis balls.

The treasurer pays for all expenditure using the club's debit card. Receipts are obtained for all expenses and these are maintained in date order in an expenses file. The treasurer also prepares the annual financial statements.

Under the rules of the club, the annual accounts must be audited by an independent auditor. The date is now 13 April 2017 and the treasurer has just prepared the financial statements for audit.

Required:

(a)   Describe the audit work that should be performed to determine the completeness of income for the FireFly Tennis Club.   (10 marks)

(b)   Describe the audit procedures that should be performed to check the completeness and accuracy of expenditure for the FireFly Tennis Club.   (5 marks)

(c)   Discuss why internal control testing has limited value when auditing not-for-profit entities such as the FireFly Tennis Club.   (5 marks)

(20 marks)

Question 68 BLUESBERRY HOSPITAL

(a)   **Explain the purpose of a value for money audit.**   (4 marks)

(b)   Bluesberry Hospital is located in a country where healthcare is free, as the taxpayers fund the hospitals which are owned by the government. Two years ago, management reviewed all aspects of hospital operations and instigated a number of measures aimed at improving overall "value for money" for the local community. Management have asked that you, an audit manager in the hospital's internal audit department, perform a review over the measures which have been implemented.

Bluesberry has one centralised buying department and all purchase requisition forms for medical supplies must be forwarded here. Upon receipt the buying team will research the lowest price from suppliers and a purchase order is raised. This is then passed to the purchasing director, who authorises all orders. The small buying team receive in excess of 200 forms a day.

The human resources department has had difficulties with recruiting suitably trained staff. Overtime rates have been increased to incentivise permanent staff to fill staffing gaps, this has been popular, and reliance on expensive temporary staff has been reduced. Monitoring of staff hours had been difficult but the hospital has implemented time card clocking in and out procedures and these hours are used for overtime payments as well.

The hospital has invested heavily in new surgical equipment, which although very expensive, has meant that more operations could be performed and patient recovery rates are faster. However, currently there is a shortage of appropriately trained medical staff. A capital expenditure committee has been established, made up of senior managers, and they plan and authorise any significant capital expenditure items.

Required:

(i)   **Identify and explain FOUR STRENGTHS within Bluesberry's operating environment; and**   (6 marks)

(ii)   **For each strength identified, describe how Bluesberry might make further improvements to provide the best value for money.**   (4 marks)

(c)   **Describe TWO substantive procedures the external auditor of Bluesberry should adopt to verify EACH of the following assertions in relation to an entity's property, plant and equipment:**

(i)   **Accuracy, valuation and allocation;**
(ii)   **Completeness; and**
(iii)   **Rights and obligations.**

Note: Assume that the hospital adopts International Financial Reporting Standards. (6 marks)

(20 marks)

Question 69 DYLAN**

The following scenario relates to questions 1–5

You are currently completing the audit of Dylan Co for the year ended 31 August. It is proposed that the financial statements will be approved on 17 November and that the auditor's report will be signed on that date. The financial statements will be issued on 5 December.

1 **Which of the following are subsequent events in line with ISA 560 *Subsequent Events*?**

 (1) Events occurring after a sale is made to a customer
 (2) Events occurring after any cash transaction
 (3) Events occurring after the period end, but before the date of the auditor's report
 (4) Facts that become known after the date of the auditor's report

 A 1 and 2
 B 1 and 4
 C 2 and 3
 D 3 and 4

2 **Which of the following statements in relation to the auditor's responsibility for subsequent events are true?**

 (1) The auditor has an active responsibility to make continuing inquiries between the date of the auditor's report and the date the financial statements are issued

 (2) The auditor has no active responsibility to make continuing inquiries after the date of the auditor's report

 (3) The auditor has an active responsibility to make continuing inquiries between the date of the financial statements and the date of the auditor's report

 (4) The auditor has an active responsibility to make continuing inquiries between the date of the financial statements and the date on which sufficient appropriate evidence has been obtained

 A 1 and 3 only
 B 1, 3 and 4
 C 2 and 4 only
 D 2, 3 and 4

3   **What actions should the auditor take if a material event occurs between 31 August and 17 November that may require amendment to, or disclosure in, Dylan's financial statements?**

(1)   Advise management how to properly account for and adequately disclose the event in the financial statements

(2)   If not amended or disclosed in the financial statements, qualify the auditor's report because the matter is material

(3)   Write a memo for the audit file because subsequent events will affect next year's financial statements but not this year's

(4)   No action is needed because it is not a subsequent event unless it is found by the auditor after the date of the auditor's report

A   1 only
B   1 and 2 only
C   1, 2 and 3
D   4 only

4   Between 17 November and 5 December, the auditor becomes aware of an event that is material and may require amendment to, or disclosure in, the financial statements of Dylan.

Which of the following are actions the auditor would most likely take?

(1)   Request that the financial statements as they currently stand and the auditor's report thereon should not be issued

(2)   Extend the subsequent event review procedures

(3)   If the financial statements are amended, provided a new auditor's report dated not earlier than the date the amended financial statements are approved

(4)   Issue a qualified auditor's report because the subsequent events were not found until after the date of the initial auditor's report

A   1 and 2 only
B   1, 2 and 3
C   2 and 3 only
D   1, 3 and 4

5   ISA 560 *Subsequent Events* sets out the auditor's responsibilities for the period between the year end and the annual general meeting (AGM).

What action is the auditor required to take after signing the auditor's report and before the AGM?

A   Obtain a representation from the directors that no material events after the reporting period have occurred in that period of time

B   Search for evidence of events after the reporting period that may change the audit opinion

C   Consult with the directors on any events after the reporting period that might change the audit opinion

D   None, because the auditor's responsibilities cease after the auditor's report is signed

(10 marks)

Question 70 SHARP *(non-exam style)*

You are responsible for completion of the fieldwork of the audit of Sharp, a private company manufacturing domestic and industrial cleaning appliances. The draft accounts have been presented to you as follows:

Statement of financial position at 30 September 2016

		2016		2015
		$000		$000
Non-current assets		170		50
Current assets:				
Inventory	103		92	
Receivables	244		231	
Cash at bank	73		99	
		420		422
Total assets		590		472
Capital and reserves:				
Share capital		10		10
Retained earnings		189		83
		199		93
Current liabilities		391		379
Total equity and liabilities		590		472

Profit before tax was $106,000 on revenue of $1.5 million for the year ended 30 September 2016.

The audit tests have been completed. It only remains for you to evaluate the effect for the following findings on the draft accounts. No adjustments have been made to the draft accounts other than as indicated below.

Findings

(1) Payments to suppliers amounting to $10,172 had been prepared and processed in the accounting records on the last day of the financial year. Due to a clerical error they had not been sent to the bank until several days after the year end.

(2) An updated price list was issued in early September 2016 to take effect from 1 October 2016. A number of invoices were issued during September using the new higher prices. Your client became aware of this after the year-end. An allowance was made against receivables in the draft accounts to account for credit notes which would have to be issued as a result after the year end. The client's estimate of the extent of the credits required was $10,000 and allowance was made for this amount. Your audit rests show that, in the event, $17,542 in credits was issued after the year end in respect of these pricing errors.

(3) Additions to plant and machinery totalled $52,000 in the year. To verify their validity a representative sampling test was conducted, selection being on a random basis. The value of the sample was $13,000. A number of repair items (total value $2,500) were found to have been incorrectly included in additions. When this was brought to the client's attention these items were corrected in the draft accounts.

(4)   Appliances are sold under a two year warranty. At each year end the company makes estimates of how much should be provided for repair work to be conducted under warranties issued but not claimed against. Client's management accept that this is a reasonably subjective area but feel that their estimates, based on sales volume, rates of claim and average repair cost, are reasonable. Your workings suggest that the current provision, which stands at $25,000, needs to be at least that much and might be as much as $5,000 understated. However, past experience shows that the client's estimate has always been reasonable. Because of this, the client disagrees stating that you are taking too pessimistic a view.

(5)   You note that your client has continued to include in liabilities an "uninsured risk" provision of $20,000. Reference to the previous year's files indicates that this provision was set up a number of years ago to provide against "unforeseen events" but as yet no amounts have been charged against it.

Required:

(a)   **Evaluate the significance of each finding and suggest how each should be dealt with.**

         (10 marks)

(b)   **Summarise, the financial effect of each finding on the draft accounts, stating which, if any, may be considered unadjusted errors.**   (10 marks)

(20 marks)

Question 71 ZEEDIEM

The following scenario relates to questions 1–5

The date is 3 July 2016. The audit of ZeeDiem Co is nearly complete and the financial statements and the auditor's report are due to be signed next week. However, the following additional information on two material events has just been presented to the auditor. The company's year end was 30 April 2016.

Event 1 – Occurred on 10 May 2016

The springs in a new type of mattress have been found to be defective making the mattress unsafe for use. There have been no sales of this mattress; it was due to be marketed in the next few weeks. The company's insurers estimate the value of inventory affected to be $750,000. The insurers also estimate that the mattresses are now only worth $225,000. No claim can be made against the supplier of springs as this company is in insolvent liquidation. The insurers will not pay ZeeDiem for the fall in value of the inventory because it was underinsured.

Event 2 – Occurred 5 June 2016

Production at the ShamEve factory was halted for one day when a container truck carrying dye used in colouring the fabric on mattresses reversed into a metal pylon. The container cracked, allowing dye to spread across the factory premises and into a local river. The Environmental Agency is currently considering whether the release of dye was in breach of environmental legislation. The company's insurers have not yet commented on the event.

1   **Which of the following options correctly summarises how Event 1 should be accounted for in the financial statements of ZeeDiem for the year ended 30 April 2016?**

        A   Inventory should be written down to $225,000 because the amount is material

        B   A disclosure note should explain the defective inventory and the expected effect on next year's financial statements

        C   Information about the inventory valuation should be provided in the management commentary, including the insurer's estimate of $225,000

        D   No amendment or disclosure is required because the inventory was not found to be defective until after the reporting date

2   **Which of the following audit procedures are appropriate to confirm the appropriate accounting treatment of Event 1?**

        (1)   Obtain documentation from the insurers confirming their estimate of the value of the mattresses

        (2)   Contact the liquidator of the spring supplier to confirm that no refund can be expected in respect of the defective springs

        (3)   Perform an additional inventory count as a surprise audit procedure

        (4)   Review production and inventory records to confirm that the defective springs were not used in any other mattresses

        A   1 and 3 only
        B   2 and 4 only
        C   1, 2 and 4
        D   1, 2 and 3

3   **Which of the following options are documents that the auditor should require to assess the potential effect of Event 2 on the financial statements?**

        (1)   Board minutes of meeting in which the event was discussed
        (2)   Personnel file for the truck driver involved in the event
        (3)   A copy of relevant environmental legislation
        (4)   Interim reports from the Environmental Agency about the damage

        A   1, 2 and 4
        B   1, 3 and 4
        C   1 and 2 only
        D   3 and 4 only

4   There are many elements within an audit that ensure the audit is completed effectively and efficiently. Four such elements are:

        (1)   Direction and supervision of audit staff
        (2)   Monitoring of time and costs
        (3)   Preparation of adequate working papers
        (4)   Review of work carried out by audit staff

What are the two most important elements relating to audit finalisation?

A   1 and 2
B   2 and 3
C   3 and 4
D   1 and 4

5   **Which of the following audit procedures is appropriate to test the OCCURRENCE assertion of subsequent events?**

A   Confirming a sample of material accounts receivable after the year end
B   Inquiring as to whether any unusual adjustments were made after the year end
C   Comparing the financial statements being reported on to those of the prior period
D   Reviewing documents from third parties obtained as evidence during the audit

(10 marks)

Question 72 HUMPHRIES *(non-exam style)*

Humphries Co operates a chain of food wholesalers across the country and its year end was 30 September. The final audit is nearly complete and it is proposed that the financial statements and auditor's report will be signed on 13 December. Revenue for the year is $78 million and profit before taxation is $7·5 million. The following events occurred subsequent to the year end.

Receivable

A customer of Humphries has been experiencing cash flow problems and its year-end balance is $0·3 million. Humphries has just become aware that its customer is experiencing significant going concern difficulties. Humphries believe that as the company has been trading for many years, they will receive some, if not full, payment from the customer; hence they have not adjusted the receivable balance.

Lawsuit

A key supplier of Humphries Co is suing them for breach of contract. The lawsuit was filed prior to the year end, and the sum claimed by them is $1 million. This has been disclosed as a contingent liability in the notes to the financial statements; however correspondence has just arrived from the supplier indicating that they are willing to settle the case for a payment by Humphries Co of $0·6 million. It is likely that the company will agree to this.

Warehouse

Humphries Co has three warehouses; following extensive rain on 20 November significant rain and river water flooded the warehouse located in Bass. All of the inventory was damaged and has been disposed of. The insurance company has already been contacted. No amendments or disclosures have been made in the financial statements.

Required:

(a)   **Describe the auditor's responsibility for subsequent events occurring between:**

     (i)   **The year-end date and the date the auditor's report is signed; and**
     (ii)   **The date the auditor's report is signed and the date the financial statements are issued.**   (5 marks)

(b)   **For each of the events above:**

      (i)   **discuss whether the financial statements require amendment;**

      (ii)   **describe audit procedures that should be performed in order to form a conclusion on the amendment; and**

      (iii)   **explain the impact on the auditor's report should the issue remain unresolved.**

      Note: The total marks will be split equally between each event.   (15 marks)

      (20 marks)

Question 73 VIOLET & CO**

The following scenario relates to questions 1–5

You are the audit manager of Violet & Co and you are currently reviewing the audit files for two of your clients for which the audit fieldwork has been completed. The audit seniors have raised the following issues:

Daisy Designs Co (Daisy)

Daisy's year end is 30 September, however, subsequent to the year end the sales ledger has been corrupted by a computer virus attack. Although Daisy's finance director was able to produce the financial statements before the attack, the audit team has been unable to access the sales ledger to undertake detailed testing of revenue or year-end receivables.

Daisy's internal auditors performed tests of control on the revenue cycle throughout the year and found them to be well-designed and working effectively. The internal auditor has confirmed that there are no backup files for the sales ledger.

All other accounting records were unaffected. Daisy's revenue is $15.6 million, its receivables are $3.4 million and profit before tax is $2 million.

Fuchsia Enterprises Co (Fuchsia)

Fuchsia has experienced difficult trading conditions and has lost significant market share. The cash flow forecast reviewed during the audit fieldwork shows a significant net cash outflow. Management is confident that further funding can be obtained and so has prepared the financial statements on the going concern basis with no additional disclosures. The audit senior is highly sceptical about this. The prior year financial statements showed a profit before tax of $1.2m; however, the current year loss before tax is $4.4 million and the forecast net cash outflow for the next 12 months is $3.2 million.

1   **Which of the following audit procedures are appropriate to confirm the revenue of Daisy Designs?**

      (1)   Examine any alternative records which detail revenue for the year

      (2)   Perform analytical procedures such as monthly comparison of revenue to the prior year

      (3)   Agree trade receivables balances with customers through direct confirmation requests

      (4)   Make inquiries of the internal auditors and rely on their evaluation of the accuracy of the reported revenue

A	1 and 2 only
B	1 and 3
C	3 and 4
D	1, 2 and 4

2   **What would be the effect on the auditor's opinion for Daisy if the auditor is unable to obtain sufficient appropriate evidence in relation to the revenue and receivables balances?**

A   Disclaimer, because the auditor is unable to form an opinion on the financial statements as a whole

B   Adverse, because the auditor cannot agree that the financial statements are fairly presented

C   Disclaimer, because the corrupted records give rise to the suspicion of fraud

D   Qualified to the effect that except for the revenue and receivables balances the financial statements are fairly presented

3   **Which of the following best describes the audit risk associated with Fuschia's cash flow forecast and whether or not it is material to the audit?**

A   The cash flow forecast is inaccurate and the amount of the forecasted cash outflow is material

B   The cash flow forecast is inaccurate, but because it is a forecast it is not material

C   Fuchsia faces going concern problems and the large decline in profits is material

D   Fuchsia is facing going concern problems but since management is confident it can obtain further funding it is not material

4   **Which of the following audit procedures are appropriate to evaluate Fuschia's ability to obtain further funding?**

(1)   Discuss with management whether any new source of finance has now been secured

(2)   Review the most recent board minutes to see if management's view on Fuchsia's future as a going concern has changed

(3)   Confirm with providers of loan finance that Fuchsia has been making timely payments on its debts

(4)   Review the cash flow forecast for the next 12 months and assess the reasonableness of the assumptions used

A	1, 2 and 3
B	1 and 3 only
C	1 and 2 only
D	2 and 4

5   Upon completion of the audit procedures, you conclude that Fuschia's use of the going
         concern basis is not appropriate.

         **If management refuses to correct the financial statements, what would be the impact on
         the auditor's report?**

         (1)   Qualified opinion
         (2)   Adverse opinion
         (3)   Emphasis of Matter paragraph added
         (4)   Key Audit Matters section added

         A   2 only
         B   1 and 4
         C   2 and 4
         D   1 and 3

                                                                                        (10 marks)

Question 74 PANDA

The following scenario relates to questions 1–5

Panda Co manufactures chemicals and has a factory and four offsite storage locations for finished
goods. Panda Co's year end was 30 April 2017. The final audit is almost complete and the financial
statements and auditor's report are due to be signed next week. Revenue for the year is $55 million and
profit before taxation is $5.6 million.

The following two events have occurred subsequent to the year end. No amendments or disclosures
have been made in the financial statements.

Event 1 – Defective chemicals

Panda Co undertakes extensive quality control checks prior to despatch of any chemicals. Testing on 3
May 2017 found that a batch of chemicals produced in April was defective. The cost of this batch was
$850,000. In its current condition it can be sold at a scrap value of $100,000. The costs of correcting
the defect are too significant for Panda Co's management to consider this an alternative option.

Event 2 – Explosion

An explosion occurred at the smallest of the four offsite storage locations on 20 May 2017. This
resulted in some damage to inventory and property, plant and equipment. Panda Co's management
have investigated the cause of the explosion and believe that they cannot make a valid insurance claim.
Management of Panda Co has estimated that the value of damaged inventory and property, plant and
equipment was $900,000 and it now has no disposal value.

1   **Which of the following options correctly describes Event 1 as a subsequent event?**

         A   It is a reportable event because it involves inventory, which is always material to the
                  financial statements

         B   It is an adjusting event because it provides further evidence of conditions that
                  existed at reporting date

         C   It is a non-adjusting event because it indicates conditions that arose after the
                  reporting date

         D   It is a favourable event because the defective materials were identified using
                  preventive measures

2   **Which of the following audit procedures are necessary to form a conclusion on whether Event 1 requires amendment to or disclosure in the financial statements?**

(1)   Review the board minutes and quality control reports to assess whether this event was the only case of defective inventory

(2)   Inquire of the factory staff what was the cause of the defect to determine the likelihood of future similar events

(3)   Perform a walkthrough of the quality control process to identify the defective inventory and make recommendations for how the process could be improved

(4)   Obtain a schedule listing the defective inventory and agree to supporting production records that it was produced prior to the reporting date

(5)   Discuss with management how the scrap value of $100,000 has been determined and agree this amount to any supporting documentation

A   1, 3 and 4
B   1, 4 and 5
C   2, 3 and 5
D   3, 4 and 5

3   **Which of the following options correctly summarises how Event 1 should be accounted for in the financial statements of Panda?**

A   Show inventory at cost and provide for a loss of $750,000

B   Disclosure should be made about the defective chemicals and the $0.75 million write-down expected on the 2018 financial statements.

C   Inventory should be written down to its net realisable value of $0.1 million.

D   No amendment or disclosure is required because the amount is not material.

4   **Which of the following audit procedures would provide the auditor with reliable audit evidence regarding the valuation of the inventory damaged by the explosion?**

A   Obtain a schedule of damaged inventory and physically inspect the inventory

B   Request a written representation from Panda's management supporting their belief that a valid claim cannot be made

C   Send an enquiry letter to Panda's insurers to confirm that Panda cannot make a valid claim

D   Recalculate its cost using year-end inventory count quantities and production costing records

5   **Which of the following options correctly summarises how Event 2 should be accounted for in the financial statements of Panda for the year ended 30 April 2017?**

A   Details of the explosion and the value of assets affected disclosed in the notes

B   Damaged assets should be written off to profit or loss as they have no scrap value

C   Damaged assets should be written off and the event disclosed to explain the nature of the loss

D   There should be no accounting for this event as only next year's financial statements will be affected

(10 marks)

Question 75 SAVAGE & CO

The following scenario relates to questions 1–5

You are the audit manager of Savage & Co and you are briefing your team on the approach to adopt in undertaking the review and finalisation stage of the audit. In particular, the audit senior is unsure about the steps to take in relation to uncorrected misstatements.

In addition, you are currently reviewing the audit files for two of your clients for which the audit fieldwork has been completed. The audit seniors have raised the following issues:

Czech Co

Czech Co is a pharmaceutical company and has incurred research expenditure of $0.5m and development expenditure of $3·2m during the year, this has all been capitalised as an intangible asset. Profit before tax is $26·3m.

Dawson Co

Dawson Co's computerised wages program is backed up daily, however for a period of two months the wages records and the back-ups have been corrupted, and therefore cannot be accessed. Wages and salaries for these two months are $1·1m. Profit before tax is $10m.

1   **Which of the following describe the auditor's responsibility in respect of misstatements?**

   (1)   The auditor should accumulate only the material misstatements that arise over the course of the audit

   (2)   Identified misstatements should be considered during the audit to assess whether the audit strategy and plan should be revised

   (3)   The auditor should obtain a written representation from management to confirm that unadjusted misstatements are immaterial

   (4)   Misstatements should be accumulated during the audit and communicated to those charged with governance at the end of the audit

   A   1 and 2
   B   2 and 3
   C   3 and 4
   D   1 and 4

2   In relation to the issues raised by the audit seniors for Czech and Dawson:

   Which of the issues should be considered material?

   A   Czech only
   B   Dawson only
   C   Both Czech and Dawson
   D   Neither Czech or Dawson

3   Assume that the issues raised by the audit seniors for Czech and Dawson are determined to be material.

What is the most likely impact on the auditor's reports if the issues are not resolved?

	Czech Co	*Dawson Co*
A	Qualified	Qualified
B	Qualified	Disclaimer
C	Adverse	Qualified
D	Disclaimer	Adverse

4   Auditors are required to undertake an overall review of the financial statements as the final step before they form their audit opinion. As part of this process they undertake a number of procedures.

Which of the following procedures would an auditor NOT undertake as part of the overall review of the financial statements?

A   Reviewing the financial statements to ensure they are consistent with the auditor's knowledge of the business and the results of their audit work

B   Performing analytical procedures on the financial statements to form an overall conclusion on the financial statements

C   Undertaking a review of subsequent events to identify whether any adjustment or disclosure is required in the financial statements

D   Reviewing the financial statements to ensure compliance with accounting standards and local legislation disclosure

5   On 25 February, Savage & Co issued an auditor's report expressing an unmodified opinion on financial statements for the year ended 31 January. On 2 March, you learned that on 11 February the entity incurred a material loss on an uncollectible trade receivable. You determined that the financial statements need revision, but management has refused to adjust the financial statements for this subsequent event. There are creditors relying on the financial statements.

What is your next course of action?

A   To revise the auditor's report and distribute it to the creditors

B   To notify the creditors that the financial statements and auditor's report cannot be relied upon

C   To discuss management's refusal to adjust the financial statements with those charged with governance

D   To revise the financial statements and distribute them to the creditors

(10 marks)

Question 76 BULLFINCH.COM

The following scenario relates to questions 1–5

Bullfinch.com is a website design company whose year end was 31 October 2016. The audit is almost complete and the financial statements are due to be signed shortly. Revenue for the year is $11.2 million and profit before tax is $3.8 million. A key customer, with a receivables balance at the year end of $283,000, has just notified Bullfinch.com that it is experiencing cash flow difficulties and so is unable to make any payments for the foreseeable future. The finance director has notified the auditor that he will write this balance off as an irrecoverable debt in the 2017 financial statements.

1   **Which of the following audit procedures should be performed in order to conclude on any required amendment to Bullfinch.com's 2016 financial statements?**

(1)   Review the correspondence with the customer to assess whether there is any likelihood of payment

(2)   Review the post-year-end period to see if any payments have been received from the customer

(3)   Recalculate the loss allowance to determine whether it is sufficient to cover the write off of the receivable balance

(4)   Discuss with management why they believe an adjustment is not required in the financial statements

A   1 and 3 only
B   1, 2 and 4
C   2, 3 and 4
D   1, 2, 3 and 4

2   Assume that the matter described above is brought to the auditor's attention *after* the date of the auditor's report but before the financial statements are issued. The auditor determines that an amendment is required to Bullfinch's 2016 financial statements and Bullfinch makes the amendment.

Which of the following actions should the auditor take in this situation?

(1)   Withdraw the old auditor's report
(2)   Extend audit procedures, including performing further subsequent events review
(3)   Issue a new auditor's report after management's approval of the financial statements
(4)   Include a disclaimer of opinion in the new auditor's report

A   1 and 3 only
B   2, 3 and 4
C   1, 3 and 4
D   1, 2 and 3

3   **Which of the following events experienced by Bullfinch are adjusting events?**

> (1)   Issue of share capital in December 2016
>
> (2)   Acquisition of a subsidiary in January 2017
>
> (3)   Settlement in January 2017 of legal proceedings that commenced in May 2016
>
> (4)   A sale in November 2016 of land last revalued on 31 October 2014 that resulted in a significant loss
>
> (5)   Damage to inventory in November 2016 caused by accidental activation of the water sprinkler system in the warehouse

> A   1, 2 and 3
> B   1, 2 and 5
> C   3 and 4 only
> D   3, 4 and 5

4   **Which of the following statements in relation to the auditor's responsibilities for subsequent events is/are correct?**

> (1)   Auditors have no responsibility to perform procedures to identify subsequent events after the date of the auditor's report
>
> (2)   Where a material adjusting event is identified after the financial statements are issued, but prior to approval by the shareholders, the auditor should include a qualified opinion in the auditor's report if management refuses to adjust the financial statements for the event

> A   1 only
> B   2 only
> C   Both 1 and 2
> D   Neither 1 nor 2

5   **Which of the following audit procedures is most likely to be performed during the final stage of an audit?**

> A   Analytical procedures to assess the reasonableness of figures presented
> B   Follow-up confirmations sent to unresponsive third parties
> C   Substantive testing of revenue transactions
> D   Reviewing documents to ensure understanding of the company's industry

(10 marks)

Question 77 CREMORNE**

The following scenario relates to questions 1–5

Cremorne is a construction company with annual sales of $350 million. Its draft financial statements shows a profit for the year ended 30 June 2016 of $40 million. This is your audit firm's first audit of Cremorne. On completing audit work at the company's premises, the following two matters are outstanding:

Inventory valuation

Inventories include $7 million, at cost, of scrap rubber which is widely used for road surfacing in many countries. The Highways Agency, which is the state authority for road construction, currently bans the use of this material. However, as this ban was known to be under review and, on being offered a special price, Cremorne speculated on a favourable outcome of the review and purchased the material. In August 2016, shortly before Cremorne's financial statements were approved, the Highways Agency reported that the ban would continue. If Cremorne uses it on non-Highways Agency contracts its net realisable value would not exceed $2 million. The finance director maintains that, as the Highways Agency' report was issued after the end of the reporting period, any write down of the inventory should be reflected only in next year's financial statements.

Depreciation

Five years ago, Cremorne purchased two earthmovers and a further two for $2.5 million each in July 2012. Depreciation has been allowed at 10% straight line. For the year just ended, Cremorne decided to scrap the first two earthmovers and replace them with the latest model at a cost of $4 million each. Cremorne's chief engineer tells you that technology is developing so rapidly that he expects such machines to be replaced every five years. The finance director claims that 10% depreciation is standard in the industry and reflects the physical life of the machines. He argues that as continued improvements in technology cannot be assumed there is no justification for increasing depreciation to 20%. If these assets are depreciated at 20% instead of 10% the additional expense would be $2 million.

1   **By what amount should inventory of scrap rubber be written down in Cremorne's financial statements for the year ended 30 June 2016?**

         A $2 million
         B $2.5 million
         C $5 million
         D $nil, with disclosure of subsequent events

2   **Which of the following benchmarks are appropriate to evaluating any identified misstatement in the valuation of inventories?**

         (1)   ½% of revenue, $350 million
         (2)   5% profit, $40 million
         (3)   1% inventory, $7 million

         A   1 and 2 only
         B   2 only
         C   1 and 3 only
         D   1, 2 and 3

3   **What adjustment for depreciation of the earthmovers, if any, should be made in the financial statements for the year ended 30 June 2016?**

         A   Increase depreciation expense by $2 million to recognise the change in depreciation from 10% to 20% on all earthmovers

         B   Increase depreciation expense by $800,000 to recognise the change in depreciation from 10% to 20% on the two new earthmovers only

         C   Make no adjustment for the current year, but disclose the effect of using 20% as the depreciation rate for all new earthmovers in the notes

         D   Recognise $2 million additional depreciation expense as a prior period adjustment as it is a change in accounting policy

4   The directors have decided not to make any changes to the draft financial statements in relation to the depreciation of earthmovers.

Assuming that there are no other uncorrected errors, what audit opinion will be issued?

A	Qualified, as the matter is material when considering its cumulative effect over time
B	Unmodified, as the matter alone is neither material nor pervasive
C	Adverse, as the matter affects both total assets and profit or loss for the year
D	Disclaimer, as the matter is disputed with management, regardless of its materiality

5   **Which of the following statements would appear in a typical unmodified auditor's report?**

(1)   Our responsibility is to express an opinion on these financial statements based on our audit

(2)   We believe that the audit evidence we have obtained is sufficient and appropriate to provide a basis for our audit opinion

(3)   We conducted our audit in accordance with International Financial Reporting Standards

(4)   From the matters communicated with those charged with governance, we determine those matters that were of most significance in the audit of the financial statements of the current period

A	1 and 2 only
B	1, 2 and 3
C	1, 3 and 4
D	2, and 4

(10 marks)

Question 78 MINNIE *(non-exam style)*

You are the audit manager of Daffy & Co and you are briefing your team on the approach to adopt in undertaking the review and finalisation stage of the audit. In particular, your audit senior is unsure about the steps to take in relation to uncorrected misstatements.

During the audit of Minnie Co the following uncorrected misstatement has been noted.

The property balance was revalued during the year by an independent expert valuer and an error was made in relation to the assumptions provided to the valuer.

Required:

(a)   **Explain the term "misstatement" and describe the auditor's responsibility in relation to misstatements.**   (4 marks)

(b)   **Describe the factors Daffy & Co should consider when placing reliance on the work of the independent valuer.**   (4 marks)

(c)   The following additional issues have arisen during the course of the audit of Minnie Co. Profit before tax is $10 million.

         (i)   Depreciation has been calculated on the total of land and buildings. In previous years it has only been charged on buildings. Total depreciation is $2·5 million and the element charged to land only is $0·7 million.   (4 marks)

(ii) Minnie Co's computerised wages program is backed up daily, however for a period of two months the wages records and the back-ups have been corrupted, and therefore cannot be accessed. Wages and salaries for these two months are $1·1 million. (4 marks)

(iii) Minnie Co's main competitor has filed a lawsuit for $5 million against them alleging a breach of copyright; this case is ongoing and will not be resolved prior to the auditor's report being signed. The matter is correctly disclosed as a contingent liability. (4 marks)

Required:

Discuss each of these issues and describe the impact on the auditor's report if the above issues remain unresolved.

Note: The mark allocation is shown against each of the three issues above. Auditor's report extracts are NOT required.

(20 marks)

Question 79 PAPRIKA

The following scenario relates to questions 1–5

You are an audit manager in Brown & Co and you are nearing completion of the audit of Paprika & Co (Paprika). The audit senior has produced extracts below from the draft auditor's report for Paprika. Some of these extracts may require amendment.

Opinion

(1) We have audited the financial statements, which comprise the statement of financial position as at 31 December 2015, and the statement of comprehensive income, statement of changes in equity and statement of cash flows for the year then ended.

In our opinion, the accompanying financial statements present fairly, in all material respects, the financial position as at 31 December 2015, and its financial performance and its cash flows for the year then ended.

Auditor's responsibility

(2) Our objectives are to obtain absolute assurance about whether the financial statements as a whole are free from all misstatement, whether due to fraud or error, and to issue an auditor's report that includes our opinion.

(3) We are responsible for the preparation and fair presentation of the financial statements in accordance with IFRSs, and for such internal control as management determines is necessary to enable to preparation of financial statements.

(4) We design and perform audit procedures responsive to those risks, and obtain audit evidence that is sufficient and appropriate to provide a basis for our opinion. The procedures selected depend on the availability and experience of audit team members. We consider internal controls relevant to the entity; and express an opinion on the effectiveness of these internal controls.

(5) We did not evaluate the overall presentation of the financial statements, as this is management's responsibility. We considered the reasonableness of any new accounting estimates made by management. We did not review the appropriateness of accounting policies as these are the same as last year. In order to confirm raw material inventory quantities, we relied on the work undertaken by an independent expert.

1 **Which of the following are factors should Brown & Co consider before relying on the work of the independent expert?**

(1)   Whether the expert has the necessary competence and capabilities to perform the work

(2)   Whether using the expert's work will increase Brown & Co's efficiency in completing the audit

(3)   The expert's independence and potential threats to independence such as self-interest due to share ownership

(4)   The nature, scope and objective of the expert's work

A   1 and 3 only
B   3 and 4 only
C   1, 2 and 4
D   1, 3 and 4

2 **Which of the following should be added to extract 1?**

(1)   Identity of the entity, Paprika & Co
(2)   Identity of the auditor, Brown & Co
(3)   Identity of the financial reporting framework
(4)   Reference to the notes to the financial statements, including significant accounting policies

A   1 and 4 only
B   2 and 3 only
C   1, 2 and 3
D   1, 3 and 4

3   Extract 2 is incorrect.

Which of the following options correctly identifies the auditor's responsibility for obtaining assurance about materials misstatements due to fraud or error?

	Error	*Fraud*
A	Absolute	Reasonable
B	Absolute	None
C	Reasonable	Reasonable
D	Reasonable	None

4 **Which of the following are responsibilities of management that should be clarified in extract 3?**

(1)   Preparation and fair presentation of financial statements
(2)   Internal control
(3)   Conclusion on the use of the going concern basis of accounting

A   1 only
B   2 only
C   1 and 2 only
D   1, 2 and 3

5 **Which of the following statements explain why extract 4 is incorrect?**

(1) It should state that the auditor is only required to obtain evidence that would more likely than not be deemed sufficient by a reasonable user of financial statements

(2) The procedures selected should be based on their effectiveness and efficiency in obtaining audit evidence, not the availability and experience of audit team members

(3) It should state that the auditor reports to management any significant deficiencies in internal controls identified rather than express an opinion on their effectiveness

A   1 and 2 only
B   2 and 3 only
C   1 and 3 only
D   1, 2 and 3

(10 marks)

Question 80 CORSCO

The following scenario relates to questions 1–5

Harris & Johnson have been the auditors of Corsco, a listed telecommunications company, for six years. It is highly geared because it borrowed a large sum to pay for a licence to operate a mobile phone network with technology that has not proved popular. The company's share price has dropped by 50% during the last three years and there have been several changes of senior management during that period. There has been considerable speculation in the press over the last six months about whether the company can survive without being taken over by a rival. Three approaches to take over the company have failed because the bidders pulled out of the deal due to the fall in share price.

The company has net assets, but has found it necessary to severely curtail its capital investment program. Some commentators consider this fundamental to the future growth of the business; others consider that the existing business is fundamentally sound. It has also been necessary for the company to restructure its finances. Detailed disclosures of all of these matters have always been made in the financial statements. No reference has been made to the going concern status of the company in previous auditor's reports and the deterioration in circumstances in the current year is no worse than it has been in previous years.

1 **Based on the information provided above, which of the following best describes the auditor's report MOST likely to be issued in respect of the current year's financial statements?**

A   Adverse because the failed takeovers are a clear indicator that the company is not a going concern

B   Unmodified with a Key Audit Matter section detailing the recent changes in share price and the press speculation about the company's future prospects

C   Unmodified without reference to the use of the going concern basis of accounting, as the deterioration in circumstances is no worse than in previous years

D   Disclaimer because without confidence in Corsco's ability to continue as a going concern, the auditor cannot issue an opinion

2   **Which of the following difficulties could be faced by Corsco if the auditor's report draws attention to the use of the going concern basis of accounting?**

(1)   The mere act of drawing attention to going concern may create a going concern problem (a self-fulfilling prophecy)

(2)   Corsco may need to find another auditor to get a second opinion on the going concern issues

(3)   Specific reference to the going concern basis of accounting may cause Corsco's share price to fall even further

(4)   Corsco may need to invest resources in an audit committee to remedy the weaknesses that led to the going concern issues

A   2 and 4
B   1 and 3
C   3 and 4
D   1 and 2

3   **In line with ISA 570 *Going Concern,* which of the following describes an auditor's responsibility relating to the going concern basis of accounting?**

A   The auditor should assume the going concern basis to be appropriate unless evidence arises that suggests otherwise, in which case the auditor should verify its use

B   If management does not assess the entity's ability to continue as a going concern, it is the auditor's responsibility to rectify that lack of analysis

C   The auditor should ask management if it knows of indicators of significant doubt beyond the period of management's going concern assessment

D   The auditor should obtain sufficient appropriate audit evidence regarding going concern only when management's assessment is explicitly required the financial reporting framework

4   **Which of the following describe management's responsibilities in assessing the company's ability to continue as a going concern?**

(1)   Management must assess the entity's ability to continue as a going concern IAS 1 *Presentation of Financial Statements*

(2)   If the company has a history of profitable operations and access to sufficient financial resources, management may conclude that the going concern basis is appropriate without detailed analysis

(3)   When making the going concern assessment, management should take into account only those future events or conditions that are certain

(4)   Management must provide the auditor with a cash forecast for a period that is at least, but not limited to, 12 months from the end of the reporting period

A   1 and 4
B   2, 3 and 4
C   1, 2 and 3
D   1 and 2 only

5   Harris & Johnson are also the auditors of Key West, a supplier of shipping materials. The following matters relate to Key West:

(1)   The chief executive officer is due to retire within six months of the year end
(2)   Adverse key financial ratios for the first time
(3)   No cash flow forecast for the next 12 months has been produced
(4)   Operating losses have continued to grow
(5)   The cash flow statement show net cash used in operating activities

Which of the above matters would be considered by the auditor during his planning of the audit as indicators of potential going concern difficulties?

A   1, 2 and 4
B   2, 4 and 5
C   1, 3 and 5
D   3, 4 and 5

(10 marks)

Question 81   MEDIMADE *(non-exam style)*

(a)   **Define the going concern assumption.**   (2 marks)

(b)   Medimade Co is an established pharmaceutical company that has, for many years, generated 90% of its revenue through the sale of two specific cold and flu remedies. Medimade has lately seen a real growth in the level of competition and demand for its products has significantly declined. To make matters worse, the company has not invested sufficiently in new product development and so has been trying to remedy this by recruiting suitably trained scientific staff, but this has proved more difficult than anticipated.

The company also needed to invest $2 million in plant and machinery. The company wanted to borrow this sum but was unable to agree suitable terms with the bank; therefore it used its overdraft facility, which carried a higher interest rate. Consequently, some of Medimade's suppliers have been paid much later than usual and hence some of them have withdrawn credit terms meaning the company must pay cash on delivery. As a result of the above, Medimade's overdraft balance has grown substantially.

The directors have produced a cash flow forecast and this shows a significantly worsening position over the coming 12 months.

The directors have informed you that the bank overdraft facility is due for renewal next month, but they are confident that it will be renewed. They also strongly believe that the new products which are being developed will be ready to market soon and hence trading levels will improve and therefore that the company is a going concern. Therefore they do not intend to make any disclosures in the accounts regarding going concern.

Required:

Identify any potential indicators that the company is not a going concern and describe why these could affect the ability of the company to continue trading on a going concern basis.   (8 marks)

(c)   **Explain the audit procedures that the auditor of Medimade should perform in assessing whether or not the company is a going concern.**   (6 marks)

(d) The auditors have been informed that Medimade's bankers will not make a decision on the overdraft facility until after the auditor's report is completed. The directors have now agreed to include going concern disclosures.

Required:

Describe the impact on the auditor's report of Medimade if the auditor believes the company is a going concern but a material uncertainty exists. (4 marks)

(20 marks)

Question 82 STRAWBERRY KITCHEN DESIGNS

The following scenario relates to questions 1–5

You are the audit manager of Kiwi & Co and you have been provided with financial statements extracts and the following information about your client, Strawberry Kitchen Designs Co (Strawberry), who is a kitchen manufacturer. The company's year end is 30 April 2016.

The kitchen manufacturing industry has many competitors. The industry is cyclical, with a high percentage of sales occurring in the fourth quarter of each year. Strawberry has recently been experiencing trading difficulties, as its major customer who owes $600,000 to Strawberry has ceased trading, and it is unlikely any of this will be received. The sales director has recently left Strawberry and has yet to be replaced.

The monthly cash flow has shown a net cash outflow for the last two months of the financial year and is forecast as negative for the forthcoming financial year. As a result of this, the company has been slow in paying its suppliers and some are threatening legal action to recover the sums owing.

Due to its financial difficulties, Strawberry missed a loan repayment and, as a result of this breach in the loan covenants, the bank has asked that the loan of $4·8 million be repaid in full within six months. The directors have decided that in order to conserve cash, Strawberry will discontinue research and development for the remainder of 2016.

1 **Which of the following are indications that Strawberry Kitchen Designs Co may not be a going concern?**

(1) The kitchen manufacturing industry has many competitors and seasonal trading

(2) A major customer has ceased trading, owing Strawberry $600,000 that is unlikely to be collected

(3) Strawberry is experiencing negative monthly cash flows and this is expected to continue

(4) Strawberry has missed a loan repayment in breach of a loan covenant and now has only six months in which to raise $4.8 million for the loan that is now repayable

A 1, 3 and 4
B 2 and 3 only
C 2, 3 and 4
D 2 and 4 only

2   **Which of the following audit procedures should be performed to assess whether Strawberry can continue as a going concern?**

(1)   Perform a sensitivity analysis on the cash flows to understand the margin of safety of its net cash in/out flow

(2)   Confirm the existence of accounts payable by sending confirmation letters to a sample of suppliers

(3)   Enquire of Strawberry's legal advisors if any legal claims have been brought and request their assessment of the likely amounts payable to the suppliers

(4)   Interview a random sample of employees to evaluate the likelihood of misappropriation of assets and other acts of fraud

A   1 and 4
B   1 and 3
C   2 and 4
D   2 and 3

3   **Which of the following factors would support the auditor's conclusion that the auditor's report should be modified in relation to going concern?**

(1)   Management's plan to dispose of assets to maintain adequate cash flows

(2)   Forecast management information, cash flows and budgets showing that the company expects to incur significant losses over the next three years

(3)   A substantial bank loan is due to be repaid 18 months after the reporting period

(4)   Guarantees of financial support given by the directors

A   1 and 4
B   2 and 4
C   2 and 3
D   1 and 3

4   **Which of the following is Kiwi & Co MOST likely to consider to be a mitigating factor when assessing Strawberry's ability to continue as a going concern?**

A   Plans to discuss with lenders the terms of all debt and loan agreements
B   Postponement of research and development expenditures
C   Plans to hire a new sales director
D   A strong relationship with its suppliers

5   Kiwi & Co determines that a material uncertainty exists that may cast doubts on Strawberry's ability to continue as a going concern.

Which of the following correctly summarises the audit opinions which can be issued depending on whether or not the uncertainty is appropriately disclosed?

	Appropriate	*Not appropriate*
A	Unmodified	Unmodified with a separate going concern section
B	Unmodified with a separate going concern section	Unmodified with a separate going concern section
C	Qualified "except for"	Adverse opinion
D	Unmodified with a separate going concern section	Qualified "except for" or adverse

(10 marks)

Question 83 CLARINET *(non-exam style)*

Clarinet Co (Clarinet) is a computer hardware specialist and has been trading for over five years. The company is funded partly through overdrafts and loans and also by several large shareholders; the year end is 30 April 2016.

Clarinet has experienced significant growth in previous years; however, in the current year a new competitor, Drums Design Co (Drums), has entered the market and through competitive pricing has gained considerable market share from Clarinet. One of Clarinet's larger customers has stopped trading with them and has moved its business to Drums. In addition, a number of Clarinet's specialist developers have left the company and joined Drums. Clarinet has found it difficult to replace these employees due to the level of their skills and knowledge. Clarinet has just received notification that its main supplier who provides the company with specialist electrical equipment has ceased to trade.

Clarinet is looking to develop new products to differentiate itself from the rest of its competitors. It has approached its shareholders to finance this development; however, they declined to invest further in Clarinet. Clarinet's loan is long term and it has met all repayments on time. The overdraft has increased significantly over the year and the directors have informed you that the overdraft facility is due for renewal next month, and they are confident it will be renewed.

The directors have produced a cash flow forecast which shows a significantly worsening position over the coming 12 months. They are confident with the new products being developed, and in light of their trading history of significant growth, believe it is unnecessary to make any disclosures in the financial statements regarding going concern.

At the year end, Clarinet received notification from one of its customers that the hardware installed by Clarinet for the customers' online ordering system has not been operating correctly. As a result, the customer has lost significant revenue and has informed Clarinet that they intend to take legal action against them for loss of earnings. Clarinet has investigated the problem post year end and discovered that other work-in-progress is similarly affected and inventory should be written down. The finance director believes that as this misstatement was identified after the year end, it can be amended in the 2017 financial statements.

Required:

(a)   **Describe the procedures the auditors of Clarinet Co should undertake in relation to the uncorrected inventory misstatement identified above.**   (4 marks)

(b)   **Explain SIX potential indicators that Clarinet Co is not a going concern.**   (6 marks)

(c)   **Describe the audit procedures which you should perform in assessing whether or not Clarinet Co is a going concern.**   (6 marks)

(d)   The auditors have been informed that Clarinet's bankers will not make a decision on the overdraft facility until after the auditor's report is completed. The directors have now agreed to include some going concern disclosures.

Required:

Describe the impact on the auditor's report of Clarinet Co if the auditor believes the company is a going concern but that this is subject to a material uncertainty.   (4 marks)

(20 marks)

Question 84 OCTBALL *(non-exam style)*

You are the senior manager in the internal audit department of Octball Co. You report to the chief internal auditor and have a staff of six junior auditors to supervise, although the budget allows for up to 10 junior staff.

In a recent meeting with the chief internal auditor, the difficulty of staff recruitment and retention was discussed. Over the past year, five junior internal audit staff have left the company, but only two have been recruited. Recruitment problems identified include location of Octball's head office in a small town over 150 kilometres from the nearest major city and extensive foreign travel, often to cold climates.

Together with the chief internal auditor you believe that outsourcing the internal audit department may be a way of alleviating the staffing problems. You would monitor the new outsourced department in a part-time role taking on additional responsibilities in other departments, and the chief internal auditor would accept the post of Finance Director (FD) on the board, replacing the retiring FD.

Two firms have been identified as being able to provide the internal audit service:

■   The NFA Partnership, a local firm specialising in provision of accountancy and internal audit services. NFA does not audit financial statements or report to members; and

■   T&M, Octball's external auditors, who have offices in 75 countries and employ in excess of 65,000 staff.

Required:

(a)   **Discuss the advantages and disadvantages of appointing NFA as internal auditors for Octball.**   (8 marks)

(b)   **Discuss the issues T&M need to consider before they could accept appointment as internal auditors for Octball.**   (7 marks)

(c)   Assume that an outsourcing company has been chosen to provide internal audit services.

Describe the control activities that Octball should apply to ensure that the internal audit service is being maintained to a high standard.   (5 marks)

(20 marks)

Question 85 SAXOPHONE *(non-exam style)*

Saxophone Enterprises Co (Saxophone) has been trading for 15 years selling insurance and has recently become a listed company. In accordance with corporate governance principles Saxophone maintains a small internal audit department. The directors feel that the team needs to increase in size and specialist skills are required, but they are unsure whether to recruit more internal auditors, or to outsource the whole function to their external auditors, Cello & Co.

Saxophone is required to comply with corporate governance principles in order to maintain its listed status; hence the finance director has undertaken a review of whether or not the company complies.

Bill Bassoon is the chairman of Saxophone, until last year he was the chief executive. Bill is unsure if Saxophone needs more non-executive directors as there are currently three non-executive directors out of the eight board members. He is considering appointing one of his close friends, who is a retired chief executive of a manufacturing company, as a non-executive director.

The finance director, Jessie Oboe, decides on the amount of remuneration each director is paid. Currently all remuneration is in the form of an annual bonus based on profits. Jessie is considering setting up an audit committee, but has not undertaken this task yet as she is very busy. A new sales director was appointed nine months ago. He has yet to undertake his board training as this is normally provided by the chief executive and this role is currently vacant.

There are a large number of shareholders and therefore the directors believe that it is impractical and too costly to hold an annual general meeting of shareholders. Instead, the board has suggested sending out the financial statements and any voting resolutions by email; shareholders can then vote on the resolutions via email.

Required:

(a)   **Explain the advantages and disadvantages for each of Saxophone Enterprises Co AND Cello & Co of outsourcing the internal audit department.**   (10 marks)

        Note: The total marks will be split as follows:

        Saxophone Enterprises Co   (8 marks)
        Cello & Co   (2 marks)

(b)   **In respect of the corporate governance of Saxophone Enterprises Co:**

        (i)   **Identify and explain FIVE corporate governance weaknesses; and**
        (ii)   **Provide a recommendation to address each weakness.**

        Note: The total marks will be split equally between each part.   (10 marks)

                                                                                    (20 marks)

Question 86 BUSH-BABY HOTELS

The following scenario relates to questions 1–5

Bush-Baby Hotels Co (BBH) operates a chain of 18 hotels located across the country. Each hotel has bedrooms, a restaurant and leisure club facilities. Most visitors to the restaurant and leisure club are hotel guests; however, these facilities are open to the public as well. Hotel guests generally charge any costs to their room but other visitors must make payment directly to the hotel staff.

During the year, senior management noticed an increased number of discrepancies in cash balances and amounts of inventory that suggests that some employees have been stealing cash and goods from the hotels. Management is keen to prevent this from recurring and is considering establishing an internal audit department to undertake a fraud investigation.

1   **Which of the following describes how a new internal audit department could assist the directors of BBH in preventing and detecting fraud and error?**

    (1)   It could assess the main areas of fraud risk, as well as assess the adequacy and effectiveness of control systems

    (2)   It could evaluate the appropriateness of a company's objectives and the board's strategies to achieve those objectives

    (3)   Having developed internal controls, it could undertake regular reviews of each hotel's compliance with these controls

    (4)   Where fraud is suspected, it could undertake an investigation to identify who is involved, the likely amounts stolen and gather evidence for any police investigation

    A   1, 2 and 3
    B   1 and 3 only
    C   1, 3 and 4
    D   3 and 4 only

2   **Which of the following are limitations of BBH establishing and maintaining an internal audit department?**

    (1)   That the internal auditors will be employees may impair their independence, as they may not report issues to those charged with governance for fear of losing their job

    (2)   As there is no requirement for internal auditors to be qualified, there may be gaps in the experience and technical knowledge of the department

    (3)   As BBH has not previously had such a department, there may be some resistance to employees having their work reviewed, especially if the department's first task is a fraud investigation

    (4)   As internal audit is required to be both objective and independent it can be difficult to find sufficient personnel to staff the department

    A   1 and 2 only
    B   1, 2 and 3
    C   1, 2 and 4
    D   2, 3 and 4

3   Once established, one of the first responsibilities of BBH's internal audit department will be to establish relevant benchmarks to compare the performance of a number of departments across a range of relevant indicators as part of the scope of a wide-ranging project to improve results.

What type of assignment will the internal audit department be carrying out?

A   Regulatory compliance
B   Value for money
C   Operational information systems
D   Best value

4   Once established, the internal audit department could undertake inventory counts at the restaurants of the 18 hotels. There is likely to be a significant level of inventory held at each hotel. Internal audit could then compare actual quantities to the hotels' records.

Which of the following conclusions could be drawn by the internal audit department as a result of the inventory counts?

(1)   If actual quantities are generally lower than recorded quantities there may be obsolete inventory

(2)   If actual quantities for a specific hotel are lower than recorded quantities this may indicate fraud

(3)   If actual quantities are higher than recorded quantities, employees may not have been adequately trained on how to record inventory movements

(4)   If there are no differences there are no inventory issues

A   2 and 3 only
B   1 and 3
C   1 and 4
D   2, 3 and 4

5   The directors would like the internal audit department to have as broad a role as possible, as this will make the decision to recruit an internal audit department more cost effective.

Which of the following are additional functions, other than the fraud investigation, that the directors of BBH could ask the internal audit department to undertake?

(1)   Testing controls over cash receipts and cash counts
(2)   Reviewing the computer environment and controls
(3)   Monitoring compliance with laws and regulations
(4)   Reviewing employees' eligibility for promotions

A   1 and 3 only
B   2 and 3 only
C   1, 2 and 3
D   1, 2 and 4

(10 marks)

Question 87 ZPM *(non-exam style)*

ISA 610 *Using the Work of Internal Auditors* states that "when the external auditor intends to use specific work of internal auditing, the external auditor should evaluate and perform audit procedures on that work to confirm its adequacy for the external auditor's purposes."

Required:

(a)   **In relation to ISA 610, explain the factors the external auditor will consider when evaluating the work of the internal auditor.**   (5 marks)

(b)   ZPM is a listed company with a year end of 30 June. ZPM's main activity is selling home improvement or "Do-It-Yourself" (DIY) products to the public. Products sold range from nails, paint and tools to doors and showers; some stores also sell garden tools and furniture. Products are purchased from approximately 200 different suppliers. ZPM has 103 stores in eight different countries.

ZPM has a well-staffed internal audit department, who report on a regular basis to the audit committee. Areas where the internal and external auditors may carry out work include:

(a)   Attending the year-end inventory count in 30 stores annually. All stores are visited on a rotational basis.

(b)   Checking the internal controls over the procurement systems (e.g. ensuring a liability is only recorded when the inventory has been received).

(c)   Reviewing the operations of the marketing department.

Required:

For each of the above three areas, discuss

(i)   **the objectives of the internal auditor;**   (5 marks)

(ii)   **the objectives of the external auditor; and**   (5 marks)

(iii)   **whether the external auditor will rely on the internal auditor, and if reliance is required, the extent of that reliance.**   (5 marks)

(20 marks)

MCQs 1 AUDIT AND OTHER ASSURANCE ENGAGEMENTS

1.1   "Based on our review, nothing has come to our attention that causes us to believe that the accompanying financial statements do not give a true and fair view in accordance with International Financial Reporting Standards."

Which of the following BEST describes the type of assurance provided by this statement?

A   Positive assurance expressed negatively
B   Negative assurance expressed positively
C   High level of assurance expressed negatively
D   Limited level of assurance expressed negatively

1.2   The level of assurance given by an assurance engagement will depend on the type of engagement. Assurance levels are often described as being either:

(1)   Absolute
(2)   Reasonable
(3)   Limited
(4)   Zero

What level of assurance would normally be given to an audit of financial statements and what level of assurance to a review of financial statements?

A   1 and 4
B   2 and 4
C   1 and 3
D   2 and 3

1.3   **Which of the following best describes professional scepticism?**

A   The assurance provider should not believe anything that management tells him

B   The assurance provider should not believe anything that management tells him, without obtaining supporting evidence

C   The assurance provider should apply a questioning mind to the information and evidence he obtains

D   The assurance provider should be prudent and always assume the worst outcome in cases of uncertainty

1.4   **Which of the following statements, relating to International Standards on Auditing (ISAs), if any, is/are correct?**

(1)   International Standards on Auditing (ISAs) are issued by the International Accounting Standards Board (IASB) and provide guidance on the performance and conduct of an audit

(2)   In the event that ISAs differ from local legislation in a specific country, auditors must comply with the requirements of the ISAs

A   1 only
B   2 only
C   Both 1 and 2
D   Neither 1 nor 2

(8 marks)

MCQs 2 EXTERNAL AUDIT

2.1 **What is the objective of the external audit of a limited company?**

A To protect the interests of minority shareholders
B To detect fraud and other irregularities
C To assess the effectiveness of the company's performance
D To provide assurance on the directors' assertions about the financial statements

2.2 **Who would approve the appointment of a company's auditor?**

A The statutory authorities
B The directors
C The shareholders
D The company's bank

2.3 **Who is ultimately responsible for ensuring that the annual financial statements of a listed company are prepared in accordance with IFRS and relevant legislation?**

A The auditors
B The board of directors
C The company secretary
D The listing exchange

2.4 **Of which international body is the International Auditing and Assurance Standards Board (IAASB) a member?**

A OECD
B IFRS Foundation
C IFAC
D WTO

2.5 The following statements relate to International Standards on Auditing (ISAs) and professional auditors:

(1) All ISAs must be applied during the course of an audit

(2) ISAs override local regulations

(3) The entire text of a standard must be understood in order to apply its requirements

(4) ISAs are rules-based and all rules must be applied

(5) An individual is appropriately qualified as an auditor on passing professional examinations

(6) In most jurisdictions, only a statutory auditor is allowed to carry out audits of companies

Which of the above statements are true?

A 1, 2, 4 and 5
B 3 and 6 only
C 1, 3 and 6
D 1, 2, 5 and 6

2.6 **Which of the following is generally accepted as a right of an auditor?**

A   To have access to the company's books, accounts and records

B   To require from company officials any information and explanations on any matter whatsoever

C   To report to any legal authority any matter the auditor considers that authority needs to know

D   To attend any board or committee meeting

(12 marks)

MCQs 3 CORPORATE GOVERNANCE

3.1 **Which of the following is NOT a principle of corporate governance?**

A   Rights of shareholders
B   Board responsibilities
C   Auditor's accountability and remuneration
D   Risk management and internal control

3.2 **Who do audit committees normally liaise between?**

A   The internal and external auditors
B   The internal auditor and entity's staff
C   The executive and non-executive directors
D   The auditors and the directors

(4 marks)

MCQs 4 PROFESSIONAL CODES OF ETHICS AND CONDUCT

4.1 The directors of Exit Co, a large unlisted company, have decided to issue an annual environmental and corporate social responsibility report as they wish to follow best corporate governance practice. They have asked the company's auditors Stu & Co to provide an assurance report on the new report. If accepted, the annual fees from Exit Co would be slightly less than 15% of Stu & Co's gross annual fee income.

Which of the following safeguards would be the most appropriate for Stu & Co to implement now?

A   Resign from Exit Co
B   Decline the additional work
C   Rotate the audit partner
D   Discuss the fee levels with Exit Co's audit committee

4.2 Auditors have a professional duty of confidentiality under ACCA's *Code of Ethics and Conduct*; voluntary disclosure of information may be necessary in certain situations.

For which TWO of the following situations should an auditor make VOLUNTARY disclosure?

(1)   If an auditor knows or suspects his client is engaged in money laundering
(2)   Where disclosure is made to non-governmental bodies
(3)   Where it is in the public interest to disclose
(4)   If an auditor suspects his client has committed terrorist offences

A	1 and 4
B	1 and 3
C	2 and 4
D	2 and 3

(4 marks)

MCQs 5 AUDITOR APPOINTMENT

5.1 A potential client has asked a firm to act as auditor to his company and wants the audit to commence immediately as the financial statements are required by the bank.

What should the auditor's response be?

A	Start work on the audit right away
B	Inform the previous auditors that they intend to commence work
C	Contact the previous auditors for professional clearance before they start work
D	Accept the assignment subject to written confirmation of appointment by the Board

5.2 **Which TWO of the following should be included in an audit engagement letter?**

(1)	Objective and scope of the audit
(2)	Results of previous audits
(3)	Management's responsibilities
(4)	Need to maintain professional scepticism

A	1 and 2
B	1 and 3
C	2 and 4
D	3 and 4

(4 marks)

MCQs 6 DOCUMENTATION

6.1 **Which of the following is an advantage of using standardised working papers?**

A	Ensures the completeness of the audit working papers by the placing of a standard programme on each section of the audit file
B	Introduces a standard approach to the conduct and documentation of the audit
C	Enables junior staff to follow properly documented and designed procedures thereby reducing the need for excessive supervision
D	Facilitates briefing, delegation, supervision, review and quality control of the audit work

6.2 Auditors' working papers are conventionally divided into current and permanent files for both convenience and control.

Which of the following is most likely to appear on the permanent audit file as opposed to the current audit file?

A	Written representations from management
B	Report to management
C	Letter of engagement
D	Receivables confirmation letter

(4 marks)

MCQs 7 AUDIT PLANNING

7.1   **What is an audit programme?**

    A   A series of detailed questions to ascertain and evaluate all important characteristics of the system of internal control in operation

    B   A list of disclosure and other requirements which must be met in order to ensure compliance with IFRS, statutes and listing rules

    C   A list of general instructions on the audit firm's methods of auditing in each area and the firm's general procedures

    D   A clear set of detailed instructions on the work to be carried out by audit staff

7.2   **Which of the following statements is FALSE with regard to audit planning?**

    A   It helps the auditors to devote appropriate attention to important areas of the financial statements

    B   It helps the auditor to properly organise and manage the audit engagement, so that it is performed in an effective manner

    C   It provides assurance to the auditor that the risk of a material misstatement in the financial statements will be reduced

    D   It facilitates the direction and supervision of audit team members and the review of their work

7.3   **Which of the following should an auditor consider when developing an overall audit strategy?**

    A   Whether the allowance for sampling risk exceeds the achieved upper precision limit

    B   Findings from substantive tests performed at interim dates

    C   Whether the inquiry of the client's solicitor identifies any litigation, claims, or assessments not disclosed in the financial statements

    D   Preliminary evaluations of materiality, audit risk, and internal control

(6 marks)

MCQs 8 UNDERSTANDING THE ENTITY

8.1   To understand an entity, auditors use various sources of information. Such sources include:

    (1)   The company's systems procedure manuals
    (2)   The internal audit function's system notes
    (3)   The prior year audit file
    (4)   Inquiries made of company staff
    (5)   The company's website

    Which would be the best sources of information about a company's financial systems?

    A   1, 2 and 4
    B   3, 4 and 5
    C   1, 3 and 5
    D   1, 2 and 3

8.2 A client high-tec company has financial problems, a dominant chief executive, poor internal control and unusual transactions.

What are all of these factors indicative of?

A   Inadequacies in the systems of reporting
B   The presence of going concern problems
C   Increased scope for potential fraud
D   Increased audit risk

(4 marks)

MCQs 9 INTERNAL CONTROL

9.1 ISA 315 *Identifying and Assessing the Risks of Material Misstatement through Understanding the Entity and Its Environment* states that an internal control system in an organisation consists of five components: the control environment, the entity's risk assessment process, the information system, control activities and monitoring of controls.

Which component would include the review by a senior financial manager of monthly bank reconciliations produced by her assistant?

A   Control environment
B   Control activity
C   Monitoring of controls
D   Risk assessment

9.2 **Which of the following is an advantage of using systems flowcharts to document internal controls instead of using internal control questionnaires?**

A   They provide a visual depiction of a client's activities
B   They identify internal control weaknesses more prominently
C   They indicate whether control activities are operating effectively
D   They are more easily updated for significant changes in controls

9.3 **An internal control questionnaire is used by the auditor to document which of the following?**

A   Control risk assessment
B   Control environment effectiveness
C   The auditor's understanding of internal controls
D   General and application controls

9.4 **Which of the following is NOT a benefit of an effective system of internal control?**

A   Enhanced profitability
B   Better management of assets and liabilities
C   Cutting down the time needed for the audit
D   Compliance with laws and regulations

(8 marks)

MCQs 10 AUDIT MATERIALITY

10.1 The external auditor of Aaron Co has set a planning materiality threshold of $40,000 and a performance materiality of $30,000. The audit testing approach to the following financial statement items is being considered:

(1)   Harry, a director of Aaron Co, owes $1,000 to the company (borrowed during the year).
(2)   Sundry income of $35,000

Which of the two items should be tested?

A   Neither 1 nor 2
B   Both 1 and 2
C   1 only
D   2 only

10.2 As an audit team member with two years of experience, you were assigned to carry out a substantive test on directors' expenses. The result of the test showed that in several cases involving the same director, the Chief Financial Officer (CFO) had authorised the over payment of his expenses. Each expense item was less than the performance materiality level.

What action should be taken?

A   Draw conclusion
B   Discuss with a senior member of the audit team
C   Extend sample
D   Discuss with the CFO

10.3 **Which is the best way of describing a material item?**

A   Its omission or disclosure would reasonably influence the decisions of a user of the financial statements

B   It is large in relation to the same figure in previous years

C   It amounts to more than 10% of the total of which it forms a part

D   It is one that would reduce a company's profits

(6 marks)

MCQs 11 FRAUD, LAW AND REGULATIONS

11.1 **Which of the following procedures is NOT likely to result in the discovery of possible non-compliance with laws and regulations?**

A   Enquiring of management or the entity's lawyer
B   Reviewing internal control questionnaires
C   Underaking tests of details on classes of transactions
D   Reading minutes of board meetings

11.2 An auditor has discovered a $10,000 wages fraud by a director of a listed company. The amount is not material in relation to the financial statements of the company and the auditor has determined that the fraud does not constitute money laundering.

To whom does the auditor have a primary duty to report this matter to?

A Those charged with governance
B The company's shareholders
C The tax authorities
D The auditor's professional body

(4 marks)

MCQs 12 TESTS OF CONTROL

12.1 The following situations are all covered by general controls:

(1) Changes to data files
(2) Program changes
(3) Continuity of operations

Which general control would be appropriate to all three scenarios above?

A Password protection
B Back-up procedures
C Authorisation
D One-for-one checking

12.2 **Which of the following is an example of a general control in a computerised accounting system?**

A The sales department matches a list of computer-produced invoices to its copies of the manual input documents from which invoices are originated

B The personnel department review a monthly printout of all changes to payroll standing data which is then checked against manual records

C The sales ledger system includes a sequence check on pre-numbered sales input documents received from the sales department

D Access to the computer facility is via a locked door and is restricted to selected personnel who are issued with a personal key

12.3 **When planning the audit of the purchases cycle, which of the following internal controls should the auditor test in order to ensure that liabilities are not understated?**

A Goods inwards records (GRNs) are matched to invoices and regularly reviewed for items in respect of which no invoice has been received. An authorised list of unmatched GRNs is produced at the end of each month

B Invoices are authorised as matched with goods inwards/service received notes before being recorded in the purchases day book

C Invoices are matched with copy purchase orders and authorised before being recorded in the purchases day book

D Periodic purchase ledger reconciliations are performed (and signed) by personnel independent of the goods inwards department

12.4 **Which of the following internal controls is most likely to contribute to the auditor's confidence that all sales have been recorded in the accounts?**

A   Matching pre-numbered sales invoices to despatch notes
B   Sales manager authorising all invoices before they are issued
C   Matching pre-numbered despatch notes to invoices
D   Preparing and following up an aged receivables analysis by someone independent of the sales ledger function

12.5 **Which of the following techniques provides the *least* assurance about the operating effectiveness of an internal control?**

A   Inquiry of client personnel
B   Inspection of documents and reports
C   Observation of client personnel
D   Preparation of system flowcharts

12.6 During the current year audit, the auditor tests a control by completing certain procedures that were done by the client as part of the internal control over the given transaction cycle.

Which of the following audit procedures is the auditor using?

A   Examination
B   Recalculation
C   Reconciliation
D   Reperformance

12.7 **In which of the following scenarios would an auditor be most likely to increase tests of controls?**

A   When the client's IT system is extensively integrated throughout the company's accounting system

B   When the client's accounting system is largely based on manual processes

C   When the auditor has decided not to rely on internal controls and instead elects to increase substantive testing

D   When the auditor's assessment of inherent risk is low

12.8 **Which TWO of the following controls of a sales system ensure that all goods despatched are completely and accurately invoiced?**

(1)   Good despatched notes are matched to sales invoices
(2)   Sales invoices are sequentially numbered
(3)   Sales invoices are matched to customer orders
(4)   Regular review of unfulfilled orders

A   1 and 2
B   2 and 4
C   2 and 3
D   1 and 4

(16 marks)

MCQs 13 COMMUNICATION ON INTERNAL CONTROL

13.1   During the audit of a new client numerous weaknesses have been identified. The auditor is considering the content and format of his report to management (letter of weakness).

Which of the following best summarises the auditor's approach to the report?

A   Include all matters of sufficient importance identified, but structure the letter to take account of the varying levels of significance of matters included

B   Report only major points to be dealt with by directors, leaving less important items to be discussed informally with members of the client's staff

C   Report only those matters which potentially have a material effect on the true and fair view shown by the financial statements, indicating that this should not be regarded as a comprehensive statement of all weaknesses that exist

D   Issue separate reports for each area to the executive directors with specific responsibility in those areas

13.2   Which of the following would NOT normally be considered a significant deficiency by an auditor?

A   No sensitivity analysis was carried out on the objective determination of estimates contained within the financial statements

B   An immaterial fraud carried out by a senior manager had not been detected by the internal control system

C   Transactions in which directors have financial interests are not being scrutinised by the audit committee

D   No action has been taken to address a significant deficiency reported during the audit of the previous year

13.3   Which of the following items may be included in the report to management?

(1)   An indication of areas in which the client can assist in improving audit efficiency
(2)   Constructive feedback on business systems, risk systems and risk management
(3)   Details of the audit work carried out to detect deficiencies
(4)   Details of additional extensive work that could have been carried to try to detect further significant deficiencies

A   1 and 2 only
B   1 and 3
C   1, 2 and 4
D   2, 3 and 4

(6 marks)

MCQs 14 SERVICE ORGANISATIONS

14.1 Alhare uses a service provider to produce its payroll. Originating documents are kept by Alhare and regularly reconciled (i.e. through control totals and reviews/re-computation of data sent to and received from the service provider). Audit approach options available to the auditor include:

(1) Assess the design and implementation of the service provider's controls relevant to the payroll processing

(2) Test the service provider's controls

(3) Assess the design and implementation of the payroll controls at Alhare

(4) Obtain a representation from the directors of Alhare concerning the operation of Alhare's payroll

Which of the following would be the most likely approach taken by the auditors of Alhare concerning the service provider?

A   1 only
B   3 only
C   1 and 2
D   3 and 4

14.2 A finance company uses a service provider to process its high volume, complex transactions.

Which of the following circumstances is most likely to affect the auditor's ability to form his opinion?

A   The possibility of loss of input documentation in transmission to the service provider

B   Inadequate back-up and reconstruction facilities at the service provider

C   Failure of service provider staff to identify exceptions in output and bring them to the attention of management

D   Refusal of permission to evaluate and test controls at the service provider

14.3 An auditor is auditing the financial statements of Aloe Co. Aloe uses a service provider to process its payroll. The auditor of the service provider recently issued a report on the design, implementation and effectiveness of the service provider's internal controls.

Which of the following procedures should the auditor of Aloe perform with respect to the assurance report issued by the service provider's auditor?

A   Perform tests of controls at the service provider
B   Assess control risk at maximum when auditing Aloe's payroll
C   Review the audit program followed by the service provider's auditor
D   Inquire concerning the competence of the service provider's auditor

14.4 It is common practice for the auditor of a service company to provide a Type 1 or Type 2 report to be used by the auditors of that service company's clients.

What is the main difference between a Type 1 and Type 2 report?

A Details of the controls tested during the service provider's annual audit

B A separate assurance report on the effectiveness of the service provider's internal control function

C Details of any modification made to the auditor's report on the financial statements

D Details of the controls tested which relate to the control objectives stated in the description of the service provider's clients' function

(8 marks)

MCQs 15 AUDIT EVIDENCE

15.1 Sufficiency of audit evidence depends, among other things, on the "risk of misstatement".

Which of the following would increase this risk, and so indicate that more evidence should be collected for "sufficiency"?

A The knowledge that the audit working papers will be reviewed by an independent external technical body

B The use of audit staff who are unfamiliar with the client

C The use of judgement sampling rather than statistical sampling

D A reporting deadline which is unusually soon after the year end

15.2 Growers Co is a garden centre with 20 locations employing over two hundred people. To cope with the current and expected future annual increase in transactions, Growers has implemented a centralised computer system linked to processing and checkout terminals at each centre. The new system will significantly improve the timing and quality of the management control information. A well-qualified and experienced internal audit team was also recently appointed.

What area of the external audit will see an increased emphasis on obtaining audit assurance?

A Walk-through testing
B Controls testing
C Substantive testing of transactions
D Substantive testing of balances

15.3 Which of the following types of evidence would an auditor be most likely to examine to determine whether internal controls are operating as designed?

A Gross margin information regarding the client's industry
B Confirmation of receivables verifying account balances
C Sales orders documenting credit approval
D Anticipated results documents in budgets or forecasts

15.4 An auditor examines a sample of sales invoices to determine if they were recorded in the correct revenue accounts.

What assertion is an auditor testing?

A   Accuracy, valuation and allocation
B   Classification
C   Completeness
D   Occurrence

15.5 As part of the substantive tests performed on the client's purchase transactions, the auditor selects a sample of payment vouchers and compares the dates on the vouchers to the dates the transactions were recorded in the purchase journal.

Which of the following assertions is the auditor testing?

A   Accuracy, valuation and allocation
B   Completeness
C   Cut-off
D   Occurrence

15.6 **Which of the following assertions would NOT be tested by an auditor who is performing substantive procedures on a client's account balances?**

A   Accuracy, valuation and allocation
B   Rights and obligations
C   Existence
D   Cut-off

15.7 **Which of the following audit procedures for obtaining audit evidence is correctly described?**

A   Recalculation involves the auditor's independent execution of procedures or controls which were originally performed as part of the entity's internal control

B   Confirmation consists of seeking information of knowledgeable persons, within the company or outside the company

C   Reperformance consists of checking the mathematical accuracy of documents or records

D   Observation consists of looking at a procedure or process being performed by others

(14 marks)

MCQs 16 ANALYTICAL PROCEDURES

16.1   A review of the revenues and expenses in the detailed profit and loss account of a company, involving investigation of significant variations in comparison with the equivalent figures for the previous year, is most likely to detect which of the following significant problems?

A   The fact that a line of inventory has become obsolete during the year and should be written off

B   A misallocation of distribution costs as advertising expenses

C   The fact that the costs of some exceptional repairs to the company's premises have not been included in the profit and loss account

D   Failure to make a provision for volume discounts which have been introduced this year for certain customers

16.2   Hardware Co has a fixed mark-up of 50% on cost. The external auditor's analytical review of the current financial statements has revealed a gross profit margin of 40% of sales.

What could this indicate?

A   Some sales have not been invoiced
B   Some purchases have not been recorded
C   Closing inventory has been undervalued
D   Goods used for personal consumption have been included in purchases

16.3   As the new auditor of Elm, a listed company, you note that the company's gross profit percentage as per the draft accounts has fallen from 30% in the previous year to 20% in the current year.

Which of the following explanations is the most plausible?

A   Errors in computation led to opening inventory being overvalued and this has been compounded by the inclusion for the first time (to comply with IAS 2) of indirect overheads in the closing inventory valuation

B   Errors in computation led to opening inventory being overvalued and Elm has increased sales as a result of a marketing drive based on undercutting competitors

C   Errors in computation led to opening inventory being undervalued and margins have fallen as a result of the entry into the market of a major new competitor

D   Errors in computation have caused opening inventory to be undervalued and this has been compounded by the inclusion for the first time (to comply with IAS 2) of indirect overheads in the closing inventory valuation

(6 marks)

MCQs 17 ACCOUNTING ESTIMATES

17.1   Which of the following procedures would an auditor ordinarily perform in evaluating management's accounting estimates for reasonableness?

(1)   Develop an independent expectation of management's estimates
(2)   Gather evidence to restate prior year estimates
(3)   Test the calculations used by management to develop the estimates

A   1 only
B   1 and 2
C   1 and 3
D   2 and 3

17.2   When evaluating the reasonableness of an accounting estimate, to which of the following should the auditor pay MOST attention?

A   Assumptions that are consistent with prior periods
B   Deviations from historical patterns
C   Industry-specific factors
D   Objective assumptions that are not susceptible to bias

17.3   Which of the following factors increase the risk of misstatement in an accounting estimate?

(1)   Simplicity of calculating the estimate
(2)   Insufficient relevant data
(3)   Assumptions that are not sensitive to variation
(4)   Degree of uncertainty associated with assumptions

A   1 and 3 only
B   1, 2 and 3
C   2 and 4 only
D   2, 3 and 4

(6 marks)

MCQs 18 USING THE WORK OF AN EXPERT

18.1   Which of the following statements is NOT correct concerning the auditor's use of the work of a specialist?

A   The specialist should have an understanding of the auditor's use of the specialist's findings

B   The auditor is required to perform substantive procedures to verify the specialist's assumptions and findings

C   The client should have an understanding of the nature of the work to be performed by the specialist

D   The auditor should obtain an understanding of the methods and assumptions used by the specialist

18.2 **Which of the following statements is correct concerning an auditor's use of the work of an appraiser in assessing the value of a client's intangible assets?**

A   The auditor is not required to understand the objectives and scope of the appraiser's work

B   The reasonableness of the appraiser's assumptions is strictly the auditor's responsibility

C   The client is required to consent to the auditor's use of the appraiser's work

D   If the appraiser is not independent of the client, the auditor may still be able to use the appraiser's work

18.3 In using the work of an audit expert, an auditor referred to the expert's findings in the auditor's report.

Under what circumstances would this be appropriate?

A   The client is not familiar with the professional certification, personal reputation, or particular competence of the auditor's expert

B   The auditor, as a result of the expert's findings, adds explanatory detail to a modified opinion regarding the reasons for the opinion

C   The auditor understands the form and content of the expert's findings in relation to the representations in the financial statements

D   The auditor, as a result of the expert's findings, decides to indicate a division of responsibility with the expert

(6 marks)

MCQs 19 AUDIT SAMPLING

19.1 As part of the audit testing to satisfy the audit objective "Receivables are not overstated", the audit senior of a manufacturing company plans a receivables confirmation.

Which of the following approaches would be the most appropriate in these circumstances?

A   A random sample selected from the population of individual customers used during the year

B   A sample selected from the population of individual customers used during the year, with a bias towards those having the highest value of transactions in the year

C   A random sample selected from the population of customers' year-end balances

D   A sample selected from the population of customers' year end balances, with a bias towards large balances

19.2 **Which of the following statements are NOT true?**

(1)   The higher the inherent risk the greater the sample size
(2)   The bigger the population the bigger the sample size
(3)   The lower the acceptable detection risk the lower the sample size
(4)   The higher the tolerable misstatement the lower the sample size
(5)   The higher the expected error the lower the sample size
(6)   The more the population is stratified the lower the sample size

A   2, 3, 5 and 6

B   2 and 5 only

C   1, 4 and 6

D   2, 3 and 5 only

19.3   An auditor selects a sample using the total value of trade receivables as the population. The sample is selected as follows:

- one dollar is selected at random and deemed as the first dollar;
- individual dollars are then selected at consecutive fixed intervals of $10,000.

Which of the following statements, in respect of this form of sample selection, is the most accurate?

A   The basis of sample selection is more suited to the detection of understatement errors than overstatement errors

B   The basis of selection would be ineffective where errors occur in the population on a systematic basis

C   The basis of selection may be preferred when the book population under examination has a highly-skewed value distribution

D   The basis of selection ensures that all errors in excess of $10,000 will be detected

19.4   In addition to evaluating the frequency of deviations in tests of controls, the auditor should also consider the qualitative aspects of deviations.

Which of the following would be most likely cause the auditor to consider the broader implications of a deviation?

A   It was the only deviation in the sample

B   It was identical to a deviation discovered in the prior year audit

C   It was initially concealed by a forged document

D   It was caused by an employee's misunderstanding of instructions

(8 marks)

MCQs 20 WRITTEN REPRESENTATIONS

20.1   ISA 580 *Written Representations* require auditors to obtain written representations to support other evidence.

For which of the following matters would a written representation NOT be suitable as audit evidence?

A   That all deficiencies in internal control known to management have been communicated to the auditor

B   That subsequent events requiring adjustment or disclosure in the financial statements have been dealt with appropriately

C   That the payroll charge for three months of the year during which the accounting records were unavailable is correctly stated

D   That management has fulfilled its responsibility for the preparation and presentation of the financial statements

(2 marks)

MCQs 21 COMPUTER-ASSISTED AUDIT TECHNIQUES

21.1   A large manufacturer has a computerised open-item sales ledger, holding 2,000 customer accounts. The principal files within the system are the customer master file, sales ledger file, and transactions history file.

What audit test could be assisted by a computer enquiry from the sales ledger files against the customer master file?

A   Checking whether customers have exceeded their credit limits
B   Extracting a monetary unit sample of sales invoices
C   Verifying large credit notes
D   Verifying the age analysis of trade receivables

21.2   During the final audit of Colossus, a large multi-national listed conglomerate, it is suspected that systematic errors that have occurred within the integrated computer system are a result of mainframe programming inadequacies.

Which tests are most likely to confirm these suspicions?

A   The use of test data together with a review of general controls over systems development and implementation

B   Integrated test facilities or other embedded facilities designed to allow a continuous review of data recorded and the manner in which it is treated by the system

C   File dumps at intervals, with manual recreation and comparison with actual output

D   Special computer audit programs to ensure the completeness of input and used to simulate programmed controls

21.3   **Which of the following most closely represents the use of audit software?**

	Auditor's program	Client's program	Auditor's data	Client's data
A	√		√	
B		√	√	
C	√			√
D		√		√

21.4   **Which of the following is NOT an audit software technique?**

A   Using computer programs to extract a sample for a receivables circularisation

B   Running a computer program to test the addition of the cash book

C   Using a computer to perform an analytical review comparison of administration expenses against the prior year

D   Entering a sample of dummy sales orders through the computer system which takes customers over their credit limit to ensure the system rejects the orders

(8 marks)

MCQs 22 NON-CURRENT ASSETS

22.1 **Which of the following describes how an auditor would confirm the existence assertion for a non-current asset?**

A   Agree the physical item to the non-current asset register
B   Agree the physical item to the financial statements
C   Agree an entry in the non-current asset register to the physical item
D   Agree an authorised capital expenditure request form to the physical item

22.2 **Which of the following audit procedures provides the most relevant evidence to verify the carrying amount of a company's fleet of cars?**

A   Checking depreciation rates and calculations for the vehicles
B   Examination of the vehicle registration documents
C   Inspection of the cars' insurance certificates
D   Physical inspection of the cars

(4 marks)

MCQs 23 INVENTORY

23.1 **An auditor analysing inventory turnover rates would NOT obtain evidence about which of the following management assertions?**

A   Existence
B   Rights and obligations
C   Completeness
D   Accuracy, valuation and allocation

23.2 An audit objective is stated as "to ensure that all inventory on hand is reflected in the inventory balance at the reporting date".

Which of the following management assertions should the auditor test?

A   Rights and obligations
B   Accuracy, valuation and allocation
C   Completeness
D   Existence

23.3 In order for a continuous inventory counting system to provide satisfactory evidence of year-end inventory levels it is essential that management maintains adequate inventory records and investigates and corrects all material differences between the inventory records and the physical counts.

How often must the inventory be counted?

A   All items at least once during the year
B   All items more than once during the year with the auditor in attendance
C   All items at the same time at least once during the year
D   All high value items at the year end

(6 marks)

MCQs 24 EXTERNAL CONFIRMATIONS, RECEIVABLES AND SALES

24.1 In order to gather sufficient, appropriate evidence, the auditor may make use of external confirmations. These may take the form of being a positive or negative request.

Which of the following statements is/are true?

(1) A positive confirmation request for trade receivables asks respondents to reply to the auditor indicating whether or not they agree with the information provided

(2) A negative confirmation request is a professional way for the auditor to ask for a response only if there is a problem

A 1 only
B 2 only
C Both 1 and 2
D Neither 2 nor 2

24.2 **How would an auditor trace transactions if the objective of the auditor's tests of details is to detect possible understatement of sales?**

A From purchase order to shipping documents
B From cash receipts to sales invoices
C From purchase order to cash receipts
D From shipping documents to sales invoices

(4 marks)

MCQs 25 SHARE CAPITAL, RESERVES AND DIRECTORS' REMUNERATION

25.1 The financial statements of a manufacturing company do not disclose a loan of $1,500 made to a director during the year and repaid in full before the year end. The company's profit for the year was $2 million.

What reference, if any, should be made to this matter in the auditor's report?

A No reference is necessary
B As an except for opinion, giving details of the loan (lack of evidence)
C As an except for opinion, giving details of the loan (material misstatement)
D An adverse opinion, giving details of the loan

25.2 A company uses the services of a company secretary agent to deal with all regulatory issues relating to share capital including maintenance of the share register, share issues and statutory returns.

What written confirmation should the auditor obtain from the company's agent?

A Details of any restrictions on the payment of dividends
B The number of shares issued and outstanding
C Guarantees of preferred share liquidation value
D The authorised share capital

25.3 An auditor is in the process of performing substantive procedures on a client's equity balances and traces share-related transactions recorded during the year to the board minutes.

Which of the following assertions is the auditor testing with this procedure?

A   Accuracy, valuation and allocation
B   Classification
C   Existence and occurrence
D   Completeness

(6 marks)

MCQs 26 LOANS, BANK AND CASH

26.1 Obtaining annual bank confirmation letters and receivable confirmation letters are standard audit procedures. The two forms of letterhead mostly used are:

(1)   Client's letterhead
(2)   Auditor's letterhead.

On whose letterhead are bank letters and receivable confirmation letters sent?

A   Both on 1
B   1 for the bank letter, 2 for the receivable confirmation
C   1 for the receivable confirmation, 2 for the bank letter
D   Both on 2

26.2 When auditing a client's year-end cash balance, an auditor uses standard bank confirmations and performs tests on the client's year-end bank reconciliations.

Which of the following assertions is tested by these procedures?

A   Accuracy, valuation and allocation
B   Classification
C   Existence
D   Rights and obligations

26.3 Farnham Co has a bank overdraft of $450,000, secured by a floating charge over its inventory. It also has a deposit with the same bank of $200,000. The bank confirmation letter states that the bank has the right to off-set these balances, and has set an overall net borrowing limit on the company of $300,000. The finance director has disclosed these amounts as "secured overdraft – $250,000" under "current liabilities", with no further description in the notes other than the nature of the security.

What steps, if any, should the auditor take in respect of this matter?

A   None, as the treatment is correct

B   Insist upon classification of $200,000 under current assets and $450,000 under current liabilities

C   Insist that the company discloses in the notes the full amount of the overdraft and that it is in breach of its borrowing limit

D   Accept the treatment but include added emphasis in the auditor's report explaining that these amounts have been off-set, and disclosing the overdraft limit

26.4 During the audit of a company's year-end bank reconciliation, the auditor discovered that a material amount of cheques to pay the company's suppliers were drawn and recorded in the books just before the year end. The cheques were sent out two weeks after the year end.

What action should be taken by the auditor?

A   Not seek to make any adjustment to the amount of trade payables or bank balance in the accounts

B   Confirm when the cheques were cleared before deciding if any adjustment is necessary

C   Request the company to adjust the amount of trade payables and bank balance by the total of the cheques

D   Request the company to adjust the amount of trade payables and bank balance by the total of the above cheques which remain unpresented at the completion of the audit

(8 marks)

MCQs 27 LIABILITIES, PROVISIONS AND CONTINGENCIES

27.1 During the course of their interim audit of a company, the auditors established that purchases may be understated because goods received at the end of one month are often not invoiced by suppliers until the following month.

Which of the following audit procedures should be used by the auditor at year end to gather evidence regarding the understatement of payables due to this problem?

A   A payables confirmation at the end of the financial year with following up of unsatisfactory replies

B   A detailed year-end inventory count in those areas where cut-off inadequacies are suspected

C   Comparing goods received notes for the last few days of the financial year with the purchase ledger records and accruals (goods received not yet invoiced)

D   Reconciling suppliers' statements as at the year end date with purchase ledger records

27.2 **What is the appropriate population to select from when using confirmations to provide evidence about the completeness assertion for accounts payable?**

A   Amounts recorded in the payables ledger
B   Invoices filed in the entity's open invoice file
C   Payees of cheques drawn in the month after the reporting date
D   Suppliers with whom the entity has previously done business

27.3 **Which of the following are appropriate audit procedures to test for COMPLETENESS of trade payables at the year end?**

(1) Review outstanding invoices in the purchase ledger greater than three months old and enquire of management whether they are valid outstanding liabilities

(2) Perform supplier statement reconciliations for a sample of suppliers

(3) Review bank statements for payments made after the year end to identify those payments relating to pre year-end liabilities

(4) Select a sample of invoices in the purchase ledger at the year end and agree payments made to bank statements post year end

A 1, 2 and 3
B 3 and 4
C 1 and 4
D 2 and 3 only

(6 marks)

MCQs 28 SMALL BUSINESS AND NOT-FOR-PROFIT ORGANISATIONS

28.1 It may be common for a professional firm to both prepare and audit the financial statements of small businesses and not-for-profit organisations.

Which of the following procedures would NOT be acceptable for the auditor of a small business to carry out as part of the accounting and auditing functions?

A Estimating the remaining useful lives of non-current assets

B Inspecting non-current assets

C Entering details of non-current assets into the books and records from purchase invoices

D Calculating the profit or loss on the disposal of non-current assets

28.2 Under International Standards on Auditing, revenue is identified as being an area of significant risk.

Which financial element of a typical not-for-profit organisation should also be considered a significant risk?

A Cash
B Receivables
C Administration expenses
D Liabilities

28.3 **Which statement on internal controls is the most relevant for small entities?**

A   There is a greater need for formal internal controls since segregation of duties will be weaker

B   The same need for formal internal controls is required since the directors' personal involvement is counteracted by weaker segregation of duties

C   There is less need to depend upon formal internal controls since the lower number of transactions will reduce the likelihood of unreliable records and other information

D   Dependence on formal internal controls can be lowered because of the directors' personal involvement in the operation of the entity

(6 marks)

MCQs 29 AUDIT FINALISATION

29.1 **Which of the following statements, relating to the auditor's responsibilities regarding subsequent events, if any, is/are correct?**

(1)   Auditors do not have a responsibility to perform procedures to identify subsequent events after the date of the auditor's report

(2)   Where a material adjusting subsequent event is identified after the financial statements are issued, but prior to approval by the shareholders, the auditor should include a qualified opinion in the auditor's report if management refuses to adjust the financial statements for the event

A   1 only
B   2 only
C   Both 1 and 2
D   Neither 1 nor 2

(2 marks)

MCQs 30 THE AUDITOR'S REPORT ON FINANCIAL STATEMENTS

30.1 Torte Co has not complied with certain aspects of an applicable financial reporting standard. The auditor concurs with the departure in that if Torte Co had applied all aspects of the standard, the company's financial statements would not have shown a true and fair view. It has not been disclosed as a departure from an applicable financial reporting standard in the accounting policy note.

What form should the auditor's report take?

A   Modified opinion for material misstatement over non-disclosure of the departure

B   Modified opinion for material misstatement over truth and fairness and non-compliance with disclosure requirements

C   Modified opinion for material misstatement over truth and fairness

D   Unmodified opinion with an Emphasis of Matter paragraph referring to the non-disclosure of the departure from the financial reporting standard

30.2 A company's financial statements include an investment of $45,000 in a company which is in liquidation. It is not yet clear what, if anything, will be recovered. Pending the final report of the liquidators, no allowance has been made in the financial statements. The situation is fully explained in a note to the financial statements. Profit before tax is $200,000.

What form should the audit opinion take?

A Adverse
B Except for – material misstatement
C Unmodified
D Disclaimer

(4 marks)

MCQs 31 GOING CONCERN

31.1 The auditor of Abrahams Co is uncertain whether the going concern assumption is an appropriate basis for the preparation of the company's financial statements. The company has incurred heavy losses for a number of years and current liabilities have this year risen above current assets for the first time. In addition, negotiations with the company's bankers for extended overdraft facilities are underway at the date on which the auditor's report must be signed. These matters are disclosed in the financial statements.

What action should the auditor take?

A Give an unmodified opinion but with reference in a Material Uncertainty Related to Going Concern section to the material uncertainty

B Issue a disclaimer of opinion on the grounds that the accounts may be fundamentally wrong

C Give an unmodified report on the grounds that the negotiations with the bankers are incomplete and that a modified report may prejudice their outcome

D Refuse to give a report unless the accounts are prepared on the basis that the company may no longer be a going concern

31.2 Which of the following statements, relating to the auditor's reporting responsibilities for going concern, if any, is/are correct?

(1) Where management is unwilling to make their assessment of the company's ability to continue as a going concern, the auditor should include an emphasis of matter paragraph in the auditor's report

(2) Where the use of the going concern basis is inappropriate, the auditor should include a qualified opinion in the auditor's report

A 1 only
B 2 only
C Both 1 and 2
D Neither 1 nor 2

(4 marks)

MCQs 32 INTERNAL AUDIT

32.1 Which of the following statements, if any, is/are correct?

(1)   Internal auditors should report to the finance director as they understand internal controls and are best placed to implement any recommendations in a timely manner

(2)   Companies are not required to establish and maintain an internal audit function

A   1 only
B   2 only
C   Both 1 and 2
D   Neither 1 nor 2

(2 marks)

MCQs 33 USING THE WORK OF INTERNAL AUDIT

33.1 During the course of his work, the external auditor performs many procedures. Three such procedures are:

(1)   Procedures performed in obtaining an understanding of internal control
(2)   Procedures performed in assessing the risk of material misstatement
(3)   Substantive procedures performed in gathering direct evidence

What procedures could be affected by the work of the internal auditor?

A   1 and 2 only
B   1 and 3 only
C   2 and 3 only
D   1, 2 and 3

33.2 For which of the following judgments may an independent auditor share responsibility with an entity's internal auditor who is assessed to be both competent and objective?

	Materiality of misstatements	*Evaluation of accounting estimates*
A	Yes	No
B	No	Yes
C	No	No
D	Yes	Yes

33.3 Which of the following statements relating to internal and external auditors is correct?

A   Internal auditors are required to be members of a professional body

B   Internal auditors' scope of work should be determined by those charged with governance

C   External auditors report to those charged with governance

D   Internal auditors can never be independent of the company

(6 marks)

Answer 1 NON-AUDIT ENGAGEMENTS AND TRUE AND FAIR

(a) **Elements of a non-audit engagement**

An assurance engagement will involve three separate parties;

- The intended user who is the person who requires the assurance report.

- The responsible party, which is the organisation responsible for preparing the subject matter to be reviewed.

- The practitioner (i.e. an accountant) who is the professional who will review the subject matter and provide the assurance.

A second element is a suitable subject matter. The subject matter is the data that the responsible party has prepared and which requires verification.

Suitable criteria are required in an assurance engagement. The subject matter is compared to the criteria in order for it to be assessed and an opinion provided.

Appropriate evidence has to be obtained by the practitioner in order to give the required level of assurance.

An assurance report is the opinion that is given by the practitioner to the intended user and the responsible party.

(b) **True and fair presentation**

Financial statements are produced by management which give a true and fair view of the entity's results. The auditor in reviewing these financial statements gives an opinion on the truth and fairness of them.

Although there is no definition in the International Standards on Auditing of true and fair it is generally considered to have the following meaning:

True – Information is factual and conforms with reality in that there are no factual errors. In addition it is assumed that to be true it must comply with accounting standards and any relevant legislation. Lastly true includes data being correctly transferred from accounting records to the financial statements.

Fair – Information is clear, impartial and unbiased, and also reflects plainly the commercial substance of the transactions of the entity.

Answer 2 SERENA

Item	Answer	Justification
1	D	(1) and (4) are benefits of forming an audit committee. (2) is not a benefit it is the remuneration committee, not the audit committee, that determines the remuneration of the executive directors. (3) is not a benefit because the audit committee reviews, but does not assume responsibility for, the company's financial statements and budget. The financial statements and budget are the responsibility of management.

2   A   The two non-executive directors (NEDs) could be included on the audit committee as the audit committee should be comprised of at least three independent NEDs. The CEO and executive directors, including the finance director should not be included on the audit committee because they are not independent. The audit committee does need at least one member with recent, relevant financial experience. But the finance director does not qualify for this position because he is a non-independent executive director.

3   A   The inclusion of share options in the directors' remuneration is an element of good corporate governance because it keeps the directors focused on the long-term. (1) does not reflect the principles of corporate governance because at least half of the board should be NEDs. (2) does not reflect the principles of corporate governance because there should be a clear division of responsibility between the CEO and the chairman of the board. (4) does not reflect the principles of corporate governance because board members should submit themselves regularly to re-election by the shareholders.

4   D   Internal audit should not have operational responsibilities so should not authorise transactions (2) or routinely prepare bank reconciliations (5).

5   A   Subject to specific regulatory requirements (e.g. specific banning of the external auditor providing other services) the internal audit function may be carried out by the external auditor when the threat to the external auditor's objectivity has been reduced to an acceptable level. The potential threats are self-interest and self-review. These can be reduced to an acceptable level where the work carried out by the external auditor does not involve any accounting and financial statement systems and members of the internal audit function are not involved in the external audit.

Answer 3 BLUEBIRD ENTERPRISES

Item   Answer   Justification

1   D   D is an advantage of an audit committee. A is not correct because the audit committee is comprised on non-executive directors (NEDs). B is not correct because the audit committee offers the external auditors a direct link to non-executive directors. C is incorrect because it enables the board (not management) to delegate a review of audit matters.

2   A   Goldfinch's work in the banking industry is a disadvantage because he may not have the relevant experience for companies such as Bluebird and may not be able to give meaningful advice to the executive directors. His experiences as a NED and audit committee member are advantageous because he is familiar with the roles that he will fill on Bluebird's board. His willingness to work for a fixed fee that is not profit related is an advantage because remuneration should be unrelated to company performance.

3   C   Mallard's work as a finance director for another company is an advantage because he possesses recent and relevant financial experience which is required for at least one member of the audit committee. Being the brother of the chief executive is not an advantage because it may make him less objective in his judgment. Contracting as a NED for seven years is not an advantage because NEDs should be subject to re-election at regular intervals not to exceed three years. Being paid only when the share price increases is not an advantage because remuneration should not be related to company performance.

| 4 | C | The expectations gap (4) relates to the expectations of shareholders and the general public about the role of the auditor. Although called corporate governance (5), the principles are applied to many entities that are not corporations (e.g. government, not-for-profit, NGOs). The remaining statements are taken from key definitions and explanations of corporate governance (e.g. OECD). |
| 5 | B | (1) is not a disadvantage but a requirement. (4) is a limitation of internal controls not a disadvantage of having financial responsibility handled by the audit committee. |

Answer 4 STARK

Item	Answer	Justification
1	C	(1) Partner has been in role for nine years, contravenes ACCA's *Code of Ethics and Conduct* and represents a *familiarity* threat. (2) Is not a threat to independence. "As a regular client" Mr Far will have paid for the advice (i.e. a normal commercial transaction). Also, his position is not one of seniority (so is unlikely to influence the audit) and his work will be reviewed (as a normal quality control procedure). (3) Acceptance of gifts from a client, unless of an insignificant amount, is not allowed. The balloon flight poses *familiarity* and *self-interest* risks. **Tutorial note:** *The fact that the flight costs less than the yacht expense is irrelevant.* (4) This represents fees on a contingent basis and raises a *self-interest* threat as Ali & Co's fee will rise if tax savings are found. There would also be a *self-review* threat since tax advice should have a bearing on calculations of current and deferred tax. **Tutorial note:** *Pressure to gain the highest tax refund for the client could tempt the audit firm to suggest illegal tax avoidance schemes.*
2	C	Mr Son should be removed from the audit team as he has been a key audit partner for longer than the permitted seven-year period. **Tutorial note:** *To show complete independence, Zoe should not be part of the audit team. However, if Mr Son is no longer the engagement partner then this removes the ethical threat and Zoe could be included in the audit team.*
3	D	(3) and (4) are valid considerations. If the advice is clearly supported by tax law it does not generally create a threat to independence. The significance of any threat should be evalated in relation to any material effect on the financial statements. The levels of tax expertise of the client's employees and members of the tax advisory team are relevant, but not the external audit team. The period of time over which tax advisory services may be provided is not relevant.
4	B	The contingent fee basis for the taxation services must be rejected.

5   B   Where taxation services involve acting as an advocate for an audit client before a court in the resolution of a tax matter that is material to the financial statements the advocacy threat created would be so significant that no safeguards could eliminate or reduce the threat to an acceptable level. Therefore, Ali & Co cannot perform this type of service for Stark.

Tutorial note: *As the dispute concerns sales tax it will almost certainly be material (e.g. since ½ – 1% revenue is generally considered material).*

Answer 5 LV FONES

Item   Answer   Justification

1   B   (1) The audit team receiving the staff discount on the luxury phone represents a *self-interest* threat and a *familiarity* threat.

(2) The audit senior's secondment as the financial controller of LV Fones represents a *self-interest* threat if he prepared records or schedules that support the year-end financial statements and then audits those documents. There is also a *familiarity* threat as the management and directors of LV Fones may still treat him as part of their management team.

(3) The total fee income from LV Fones is 16% of the total fees for the audit firm. If the fees for audit and recurring work exceed 15% there is a *self-interest* threat.

(4) Personal relationships between the client and members of the audit team can create a *familiarity* or *self-interest* threat.

2   C   In relation to the self-review threat, the firm should clarify exactly what areas the senior assisted the client on. If he worked on areas not related to the financial statements then he may be able to remain in the audit team. However, it is likely that he has worked on some related schedules and therefore he should be removed from the audit team to ensure that independence is not threatened. In relation to the familiarity threat, there is no safeguard that could reduce this threat to an acceptable level. The senior should not be a member of the audit team.

3   D   Jones & Co should chase the outstanding fees. If they remain outstanding, the firm should discuss with those charged with governance the reasons for the continued non-payment, and ideally agree a payment schedule which will result in the fees being settled before much more work is performed for the current year audit.

4   C   Self-review threat – the audit firm will audit the system it has implemented.

5   D   Decline Titania Co as it is not acceptable to prepare and audit the financial statements of a listed company (because of self-review threat and the specific public interest of a listed company).

Accept Puck Co with safeguards (e.g. not letting the FD's brother have any direct (e.g. team member) or indirect (e.g. unofficial advisor) part in the audit). The brother is a close family member (parent, child or sibling) as opposed to an immediate family member (spouse, partner or dependent).

Tutorial note: *The closer the key players are to influencing the audit or the financial decisions of the entity, the higher the probability that no safeguard would be adequate.)*

Answer 6 GOOFY

Tutorial note: *This 20-mark question relates to syllabus area A and is therefore non-exam style. Section B will predominantly examine one or more aspects of syllabus areas B, C or D.*

(a)   Conflict of interest

Safeguards to be adopted to address the conflict of interest of auditing both Goofy and Mickey:

- Both Goofy and Mickey should be notified that NAB & Co would be acting as auditors for each company and, if necessary, consent obtained.

- Advising one or both clients to seek additional independent advice.

- The use of separate engagement teams, with different engagement partners and team members; once an employee has worked on one audit such as Goofy then they would be prevented from being on the audit of Mickey for a period of time. This separation of teams is known as building a "Chinese wall".

- Procedures to prevent access to information, for example, strict physical separation of both teams, confidential and secure data filing.

- Clear guidelines for members of each engagement team on issues of security and confidentiality. These guidelines could be included within the audit engagement letters.

- Potentially the use of confidentiality agreements signed by employees and partners of the firm.

- Regular monitoring of the application of the above safeguards by a senior individual in NAB & Co not involved in either audit.

(b)   Advantages of outsourcing Goofy's internal audit department

Staffing

Goofy needs to expand its internal audit department from five employees as it is too small; however, if they outsource there will be no need to recruit as NAB & Co will provide the staff members and this will be an instant solution.

Skills and experience

NAB & Co is a large firm and so will have a large pool of staff available to provide the internal audit service. In addition, Goofy has requested that ad hoc reviews are performed and, depending on the nature of these, it may find that the firm has specialist skills that Goofy may not be able to afford if the internal audit department continues to be run internally.

Costs

Any associated costs such as training will be eliminated as NAB & Co will train its own employees. In addition, the costs for the internal audit service will be agreed in advance. This will ensure that Goofy can budget accordingly.

As NAB & Co will be performing both the external and internal audit there is a possibility that the fees may be reduced.

Flexibility

With the department being outsourced Goofy will have total flexibility in its internal audit service. Staff can be requested from NAB & Co to suit Goofy's workloads and requirements. This will ensure that, when required, extra staff can be used to visit a large number of shops and in quieter times there may be no internal audit presence.

Additional fees

NAB & Co will benefit from the internal audit service being outsourced as this will generate additional fee income. However, the firm will need to monitor the fees to ensure that they do not represent too high a percentage of their total fee income.

Disadvantages of outsourcing Goofy's internal audit department.

Knowledge of systems

NAB & Co will allocate available staff members to work on the internal audit assignment, this may mean that each month the staff members are different and hence they may not understand the systems of Goofy. This will decrease the quality of the services provided and increase the time spent by Goofy employees explaining the system to the auditors.

Independence

If NAB & Co continues as external auditor as well as providing the internal audit service, there may be a self-review threat, where the internal audit work is relied upon by the external auditors. NAB & Co would need to take steps to ensure that separate teams were put in place as well as additional safeguards.

Existing internal audit department

Goofy has an existing internal audit department of five employees. If they cannot be redeployed elsewhere in the company then they may need to be made redundant and this could be costly for the company. Staff may oppose the outsourcing if it results in redundancies.

Cost

As well as the cost of potential redundancies, the internal audit fee charged by NAB & Co may, over a period of time, prove to be very expensive.

Loss of in-house skills

If the current internal audit team is not deployed elsewhere in the company valuable internal audit knowledge and experience may be lost; if Goofy then decided at a future date to bring the service back in-house this might prove to be too difficult.

Timing

NAB & Co may find that Goofy requires internal audit staff at the busy periods for the audit firm, and hence it might prove difficult to actually provide the required level of resource.

Confidentiality

Knowledge of company systems and confidential data will be available to NAB & Co. Although the engagement letter would provide confidentiality clauses, this may not stop breaches of confidentiality.

Control

Goofy will currently have more control over the activities of its internal audit department; however, once outsourced it will need to discuss areas of work and timings well in advance with NAB & Co.

(c)   **Ethical threats and how they may be reduced**

Ethical threat	*How reduced*
A familiarity threat arises where an engagement partner is associated with a client for a long period of time. NAB & Co's partner has been involved in the audit of Goofy for six years and hence may not maintain her professional scepticism and objectivity.	NAB & Co should monitor the relationship between engagement and client staff, and should consider rotating engagement partners when a long association has occurred. In addition, *ACCA's Code of Ethics and Conduct* recommends that engagement partners rotate off an audit after seven years for listed and public interest entities. Therefore consideration should be given to appointing an alternative audit partner in the near future.
The engagement partner's son has accepted a job as a sales manager at Goofy. This could represent a self-interest/familiarity threat if the son was involved in the financial statement process.	It is unlikely that as a sales manager the son would be in a position to influence the financial statements and hence additional safeguards would not be necessary.
A self-interest threat can arise when an audit firm has a financial interest in the company. In this case the partner's son will receive shares as part of his remuneration. As the son is an immediate family member of the partner then if he holds the shares it will be as if the partner holds these shares, and this is prohibited.	In this case as holding shares is prohibited by *ACCA's Code of Ethics and Conduct* then either the son should refuse the shares or more likely the engagement partner will need to be removed from the audit.
Fees based on the outcome or results of work performed are known as contingent fees and are prohibited by *ACCA's Code of Ethics and Conduct*. Hence Goofy's request that 20% of the external audit fee is based on profit after tax would represent a contingent fee.	NAB & Co will not be able to accept contingent fees and should communicate to Goofy that the external audit fee needs to be based on the time and level of work performed.

Answer 7 ORANGE FINANCIALS

Tutorial note: *This 20-mark question relates to syllabus area A and is therefore non-exam style. Section B will predominantly examine one or more aspects of syllabus areas B, C or D.*

(a) **Responsibilities of auditor in relation to fraud and error**

An auditor conducting an audit in accordance with ISA 240 The Auditor's Responsibilities Relating to Fraud in an Audit of Financial Statements is responsible for obtaining reasonable assurance that the financial statements taken as a whole are free from material misstatement, whether caused by fraud or error.

In order to fulfil this responsibility auditors are required to identify and assess the risks of material misstatement of the financial statements due to fraud.

The auditor will need to obtain sufficient appropriate audit evidence regarding the assessed risks of material misstatement due to fraud, through designing and implementing appropriate responses.

In addition, the auditor must respond appropriately to fraud or suspected fraud identified during the audit.

When obtaining reasonable assurance, the auditor is responsible for maintaining professional scepticism throughout the audit, considering the potential for management override of controls and recognising the fact that audit procedures that are effective in detecting error may not be effective in detecting fraud.

To ensure that the whole engagement team is aware of the risks and responsibilities for fraud and error, ISAs require that a discussion is held within the team. For members not present at the meeting the engagement partner should determine which matters are to be communicated to them.

(b) **Ethical threats**

(i) *Explanation*	*(ii)* *How reduced*
■ Orange has asked the engagement partner of Currant & Co to attend meetings with potential investors. This represents an advocacy threat as the audit firm may be perceived as promoting investment in Orange and this threatens objectivity.	■ The engagement partner should politely decline this request from Orange, as it represents too great a threat to independence.
■ Due to the stock exchange listing, Orange has requested that Currant & Co produce the financial statements. This represents a self-review threat. As Orange is currently not a listed company then Currant & Co are permitted to produce the financial statements and also audit them.	■ Ideally, Currant & Co should not undertake the preparation of the financial statements. Due to the imminent listing, this would probably represent too high a risk.
■ However, Orange is seeking a listing and therefore these financial statements will be critical to the potential investors and this increases audit risk.	■ If Currant & Co chooses to produce the financial statements then separate teams should undertake each assignment and the audit team should not be part of the accounts preparation process.

(i)	*Explanation*	*(ii)*	*How reduced*

■ The assistant finance director of Orange has joined Currant & Co as a partner and has been proposed as the review partner.

■ This represents a self-review threat, as he was in a position to influence the financial statements whilst working at Orange; if he is the review partner there could be a risk of him reviewing his own work.

■ This partner must not be involved in the audit of Orange for a period of at least two years. An alternative review partner should be appointed.

■ Orange has several potential assurance assignments available and Currant & Co wish to be appointed to these. There is a potential self-interest threat as these assurance fees along with the external audit fee could represent a significant proportion of Currant & Co's fee income.

■ The firm should assess whether these assignments along with the audit fee would represent more than 15% of gross practice income for two consecutive years. These assurance assignments will only arise if the company obtains its listing and hence will be a public interest company.

■ If the recurring fees are likely to exceed 15% of annual practice income then additional consideration should be given as to whether these assignments should be sought by the firm.

■ Orange has implied to Currant & Co that the audit must be completed quickly and with minimal queries/ issues if Currant & Co wishes to obtain the assurance assignments.

■ This creates an intimidation threat on the team as they may feel pressure to cut corners and not raise issues, and this could compromise the objectivity of the audit team.

■ The engagement partner should politely inform the finance director that the team will undertake the audit in accordance with all relevant ISAs and their own quality control procedures. Therefore the audit will take as long as is necessary to obtain sufficient, appropriate evidence to form an opinion. If any residual concerns remain or the intimidation threat continues then Currant & Co may need to consider resigning from the engagement.

■ The finance director has offered the team a free weekend away at a luxury hotel. This represents a self-interest threat as the acceptance of goods and services, unless insignificant in value, is not permitted.

■ As it is unlikely that a weekend at a luxury hotel for the whole team has an insignificant value, then this offer should be politely declined.

■ The finance director has offered a senior team member a loan at discounted interest rates.

■ Orange does provide loans and hence the provision of a loan is within the normal course of business. However, if the loan is on preferential rates, as this is, then it would represent a self-interest threat.

■ This loan must not be accepted by the audit senior due to the preferential terms.

■ However, if the terms of the loan are amended so that the interest rate charged is in line with Orange's normal levels, then the provision of the loan is acceptable.

(c)   **Benefits of audit committee for Orange Financials**

- It will help to improve the quality of the financial reporting of Orange; whilst the company already has a finance director, the audit committee will assist by reviewing the financial statements.

- The establishment of an audit committee can help to improve the internal control environment of the company. The audit committee is able to devote more time and attention to areas such as internal controls.

- Orange does not currently have any non-executive directors, hence once appointed, they will bring considerable outside experience to the executive directors as well as challenging their decisions and contributing to an independent judgement.

- The finance director will benefit in that he will be able to raise concerns and discuss accounting issues with the audit committee.

- The audit committee will be responsible for appointing the external auditors and this will strengthen the auditors' independence and contribute to a channel of communication and forum of issues.

- If Orange has an internal audit (IA) department, then establishing an audit committee will also improve the independence of IA.

- The audit committee can also provide advice on risk management to the executive directors. They can create a climate of discipline and control and reduce the opportunity for fraud, and increase the public confidence in the credibility and objectivity of the financial statements.

Answer 8   WILLOW WANDS

Item	Answer	Justification
1	D	The proposal for the former engagement partner to undertake the role of independent review partner represents a familiarity threat as the partner will have been associated with Willow for a long period of time and so may not retain professional scepticism and objectivity. The other three potential risks represent self-interest threats.
2	B	It is not necessary for Beech & Co to resign from the engagement because a close family member of an audit team member (and a very junior one at that) owns a financial interest in a client, although this would be an appropriate response if a family member of the *partner* owned the financial interest. The other three options listed are appropriate safeguards for this treat to independence.
3	C	Beech would not be required to resign from the engagement due to the audit manager leaving Beech to join Willow because the risks can be mitigated through quality control procedures. As the audit manager will leave before the current period audit begins there will be no work by him to be reviewed.
4	C	The UK Corporate Governance Code states that no director should be involved in setting their own remuneration. Hence the non-executive chairman cannot set his own remuneration.
5	D	Under the confidentiality provisions of the ACCA's *Code of Ethics and Conduct*, disclosure should be made where there is a legal right or duty to do so. There may also be a professional duty or right to do so (e.g. to respond to an ACCA inquiry). This overrides option A.

Answer 9 ZIRCON, RIVET AND PLUSHY

(a)   **Engagement quality control review**

The purpose of the review is to provide an objective evaluation, on or before the date of the auditor's report, of the significant judgments the engagement team made and the conclusions it reached in formulating the auditor's report.

The process is only for audits of financial statements of listed entities and other audit engagements, if any, for which the firm has determined that such a review is required.

The reviewer, who is not part of the engagement team, must have sufficient and appropriate experience and authority to objectively evaluate the engagement team's judgments and conclusions in formulating the auditor's report.

The reviewer's evaluation should include:

- ■   Discussion of significant matters with the engagement partner;
- ■   Review of the financial statements and the proposed auditor's report;
- ■   Review of selected working papers relating to significant judgments and conclusions;
- ■   Evaluation of the conclusions reached and consideration whether the proposed auditor's report is appropriate.

For listed entities the reviewer should evaluate:

- ■   the firm's independence;
- ■   whether there has been appropriate consultation on contentious matters; and
- ■   whether audit documentation selected for review reflects the work performed in relation to the significant judgments and supports the conclusions reached.

(b)   **Zircon Co**

(i)   Significant risks

The auditor's independence may be challenged because investment advice to a client is beyond the scope of the audit, particularly when the recommendations include specific investments in other clients.

The manager could be accused of insider dealing since he recommended investments in client companies. As he may have access to price-sensitive information he could be criminally liable under insider dealing legislation. Any legal action against the manager may also bring the firm into disrepute.

(ii)   Steps to be taken

The matter must be discussed with the audit partner and manager to discover why the manager thought it appropriate to make the recommendations and whether the audit manager has made similar recommendations to other clients.

Enquiries should be made to find out whether Zircon has acted on the recommendation. If not, a corrective letter should be sent out stating that the recommendations should be disregarded.

(iii) *Quality control procedures*

A briefing note should be circularised to all professional staff clarifying the firms procedures with respect to correspondence with clients and in particular the approval required.

The quality control procedures manual should be reviewed regarding the firm's ethical requirements (on independence in particular) and the risks and safeguards relating to insider dealing and updated if necessary.

Rivet

(i) *Significant risks*

Inventory is invariably material to the financial statements of a manufacturing company. Therefore, the absence of inventory files means that there is insufficient (no) evidence on which to conclude that the financial statements are free from material misstatement.

The auditor has a duty of confidentiality to the client and is solely responsible for the safe custody of audit documentation. Leaving working papers unattended is negligent and if Rivet were to suffer any loss as a result of the theft the auditor could be liable for damages.

Whether the objective of the theft was for the car, the laptop or the files on the laptop. The latter might have been the target if, for example, the audit documentation contained evidence of fraud or other irregularity.

(ii) *Steps to be taken*

Assuming inventory to be material the audit documentation will need to be recreated with the help of the audit senior. However, it is unlikely that audit evidence documented at the physical inventory count can be sufficiently reproduced. Especially if problems were encountered during attendance at the year-end count, it may be necessary to arrange another one. The result of this would require verification of movements since the year end.

Rivet should be informed about the missing files so the client is aware of the risk that confidential information might fall into the hands of competitors (e.g. on pricing).

(iii) *Quality control procedures*

The firm's policies and procedures for maintaining the confidentiality, safe custody, integrity, accessibility and retrievability of engagement documentation must be reviewed. In particular, back-up routines for electronic engagement documentation at appropriate stages during the audit.

All personnel should be reminded of the firm's policy that engagement documentation should never be left unattended outside of the firm's premises. If appropriate, the audit senior may be reprimanded for his lack of due care.

Plushy

(i) *Significant risks*

Bringing forward the publication deadline for the financial statement increases the risk that insufficient attention will be given to significant judgements and inappropriate conclusions may be drawn. The additional time pressure increases the need for the quality control review.

Plushy has made the auditor aware that a potential investor will be placing reliance on the financial statements. The auditor will therefore owe a duty of care to that investor.

(ii)   *Steps to be taken*

The audit partner should discuss the final dates with the client and agree a mutually convenient timetable. This amended timetable must ensure that the firm's quality control procedures are in no way sacrificed, particularly as a third party is known to be placing reliance on these financial statements.

Dates for the quality control review must be agreed with the engagement partner and due to the urgency given a high priority.

(iii)   *Quality control procedures*

As Plushy is the office's major audit client the engagement quality control review will be required. Another partner other than the engagement partner or a suitably qualified external person may team up with the firm's quality control reviewer for review of this engagement.

Although the auditor's report cannot be dated until this review has been completed, documentation of the review may be completed after the date of the report. The review can be conducted in stages while the audit fieldwork is still in progress to allow significant matters to be resolved.

Answer 10 BONDI

(a)   **Arguments against acceptance of nomination**

- Rapid growth is often accompanied by inadequate accounting systems and weak internal controls. However, rapid growth is not sufficient reason to decline an audit although it increases inherent risk.

- Rapid growth through aggressive takeovers implies a management philosophy that is willing to accept risks and this is likely to apply to controls as well. Again this increases inherent risk.

- Failure to take action against employee fraud brought to the directors' notice by the auditors is more serious. This fosters a visible culture of unethical behaviour that is likely to permeate the company and to be shared by other employees. This will result in a weak control environment.

- Introduction of a new computer system must be undertaken very carefully. In addition, an unnecessarily complicated system is one of the warning signs of fraud. Such a computer system may be difficult to audit.

- Aggression against audit staff is a well-known device for concealment of top management fraud. There are many documented examples of audit failure through fear of the audit staff to query management explanations.

- The impending public listing means that the company is under pressure to show an improving performance but also means that the work of the auditor will come under increasing scrutiny. There are always significant risks in accepting an audit under such terms.

Arguments for accepting nomination

As a larger firm your firm is likely to have the capability of influencing the directors of Bondi and persuading them of the benefits of a more ethical style of business. This will benefit the company's shareholders. If your firm rejects the audit they are likely to appoint a less competent firm. This will not be in the shareholders' interest and may discredit the profession.

(b) **Matters relevant to obtaining knowledge for development of the audit plan**

Employee frauds

■ More information is needed about the alleged employee frauds. In particular the specific control weaknesses that were exploited and whether any changes have since been made to the accounting and internal control systems.

■ The current positions held by the guilty employees and whether they have access to assets and accounting records. Also, whether they are adequately supervised especially if a lack of segregation of duties is apparent.

Computer system

■ Particular attention should be given to the control environment relating to computer systems and to the evaluation of general (IT) and application controls.

■ The audit team should include sufficient computer audit specialists.

■ Due to the complicated nature of the system, tests of controls could include the use of test data or other computer assisted audit techniques.

Contracts with manufacturers

■ Examine the terms of contracts and the strategies adopted by the company for securing maximum benefit from them.

■ An industry specialist may provide evidence regarding the problems encountered by manufacturers and dealers in confirming compliance with these contracts.

■ As the incentive schemes may have accounting implications (e.g. discounts and 0% finance) the commercial substance as well as the legal form of the transactions with the manufactures must be understood and the impact on the financial statements assessed.

(c) **Misstatement**

■ As this appears to be a fraud against the government through falsification of accounting records, the evidence that the falsification of the records is deliberate and not an accidental consequence of a poorly designed computer system, must be documented.

■ The matter must be discussed with management. Management must be asked to:

❑ correct the fictitious records;

❑ make full provision for all taxes including any penalties for which they are potentially liable; and

❑ make a full disclosure to the taxation authorities.

■ If management refuse, the audit opinion should be modified if the amount of taxes not provided for is material (qualified "except for" opinion).

■ The auditor's duty of confidentiality prevents the auditor from raising the matter with the taxation authorities. Therefore, it may be most appropriate to resign from the audit if management refuses to put a stop to the malpractice. Any written "statement of circumstances" required on ceasing to hold office could allude to the matter but would need to be carefully worded, probably with legal advice, to avoid accusing the directors of fraud and exposing the firm to a charge of defamation (i.e. causing damage to reputation).

Answer 11 AGNESAL

(a)   **Quality control procedures**

Tutorial note: *The aspects of quality control are direction, supervision and performance and review.*

■ Work delegated to assistants should be directed, supervised and reviewed to ensure the audit is conducted in compliance with ISAs.

■ Assistants should be professionally competent to perform the work delegated to them with due care.

■ Direction of the engagement team includes informing team members of:

– their responsibilities (including compliance with ethical requirements);
– the nature of the entity's business; and
– the detailed approach to the performance of the engagement.

■ Supervisory responsibilities include tracking the progress of the audit to ensure that assistants are competent, understand their tasks and are carrying them out as directed.

■ The work of assistants must be reviewed to assess whether:

– it is in accordance with the audit program;
– it is adequately documented;
– significant matters have been resolved;
– objectives have been achieved;
– conclusions are appropriate (i.e. consistent with results).

(b)   **Weaknesses in quality control procedures**

Tutorial note: *"Planning an answer" means, as a minimum, deciding how marks are likely to be allocated and structuring the answer accordingly. In general, the more a question is broken down into parts, the less time needs to be spent on "formal" writing out of an answer plan. In this Q there are 16 marks for addressing 4 matters (i.e.4 marks of answer for each).*

(1)   Analytical procedures

Carla did not perform analytical procedures. She stated that they were not required for the new client. Applying analytical procedures at the planning stage to assist in understanding the business and in identifying areas of potential risk, is required (ISA 520). An audit senior should understand that analytical procedures are required. The fact that Carla did not think that the procedures were necessary is an indicator that she may not be professionally competent to do the work delegated to her. It is also suggests that Carla was not given proper direction or supervision.

The audit supervisor did not sign off that he had reviewed the audit planning checklist, in breach of the quality control requirement that work of assistants must be reviewed. As a result, the audit has been inadequately planned and the audit may not be carried out effectively and efficiently.

(2)   Supervisor's assignments

The audit supervisor has not been present to supervise the audit because he has been working on three other jobs. It appears that the firm does not have sufficient audit staff with relevant competencies to meet its supervisory needs. In addition, audit work has been delegated inappropriately. The senior has performed work on tangible non-current assets which is a less material (18% of total assets) audit area than trade receivables (57% of total assets) which has been assigned to an audit trainee. Tangible non-current assets also appear to be a lower risk audit areas than trade receivables because the carrying amount of tangible non-current assets is comparable with the prior year ($1.1m at both year ends), whereas trade receivables have more than doubled (from $1.6m to $3.5m).

(3)   Direct confirmation

It is usual for direct confirmation of accounts receivable to be obtained where accounts receivable are material and it is reasonable to expect customers to respond. However, as it is already sometime after the end of the reporting period (the final audit commenced two weeks ago) and, although trade receivables are clearly material (57% of total assets), an alternative approach may be more efficient (and cost effective). For example, monitoring of after-date cash will provide evidence about the collectability of accounts receivable (as well as corroborate their existence).

This may be a further consequence of the audit having been inadequately planned.

Alternatively, monitoring of the audit may be inadequate. For example, if the audit trainee did not understand the alternative approach but mechanically followed external confirmation procedures.

(4)   Inventory

Inventory is relatively immaterial from an auditing perspective, being less than 2.5% of total assets (2015 2.1%). Although it therefore seems appropriate that a trainee should be auditing it, the audit approach appears highly inefficient. Such in-depth testing (of controls and details) on an immaterial area provides further evidence that the audit has been inadequately planned, directed and supervised.

This also demonstrates a lack of knowledge and understanding about Agnesal's business – the company has no stock-in-trade, only consumables used in the supply of services.

Answer 12 SALT & PEPPER

Tutorial note: *This 20-mark question relates to syllabus area A and is therefore non-exam style. Section B will predominantly examine one or more aspects of syllabus areas B, C or D.*

(a)   New audit engagement

(i)   Steps prior to accepting the audit of Cinnamon Brothers

ISA 210 *Agreeing the Terms of Audit Engagements* provides guidance to Salt & Pepper on the steps they should take in accepting the new audit client, Cinnamon. It sets out a number of processes that the auditor should perform prior to accepting a new engagement, in addition to considering whether preconditions for the audit are in place.

Salt & Pepper should consider any issues which might arise which could threaten compliance with ACCA's *Code of Ethics and Conduct* or any local legislation, including conflict of interest with existing clients. If issues arise, then their significance must be considered.

In addition, they should consider whether they are competent to perform the work and whether they would have appropriate resources available, as well as any specialist skills or knowledge required for the audit of Cinnamon.

Salt & Pepper should consider what they already know about the directors of Cinnamon; they need to consider the reputation and integrity of the directors. If necessary, the firm may want to obtain references if they do not formally know the directors.

Additionally, Salt & Pepper should consider the level of risk attached to the audit of Cinnamon and whether this is acceptable to the firm. As part of this, they should consider whether the expected audit fee is adequate in relation to the risk of auditing Cinnamon.

Salt & Pepper should communicate with the outgoing auditor of Cinnamon to assess if there are any ethical or professional reasons why they should not accept appointment. They should obtain permission from Cinnamon's management to contact the existing auditor; if this is not given, then the engagement should be refused.

If given permission to respond, the auditors should reply to Salt & Pepper, who should carefully review the response for any issues that could affect acceptance.

(ii)   Preconditions for the audit

ISA 210 *Agreeing the Terms of Audit Engagements* requires auditors to only accept a new audit engagement when it has been confirmed that the preconditions for an audit are present.

To assess whether the preconditions for an audit are present, Salt & Pepper must determine whether the financial reporting framework to be applied in the preparation of Cinnamon's financial statements is acceptable. In considering this, the auditor should assess the nature of the entity, the nature and purpose of the financial statements and whether law or regulations prescribes the applicable reporting framework.

In addition, they must obtain the agreement of Cinnamon's management that it acknowledges and understands its responsibility for the following:

■   Preparation of the financial statements in accordance with the applicable financial reporting framework, including where relevant their fair presentation;

■ For such internal control as management determines is necessary to enable the preparation of financial statements which are free from material misstatement, whether due to fraud or error; and

■ To provide Salt & Pepper with access to all relevant information for the preparation of the financial statements, any additional information that the auditor may request from management and unrestricted access to persons within Cinnamon from whom the auditor determines it necessary to obtain audit evidence.

If the preconditions for an audit are not present, Salt & Pepper shall discuss the matter with Cinnamon's management. Unless required by law or regulation to do so, the auditor shall not accept the proposed audit engagement:

■ If the auditor has determined that the financial reporting framework to be applied in the preparation of the financial statements is unacceptable; or

■ If management agreement of their responsibilities has not been obtained.

(b) **Engagement letters**

Matters to be included in an audit engagement letter:

■ The objective and scope of the audit;

■ The responsibilities of the auditor;

■ The responsibilities of management;

■ Identification of the financial reporting framework for the preparation of the financial statements;

■ Expected form and content of any reports to be issued;

■ Elaboration of the scope of the audit with reference to legislation;

■ The form of any other communication of results of the audit engagement;

■ The fact that some material misstatements may not be detected;

■ Arrangements regarding the planning and performance of the audit, including the composition of the audit team;

■ The expectation that management will provide written representations;

■ The basis on which fees are computed and any billing arrangements;

■ A request for management to acknowledge receipt of the audit engagement letter and to agree to the terms of the engagement;

■ Arrangements concerning the involvement of internal auditors and other staff of the entity;

■ Any obligations to provide audit working papers to other parties;

■ Any restriction on the auditor's liability; and

■ Arrangements to make available draft financial statements and any other information.

(c)   **(i)**   **Ethical risks**   **(ii)**   **Steps to reduce the risks**

Ethical risks	Steps to reduce the risks
Salt & Pepper has guaranteed that their audit will not last longer than two weeks and will minimise disruption to companies.	Salt & Pepper should cease this advertising campaign immediately as it is not in compliance with ACCA's *Code of Ethics and Conduct*.
Every audit engagement is different and hence will require a differing amount of time. Complex audits cannot possibly be completed within two weeks as the team would not be able to gather sufficient and appropriate audit evidence in this time, leading to an incorrect opinion.	For any potential clients who have approached Salt & Pepper as a result of this advert, the firm should inform them that the audit duration will be based on the level of audit risk present, and this could be considerably longer than two weeks.
Salt & Pepper has offered all new audit clients a free accounts preparation service for the first year of the engagement.	For engagements where Salt & Pepper is to prepare the accounts, they must ensure that this work is undertaken by a team separate to the audit team.
Whilst Salt & Pepper is able to prepare accounts for unlisted clients, this does increase the risk of self-review as the audit team could be auditing their own work.	
Additionally, if this service is offered for free, then in order to make a profit on the total engagement, Salt & Pepper could be inclined to substantially reduce the procedures undertaken on the audit engagement.	In addition, the firm should ensure that all audit engagements are conducted in accordance with International Standards on Auditing.
The firm is not updating engagement letters for existing clients on the basis that they do not change much on a yearly basis.	Salt & Pepper should comply fully with ISA 210 and annually review the need for revising the engagement letters.
This is not in accordance with ISA 210 *Agreeing the Terms of Audit Engagements* as even if engagement letters are not changed, they should still be reviewed to ensure that they are still relevant and up to date.	
An existing client of Salt & Pepper has proposed an audit fee based on a percentage of the client's final pre-tax profit.	Salt & Pepper should politely decline the proposed contingent fee arrangement as it would be a breach of ACCA's *Code of Ethics and Conduct*. Instead they should inform the client that the fees will be based on the level of work required to obtain sufficient and appropriate audit evidence.
This is a contingent fee arrangement and is prohibited as it creates a self-interest threat which cannot be reduced to an adequate level.	

Ethical risks	Steps to reduce the risks
Salt & Pepper intends to use junior staff for the audit of their new client Cinnamon as the timing of the audit is when the firm is very busy. As a new engagement, Salt & Pepper has little knowledge of the risks associated with this audit. If they use too junior staff, they will not be competent enough to assess whether they have performed adequate work, and the risk of giving an incorrect audit opinion is increased.	Salt & Pepper should review the staffing of Cinnamon and make changes to increase the amount of experienced team members. If this is not possible, they should discuss with the directors of Cinnamon to see whether the timing of the audit could be moved to a point where the firm has adequate staff resources.
Salt & Pepper has not contacted Cinnamon's previous auditors. Contacting the previous auditors is important as the firm needs to understand why Cinnamon has changed their auditors. They may have been acting unethically and their previous auditors therefore refused to continue. In addition, it is professional courtesy to contact the previous auditors.	Salt & Pepper should contact the previous auditors to identify if there are any ethical issues which would prevent them from acting as auditors of Cinnamon.

Answer 13 SPECS4YOU

(a) **The purposes of audit working papers**

- To assist with the planning and performance of the audit.
- To assist in the supervision and review of audit work.
- To record the audit evidence resulting from the audit work performed to support the auditor's opinion.

(b)

Documentation required	Information obtained
Memorandum and articles of association.	Details of the objectives of Specs4You, its permitted capital structure and the internal constitution of the company.
Most recent published financial statements.	Provide detail on the size of the company, profitability, etc as well as any unusual factors such as loans due for repayment.
Most recent management accounts/budgets/ cash flow information.	Determine the current status of the company including on-going profitability, ability to meet budget, etc as well as identifying any potential going concern problems.
Organisation chart of Spec4You.	To identify the key managers and employees in the company and other people to contact during the audit.

Industry data on spectacle sales.	To find out how Specs4You is performing compared to the industry standards. This will help to highlight any areas of concern for example, higher than expected cost of sales, for investigation on the audit.
Financial statements of similar entities.	To compare the accounting policies of Specs4You and obtain additional information on industry standards.
Prior year audit file.	To establish what problems were encountered in last year's audit, how those problems were resolved and identify any areas of concern for this year's audit.
Internet news sites.	To find out whether the company has any significant news stories, (good or bad) which may affect the audit approach.

(c)   **Working paper standards**

The audit working paper does not meet the standards normally expected in a working paper because:

- The page reference is unclear making it very difficult to either file the working paper in the audit file or locate the working paper should there be queries on it.

- It is not clear what the client year end date is – the year is missing. The working paper could easily be filed in the wrong year's audit file.

- There is no signature of the person who prepared the working paper. This means it is unclear who to address queries to regarding the preparation or contents of the working paper.

- There is evidence of a reviewer's signature. However, given that the reviewer did not query the lack of preparer's signature or other omissions noted below, the effectiveness of the review must be put in question.

- The test "objective" is vague – it is not clear what "correct" means for example, it would be better to state the objective in terms of assertions such as completeness or accuracy.

- The test objective is also stated as an audit assertion. This is not the case as no audit assertions are actually listed here.

- It is not clear how the number for testing was determined. This means it will be very difficult to determine whether sufficient audit evidence was obtained for this test.

- Stating that details of testing can be found on another working paper is insufficient – time will be wasted finding the working paper, if it has, in fact, been included in the audit working paper file.

- Information on the results of the test is unclear – the working paper should clearly state the results of the test without bias. The preparer appears to have used personal judgement which is not appropriate as the opinion should be based on the facts available, not speculation.

- The conclusion provided does not appear to be consistent with the results of the test. Five errors were found therefore it is likely that there are some systems weaknesses.

Answer 14 DASH

(a)   Information required

An analysis of the statement of profit and loss and statement of financial position between the three divisions. Each division has different profit margins and a divisional analysis of inventory and receivables will allow inventory and trade receivable days to be calculated for each division.

Budget information for each division. The date from which the machine manufacture division commenced trading is required, so that amounts for this division can be adjusted to take account of a trading period of less than one year.

Corresponding information for the sports retail and fitness divisions from Dash's previous year's financial statements will be needed for comparison with actual and budget performance. This could identify material or significant items, potential misstatements or variations from expected results.

If available, financial information from companies in the same industries could be used to identify where the company has performed well or badly and prompt areas for further investigation by the auditor.

Tutorial note: *Generally, only data aggregated at a high level will be used in analytical procedures at the planning stage. More detailed data (e.g. production cost per unit, number of machines sold, etc) relevant to substantive analytical procedures are not relevant here.*

(b)   Limitations of using analytical procedures at the planning stage

■   The auditor needs a good understanding of the business to interpret the results of analytical procedures. This may take some time to acquire for a new client.

■   If analytical procedures are performed mechanically, apparent consistency of results from one year to the next may in fact conceal a material error which may not be identified.

■   Effective analytical procedures rely on good quality and reliable information being available from the client which may not always be available.

■   When planning is before the end of the reporting period available information is likely to be incomplete. For example, revenue and expense accounts will include transactions for less than the entire period and period-end adjustments (e.g. allowances for depreciation, inventory and trade receivables) have still to be made.

Tutorial note: *Again note that the requirement is very specific about limitations at the planning stage. The limitations that analytical procedures provide only conclusions on reasonableness or less persuasive evidence than tests of details are relevant to substantive, evidence-gathering stage.*

(c)

Audit risks	Auditor's response
This is a new audit client which means that there is a lack of cumulative prior knowledge which in turn increases the risk of an undetected misstatement in the financial statements.	The auditor should obtain and document a thorough understanding of the entity and its environment (including the nature of the entity, relevant industry, regulatory and external factors, the selection and application of accounting policies, its objectives and strategies) and review its financial performance using analytical procedures. Obtaining an understanding would include evaluating Dash's accounting systems and internal controls.
	Adequate planning will be essential to avoid over-auditing in the first year.
Dash operates from 35 locations which hold material balances of inventory and non-current assets.	The auditor should arrange year-end attendance at physical inventory counts at all material locations. The auditor should inspect material non-current assets and carry out selected cash counts during these visits.
The risk of a breakdown in head office controls is higher in multi-site locations.	If the audit approach is to rely on controls, the auditor should undertake tests of controls using samples that cover all major locations.
Dash makes cash sales in its retail outlets and fitness clubs and it pays its casual staff in cash. Cash transactions increase the risk of misappropriation of cash and the understatement of revenue in the financial statements.	The auditor should evaluate the effectiveness of controls over cash, including the daily reconciliation of the till balance at each retail outlet and fitness club.
Paying the casual staff in cash may result in Dash failing to account for the appropriate amounts of income tax, which could lead to penalties from the tax authorities.	The auditor should assess Dash's compliance with personal tax regulations. A sample of cash payments to casual employees should be compared to payroll records to confirm inclusion in payroll expense and that appropriate taxes were withheld and submitted to the relevant taxing authorities.
Dash has received adverse publicity over the use of "sweatshops". This may damage Dash's reputation, brand name and image which could in turn affect the status of Dash as a going concern.	The auditor should assess the effect of the publicity on Dash's business. If there has been a significant decrease in sales at the retail outlets and/or a significant increase in inventory costs due to the switch to national suppliers, the auditor should determine whether this raises a significant doubt about Dash's ability to continue as a going concern. If so, the auditor should inquire about and document any mitigating factors and consider the impact on the auditor's report.

The fitness clubs receive annual subscriptions which may cause revenue to be recognised in the wrong accounting year.	Dash's accounting policy for revenue recognition will need to be reviewed to determine whether the performance obligations are properly identified. A sample of contracts with customers should be tested to determine whether revenue was properly recognised as the performance obligations were satisfied (in accordance with IFRS 15).
The profit-related bonus scheme increases the risk of manipulation of profit by divisional management by recording revenue before it is earned or deferring the recognition of expenses.	Audit work should include testing the recognition of revenue and related expenses before and after each period end for recording in the proper period. Purchase cut-off should be checked to identify any potential suppressed invoices.
Payments to overseas suppliers in instalments may lead to cut off errors arising from incorrect treatment of the first 50% paid with each order.	A sample of purchase orders and related invoices for components purchased shortly before the year end should be examined to determine whether the 50% paid on ordering was accounted for correctly.
20% of the manufactured machines are transferred to the company's retail outlets at cost plus 10%. This inter-divisional trading means that the cost of inventory held at the outlets will include some unrealised profit.	The audit approach should ensure all inter-divisional trading is separately analysed so that any unrealised profit can be identified. The "Dash" brand retail outlet inventory balance should be recalculated and compared to the amount recorded to determine whether unrealised profit has been properly eliminated.

(d) **Quality control system**

(i) *Objectives*

The objective of a system of quality control is to provide the audit firm with reasonable assurance that:

■ The firm and its personnel comply with professional standards and applicable legal and regulatory requirements; and

■ Reports issued by the firm or engagement partners are appropriate in the circumstances.

(ii) *Elements relevant to the audit of Dash*

■ Acceptance and continuance of client relationships and specific engagements. Dash is a new audit client and appropriate acceptance procedures have been followed. The team assigned to the engagement must be competent to perform it even though they have no previous experience of this specific client engaged in diverse activities.

■ Engagement performance. Direction, supervision and performance and review are particularly relevant to the first audit of this new client. Supervision includes tracking the progress of the audit engagement which will be conducted at multiple locations. Significant matters arising during this first engagement may require the auditor to modify the planned approach.

Tutorial note: *Other elements that would be given credit if explained in the context of Dash are leadership responsibilities for quality within the firm, relevant ethical requirements, human resources and monitoring.*

Answer 15 URBAN ROCK

(a)   **Factors to consider**

   (i)   Appointment as external auditor

The reasons for the previous auditors not being reappointed should be determined. The firm should establish whether the preconditions for an audit are present by inquiring about the financial reporting framework used in preparing the financial statements and should obtain management's agreement that it acknowledges and understands its responsibilities for the financial statements, internal controls, and providing the auditors with the information and access to persons in the entity necessary to complete the audit. Consideration should be given to the firm's ability to undertake the external audit engagement, including factors such as the level of experience within the firm of music events companies, ability to deal with online sales processes and availability of staff to undertake the necessary level of work, particularly in light of the time pressure. The firm may conclude that an opinion cannot be reached in the timeframe available as no assurance can be gained from procedures or attendance at festivals for 2016 (as appointment is post year end). The prevalence of cash-based transactions may also limit the firm's ability to reach an opinion.

The firm should consider whether Urban is a client with which it wishes to be associated. The adverse publicity arising from the legal claim may impact the firm's own reputation. In addition, issues raised regarding going concern, the possibility of internal control weaknesses at festivals as cited by Sam Smith and the reliance by the bank on the financial statements increases the risk associated with this audit.

Ethical issues surrounding acceptance should be considered, particularly whether any conflicts of interest are likely to arise with existing clients (given firm's current specialism in entertainment industry) and the likely proportion of total fee income that will be generated from Urban.

   (ii)   Additional work on controls

Attendance at board meetings may be perceived as undertaking a management role. It is also unclear what level of assurance is required by the directors in respect of this work.

Work on controls may lead to a self-review threat if the work is relied on as part of the external audit.

Whether sufficient staff with required expertise will be available on appropriate weekends and in appropriate locations.

(b)

Audit risks	Auditor's response
The going concern basis may be inappropriate/issue not adequately disclosed due to:	The auditor should review:

The going concern basis may be inappropriate/issue not adequately disclosed due to:

- Falling ticket sales/adverse weather;
- Increased supplier costs;
- Adverse press re injured customer;
- Reliance on online ticket sales (risk re system failure);
- Lost revenue if police/municipal authority refuse permission or reduce ticket numbers;
- Bank loan increases debt (and gearing).

The auditor should review:

- Level of advanced ticket sales and compare to forecast/prior year;
- Press and other media for further adverse publicity;
- Correspondence with police/municipal authority to ascertain if permission granted/ticket volumes changed;
- Management forecast for working capital requirements in light of increased debt.

Errors/omissions may be undetected by audit procedures due to:

- First year audit – lack of cumulative audit knowledge and experience;
- Tight reporting deadline;
- Concerns about the adequacy of controls at events.

The auditor should assign an audit team to complete audit work to an agreed timetable.

The auditor should thoroughly research Urban to gain an understanding of the business.

The auditor should include in the timescale a second partner review of areas of subjectivity/estimation.

Unrecorded liabilities and/or undisclosed contingent liabilities may arise due to:

- Possible liability relating to injured customer;
- Nature of events give rise to risk of non-compliance with health and safety standards;
- Risk of breaching maximum customer numbers allowed by municipal authority;
- Casual staff employed – risk of non-compliance with tax and employment laws.

Review correspondence with lawyers regarding the claim for damages and likely outcome.

Review events after the reporting date that indicate a liability (e.g. out-of-court settlement).

Ascertain if the claim is covered by insurance policy.

Review correspondence with authorities to ascertain if any other disputes/liabilities regarding health and safety have arisen.

Compare total actual ticket sales to maximum numbers permitted.

Review personnel and payroll records to ascertain whether appropriate taxes are deducted for stewards and casual staff.

Revenue may be overstated as tickets for next year's events are on sale in current year (cut-off error).

Perform cut-off tests to confirm that sales of tickets for next year are treated as deferred income.

Revenue will be understated if ticket sales for cash are not all recorded.

Ascertain what controls were in place over cash takings recorded – obtain evidence that those controls were exercised at events in the current year.

Expenses and revenue will be unrecorded (understated) if cash receipts and payments are netted off.	Review reconciliations of cash received/paid by the on-site office. Review records from on-site cash offices and compare to: ■ Agreements with agents for payments to musicians on site; ■ Number of casual staff hired and paid; ■ Level of ticket sales recorded at entrance gate.
Cut off errors in expenditure may arise through advance payments made to musicians' agents.	Review pre- and post year-end payments to agents and trace to appropriate accounting period. Compare actual musician costs for the year to budget.

(c)   **Internal controls**

     (i)   *Over cash*

■ Cash kept in a safe at the on-site cash office.

■ Security around cash office and ticket offices (e.g. locked, coded-entry, locked tills, CCTV, supervision).

■ Cash collected regularly from ticket offices and transferred to cash office by event supervisor or security.

■ Cash counted in ticket office by two members of staff, record made and signed.

■ Cash checked to record when received in cash office.

■ Cash regularly taken off site by security company.

■ List of musicians/agents due to be paid cash on day of performance maintained in on-site cash office.

■ Cash collected by artists, agents and casual staff signed for,

■ Cash payments authorised by event supervisor.

■ Identification obtained where cash collected in person.

■ Reconciliation of cash takings to wristbands at end of each day.

■ Spot counts of cash at ticket box and cash office.

■ Segregation of duties between collecting and counting cash.

■ Use of cash counting machines in cash office.

(ii)   Over wristband exchange

■   Staff appropriately trained in how to manage wristband exchange.

■   Advance ticket holders must hand over ticket booking confirmation before receiving wristband.

■   Booking confirmations retained (to prevent reuse) and number of confirmations agreed to number of advance ticket sales and wristbands issued.

■   Customer's unique booking reference checked off against online system to ensure no duplicate use of confirmations.

■   Wristbands should be kept securely (e.g. safe or released by cash office in stages)/security around wristband exchange.

■   Wristbands available for sale on day only up to the maximum number of customers allowed by municipal authority.

■   Wristbands physically counted at start of each event by Urban staff.

■   Wristbands designed so they cannot be counterfeited (e.g. hologram).

■   Wristbands secured on customers by exchange staff (to prevent reselling).

■   Customers show ID or credit card used for payment with booking confirmation.

Answer 16 BRIDGFORD PRODUCTS

(a)   Importance of planning

ISA 300 *Planning an Audit of Financial Statements* requires that "The auditor should plan the audit work so that the audit will be performed in an effective manner". It goes on to say that "planning means developing a general strategy and a detailed approach for the expected nature, timing and extent of the audit".

Planning will address the appropriate approach to the components of the company, preliminary risk assessment and materiality assessment. It will include the timing of the audit work. It will be necessary to agree a timetable with the company of when information will be available. For example:

■   the inventory count;
■   when the full financial statements are available for audit;
■   when the financial statements are agreed and signed by the directors and the auditor.

The necessary level of skills (both internal and, if necessary, external) will be determined and staff booked and external experts contracted.

A budget will be prepared which sets the time which should be spent on each aspect of the audit and the completion dates of each part of the audit.

During the audit, progress will be compared with the audit plan. Any adverse (and favourable) variances against the plan will be investigated, and the plan amended if it is considered appropriate.

The requirement to plan an audit ensures senior audit staff have considered the work which is required to complete the audit and the timing of that work so that it fits in with the dates information is available from the company and the review and planned completion dates.

By having a plan, the auditor will take a more considered and efficient approach to the audit, which will improve the quality of the audit, and thus both minimise the time spent on the audit and the overall audit risk.

(b)   **Audit risks and responses**

Sales and profits

Audit risk: The company's sales for 10 months are $130 million, which given an annualised sales of $156 million, is a 41.8% increase over the previous years. The annualised profit before tax is $4.8 million, compared with $8 million last year, which is a fall of 40%. It appears the company is increasing sales at the expense of profits.

Audit response: During the audit a detailed breakdown of sales and expenses will be obtained, discussed with management and tested in order to understand the increases in both sales and expenses.

New computerised inventory system

Audit risk: Relying only on the new inventory control system to determine the value of year-end inventory may result in a misstatement of the inventory balance that would be detected only by inventory count.

Audit response: Audit work will have to be carried out on the new computerised inventory control system. Computer audit specialists within the audit firm will probably have to be used. It may be appropriate to carry out this work before the year end, so that any problems with the system can be highlighted and either overcome or allowed for at the year end.

Since the company intends not to carry out an inventory count at the year end, the auditor will have to place considerable reliance on the accuracy of the inventory quantities reported by the inventory control system. He will need to review and test the new system, check the changeover and determine from the company how frequently they count the inventory, the proportion of the inventory counted at each inventory count, and the checks they make to the inventory quantities on the computerised system and the frequency and size of errors.

This work will have to be concluded before the year end, as, if differences are frequent, it may be necessary to carry out a full inventory count at the year end.

Product reliability

Reliability problems with the company's products could result in the following:

- certain inventory being unsaleable, and thus worth less than cost;
- legal claims against the company; and
- customers not paying for the products.

The **audit risks** associated with these problems include:

■   The risk that there may be more claims and irrecoverable debts relating to the year under review which may not become apparent until after the auditor's report is signed.

■   The difficulty in estimating the costs of defending legal claims and damages which may have to be paid as well as the impairment of trade receivables. If the costs are too high, there may be significant uncertainty about the company's ability to continue as a going concern.

Any faulty inventory may be overvalued.

Audit responses

■   Further details will have to be obtained about any legal claims against the company and customers refusing to pay their outstanding balances. Information can be obtained for this by inspecting correspondence with customers and discussing the matter with the company's staff.

■   Procedures should be performed to assess whether there is significant doubt about the entity's ability to continue as a going concern and, if so, to document any mitigating factors and determine the possible effect on the auditor's report.

■   The selling price of inventory sold after the year end should be compared with cost to ensure it is valued at the lower of cost and net realisable value. The physical condition of unsold, slow-moving items should be examined and, if faulty, included in the calculation of inventory allowance.

Extended credit

Audit risks: The large increase in receivables age has caused a very large increase in receivables, from \$14.7 million ($^{110}/_{12} \times 1.6$) at 30 June 2015 to an estimated \$53.3 million ($^{156\ (\text{per (i)})}/_{12} \times 4.1$) at 30 June 2016. In addition, the actual age of receivables is 1.1 months in excess of the current credit limit (of three months) compared with 0.6 months over the credit limit in the previous year.

The increase in the credit period and sales to new customers will result in the following audit risks:

■   Decrease in available cash due to prolonged collection period.

■   New customers may be low quality and tend to have a higher risk than existing ones, thus increasing the risk of bad debts; increasing the credit period tends to attract customers who are a poor credit risk.

■   There may be problems with collection of receivables from customers and thus an increase in bad debts. A potential bad debt may not become apparent until after the credit period has been exceeded.

Audit response

- The financing of the increase may have come from increased borrowings which need to be verified.

- A sample of new customers should be selected and reviewed to determine whether the new customers are paying according to the credit terms or are more likely to be delinquent.

- A sample of receivables outstanding at year end should be tested for subsequent cash receipts.

More audit effort and more time after the year end is required to conclude adequately on recoverability.

Staff dismissals

Audit risks: The effect of there being no chief financial officer between 15 January and the year end may mean that financial records and controls may not be as effective as in previous years. If the chief financial officer prepared the annual draft financial statements in previous years, does the chief accountant have the skills and experience to prepare this year's financial statements?

In addition the consequences of the company being without a purchasing manager from 15 January until the new purchasing manager was appointed must be considered. There is the risk that controls during this period will not have operated well, thus increasing the risk of fraud.

Audit responses: The reasons for the dismissal of the chief financial officer and purchasing manager will have to be ascertained. Were they carrying out a fraud? If this was happening, what are the financial consequences? Is it possible for this type of fraud to recur? Could the audit firm be liable for not detecting these events? The assessment of inherent risk may be increased in any areas under their control.

If the dismissed employees are claiming compensation for unfair dismissal and compensation from the company, the likely outcome from these claims would have to be investigated and an appropriate provision included in the financial statements.

Answer 17 EUKARE CHARITY

(a) **Audit risk**

Audit risk is the risk that an auditor gives an inappropriate opinion on the financial statements being audited. It comprises three elements:

- Inherent risk – the susceptibility of an assertion to a misstatement that could be material individually or when aggregated with misstatements, assuming that there are no related controls. The risk of such misstatement is greater for some assertions and related classes of transactions, account balances, and related disclosures than for others.

- Control risk – the risk that a material error could occur in an assertion that could be material, individually or when aggregated with other misstatements, will not be prevented or detected on a timely basis by the company's internal control systems.

- Detection risk – the risk that the auditors' procedures will not detect a misstatement that exists in an assertion that could be material, individually or when aggregated with other misstatements.

(b) **Inherent risks in charity**

Area of inherent risk	*Effect on audit approach*
Income is from voluntary donations only. There is a risk that donations will fall, especially where donors' own income is limited by the "credit crunch" etc.	It is difficult to estimate that income in the future will be sufficient to meet the expenditure of the charity. Audit of the going concern concept (as in ensuring that the charity can still operate) will therefore be quite difficult.
Completeness of income – where there are no controls to ensure income is complete for example sales invoices are not raised to obtain donations and donations could be stolen by staff.	Audit tests are unlikely to be effective to meet the assertion of completeness. The audit opinion may need to be modified to explain the lack of evidence stating that completeness of income cannot be confirmed.
Funds can only be spent in accordance with the aims of the charity. There is a risk that funds are spent outside the aims of the charity.	Careful review of expenditure will be necessary to ensure that expenditure is not *ultra vires* the objectives of the charity. The auditor will need to review the constitution of the EuKaRe charity carefully in this respect.
Taxation rules relevant to charities. There is a risk that the rules will be broken due to lack of correct analysis of income/expenditure.	The auditor will need to ensure that staff familiar with the taxation rules affecting the charity are on the audit team.
Requirement to report expenditure in accordance with the constitution – administration expenditure can be no more than 10% of total income. Risks here include income being overstated to allow expenditure to be overstated.	The trustees may attempt to hide "excessive" expenditure on administration under other expense headings. As the auditor has to report on the accuracy of income and expenditure then audit procedures must focus on the accuracy of recording of expenditure.
Donations to charity for specific activities for example provision of sports equipment. There is a risk that donations are not spent in accordance with donors' instructions.	Documentation for any donation will need to be obtained and then expenditure agreed to the terms of the documentation. Any discrepancies will have to be reported to management.

(c)   **Weak control environment**

Lack of segregation of duties/responsibilities

There is normally a limited number of staff working in the charity meaning that a full system of internal control including segregation of duties cannot be implemented. Staff are likely to be unclear as to their exact responsibilities as they are not formal "employees" and are not part of the formal authority structure in the charity.

Volunteer staff

Many staff are volunteers and so will only work at the charity on an occasional basis. Controls will be performed by different staff on different days making the system unreliable.

Lack of qualified staff (human resource issues)

Selection of staff is limited – people tend to volunteer for work when they have time – and so they are unlikely to have professional qualifications or experience to implement or maintain good control systems.

No internal audit department (lack of organisational structure)

Any control system will not be monitored effectively, mainly due to the lack of any internal audit department. The charity will not have the funds or experience to establish internal audit.

Attitude of the trustees

It is not clear how the charity's trustees view risk. However, where trustees are not professionally trained or have little time to devote to the charity, there may be an impression that controls are not important. The overall control environment may therefore be weak as other charity workers do not see the importance of maintaining good controls.

Answer 18 ABRAHAMS

(a)   **Components of audit risk**

> **Tutorial note:** *The requirement to this part is general. The scenario of Abrahams is only relevant from part (b) which starts "Using the information provided ...".*

Inherent risk

The susceptibility of an assertion about a class of transaction, account balance or related disclosure to a misstatement that could be material, either individually or when aggregated with other misstatements, before consideration of any related controls. Inherent risk is affected by the nature of an entity. Factors which can result in an increase include:

- Changes in the industry it operates in.
- Operations that are subject to a high degree of regulation.
- Going concern and liquidity issues including loss of significant customers.
- Developing or offering new products or services or moving into new lines of business.
- Expanding into new locations.
- Application of new accounting standards.
- Accounting measurements that involve complex processes.
- Events or transactions that involve significant accounting estimates.
- Pending litigation and contingent liabilities.

Control risk

The risk that a misstatement that could occur in an assertion about a class of transaction, account balance or related disclosure and that could be material, either individually or when aggregated with other misstatements, will not be prevented, or detected and corrected, on a timely basis by the entity's internal control. Factors that can result in an increase in control risk include:

■ Lack of personnel with appropriate accounting and financial reporting skills.
■ Changes in key personnel including departure of key management.
■ Deficiencies in internal control, especially those not addressed by management.
■ Changes in the information technology (IT) environment.
■ Installation of significant new IT systems related to financial reporting.

Detection risk

The risk that the procedures performed by the auditor to reduce audit risk to an acceptably low level will not detect a misstatement that exists and that could be material, either individually or when aggregated with other misstatements. Detection risk is affected by sampling and non-sampling risk. Factors which can result in an increase include:

■ Inadequate planning.
■ Inappropriate assignment of personnel to the engagement team.
■ Failing to apply professional scepticism.
■ Inadequate supervision and review of the audit work performed.
■ Incorrect sampling techniques performed.
■ Incorrect sample sizes.

Tutorial note: *Only* **one** *example for each component of risk was required for full marks.*

(b) **Audit risks and responses**

Audit risk	*Audit response*
The finance director is planning to capitalise, as an asset, the full $2·2 million of development expenditure incurred. However, in order to do this all the criteria of IAS 38 *Intangible Assets* must be met.	A breakdown of the development expenditure should be reviewed and tested in detail to ensure that only projects which meet the capitalisation criteria are included as an intangible asset, with the balance being expensed.
Some projects may not reach final development stage and hence should be expensed rather than capitalised. The risk of overstating intangible assets is increased due to the loan covenant requirements to maintain a minimum level of assets.	

Audit risk	*Audit response*
The inventory valuation method used is standard costing. This is acceptable under IAS 2 *Inventories* if standard cost is a close approximation to actual cost. Abrahams has not updated the standard costs from when the product was first developed and hence there is a risk that the standard costs could be out of date, resulting in over or undervalued inventory.	The standard costs used for the inventory valuation should be tested in detail and compared to actual cost. If there are significant variations this should be discussed with management, to ensure that the valuation is appropriate.
The work in progress balance at the year end is likely to be material; however there is a risk that due to the nature of the production process the audit team may not be sufficiently qualified to assess the quantity and value of work in progress leading to misstated work in progress.	Consideration should be given to whether an independent expert is required to value the work in progress. If so this will need to be arranged with consent from management and in time for the year-end count.
Over one-third of the warehouses of Abrahams belong to third parties. Sufficient and appropriate evidence will need to be obtained to confirm the quantities of inventory held in these locations in order to verify completeness and existence.	Additional procedures will be required to ensure that inventory quantities have been confirmed for both third party and company owned locations.
In September Abrahams introduced a new accounting system. This is a critical system for the accounts preparation and if there were any errors that occurred during the changeover process, these could affect the final amounts in the trial balance.	The new system will need to be documented in full and testing should be performed over the transfer of data from the old to the new system.
The new accounting system is bespoke and the IT manager who developed it has left the company already and his replacement is not due to start until just before the year end. The accounting personnel who are using the system may have encountered problems and without the IT manager's support, errors could be occurring in the system due to a lack of knowledge and experience. This could result in significant errors arising in the financial statements.	This issue should be discussed with the finance director to understand how he is addressing this risk of misstatement. In addition, the team should remain alert throughout the audit for evidence of such errors.
Significant finance has been obtained in the year, $1 million of equity finance and $2·5 million of long-term loans. This finance needs to be accounted for correctly, with adequate disclosure made. The equity finance needs to be allocated correctly between share capital and share premium, and the loan should be presented as a non-current liability.	Check that the split of the equity finance is correct and that total financing proceeds of $3·5 million were received. In addition, the disclosures for this finance should be reviewed in detail to ensure compliance with relevant accounting standards.

Audit risk	Audit response
The loan has a number of covenants attached to it. If these are breached then the loan would be instantly repayable and would be classified as a current liability. This could result in the company being in a net current liability position. If the company did not have sufficient cash flow to meet this loan repayment there could be going concern implications.	Review the covenant calculations prepared by Abrahams and identify whether any defaults have occurred; if so then determine the effect on the company. The team should maintain their professional scepticism and be alert to the risk that assets have been overstated to ensure compliance with covenants.
The land and buildings are to be revalued at the year end; it is likely that the revaluation surplus/deficit will be material. The revaluation needs to be carried out and recorded in accordance with IAS 16 *Property, Plant and Equipment*; otherwise non-current assets may be incorrectly valued.	Review the reasonableness of the valuation and recalculate the revaluation surplus/deficit to ensure that land and buildings are correctly valued.
The reporting timetable for Abrahams is likely to be reduced. The previous timetable was already quite short and any further reductions will increase detection risk and place additional pressure on the team in obtaining sufficient and appropriate evidence.	The timetable should be confirmed with the finance director. If it is to be reduced then consideration should be given to performing an interim audit in late December or early January, this would then reduce the pressure on the final audit.

(c)   **Substantive procedures**

(i)   *Inventory held at third party warehouses*

■   Send a letter requesting direct confirmation of inventory balances held at year end from the third party warehouse providers used by Abrahams regarding quantities and condition.

■   Attend the inventory count (if one is to be performed) at the third party warehouses to review the controls in operation to ensure the completeness and existence of inventory.

■   Inspect any reports produced by the auditors of the warehouses in relation to the adequacy of controls over inventory.

■   Inspect any documentation in respect of third party inventory.

(ii)   *Use of standard costs for inventory valuation*

■   Discuss with management the basis of the standard costs applied to the inventory valuation, and how often these are reviewed and updated.

■   Review the level of variances between standard and actual costs and discuss with management how these are treated.

■   Obtain a breakdown of the standard costs and agree a sample of these costs to actual invoices or wage records to assess their reasonableness.

Answer 19 SUNFLOWER STORES

(a)   **Understanding an entity**

Source of information	Information expect to obtain
Prior year audit file	Identification of issues that arose in the prior year audit and how these were resolved. Also whether any points brought forward were noted for consideration for this year's audit.
Prior year financial statements	Provides information in relation to the size of the entity as well as the key accounting policies and disclosure notes.
Accounting systems notes	Provides information on how each of the key accounting systems operates.
Discussions with management	Provides information in relation to any important issues which have arisen or changes to the company during the year.
Current year budgets and management accounts of Sunflower Stores (Sunflower)	Provides relevant financial information for the year to date. Will help the auditor to identify whether Sunflower has changed materially since last year. In addition, this will be useful for preliminary analytical review and risk identification.
Permanent audit file	Provides information in relation to matters of continuing importance for the company and the audit team, such as statutory books information or important agreements.
Sunflower's website	Recent press releases from the company may provide background on changes to the business during the year as this could lead to additional audit risks.
Prior year report to management	Provides information on the internal control deficiencies noted in the prior year; if these have not been rectified by management then they could arise in the current year audit as well.
Financial statements of competitors	This will provide information about Sunflower's competitors, in relation to their financial results and their accounting policies. This will be important in assessing Sunflower's performance in the year and also when undertaking the going concern review.

(b)   **Audit risks and auditor responses**

Audit risk	Auditor response
Sunflower has spent $1·6m on refurbishing its 25 food supermarkets. This expenditure needs to be reviewed to assess whether it is of a capital nature and should be included within non-current assets or expensed as repairs.	Review a breakdown of the costs and agree to invoices to assess the nature of the expenditure. If capital, agree inclusion in the asset register. If repairs, agree inclusion in expense to profit or loss.

Audit risk	*Auditor response*
During the year a small warehouse has been disposed of at a profit. The asset needs to have been correctly removed from property plant and equipment to ensure the non-current asset register is not overstated, and the profit on disposal should be included in profit or loss.	Review the non-current asset register to ensure that the asset has been removed. Also confirm the disposal proceeds as well as recalculating the profit on disposal.
	Consideration should be given as to whether the profit on disposal is significant enough to warrant separate disclosure in the statement of profit or loss.
Sunflower has borrowed $1·5m from the bank via a five year loan. This loan needs to be correctly split between current and non-current liabilities.	During the audit the team would need to confirm that the $1·5m loan finance was received. In addition, the split between current and non-current liabilities and the disclosures for this loan should be reviewed in detail to ensure compliance with relevant accounting standards.
In addition, Sunflower may have given the bank a charge over its assets as security for the loan. There is a risk that the disclosure of any security given is not complete.	The loan agreement should be reviewed to ascertain whether any security has been given, and this bank should be circularised as part of the bank confirmation process.
Sunflower will be undertaking a number of simultaneous inventory counts on 31 December including the warehouse and all 25 supermarkets. It is not practical for the auditor to attend all of these counts; hence it may not be possible to gain sufficient appropriate audit evidence over inventory counts.	The team should select a sample of sites to visit. It is likely that the warehouse contains most goods and therefore should be selected. In relation to the 25 supermarkets, the team should visit those with material inventory balances and/or those with a history of inventory count issues.
Sunflower's inventory valuation policy is selling price less average profit margin. Inventory should be valued at the lower of cost and net realisable value (NRV) and if this is not the case, then inventory could be under or overvalued.	Testing should be undertaken to confirm cost and NRV of inventory and that on a line-by-line basis the goods are valued correctly.
IAS 2 *Inventories* allows this as an inventory valuation method as long as it is a close approximation to cost. If this is not the case, then inventory could be under or overvalued.	In addition, valuation testing should focus on comparing the cost of inventory to the selling price less margin to confirm whether this method is actually a close approximation to cost.
The opening balances for each supermarket have been transferred into the head office's accounting records at the beginning of the year. There is a risk that if this transfer has not been performed completely and accurately, the opening balances may not be correct.	Discuss with management the process undertaken to transfer the data and the testing performed to confirm the transfer was complete and accurate.
	Computer-assisted audit techniques could be utilised by the team to sample test the transfer of data from each supermarket to head office to identify any errors.

Audit risk	*Auditor response*
There has been an increased workload for the finance department, the financial controller has left and his replacement will only start in late December.	The team should remain alert throughout the audit for additional errors within the finance department.
This increases the inherent risk within Sunflower as errors may have been made within the accounting records by the overworked finance team members. The new financial controller may not be sufficiently experienced to produce the financial statements and resolve any audit issues.	In addition, discuss with the finance director whether he will be able to provide the team with assistance for any audit issues the new financial controller is unable to resolve.

(c) **Internal audit department**

Prior to establishing an internal audit (IA) department, the finance director of Sunflower should consider the following:

■   The costs of establishing an IA department will be significant, therefore prior to committing to these costs and management time, a cost benefit analysis should be performed.

■   The size and complexity of Sunflower should be considered. The larger, more complex and diverse a company is, then the greater the need for an IA department. At Sunflower there are 25 supermarkets and a head office and therefore it would seem that the company is diverse enough to gain benefit from an IA department.

■   The role of any IA department should be considered. The finance director should consider what tasks he would envisage IA performing. He should consider whether he wishes them to undertake inventory counts at the stores, or whether he would want them to undertake such roles as internal controls reviews.

■   Having identified the role of any IA department, the finance director should consider whether there are existing managers or employees who could perform these tasks, therefore reducing the need to establish a separate IA department.

■   The finance director should assess the current control environment and determine whether there are departments or stores with a history of control deficiencies. If this is the case, then it increases the need for an IA department.

■   If the possibility of fraud is high, then the greater the need for an IA department to act as both a deterrent and also to possibly undertake fraud investigations. As Sunflower operates 25 food supermarkets, it will have a significant risk of fraud of both inventory and cash.

Answer 20 RECORDER COMMUNICATIONS

(a)

Audit risk	Auditor's response
Recorder is a new client for Piano & Co. As the team is not so familiar with the accounting policies, transactions and balances of Recorder, there will be an increased detection risk on the audit.	Piano & Co should ensure they have a suitably experienced team. Also, adequate time should be allocated for team members to obtain an understanding of the company and the risks of material misstatement.
Recorder purchases their goods from South Asia and the goods are in transit for two weeks. At the year end there is a risk that the cut-off of inventory, purchases and payables may not be accurate. The company correctly accounts for goods when they receive them. Therefore at the year end only goods which have been received into the warehouse should be included in the inventory balance and a respective payables balance recognised.	The audit team should undertake detailed cut-off testing of goods in transit from the suppliers in South Asia to ensure that the cut-off is complete and accurate.
The company undertakes continuous (perpetual) inventory counts at its central warehouse. Under such a system all inventory must be counted at least once a year with adjustments made to the inventory records. Inventory could be under or overstated if the continuous (perpetual) inventory counts are not complete and the inventory records accurately updated for adjustments.	The completeness of the continuous (perpetual) inventory counts should be reviewed. In addition, the level of adjustments made to inventory should be considered to assess whether reliance on the inventory records at the year end will be acceptable.
A sales-related bonus scheme has been introduced in the year; this may lead to sales cut-off errors with employees aiming to maximise their current year bonus.	Increased sales cut-off testing will be performed along with a review of any post year-end cancellations of contracts as they may indicate cut-off errors.
Receivables are considerably higher than the prior year and there are concerns about the creditworthiness of some customers. There is a risk that some receivables may be overvalued as they are not recoverable.	Extended post year-end cash receipts testing and a review of the aged receivables ledger to be performed to assess valuation. Also consider the adequacy of any allowance for receivables.
In addition, receivables could be overstated as a result of the bonus scheme; some of the customers signed up for contracts may not actually exist.	External confirmation of receivables to confirm that customers exist and represent valid amounts due.

Audit risk	Auditor's response
Recorder has a policy of revaluing its land and buildings and these valuations have been updated during the year.	Discuss with management the process adopted for undertaking the valuation, including whether the whole class of assets was revalued and if the valuation was undertaken by an expert. This process should be reviewed for compliance with IAS 16.
Property, plant and equipment could be under or overvalued if the recent valuation has not been carried out in accordance with IAS 16 *Property, Plant and Equipment* and adequate disclosures may not have been made in the financial statements.	Review the disclosures of the revaluation in the financial statements for compliance with IAS 16.
The directors have each been paid a significant bonus and separate disclosure of this in the financial statements is required by local legislation.	Discuss this matter with management and review the disclosure in the financial statements to ensure compliance with local legislation.
The directors' remuneration disclosure will not be complete and accurate if the bonus paid is not disclosed in accordance with the relevant local legislation.	

(b)   **Audit procedures for continuous (perpetual) inventory counts**

■   The audit team should attend at least one of the continuous (perpetual) inventory counts to review whether the controls over the inventory count are adequate.

■   The audit team should confirm that all of the inventory lines have been counted or are due to be counted at least once a year by reviewing the schedules of counts undertaken/due to be undertaken.

■   Review the adjustments made to the inventory records on a monthly basis to gain an understanding of the level of differences arising on a month by month basis.

■   If significant differences consistently arise, this could indicate that the inventory records are not adequately maintained. Discuss with management how they will ensure that year-end inventory will not be under or overstated.

■   Consider attending the inventory count at the year end to undertake test counts of inventory from records to floor and from floor to records in order to confirm the existence and completeness of inventory.

(c)   **Substantive procedures for directors' bonus and remuneration**

■   Obtain a schedule of the directors' remuneration including the bonus paid and cast the addition of the schedule.

■   Agree the individual bonus payments to the payroll records.

■   Confirm the amount of each bonus paid by agreeing to the cash book and bank statements.

■   Review the board minutes to confirm whether any additional bonus payments relating to this year have been agreed.

■ Obtain a written representation from management confirming the completeness of directors' remuneration including the bonus.

■ Review any disclosures made of the bonus and assess whether these are in compliance with local legislation.

(d) **Conflicts of interest**

■ Both Recorder and its competitor should be notified that Piano & Co would be acting as auditors for each company and, if necessary, consent obtained.

■ Advising one or both clients to seek additional independent advice.

■ The use of separate engagement teams, with different engagement partners and team members; once an employee has worked on one audit, such as Recorder, then they would be prevented from being on the audit of the competitor for a period of time. This separation of teams is known as building a "Chinese wall".

■ Procedures to prevent access to information, for example, strict physical separation of both teams, confidential and secure data filing.

■ Clear guidelines for members of each engagement team on issues of security and confidentiality. These guidelines could be included within the audit engagement letters.

■ Potentially the use of confidentiality agreements signed by employees and partners of the firm.

■ Regular monitoring of the application of the above safeguards by a senior individual in Piano & Co not involved in either audit.

Answer 21 WALTERS

(a)(i) **Ratios to assist in planning the audit**

	2016	*2015*
Operating margin	$4 \cdot 5 \div 23 = 19 \cdot 6\%$	$4 \div 18 = 22 \cdot 2\%$
Inventory days	$2 \cdot 1 \div 11 \times 365 = 70$ days	$1 \cdot 6 \div 10 \times 365 = 58$ days
Payable days	$1 \cdot 6 \div 11 \times 365 = 53$ days	$1 \cdot 2 \div 10 \times 365 = 44$ days
Current ratio	$6 \cdot 6 \div 2 \cdot 5 = 2 \cdot 6$	$6 \cdot 9 \div 1 \cdot 2 = 5 \cdot 8$
Quick ratio	$(6 \cdot 6 - 2 \cdot 1) \div 2 \cdot 5 = 1 \cdot 8$	$(6 \cdot 9 - 1 \cdot 6) \div 1 \cdot 2 = 4 \cdot 4$

(ii)

Audit risk	Audit response
Management were disappointed with 2015 results and hence undertook strategies to improve the 2016 trading results. There is a risk that management might feel under pressure to manipulate the results through the judgements taken or through the use of provisions.	Throughout the audit the team will need to be alert to this risk. They will need to carefully review judgemental decisions and compare treatment against prior years.
A generous sales-related bonus scheme has been introduced in the year, this may lead to sales cut-off errors with employees aiming to maximise their current year bonus.	Increased sales cut-off testing will be performed along with a review of post year-end sales returns as they may indicate cut-off errors.

Audit risk	**Audit response**
Revenue has grown by 28% in the year however, cost of sales has only increased by 10%. This increase in sales may be due to the bonus scheme and the advertising however, this does not explain the increase in gross margin. There is a risk that sales may be overstated.	During the audit a detailed breakdown of sales will be obtained, discussed with management and tested in order to understand the sales increase.
Gross margin has increased from 44·4% to 52·2%. Operating margin has decreased from 22·2% to 19·6%. This movement in gross margin is significant and there is a risk that costs may have been omitted or included in operating expenses rather than cost of sales. There has been a significant increase in operating expenses which may be due to the bonus and the advertising campaign but could be related to the misclassification of costs.	The classification of costs between cost of sales and operating expenses will be compared with the prior year to ensure consistency.
The finance director has made a change to the inventory valuation in the year with additional overheads being included. In addition inventory days have increased from 58 to 70 days. There is a risk that inventory is overvalued.	The change in the inventory policy will be discussed with management and a review performed of the additional overheads included to ensure that these are of a production nature. Detailed cost and net realisable value testing to be performed and the aged inventory report to be reviewed to assess whether inventory requires writing down.
Receivables days have increased from 61 to 71 days and management have extended the credit period given to customers. This leads to an increased risk of recoverability of receivables.	Extended post year-end cash receipts testing and a review of the aged receivables ledger to be performed to assess valuation.
The current and quick ratios have decreased from 5·8 to 2·6 and 4·4 to 1·8 respectively. In addition, the cash balances have decreased significantly over the year. Although all ratios are above the minimum levels, this is still a significant decrease and along with the increase of sales could be evidence of overtrading which could result in going concern difficulties.	Detailed going concern testing to be performed during the audit and discussed with management to ensure that the going concern basis is reasonable.

(b) **Going concern procedures**

- Obtain Walters' cash flow forecast and review the cash in and out flows. Assess the assumptions for reasonableness and discuss the findings with management to understand if the company will have sufficient cash flows.

- Review any current agreements with the bank to determine whether any key ratios have been breached with regards to the bank overdraft.

- Review the company's post year-end sales and order book to assess the levels of trade and if the revenue figures in the cash flow forecast are reasonable.

- Review post year end correspondence with suppliers to identify whether any restriction in credit have arisen, and if so ensure that the cash flow forecast reflects an immediate payment for trade payables.

- Inquire of the lawyers of Walters as to the existence of litigation and claims; if any exist then consider their materiality and impact on the going concern basis.

- Perform audit tests in relation to subsequent events to identify any items that might indicate or mitigate the risk of going concern not being appropriate.

- Review the post year end board minutes to identify any other issues that might indicate financial difficulties for the company.

- Review post year end management accounts to assess if in line with cash flow forecast.

- Consider whether any additional disclosures as required by IAS 1 *Presentation of Financial Statements* in relation to material uncertainties over going concern should be made in the financial statements.

- Obtain a written representation confirming the director's view that Walters is a going concern.

Answer 22 EAGLE HEATING

Item	Answer	Justification
1	B	(1) is incorrect. It is possible that the selling price may have fallen so low that the net realisable value of the inventory is below cost. Hence it is possible that inventory is overvalued, not undervalued. (2) is correct. There is an increased risk that the receivables are overvalued because of the receivable that may not be recoverable. (3) is all correct. There is an increased risk that Eagle is facing going concern difficulties given the increase in competition, the decrease in selling price and the financial difficulties of one of its key customers. (4) is also correct. There is an increased risk that administrative expenses are understated because administrative expenses are fixed costs that are unlikely to fluctuate significantly with changes in sales volume.
2	C	Appropriate audit responses include discussing with the finance director whether he will be able to provide the audit team with assistance in the absence of a financial controller and remaining alert throughout the audit for errors. Visiting the company's lawyers is not an appropriate response. It is sufficient to write to the lawyers to enquire of the existence and likelihood of success of the former controllers claims. It is not appropriate to offer assistance to Eagle in recruiting a new controller as this would give rise to a self-interest threat to the auditor's independence.
3	B	Procedures 2 and 3 are substantive procedures rather than tests of control.
4	C	Substantive procedure 1 provides evidence over the assertion of completeness as the direction of the test is from source documents to accounting records. Substantive procedure 4 provides evidence over accuracy, valuation and allocation rather than existence.
5	C	Statement 1 refers to the use of analytical procedures at the final review or completion stage of the audit. Statement 2 refers to the use of analytical procedures to obtain substantive evidence during the fieldwork stage of the audit.

Answer 23 KANGAROO CONSTRUCTION

(a)   **Materiality and performance materiality**

Materiality and performance materiality are dealt with under ISA 320 *Materiality in Planning and Performing an Audit*.

Auditors need to establish the materiality level for the financial statements as a whole, as well as assess performance materiality levels, which are lower than the overall materiality.

Materiality is defined in ISA 320 as follows:

"Misstatements, including omissions, are considered to be material if they, individually or in the aggregate, could reasonably be expected to influence the economic decisions of users taken on the basis of the financial statements."

In assessing the level of materiality, there are a number of areas that should be considered. First the auditor must consider both the amount (quantity) and the nature (quality) of any misstatements, or a combination of both. The quantity of the misstatement refers to the relative size of it and the quality refers to an amount that might be low in value but due to its prominence could influence the user's decision, for example, directors' transactions.

As per ISA 320, materiality is often calculated using benchmarks such as 5% of profit before tax or 1% of total revenue or total expenses. These values are useful as a starting point for assessing materiality.

The assessment of what is material is ultimately a matter of the auditor's professional judgement, and it is affected by the auditor's perception of the financial information needs of users of the financial statements and the perceived level of risk; the higher the risk, the lower the level of overall materiality.

In assessing materiality, the auditor must consider that a number of errors each with a low value may, when aggregated, amount to a material misstatement.

In calculating materiality, the auditor should also set the performance materiality level. Performance materiality is normally set at a level lower than overall materiality. It is used for testing individual transactions, account balances and related disclosures. The aim of performance materiality is to reduce the risk that the total of errors in balances, transactions and related disclosures does not in total exceed overall materiality.

Tutorial note: *Marks were also available for the ISA 320 definition of performance materiality:*

"Performance materiality means the amount or amounts set by the auditor at less than materiality for the financial statements as a whole to reduce to an appropriately low level the probability that the aggregate of uncorrected and undetected misstatements exceeds materiality for the financial statements as a whole. If applicable, performance materiality also refers to the amount or amounts set by the auditor at less than the materiality level or levels for particular classes of transactions, account balances or related disclosures."

(b) **Planning the audit**

(i) *Ratios*

Ratios to assist the audit supervisor in planning the audit:

	2017	2016
Gross margin	$5 \cdot 5 \div 12 \cdot 5 = 44\%$	$7 \div 15 = 46 \cdot 7\%$
Operating margin	$0 \cdot 5 \div 12 \cdot 5 = 4\%$	$1 \cdot 9 \div 15 = 12 \cdot 7\%$
Inventory days	$1 \cdot 9 \div 7 \times 365 = 99$ days	$1 \cdot 4 \div 8 \times 365 = 64$ days
Inventory turnover	$7 \div 1 \cdot 9 = 3 \cdot 7$	$8 \div 1 \cdot 4 = 5 \cdot 7$
Receivable days	$3 \cdot 1 \div 12 \cdot 5 \times 365 = 91$ days	$2 \cdot 0 \div 15 \times 365 = 49$ days
Payable days	$1 \cdot 6 \div 7 \times 365 = 83$ days	$1 \cdot 2 \div 8 \times 365 = 55$ days
Current ratio	$5 \cdot 8 \div 2 \cdot 6 = 2 \cdot 2$	$5 \cdot 3 \div 1 \cdot 2 = 4 \cdot 4$
Quick ratio	$(5 \cdot 8 - 1 \cdot 9) \div 2 \cdot 6 = 1 \cdot 5$	$(5 \cdot 3 - 1 \cdot 4) \div 1 \cdot 2 = 3 \cdot 3$

(ii) *Audit risk*

Audit risk	*Audit response*
Receivable days have increased from 49 to 91 days and management has significantly extended the credit terms given to customers. This leads to an increased risk of recoverability of receivables as they may be overvalued.	Extended post year-end cash receipts testing and a review of the aged receivables ledger to be performed to assess valuation.
Due to the fall in demand for Kangaroo's houses, there are some houses where the selling price may be below cost. IAS 2 *Inventories* requires that inventory should be stated at the lower of cost and NRV.	Detailed cost and net realisable value (NVR) testing to be performed and the aged inventory report to be reviewed to assess whether inventory requires writing down.
In addition, inventory days have increased from 64 to 99 days and inventory turnover has fallen from $5 \cdot 7$ in 2016 to $3 \cdot 7$ in the current year. There is a risk that inventory is overvalued.	
The directors have extended the useful lives of plant and machinery from three to five years, resulting in the depreciation charge reducing. Under IAS 16 *Property, Plant and Equipment*, useful lives are to be reviewed annually, and if asset lives have genuinely increased, then this change is reasonable.	Discuss with the directors the rationale for extending the useful lives. Also, the five year life should be compared to how often these assets are replaced, as this provides evidence of the useful life of assets.
However, there is a risk that this reduction has occurred in order to achieve profit targets. If this is the case, then plant and machinery is overvalued and profit overstated.	

Audit risk

The directors need to reach a profit level of $0·5 million in order to receive their annual bonus. There is a risk that they might feel under pressure to manipulate the results through the judgements taken or through the use of provisions.

Due to a change in material supplier, the quality of products used has deteriorated and this has led to customers claiming on their five-year building warranty. If the overall number of people claiming on the warranty is likely to increase, then the warranty provision should possibly be higher. If the directors have not increased the level of the provision, there is a risk the provision is understated.

Kangaroo has borrowed $1·0m from the bank via a short-term loan. This loan needs to be repaid in the current year and so should be disclosed as a current liability.

In addition, Kangaroo may have given the bank a charge over its assets as security for the loan. There is a risk that the disclosure of any security given is not complete.

The current and quick ratios have decreased from 4·4 to 2·2 and 3·3 to 1·5 respectively. In addition, the cash balances have decreased over the year, there is a fall in demand and Kangaroo have taken out a short-term loan of $1 million, which needs to be repaid in in the current year.

Although all ratios are above the minimum levels, this is still a significant decrease and along with the fall in both operating and gross profit margins, as well as the significant increase in payable days could be evidence of going concern difficulties.

Audit response

Throughout the audit, the team will need to be alert to this risk and maintain professional scepticism. They will need to carefully review judgemental decisions and compare treatment against prior years. In addition, a written representation should be obtained from management confirming the basis of any significant judgements.

Review the level of the warranty provision in light of the increased level of claims to confirm completeness of the provision.

During the audit, the team would need to check that the $1·0m loan finance was received. In addition, the disclosures for this loan should be reviewed in detail to ensure compliance with relevant accounting standards and legislation.

The loan correspondence should be reviewed to ascertain whether any security has been given, and this bank should be circularised as part of the bank confirmation process.

Detailed going concern testing to be performed during the audit and discussed with the directors to ensure that the going concern basis is reasonable.

The team should discuss with the directors how the short-term loan of $1·0 million will be repaid later in the year.

Tutorial note: *It has been assumed that customers do not pay in advance for houses and hence the company has receivable balances.*

Answer 24 BESTWOOD ENGINEERING

(a)   **Purchase and receipt of goods**

> **Tutorial note:** *The question specifically refers to controls to be exercised in the purchasing department.*

For all goods ordered, there should be a purchase requisition from a user department. The purchasing department should not be permitted to raise purchase requisitions as this would create a weakness in the division of duties.

The purchasing department should check the purchase requisition is for goods the user department is authorised to buy or consume. If the value of the order is substantial, the purchasing department should ensure there is a need for such a large order by checking current inventory levels and future orders to determine whether so large a quantity or value is required.

The purchase requisition should use a standard form and be signed by an authorised signatory.

The purchasing department should order the goods from an authorised vendor. Where there is a choice of vendor or a new vendor is required, the purchasing department should obtain the product from the vendor who provides the product or service at the best price, quality and delivery.

The purchasing department should raise the purchase order which should be signed by the purchasing manager. For large value purchases, a director may be required to sign the purchase order. The purchase order should be sent to the vendor, the goods received department, the user department and the accounts department.

The purchasing department should ensure the goods are received on time. This may require them to contact the vendor a week before the expected delivery date to ensure they are received on time, and allow action to be taken if the delivery date is later than specified on the purchase order.

When the goods are received the purchasing department should receive a copy of the goods received note (GRN) from the goods received department. They should record the goods received against the order.

The purchasing department may be part of the system which authorises purchase invoices. They should check the goods on the invoice are consistent with the purchase order/GRN and the price per unit is correct.

The purchasing department should be informed about short deliveries (i.e. the quantity of goods received is less than on the purchase order or advice note) and when there are quality problems. From this information, they can contact the vendor so that corrective action is taken. Also, such details may be helpful in determining whether the vendor should be used for future orders.

The purchasing department should be informed of situations when goods or services are received but no purchase order has been raised. With this information, the purchasing department should contact the "offending" department and ensure that in future a purchase order is raised for all the goods they order.

(b) **Authorisation of purchase invoices**

Tutorial note: *The question calls for control procedures in the accounts department before the purchase invoice is processed.*

The accounts department will receive the purchase invoice, which they should record in a register.

The expense code will be entered on the invoice (for posting to the general ledger).

The accounts department will either match the purchase invoice to the goods received note and delivery note or ask the goods received department to check and authorise the purchase invoice.

The purchasing department will be asked to confirm the goods are as described on the purchase order and the price per unit is correct.

The user department may be asked to authorise the purchase invoice.

An appropriate responsible official will be asked to finally approve the purchase invoice.

Provided these checks are satisfactory, the accounts department should input the invoice details into the computer which will post it to the accounts payable ledger and the general ledger.

An independent person should check monthly supplier statements against the balances on the accounts payable ledger. Differences between these two balances should be investigated for correction of possible error or omission.

(c) **Controls over purchase of services**

Procedures over receiving services are inherently different to those over receiving goods.

For some types of service there may be no system for raising purchase orders (e.g. electricity, gas, water and telephone charges). However there should be a system for reviewing these costs, by comparing them with the previous year (or period), with budget and with amounts charged by alternative vendors. In this way, the company can ensure these services are received at the most economical cost.

For receipt of all other services, before the service is obtained, a purchase requisition could be raised by the user department, and the purchasing department should raise a purchase order. In emergency situations, it may be acceptable to raise a purchase requisition and order after the service has been received (e.g. the repair of a vehicle which has broken down).

There should be a system whereby action is taken when no purchase order has been raised for a service which has been received.

The major controls over validity and cost of services (e.g. advertising, training, etc) will be monitoring and control over cost:

- Budgets set for major activities, suitably analysed;
- Monitoring of actual cost against budget;
- Informing cost centres of charges allocated to them from incoming invoices;
- Cost centre approval of invoices;
- Management review of performance including efficiency and effectiveness of the services received.

Answer 25 PEAR INTERNATIONAL I

(a) **Internal control**

(i) Deficiency	*(ii)* Control	*(iii)* Test of control
Currently the website is not integrated into inventory system. This can result in Pear accepting customer orders when they do not have the goods in inventory. This can cause them to lose sales and customer goodwill.	The website should be updated to include an interface into the inventory system; this should check inventory levels and only process orders if adequate inventory is held. If inventory is not available, this should appear on the website with an approximate waiting time.	Test data could be used to attempt to process orders via the website for items which are not currently held in inventory. The orders should be flagged as currently unavailable and indicate an approximate waiting time.
For goods despatched by local couriers, customer signatures are not always obtained. This can lead to customers falsely claiming that they have not received their goods. Pear would not be able to prove that they had in fact despatched the goods and may result in goods being despatched twice.	Pear should remind all local couriers that customer signatures must be obtained as proof of despatch and payment will not be made for any despatches with missing signatures.	Select a sample of despatches by couriers and ask Pear for proof of despatch by viewing customer signatures.
There have been a number of situations where the sales orders have not been fulfilled in a timely manner. This can lead to a loss of customer goodwill and if it persists will damage the reputation of Pear as a reliable supplier.	Once goods are despatched they should be matched to sales orders and flagged as fulfilled. The system should automatically flag any outstanding sales orders past a predetermined period, such as five days. This report should be reviewed by a responsible official.	Review the report of outstanding sales orders. If significant, discuss with a responsible official to understand why there is still a significant time period between sales order and despatch date. Select a sample of sales orders and compare the date of order to the goods despatch date to ascertain whether this is within the acceptable predetermined period.

AUDIT AND ASSURANCE (F8) – REVISION QUESTION BANK

(i) Deficiency	(ii) Control	(iii) Test of control
Customer credit limits are set by sales ledger clerks. Sales ledger clerks are not sufficiently senior and so may set limits too high, leading to irrecoverable debts, or too low, leading to a loss of sales.	Credit limits should be set by a senior member of the sales ledger department and not by sales ledger clerks. These limits should be regularly reviewed by a responsible official.	For a sample of new customers accepted in the year, review the authorisation of the credit limit, and ensure that this was performed by a responsible official. Enquire of sales ledger clerks as to who can set credit limits.
Sales discounts are set by Pear's sales team. In order to boost their sales, members of the sales team may set the discounts too high, leading to a loss of revenue.	All members of the sales team should be given authority to grant sales discounts up to a set limit. Any sales discounts above these limits should be authorised by sales area managers or the sales director.	Discuss with members of the sales team the process for setting sales discounts.
	Regular review of sales discount levels should be undertaken by the sales director, and this review should be evidenced.	Review the sales discount report for evidence of review by the sales director.
Supplier statement reconciliations are no longer performed. This may result in errors in the recording of purchases and payables not being identified in a timely manner.	Supplier statement reconciliations should be performed on a monthly basis for all suppliers and these should be reviewed by a responsible official.	Review the file of reconciliations to ensure that they are being performed on a regular basis and that they have been reviewed by a responsible official.
Changes to supplier details in the purchase ledger master file can be undertaken by purchase ledger clerks. This could lead to key supplier data being accidently amended or fictitious suppliers being set up, which can increase the risk of fraud.	Only purchase ledger supervisors should have the authority to make changes to master file data. This should be controlled via passwords.	Request a purchase ledger clerk to attempt to access the master file and to make an amendment, the system should not allow this.
	Regular review of any changes to master file data by a responsible official and this review should be evidenced.	Review a report of master data changes and review the authority of those making amendments.

1052

(i) Deficiency	*(ii)* Control	*(iii)* Test of control
Pear has considerable levels of surplus plant and equipment. Surplus unused plant is at risk of theft. In addition, if the surplus plant is not disposed of then the company could lose sundry income.	Regular review of the plant and equipment on the factory floor by senior factory personnel to identify any old or surplus equipment. As part of the capital expenditure process there should be a requirement to confirm the treatment of the equipment being replaced.	Observe the review process by senior factory personnel, identifying the treatment of any old equipment. Review processed capital expenditure forms to ascertain if the treatment of replaced equipment is stated.
Purchase requisitions are authorised by production supervisors. Production supervisors are not sufficiently independent or senior to authorise capital expenditure.	Capital expenditure authorisation levels to be established. Production supervisors should only be able to authorise low value items, any high value items should be authorised by the board.	Review a sample of authorised capital expenditure forms and identify if the correct signatory has authorised them.

(b) **Internal and external audit**

(i) *Differences*

External Audit	**Internal Audit**

Objective

The main objective of the external auditor is to express an opinion on the truth and fairness of the financial statements.	The main objective of internal audit is to improve a company's operations, by reviewing the efficiency and effectiveness of the company's internal controls.

Reporting

External auditors report to the shareholders or members of the company. External audit reports are contained within the financial statements and hence are publicly available.	Internal auditors normally report to management or those charged with governance. Internal audit reports not publicly available and are only intended to be seen by the addressee of the report. The reports are normally provided to the board of directors and those charged with governance such as the audit committee.

Scope of work

The external auditor's work is limited to verifying the truth and fairness of the financial statements of the company.	The internal auditor can have a wide scope of work and it is determined by the requirements of management or those charged with governance. Commonly internal audit focus on the company's internal control environment, but any other area of a company's operations can be reviewed.

Relationship with company

External auditors are appointed by the company's shareholders. They are independent of the company.	Internal auditors are appointed by management. As internal auditors are normally employees of the company they lack independence. However, the internal audit department can be outsourced and this can increase their independence.

(ii) *Impact of work performed*

Interim audit

Apple & Co could look to rely on any internal control documentation produced by internal audit (IA) as they would need to assess whether the control environment has changed during the year.

If the IA department has performed testing during the year on internal control systems, such as the payroll, sales and purchase systems, then Apple & Co could review and possibly place reliance on this work. This may result in the workload reducing and possibly a decrease in the external audit fee.

During the interim audit, Apple & Co would need to perform a risk assessment to assist in the planning process. It is possible that the IA department may have conducted a risk assessment and so Apple could use this as part of their initial planning process.

Apple & Co would need to consider the risk of fraud and error and non-compliance with law and regulations resulting in misstatements in the financial statements. This is also an area for IA to consider, hence there is scope for Apple & Co to review the work and testing performed by IA to assist in this risk assessment.

Final audit

It is possible that the IA department may assist with year-end inventory counting and controls and so Apple & Co can place some reliance on the work performed by them, however, they would still need to attend the count and perform their own reduced testing.

Answer 26 OREGANO

(a)   Documenting the sales and despatch system

There are several methods which can be used by the internal audit department of Oregano to document its system.

Narrative notes

Narrative notes consist of a written description of the system; they would detail what occurs in the system at each stage and would include any controls which operate at each stage.

Advantages

■   They are simple to record; after discussion with staff members of Oregano, these discussions are easily written up as notes.

■   They can facilitate understanding by all members of the internal audit team, especially more junior members who might find alternative methods too complex.

Disadvantages

■   Narrative notes may prove to be too cumbersome, especially if the sales and distribution system is complex.

■   This method can make it more difficult to identify missing internal controls as the notes record the detail but do not identify control exceptions clearly.

Questionnaires

Internal control questionnaires (ICQ) or internal control evaluation questionnaires (ICEQ) contain a list of questions; ICQs are used to assess whether controls exist whereas ICEQs test the effectiveness of the controls.

Advantages

■   Questionnaires are quick to prepare, which means they are a timely method for recording the system.

■   They ensure that all controls present within the system are considered and recorded; hence missing controls or deficiencies are clearly highlighted by the internal audit team.

Disadvantages

- It can be easy for the staff members of Oregano to overstate the level of the controls present as they are asked a series of questions relating to potential controls.

- A standard list of questions may miss out unusual controls of Oregano.

Flowcharts

Flowcharts are a graphic illustration of the internal control system for the sales and despatch system. Lines usually demonstrate the sequence of events and standard symbols are used to signify controls or documents.

Advantages

- It is easy to view the sales system in its entirety as it is all presented together in one diagram.

- Due to the use of standard symbols for controls, they are easy to spot as are any missing controls.

Disadvantages

- They can sometimes be difficult to amend, as any amendments may require the whole flowchart to be redrawn.

- There is still the need for narrative notes to accompany the flowchart and hence it can be a time consuming method.

Tutorial note: *Full marks will be awarded for describing TWO methods for documenting the sales and despatch system and explaining ONE advantage and ONE disadvantage for each method.*

(b) **Control objectives for sales and despatch system**

- To ensure that orders are only accepted if goods are available to be processed for customers.

- To ensure that all orders are recorded completely and accurately.

- To ensure that goods are not supplied to poor credit risks.

- To ensure that goods are despatched for all orders on a timely basis.

- To ensure that goods are despatched correctly to customers and that they are of an adequate quality.

- To ensure that all goods despatched are correctly invoiced.

- To ensure completeness of income for goods despatched.

- To ensure that sales discounts are only provided to valid customers.

Tutorial note: *Only two were required for full marks.*

(c) **Deficiencies and controls for Oregano sales and despatch system**

Deficiency	*Control*
Inventory availability for telephone orders is not checked at the time the order is placed. The order clerks manually check the availability later and only then inform customers if there is insufficient inventory available. There is the risk that where goods are not available, order clerks could forget to contact the customers, leading to unfulfilled orders. This could lead to customer dissatisfaction, and would impact Oregano's reputation.	When telephone orders are placed, the order clerk should check the inventory system whilst the customer is on the phone; they can then give an accurate assessment of the availability of goods and there is no risk of forgetting to inform customers.
Telephone orders are not recorded immediately on the three part pre-printed order forms; these are completed after the telephone call. There is a risk that incorrect or insufficient details may be recorded by the clerk and this could result in incorrect orders being despatched or orders failing to be despatched at all, resulting in a loss of customer goodwill.	All telephone orders should be recorded immediately on the three part pre-printed order forms. The clerk should also double check all the details taken with the customer over the telephone to ensure the accuracy of the order recorded.
Telephone orders are not sequentially numbered. Therefore if orders are misplaced whilst in transit to the despatch department, these orders will not be fulfilled, resulting in dissatisfied customers.	The three part pre-printed orders forms should be sequentially numbered and on a regular basis the despatch department should run a sequence check of orders received. Where there are gaps in the sequence, they should be investigated to identify any missing orders.
Customers are able to place online orders which will exceed their agreed credit limit by 10%. This increases the risk of accepting orders from bad credit risks.	Customer credit limits should be reviewed more regularly by a responsible official and should reflect the current spending pattern of customers. If some customers have increased the level of their purchases and are making payments on time, then these customers' credit limits could be increased. The online ordering system should be amended to not allow any orders to be processed which will exceed the customer's credit limit.
A daily pick list is used by the despatch department when sending out customer orders. However, it does not appear that the goods are checked back to the original order; this could result in incorrect goods being sent out.	In addition to the pick list, copies of all the related orders should be printed on a daily basis. When the goods have been picked ready to be despatched, they should be cross checked back to the original order. They should check correct quantities and product descriptions, as well as checking the quality of goods being despatched to ensure they are not damaged.

Deficiency	Control
Additional staff have been drafted in to help the two sales clerks produce the sales invoices. As the extra staff will not be as experienced as the sales clerks, there is an increased risk of mistakes being made in the sales invoices. This could result in customers being under or overcharged.	Only the sales clerks should be able to raise sales invoices. As Oregano is expanding, consideration should be given to recruiting and training more permanent sales clerks who can produce sales invoices.
Discounts given to customers are manually entered onto the sales invoices by sales clerks. This could result in unauthorised sales discounts being given as there does not seem to be any authorisation required.	For customers who are due to receive a discount, the authorised discount levels should be updated to the customer master file. When the sales invoices for these customers are raised, their discounts should automatically appear on the invoice.
In addition, a clerk could forget to manually enter the discount or enter an incorrect level of discount for a customer, leading to the sales invoice being overstated and a loss of customer goodwill.	The invoicing system should be amended to prevent sales clerks from being able to manually enter sales discounts onto invoices.

Answer 27 CHERRY BLOSSOM

Item	Answer	Justification
1	A	It is not a control deficiency for production supervisors to complete requisitions and submit them to the purchase ordering department. This is generally how purchases are initiated. The other three options are control deficiencies. The warehouse department should check goods received against the original purchase order as well as the supplier's despatch note. Purchase invoices should be numbered sequentially, not based on supplier code. Payment should be in accordance with supplier's terms and take account of early settlement discounts.
2	D	Statement (2) is not a control that should be used to address the purchase ordering department control deficiencies because the finance director should only be responsible for authorising payments. Statements (1), (3) and (4) are all controls that address the purchasing department's control deficiencies.
3	B	(1) is an example of authorisation (showing that the financial accountant has reviewed the reconciliation). (2) Is an example of performance reviews which includes reviews and analyses of actual performance against budgets (as here), forecasts and prior period performance.
4	A	Authorisation of transactions, custody or handling of assets and recording of transactions are the three functions which should ideally be separated such that no-one person can initiate the transaction, record that transaction in the accounting records and have custody of assets which arise from that transaction.
5	C	The goods received note is only raised when quality has been checked and confirmed to be satisfactory. Therefore, matching purchase invoices with invoices with good received notes will identify goods that have been returned/rejected (e.g. due to poor quality).
		Tutorial note: *Since unmatched invoices would not then be processed they could not then be paid.*

Answer 28 DOCUMENTATION AND MATERIALITY

(a)   **Documenting audit work**

- Provides evidence of the auditor's basis for a conclusion about the achievement of the overall objective of the audit.

- Provides evidence that the audit was planned and performed in accordance with ISAs and applicable legal and regulatory requirements.

- Assists the engagement team to plan and perform the audit.

- Assists members of the engagement team responsible for supervision to direct, supervise and review the audit work.

- Enables the engagement team to be accountable for its work.

- Retains a record of matters of continuing significance to future audits.

(b)   **Materiality**

Materiality is defined as "misstatements, including omissions, are considered to be material if they, individually or in the aggregate, could reasonably be expected to influence the economic decisions of users taken on the basis of the financial statements".

In assessing the level of materiality there are a number of areas that should be considered. Firstly the auditor must consider both the amount (quantity) and the nature (quality) of any misstatements, or a combination of both. The quantity of the misstatement refers to the relative size of it and the quality refers to an amount that might be low in value but due to its prominence could influence the user's decision (e.g. directors' transactions).

In assessing materiality the auditor must consider that a number of errors each with a low value may when aggregated amount to a material misstatement.

The assessment of what is material is ultimately a matter of the auditors' professional judgement, and it is affected by the auditor's perception of the financial information needs of users of the financial statements.

In calculating materiality the auditor should also consider setting the performance materiality level. This is the amount set by the auditor, it is below materiality, and is used for particular transactions, account balances and disclosures.

As per ISA 320 materiality is often calculated using benchmarks such as 5% of profit before tax or 1% of gross revenue. These values are useful as a starting point for assessing materiality.

Answer 29 TYE

Tutorial note: *This 20-mark question relates mainly to syllabus area A and is therefore non-exam style. Section B will predominantly examine one or more aspects of syllabus areas B, C or D.*

(a) **Valuation of aviation inventory**

- Review GAAP to ensure that there are no exceptions for aviation fuel or inventory held for emergency purposes which would suggest a market valuation should be used.

- Calculate the difference in valuation. The error in inventory valuation is $105 * 6,000 barrels or $630k, which is a material amount compared to profit.

- Review prior year working papers to determine whether a similar situation occurred last year and ascertain the outcome at that stage.

- Discuss the matter with the directors to obtain reasons why they believe that market value should be used for the inventory this year.

- Warn the directors that in your opinion, aviation fuel should be valued at the lower of cost or net realisable value (that is $15/barrel) and that using market value will result in a modification to the audit report.

- If the directors now amend the financial statements to show inventory valued at cost, then consider mentioning the issue in the weakness letter and do not modify the audit report in respect of this matter.

- If the directors will not amend the financial statements, quantify the effect of the disagreement in the valuation method – the sum of $630,000 is material to the financial statements as Tye's loss is decreased from a small loss to a loss of $130,000 although net assets decrease by only about 0·3%.

- Obtain written representations from the directors of Tye confirming that market value is to be used for the emergency inventory of aviation fuel.

- If the directors will not amend the financial statements, draft the relevant sections of the audit report, showing a qualification on the grounds of disagreement with the accounting policy for valuation of inventory.

(b) **Audit procedures and actions**

(i) *External auditor responsibilities regarding detection of fraud*

Overall responsibility of auditor

The external auditor is primarily responsible for the audit opinion on the financial statements following the international auditing standards (ISAs). ISA 240 *The Auditor's Responsibilities Relating to Fraud in an Audit of Financial Statements* is relevant to audit work regarding fraud.

The main focus of audit work is therefore to ensure that the financial statements show a true and fair view. The detection of fraud is therefore not the main focus of the external auditor's work. An auditor is responsible for obtaining reasonable assurance that the financial statements as a whole are free from material misstatement, whether caused by fraud or error.

The auditor is responsible for maintaining an attitude of professional scepticism throughout the audit, considering the potential for management override of controls and recognising the fact that audit procedures that are effective for detecting error may not be effective for detecting fraud.

Materiality

ISA 240 states that the auditor should reduce audit risk to an acceptably low level.

Therefore, in reaching the audit opinion and performing audit work, the external auditor takes into account the concept of materiality. In other words, the external auditor is not responsible for checking all the transactions. Audit procedures are planned to have a reasonable likelihood of identifying material fraud.

Discussion among the audit team

A discussion is required among the engagement team placing particular emphasis on how and where the entity's financial statements may be susceptible to material misstatement due to fraud, including how fraud might occur.

Identification of fraud

In situations where the external auditor does detect fraud, then the auditor will need to consider the implications for the entire audit. In other words, the external auditor has a responsibility to extend testing into other areas because the risk of providing an incorrect audit opinion will have increased.

(ii)   Groups to report fraud to

Report to audit committee

Disclose the situation to the audit committee as they are charged with maintaining a high standard of governance in the company.

The committee should be able to discuss the situation with the directors and recommend that they take appropriate action (e.g. amend the financial statements).

Report to government

As Tye is acting under a government contract, and the over-statement of inventory will mean Tye breaches that contract (the reported profit becoming a loss), then the auditor may have to report the situation directly to the government. The auditor of Tye needs to review the contract to confirm the reporting required under that contract.

Report to members

If the financial statements do not show a true and fair view then the auditor needs to report this fact to the members of Tye. The audit report will be modified with an except for or adverse opinion (depending on materiality) and information concerning the reason for the disagreement given. In this case the auditor is likely to state factually the problem of inventory quantities being incorrect, rather than stating or implying that the directors are involved in fraud.

Report to professional body

If the auditor is uncertain as to the correct course of action, advice may be obtained from the auditor's professional body. Depending on the advice received, the auditor may simply report to the members in the audit report, although resignation and the convening of a general meeting is another reporting option.

(iii)   *Intimidation threat – safeguards*

In response to the implied threat of dismissal if the audit report is modified regarding the potential fraud/error, the following safeguards are available to the auditor.

Discuss with audit committee

The situation can be discussed with the audit committee. As the audit committee should comprise non-executive directors, they will be able to discuss the situation with the finance director and point out clearly the auditor's opinion.

They can also remind the directors as a whole that the appointment of the auditor rests with the members on the recommendation of the audit committee. If the recommendation of the audit committee is rejected by the board, good corporate governance requires disclosure of the reason for rejection.

Obtain second partner review

The engagement partner can ask a second partner to review the working papers and other evidence relating to the issue of possible fraud. While this action does not resolve the issue, it does provide additional assurance that the findings and actions of the engagement partner are valid.

Resignation

If the matter is serious, then the auditor can consider resignation rather than not being re-appointed. Resignation has the additional safeguard that the auditor can normally require the directors to convene a general meeting to consider the circumstances of the resignation.

Answer 30 BESTWOOD TRADING

Item	Answer	Justification
1	D	(1), (2) and (3) are all reasons why auditors use working papers. (4) is not correct because the existence of working papers does not necessarily enable the auditor to escape liability in a subsequent lawsuit, especially if the working papers reveal that the auditor did not comply with audit regulations or show that conclusions were unreasonable.
2	B	(A), (C) and (D) must be tailored to suit each individual audit client and for each client they must be reviewed and updated for the circumstances of each year. Once set up, the bank confirmation letter (B) follows a standard format each year.
3	A	The late banking of cash receipts should have been reported to management and those charged with governance even though it was immaterial.
4	D	The discovery of unexplained payments to government employees is a possible indicator of non-compliance with laws and regulations. (A) is an internal control weakness. (B) and (C) are not indicators of non-compliance.
5	D	All can be used as a defence in this situation. Note that (1) is the best defence because it would encompass (2) and (3). Denial of responsibility can be a defence, although it is not as good as having evidence to show that the audit was properly conducted.

Answer 31 SYCAMORE SCIENCE

(a)   **Fraud responsibility**

Maple & Co must conduct an audit in accordance with ISA 240 *The Auditor's Responsibilities Relating to Fraud in an Audit of Financial Statements* and are responsible for obtaining reasonable assurance that the financial statements taken as a whole are free from material misstatement, whether caused by fraud or error.

In order to fulfil this responsibility, Maple & Co is required to identify and assess the risks of material misstatement of the financial statements due to fraud.

They need to obtain sufficient appropriate audit evidence regarding the assessed risks of material misstatement due to fraud, through designing and implementing appropriate responses. In addition, Maple & Co must respond appropriately to fraud or suspected fraud identified during the audit.

When obtaining reasonable assurance, Maple & Co is responsible for maintaining professional scepticism throughout the audit, considering the potential for management override of controls and recognising the fact that audit procedures which are effective in detecting error may not be effective in detecting fraud.

To ensure that the whole engagement team is aware of the risks and responsibilities for fraud and error, ISAs require that a discussion is held within the team. For members not present at the meeting, Sycamore's audit engagement partner should determine which matters are to be communicated to them.

(b)

Audit risks	Auditors' responses
Sycamore's previous finance director left in December after it was discovered that he had been committing fraud with regards to expenses claimed.	Discuss with the new finance director what procedures they have adopted to identify any further frauds by the previous finance director.
There is a risk that he may have undertaken other fraudulent transactions; these would need to be written off in the statement of profit or loss. If these have not been uncovered, the financial statements could include errors.	In addition, the team should maintain their professional scepticism and be alert to the risk of further fraud and errors.
The new finance director was appointed in January 2016 and was previously a financial controller of a bank. Sycamore is a pharmaceutical company which is very different to a bank; there is a risk that the new finance director is not sufficiently competent to prepare the financial statements, leading to errors.	During the audit, careful attention should be applied to any changes in accounting policies and in particular any key judgemental decisions made by the finance director.

Audit risks	Auditors' responses
During the year, Sycamore has spent $1·8 million on developing new products; these are at different stages and the total amount has been capitalised as an intangible asset. However, in order to be capitalised it must meet all of the criteria under IAS 38 *Intangible Assets*. There is a risk that some projects may not reach final development stage and hence should be expensed rather than capitalised. Intangible assets and profit could be overstated.	A breakdown of the development expenditure should be reviewed and tested in detail to ensure that only projects which meet the capitalisation criteria are included as an intangible asset, with the balance being expensed.
Sycamore has borrowed $2·0 million from the bank via a ten-year loan. This loan needs to be correctly split between current and non-current liabilities in order to ensure correct disclosure.	During the audit, the team would need to confirm that the $2·0 million loan finance was received. In addition, the split between current and non-current liabilities and the disclosures for this loan should be reviewed in detail to ensure compliance with relevant accounting standards.
Also as the level of debt has increased, there should be additional finance costs. There is a risk that this has been omitted from the statement of profit or loss, leading to understated finance costs and overstated profit.	The finance costs should be recalculated and any increase agreed to the loan documentation for confirmation of interest rates and cashbook and bank statements to confirm the amount was paid and is not therefore a year-end payable.
The loan has a minimum profit target covenant. If this is breached, the loan would be instantly repayable and would be classified as a current liability.	Review the covenant calculations prepared by Sycamore and identify whether any defaults have occurred; if so, determine the effect on the company.
If the company does not have sufficient cash flow to meet this loan repayment, there could be going concern implications. In addition, there is a risk of manipulation of profit to ensure that covenants are met.	The team should maintain their professional scepticism and be alert to the risk that profit has been overstated to ensure compliance with the covenant.
There have been a significant number of sales returns made subsequent to the year end. As these relate to pre year-end sales, they should be removed from revenue in the draft financial statements and the inventory reinstated.	Review a sample of the post year-end sales returns and confirm if they relate to pre year-end sales, that the revenue has been reversed and the inventory included in the year-end ledgers.
If the sales returns have not been correctly recorded, then revenue will be overstated and inventory understated.	In addition, the reason for the increased level of returns should be discussed with management. This will help to assess if there are underlying issues with the net realisable value of inventory.
During Sycamore's year-end inventory count there were movements of goods in and out. If these goods in transit were not carefully controlled, then goods could have been omitted or counted twice. This would result in inventory being under or overstated.	During the final audit, the goods received notes and goods despatched notes received during the inventory count should be reviewed and followed through into the inventory count records as correctly included or not.

Audit risks	Auditors' responses
Surplus plant and equipment was sold during the year, resulting in a profit on disposal of $210,000. As there is a minimum profit loan covenant, there is a risk that this profit on disposal may not have been correctly calculated, resulting in overstated profits.	Recalculate the profit and loss on disposal calculations and agree all items to supporting documentation.
In addition, significant profits or losses on disposal are an indication that the depreciation policy of plant and equipment may not be appropriate. Therefore depreciation may be overstated.	Discuss the depreciation policy for plant and equipment with the finance director to assess its reasonableness.

(c) **Review engagements**

(i) *Purpose and how differ from external audit*

Review engagements are often undertaken as an alternative to an audit, and involve a practitioner reviewing financial data, such as six-monthly figures. This would involve the practitioner undertaking procedures to state whether anything has come to their attention which causes the practitioner to believe that the financial data is not in accordance with the financial reporting framework.

A review engagement differs to an external audit in that the procedures undertaken are not nearly as comprehensive as those in an audit, with procedures such as analytical review and enquiry used extensively. In addition, the practitioner does not need to comply with ISAs as these only relate to external audits.

(ii) *Levels of assurance provided*

External audit – A high but not absolute level of assurance is provided, this is known as reasonable assurance. This provides comfort that the financial statements present fairly in all material respects (or are true and fair) and are free of material misstatements.

Review engagements – where an opinion is being provided, the practitioner gathers sufficient evidence to be satisfied that the subject matter is plausible; in this case negative assurance is given whereby the practitioner confirms that nothing has come to their attention which indicates that the subject matter contains material misstatements.

Answer 32 TINKERBELL

(a) **Sales cycle**

Tutorial note: *It is essential to give only tests of **control**, as asked for.*

Test of control	Objective of test
Attempt to enter an order for a fictitious customer account number. The system should not accept this order.	To ensure that orders are only accepted and processed for valid customers.
With the client's permission, attempt to enter a sales order which will take a customer over the agreed credit limit. The system should reject the order.	To ensure that goods are not supplied to poor credit risks.

Test of control	*Objective of test*
Inspect a sample of processed credit applications from the credit agency and follow through the credit limit agreed to the sales system.	To ensure that goods are only supplied to customers with good credit ratings.
Obtain a copy of the current price list and agree for a sample of invoices that relevant/current prices have been used.	To ensure that goods are only sold at authorised prices.
Confirm discounts applied to invoices agree to the customer master file.	To ensure that sales discounts are only provided to valid customers.
Attempt to process an order with a sales discount for a customer not normally entitled to discounts to assess the application controls.	
Inspect a sample of orders to confirm that an order acceptance email/letter has been generated.	To ensure that all orders are recorded completely and accurately.
Observe the sales order clerk processing orders and assess whether the order acceptance is automatically generated.	
Visit a warehouse and observe the goods despatch process to assess whether all goods are double checked against the goods despatch note (GDN) and the despatch list prior to sending out.	To ensure that goods are despatched correctly to customers and that they are of an adequate quality.
Inspect a sample of GDNs and agree that a valid sales invoice has been correctly raised.	To ensure that all goods despatched are correctly invoiced.
Review the last system generated sequence check of sales invoices to identify any omissions.	To ensure completeness of income for goods despatched.

(b)   Substantive procedures to confirm receivables balance

- Perform a positive confirmation request of a representative sample of year-end balances of trade receivables. For any non-replies, with Tinkerbell's permission, send a reminder letter to follow up.

- Review the after date cash receipts and follow through to pre-year-end receivable balances.

- Calculate average receivable days and compare this to prior year, investigate any significant differences.

- Review the reconciliation of sales ledger control account to the sales ledger list of balances.

- Select a sample of goods despatched notes (GDN) before and just after the year end and follow through to the sales invoice to ensure they are recorded in the correct accounting period.

- Inspect the aged receivables report to identify any slow moving balances, discuss these with the credit control manager to assess whether an allowance or write down is necessary.

- For any slow moving/aged balances review customer correspondence to assess whether there are any invoices in dispute.

- Review company board minutes to assess whether there are any material disputed receivables.

- Review a sample of post year-end credit notes to identify any that relate to pre-year-end transactions to verify that they have not been included in receivables.

- Review the sales ledger for any credit balances and discuss with management whether these should be reclassified as payables.

- Select a sample of year-end receivable balances and agree back to valid supporting documentation of GDN and sales order to ensure existence.

(c)

Controls to be implemented	How risk mitigated
Members of staff who are related should not be permitted to work in the same department whereby they can breach segregation of duty controls.	This should reduce the risk of staff colluding and being able to commit a fraud without easily being discovered.
Cash receipts should be processed by two members of staff.	This should reduce the risk of one person being able to steal cash receipts. In order to commit the fraud these two members of staff would need to collude and to avoid detection, also collude with other members of the finance team.
Monthly customer statements should be sent out promptly to all customers. The sales ledger supervisor should review to ensure that all customers have been sent statements.	If customers receive regular statements then they would be in a position to flag to Tinkerbell that there was a delay in their payments being credited to their accounts. This should then flag any possible "teeming and lading" fraud.
Bank reconciliations should be reviewed by a responsible official (different to the preparer of the reconciliation) on a regular basis. Any unreconciled amounts should be promptly investigated and resolved.	A small unreconciled amount can actually represent two large balances which almost cancel each other out and hence could indicate significant problems with cash and bank. Where fraud arises it can often be quickly spotted by performing and reviewing a bank reconciliation.
On a regular basis staff within the finance department should rotate duties.	If staff members know that they will need to rotate their roles then they will be less inclined to commit fraudulent activities, as the chances of them being caught increase significantly.
The sales ledger should be reconciled to the sales ledger control account on a monthly basis, and this reconciliation should be reviewed by a responsible official.	This will increase the likelihood of spotting errors in the receivable balances and help to create an environment of controls, which will decrease the likelihood of frauds occurring.

Controls to be implemented	How risk mitigated
Management should consider establishing an internal audit department which could assess the effectiveness of controls and identify areas of weaknesses, as well as perform specific fraud investigations.	As there has been a significant breakdown in the internal controls then the mere presence of an internal audit department would help to deter employees committing fraud. In addition, fraudulent activities would be more likely to be identified quicker as internal controls would be tested.

Tutorial note: The type of fraud is known as a "teeming and lading" fraud. Marks would be awarded for any additional general (but relevant) fraud points made.

(d) **Substantive procedures for revenue**

■ Compare the overall level of revenue against prior years and budget and investigate any significant fluctuations.

■ Obtain a schedule of sales for the year broken down into the major categories of toys manufactured and compare this to the prior year breakdown and for any unusual movements discuss with management.

■ Calculate the gross margin for Tinkerbell and compare this to the prior year and investigate any significant fluctuations.

■ Select a sample of sales invoices for larger customers and recalculate the discounts allowed to ensure that these are accurate.

■ Recalculate for a sample of invoices that the sales tax has been correctly applied to the sales invoice.

■ Select a sample of customer orders and agree these to the despatch notes and sales invoices through to inclusion in the sales ledger to ensure completeness of revenue.

■ Select a sample of despatch notes, both pre and post the year end, and follow these through to sales invoices in the correct accounting period to ensure that cut-off has been correctly applied.

■ Select a sample of credit notes issued after the year end and follow through to sales invoice to ensure the returns were recorded in the proper period.

Answer 33 BONSAI TRADING

Item	Answer	Justification
1	B	Statements (1) and (3) are tests of control. Statements (2) and (4) are substantive procedures.
2	A	Interviewing the controller is inquiry and verifying the proper preparation of a bank reconciliation by reviewing the signatures is inspection of records.
3	B	Interim substantive procedures should only be performed when the risk of material misstatement is low, such as when an account has little activity from year to year. A, C and D all have a high risk of material misstatement.

4   A   The auditor cannot assist Bonsai in implementing better internal controls (Statement (3)) as this would create a self-interest threat as the audit firm may be perceived as performing the role of management. Management is responsible for internal control. Statement (4) is not appropriate because the auditor's duty of confidentiality normally precludes any reporting to third parties.

5   B   B is the most accurate statement as the auditor clearly suspected possible fraud but failed to sufficiently investigate. A is incorrect as the engagement letter refers to "reasonable expectation". D is incorrect as the auditor has specific duties in relation to fraud and error and cannot pass them onto management. C is not appropriate as the auditor should design his tests to have "reasonable expectation" for those areas he considers to be at risk from fraud (not all areas).

Answer 34 BLAKE

(a)   **Control objectives – wages system**

- Employees are only paid for work that they have done.
- Gross pay has been calculated correctly.
- Gross pay has been authorised.
- Net pay has been calculated correctly.
- Gross and net pay have been recorded accurately in the general ledger.
- Only genuine employees are paid.
- Correct amounts are paid to taxation authorities.

Tutorial note: *Only four were required for full marks.*

(b)   **The Directors**
Blake Co
1701 Any Street
Big Town 31911

3 December 20XX

Dear Sirs
Report to Management

We write to bring to your attention weaknesses in your company's internal control systems and provide recommendations to alleviate those weaknesses.

(i) Weakness	*(ii) Possible effect*	*(iii) Recommendation*
The logging in process for employees is not monitored.	Employees could bring cards for absent employees to the assembly plant and scan that card for the employee; absent employees would effectively be paid for work not done.	The shift manager should reconcile the number of workers physically present on the production line with the computerised record of the number of employees logged in for work each shift.

(i) Weakness	(ii) Possible effect	(iii) Recommendation
Overtime is not authorised by a responsible official.	Employees may get paid for work not done (e.g. they may clock-off late in order to receive "overtime" payments).	All overtime should be authorised, either by the shift manager authorising an estimated amount of overtime prior to the shift commencing or by the manager confirming the recorded hours in the payroll department computer system after the shift has been completed.
The code word authorising the accuracy of time worked to the wages system is the name of the cat of the department head.	The code word is not secure and could be easily guessed by an employee outside the department (names of pets are commonly used passwords).	The code word should be based on a random sequence of letters and numbers and changed on a regular basis.
The total amount of net wages transferred to employees is not agreed to the total of the list of wages produced by the payroll department.	"Dummy" employees – payments that do not relate to any real employee – could be added to the payroll payments list in the accounts department.	Prior to net wages being sent to the bank for payment, the financial accountant should agree the total of the payments list to the total of wages from the payroll department.
Details of employees leaving the company are sent on an e-mail from the personnel department to payroll.	There is no check to ensure that all e-mails sent are actually received in the payroll department.	There needs to be a control to ensure all e-mails are received in personnel – pre-numbering of e-mails or tagging the e-mail to ensure a receipt is sent back to the personnel department will help meet this objective.
In the accounts department, the accounts clerk authorises payment of net wages to employees.	It is inappropriate that a junior member of staff should sign the payroll; the clerk may not be able to identify errors in the payroll or could even have included "dummy employees" and is now authorising payments to those "people".	The payroll should be authorised by a senior manager or finance director.

If you require any further information on the above, please do not hesitate to contact us.

Yours faithfully

Global Audit Co

Tutorial note: *Only five weaknesses were required to be addressed*

(c)   **Substantive analytical procedures**

Substantive analytical procedure	*Expectation*
Compare total salaries cost this year to total salaries cost last year.	Assuming that the number of shift managers has remained unchanged, the total salary expenditure should have increased by inflation only.
Ascertain how many shift managers are employed by Blake and the total salary from the personnel department. Calculate total salary and compare to the salary disclosed in the financial statements.	Total salary should be approximately number of managers multiplied by average salary.
Obtain a listing of total salary payments made each month.	The total payments should be roughly the same apart from July onwards when salaries increased and November when the annual bonus was paid.

(d)   **Collecting audit evidence**

Audit procedure	*Benefit to auditor in testing accuracy of time recording system*
Confirmation	
Confirmation is the process of obtaining a representation of information or of an existing condition directly from a third party.	Obtaining information from a third party will be difficult. The manufacturer of the time recording system could be approached to discuss known errors with the system; however, information provided may be limited by the need to protect the manufacturer's integrity.
	It is therefore unlikely that the auditor will benefit from this procedure.
Observation	
This procedure involves watching a procedure being performed by others – in this case watching shift-workers using the time recording system.	Testing will be limited to ensuring all shift-workers actually clock in and out when they arrive to and depart from work. The procedure has limited use as it only confirms it worked when shift-workers were observed. It also cannot confirm that hours have been recorded accurately.
Inquiry	
Inquiry involves obtaining information from client staff or external sources.	Inquiry only confirms that shift-workers confirm they clock-in or out. It does not directly confirm the action actually happened or the accuracy of the recording of hours worked.

Answer 35 GREYSTONE

(a)   **Matters to consider to determine significance of internal control deficiencies**

■   The likelihood of the deficiencies leading to material misstatements in the financial statements in the future.

■   The susceptibility to loss or fraud of the related asset or liability.

■   The subjectivity and complexity of determining estimated amounts.

■   The financial statement amounts exposed to the deficiencies.

■   The volume of activity that has occurred or could occur in the account balance or class of transactions exposed to the deficiency or deficiencies.

■   The importance of the controls to the financial reporting process.

■   The cause and frequency of the exceptions detected as a result of the deficiencies in the controls.

■   The interaction of the deficiency with other deficiencies in internal control.

Tutorial note: *ISA 265 "Communicating Deficiencies ... "states that a significant deficiency is one (or more in combination) that, in the auditor's professional judgement, is of sufficient importance to merit the attention of those charged with governance.*

(b)   **Report to management**

Board of Directors
Greystone Co
30 Any Street
A Town
X Country

8 December 2016

Dear Sirs

Audit of Greystone Co for year ended 30 September 2016

Please find enclosed the report to management on significant deficiencies in internal controls identified during the audit for the year ended 30 September 2016. The report considers deficiencies in the purchases system, implications of those deficiencies and provides recommendations to address those deficiencies.

(i) Deficiency	(ii) Implication	(iii) Recommendation
The purchasing manager decides on the inventory levels for each store without discussion with store or sales managers. The purchasing manager may not have the appropriate knowledge of the local market for a store.	This could result in stores ordering goods that are not likely to sell and hence require heavy discounting. In addition as a fashion chain, if customers perceive that the goods are not meeting the key fashion trends then they may cease to shop at Greystone at all.	The purchasing manager should initially hold a meeting with area managers of stores; if meeting all store managers is not practical, he should understand the local markets before agreeing jointly goods to be purchased.
The purchase orders are only reviewed and authorised by a purchasing director in a wholly aggregated manner (by specified regions of countries).	It will be difficult for the purchasing director to assess whether overall the correct buying decisions are being made as the detail of the orders is not being presented and he is the only level of authorisation.	A purchasing senior manager should review the information prepared for each country and discuss with local purchasing managers the specifics of their orders. These should then be authorised and passed to the purchasing director for final review and sign off.
	This could result in significant levels of goods being purchased that are not right for particular market sectors.	
The store managers are responsible for re-ordering goods through the purchasing manager.	If the store managers forget or order too late, then as the ordering process can take up to four weeks, the store could experience significant stock outs leading to loss of income.	Automatic re-order levels should be set up in the inventory management systems. As the goods sold reach the re-order levels the purchasing manager should receive an automatic re-order request.
It is not possible for a store to order goods from other local stores for customers who request them. Instead they are told to contact the stores themselves, or use the company website.	Customers are less likely to contact individual stores themselves and this could result in the company losing out on valuable sales.	An inter-branch transfer system should be established between stores. This should help stores whose goods are below the re-order level but are awaiting their deliveries from the suppliers.
	In addition some goods which are slow moving in one store may be out of stock at another, if goods could be transferred between stores then overall sales may be maximised.	

(i) Deficiency	(ii) Implication	(iii) Recommendation
Deliveries from suppliers are accepted without being checked first.	The stores are receiving goods without checking that these are correct. Hence if a delivery is subsequently disputed there may be little recourse for the company.	Deliveries from suppliers should only be accepted between designated hours such as the first two hours of the morning when it is quieter. The goods should then be checked on arrival for quantity and quality prior to acceptance from the supplier. A responsible official at each store should produce the GRN from the supplier's delivery information.
In addition they are then checked by sales assistants to the supplier's delivery note to agree quantities but not quality.	If the sales assistants are only checking quantities then goods which are not of a saleable condition may be accepted.	
Sales assistants are producing the goods received note (GRN) on receipt of a supplier's delivery note.	The assistants may not be adequately experienced to produce the GRN, and this is an important document used in the invoice authorisation process. Errors could lead to under or overpayments.	
Goods are being received without any checks being made against purchase orders.	This could result in Greystone receiving and subsequently paying for goods it did not require. In addition if no check is made against order then the company may have significant purchase orders which are outstanding, leading to lost sales.	A copy of the authorised order form should be sent to the store. This should then be checked to the GRN. Once checked the order should be sent to head office and logged as completed. On a regular basis the purchasing clerk should review the order file for any outstanding items.
Purchase invoices are manually matched to a high volume of GRNs from the individual stores.	A manual checking process increases the risk of error, resulting in invoices being accepted or rejected erroneously.	The checked GRNs should be logged onto the purchasing system, matched against the relevant order number, then as the invoice is received this should be automatically matched. The purchasing clerk should then review for any unmatched items.
The purchase invoice is only logged onto the system as it is being authorised by the purchasing director.	If the invoice is misplaced then payables may not be settled on a timely basis. In addition at the year end the purchase ledger may be understated as invoices relating to the current year have been received but are not in the purchase ledger.	Upon receipt of an invoice this should be logged into a file of unmatched invoices. As it is matched and authorised it should then be moved into the purchase ledger. At the year end, items in the unmatched invoices file should be accrued for, to ensure liabilities are not understated.

Please note that this report only addresses any significant deficiencies identified during the audit and if further testing had been performed then more deficiencies may have been reported.

This report is solely for the use of management and if you have any further questions then please do not hesitate to contact us.

Yours faithfully

An audit firm

(c)   **Substantive procedures over year-end trade payables**

- Obtain a listing of trade payables from the purchase ledger and agree to the general ledger and the financial statements.

- Reconcile the total of purchase ledger accounts with the purchase ledger control account, and cast the list of balances and the purchase ledger control account.

- Review the list of trade payables against prior years to identify any significant omissions.

- Calculate the trade payable days for Greystone and compare to prior years, investigate any significant differences.

- Review after date payments, if they relate to the current year then follow through to the purchase ledger or accrual listing to ensure completeness.

- Review after date invoices and credit notes to ensure no further items need to be accrued.

- Obtain supplier statements and reconcile these to the purchase ledger balances, and investigate any reconciling items.

- Select a sample of payable balances and perform trade payables' confirmation procedures. Follow up any non-replies and any reconciling items between balance confirmed and trade payables' balance.

- Enquire of management their process for identifying goods received but not invoiced or logged in the purchase ledger and ensure that it is reasonable to ensure completeness of payables.

- Select a sample of goods received notes before the year end and follow through to inclusion in the year-end payables balance, to ensure correct cut-off.

- Review the purchase ledger for any debit balances, for any significant amounts discuss with management and consider reclassification as current assets.

- Ensure payables included in financial statements as current liabilities.

(d)   **Additional assignments for Greystone's internal audit department**

Testing cash controls at stores

Currently the internal audit department undertake inventory counts at each of the stores. This role could be increased to include controls testing over cash receipts and cash counts. As a retailer the stores will have a significant amount of cash at each premise and will have tight controls over the cash receipts process. These controls should be tested at each location as well as performance of a cash count to reduce the level of fraud and error reported.

Mystery shopper reviews

In order to improve the customer experience in stores, internal audit department members could undertake "mystery shopper" reviews, where they enter the store as a customer, purchase goods and rate the overall shopping experience. This is then fed back to each shop to improve customer service and can provide the basis for further training if necessary.

Overall review of financial/operational controls

The department could undertake reviews of controls at head office, as well as individual stores and make recommendations to management over such areas as the purchasing process as well as the sales cycle.

Fraud investigations

It is likely that as a retailer, Greystone would have problems with theft of inventory as well as cash. Internal audit could be asked to review the main areas of fraud risk and develop controls to mitigate these risks. If fraud is suspected then internal audit could be asked to investigate these cases further.

IT system reviews

Greystone is likely to have a relatively complex computer system linking all of the tills in the stores to head office. The internal audit department could be asked to perform a review over the computer environment and controls.

Value for money review

The internal audit department could be asked to assess whether Greystone are obtaining value for money in areas such as the just in time ordering system recently introduced.

Regulatory compliance

Greystone operates in countries throughout the world and hence will be subject to varying degrees of law and regulation. The internal audit department could help ensure compliance with those regulations.

Answer 36 FOX INDUSTRIES

(a) **ISA 260 *Communication with Those Charged with Governance***

    (i)   *Importance of reporting to those charged with governance*

In accordance with ISA 260, it is important for the auditors to report to those charged with governance as it helps in the following ways:

    (1)   It assists the auditor and those charged with governance in understanding matters related to the audit, and in developing a constructive working relationship. This relationship is developed while maintaining the auditor's independence and objectivity.

    (2)   It helps the auditor in obtaining, from those charged with governance, information relevant to the audit. For example, those charged with governance may assist the auditor in understanding the entity and its environment, in identifying appropriate sources of audit evidence and in providing information about specific transactions or events.

    (3)   It helps those charged with governance in fulfilling their responsibility to oversee the financial reporting process, thereby reducing the risks of material misstatement of the financial statements.

    (ii)   *Matters to be communicated to those charged with governance*

- The auditor's responsibilities with regards to providing an opinion on the financial statements and that they have carried out their work in accordance with International Standards on Auditing.

- The auditor should explain the planned approach to the audit as well as the audit timetable.

- Any key audit risks identified during the planning stage should be communicated.

- In addition, any significant difficulties encountered during the audit should be communicated.

- Also significant matters arising during the audit, as well as significant accounting adjustments.

- During the audit any significant deficiencies in the internal control system identified should be communicated in writing or verbally.

- Those charged with governance should be notified of any written representations required by the auditor.

- Other matters arising from the audit that are significant to the oversight of the financial reporting process.

- If any suspected frauds are identified during the audit, these must be communicated.

- If the auditors are intending to make any modifications to the audit opinion, these should be communicated to those charged with governance.

- For listed entities, a confirmation that the auditors have complied with ethical standards and appropriate safeguards have been put in place for any ethical threats identified.

(b)   **Report to management**

Board of directors
Fox Industries
15 Dog Street
Cat Town
X Country
6 June 2016

Dear Sirs

Audit of Fox Industries Co (Fox) for the year ended 30 April 2016

Please find enclosed the report to management on deficiencies in internal controls identified during the audit for the year ended 30 April 2016. The appendix to this report considers deficiencies in the purchasing and payments system, the implications of those deficiencies and recommendations to address those deficiencies.

Please note that this report only addresses the deficiencies identified during the audit and if further testing had been performed, then more deficiencies may have been reported.

This report is solely for the use of management and if you have any further questions, then please do not hesitate to contact us.

Yours faithfully

An audit firm

APPENDIX

(i) Deficiency	(ii) Implication	(iii) Recommendation
When raising purchase orders, the clerks choose whichever supplier can despatch the goods the fastest.	This could result in Fox ordering goods at a much higher price or a lower quality than they would like, as the speed of delivery.	An approved supplier list should be compiled; this should take into account the price of goods, their quality and also the speed of delivery.
	It is important that goods are despatched promptly, but this is just one of many criteria that should be used in deciding which supplier to use.	Once the list has been produced, all orders should only be placed with suppliers on the approved list.
Purchase orders are not sequentially numbered.	Failing to sequentially number the orders means that Fox's ordering team are unable to monitor if all orders are being fulfilled in a timely manner; this could result in stock outs.	All purchase orders should be sequentially numbered and on a regular basis a sequence check of unfulfilled orders should be performed.
	If the orders are numbered, then a sequence check can be performed for any unfulfilled orders.	
Purchase orders below $5,000 are not authorised and are processed solely by an order clerk.	This can result in goods being purchased which are not required by Fox. In addition, there is an increased risk as an order clerk could place orders for personal goods up to the value of $5,000, which is significant.	All purchase orders should be authorised by a responsible official. Authorised signatories should be established with varying levels of purchase order authorisation.
Purchase invoices are input daily by the purchase ledger clerk and due to his experience, he does not utilise any application controls.	Without application controls there is a risk that invoices could be input into the system with inaccuracies or they may be missed out entirely.	The purchase ledger clerk should input the invoices in batches and apply application controls, such as control totals, to ensure completeness and accuracy over the input of purchase invoices.
	This could result in suppliers being paid incorrectly or not all, leading to a loss of supplier goodwill.	
The purchase day book automatically updates with the purchase ledger but this ledger is manually posted to the general ledger.	Manually posting the amounts to the general ledger increases the risk of errors occurring. This could result in the payables balance in the financial statements being under or overstated.	The process should be updated so that on a regular basis the purchase ledger automatically updates the general ledger.
		A responsible official should then confirm through purchase ledger control account reconciliations that the update has occurred correctly.

AUDIT AND ASSURANCE (F8) – REVISION QUESTION BANK

(i)	*Deficiency*	(ii)	*Implication*	(iii)	*Recommendation*
	Fox's saving (deposit) bank accounts are only reconciled every two months.		If these accounts are only reconciled periodically, there is the risk that errors will not be spotted promptly.		All bank accounts should be reconciled on a regular basis, and at least monthly, to identify any unusual or missing items.
			Also, this increases the risk of employees committing fraud. If they are aware that these accounts are not regularly reviewed, then they could use these cash sums fraudulently.		The reconciliations should be reviewed by a responsible official and they should evidence their review.
	Fox has a policy of delaying payments to their suppliers for as long as possible.		Whilst this maximises Fox's bank balance, there is the risk that Fox is missing out on early settlement discounts. Also, this can lead to a loss of supplier goodwill as well as the risk that suppliers may refuse to supply goods to Fox.		Fox should undertake cash flow forecasting/budgeting to maximise bank balances. The policy of delaying payment should be reviewed, and suppliers should be paid in a systematic way, such that supplier goodwill is not lost.
	The finance director authorises the bank transfer payment list for suppliers; however, he only views the total amount of payments to be made.		Without looking at the detail of the payments list, as well as supporting documentation, there is a risk that suppliers could be being paid an incorrect amount, or that sums are being paid to fictitious suppliers.		The finance director should review the whole payments list prior to authorising. As part of this, he should agree the amounts to be paid to supporting documentation, as well as reviewing the supplier names to identify any duplicates or any unfamiliar names. He should evidence his review by signing the bank transfer list.

(c) **Application controls**

Document counts – the number of invoices to be input are counted, the invoices are then entered one by one, at the end the number of invoices input is checked against the document count. This helps to ensure completeness of input.

Control totals – here the total of all the invoices, such as the gross value, is manually calculated. The invoices are input, the system aggregates the total of the input invoices' gross value and this is compared to the control total. This helps to ensure completeness and accuracy of input.

One for one checking – the invoices entered into the system are manually agreed back one by one to the original purchase invoices. This helps to ensure completeness and accuracy of input.

Review of output to expected value – an independent assessment is made of the value of purchase invoices to be input, this is the expected value. The invoices are input and the total value of invoices is compared to the expected value. This helps to ensure completeness of input.

Check digits – this control helps to reduce the risk of transposition errors. Mathematical calculations are performed by the system on a particular data field, such as supplier number, a mathematical formula is run by the system, this checks that the data entered into the system is accurate. This helps to ensure accuracy of input.

Range checks – a pre-determined maximum is input into the system for gross invoice value, for example, $10,000; when invoices are input if the amount keyed in is incorrectly entered as being above $10,000, the system will reject the invoice. This helps to ensure accuracy of input.

Existence checks – the system is set up so that certain key data must be entered, such as supplier name, otherwise the invoice is rejected. This helps to ensure accuracy of input.

Tutorial note: *Marks would be awarded for any other relevant application controls. Only four were asked for.*

(d) **Substantive procedures over bank and cash balance**

■ Obtain Fox's current bank account reconciliation and check the additions to ensure arithmetical accuracy.

■ Obtain a bank confirmation letter from Fox's bankers for all of its accounts.

■ For the current account, agree the balance per the bank statement to an original year-end bank statement and also to the bank confirmation letter.

■ Agree the reconciliation's balance per the cash book to the year-end cash book.

■ Trace all of the outstanding lodgements to the pre year-end cash book, post year-end bank statement and also to paying-in-book pre year end.

■ Trace all unpresented cheques through to a pre year-end cash book and post year-end statement. For any unusual amounts or significant delays obtain explanations from management.

- Examine any old unpresented cheques to assess if they need to be written back into the purchase ledger as they are no longer valid to be presented.

- Agree all balances listed on the bank confirmation letter to Fox's bank reconciliations or the trial balance to ensure completeness of bank balances.

- Review the cash book and bank statements for any unusual items or large transfers around the year end, as this could be evidence of window dressing.

- Examine the bank confirmation letter for details of any security provided by Fox or any legal right of set-off as this may require disclosure.

- For the saving (deposit) bank accounts, review any reconciling items on the year-end bank reconciliations and agree to supporting documentation.

- In respect of material cash balances, count cash balances at the year end and agree to petty cash records, such as the petty cash book.

- Review the financial statements to ensure that the disclosure of cash and bank balances are complete and accurate.

Tutorial note: *Marks would be awarded for any other relevant bank and cash tests.*

Answer 37 TROMBONE

(a) **Payroll system deficiencies, controls and test of controls**

Deficiencies	Controls	Test of controls
The wages calculations are generated by the payroll system and there are no checks performed. Therefore, if system errors occur during the payroll processing, this would not be identified. This could result in wages being over or under calculated, leading to an additional payroll cost or loss of employee goodwill.	A senior member of the payroll team should recalculate the gross to net pay workings for a sample of employees and compare their results to the output from the payroll system. These calculations should be signed as approved before payments are made.	Review a sample of the gross to net pay calculations for evidence that they are undertaken and signed as approved.
Annual wages increases are updated in the payroll system standing data by clerks.	Payroll clerks should not have access to standing data changes within the system.	Ask a clerk to attempt to make a change to payroll standing data; the system should reject this attempt.
Payroll clerks are not senior enough to be making changes to standing data as they could make mistakes leading to incorrect payment of wages. In addition, if they can access standing data, they could make unauthorised changes.	The annual wages increase should be performed by a senior member of the payroll department and this should be checked by another responsible official for errors.	Review the log of standing data amendments to identify whether the wage rate increases were changed by a senior member of payroll.
Overtime worked by employees is not all authorised by the relevant department head, as only overtime in excess of 30% of standard hours requires authorisation. This increases the risk that employees will claim for overtime even though they did not work these additional hours resulting in additional payroll costs for Trombone.	All overtime hours worked should be authorised by the relevant department head. This should be evidenced by signature on the employees' weekly overtime sheets.	Review a sample of employee weekly overtime sheets for evidence of signature by relevant department head.

Deficiencies	Controls	Test of controls
Time taken off as payment for overtime worked should be agreed by payroll clerks to the overtime worked report; however, this has not always occurred.

Employees could be taking unauthorised leave if they take time off but have not worked the required overtime. | Payroll clerks should be reminded of the procedures to be undertaken when processing the overtime sheets. They should sign as evidence on the overtime sheets that they have agreed any time taken off to the relevant overtime report. | Select a sample of overtime sheets with time taken off and confirm that there is evidence of a check by the payroll clerk to the overtime worked report. |
| The overtime worked report is emailed to the department heads and they report by exception if there are any errors.

If department heads are busy or do not receive the email and do not report to payroll on time, then it will be assumed that the overtime report is correct even though there may be errors. This could result in the payroll department making incorrect overtime payments. | All department heads should report to the payroll department on whether or not the overtime report is correct. The payroll department should follow up on any non-replies and not make payments until agreed by the department head. | For a sample of overtime reports emailed to department heads confirm that a response has been received from each head by reviewing all responses. |
| Department heads are meant to arrange for annual leave cover so that overtime sheets are authorised on a timely basis; however, this has not always happened.

If overtime sheets are authorised late, then this can lead to employee dissatisfaction as it will delay payment of the overtime worked. | Department heads should be reminded of the procedures with regards to annual leave and arrangement of suitable cover.

During annual leave periods, payroll clerks should monitor that overtime sheets are being submitted by department heads on a timely basis and follow up any late sheets. | Discuss with payroll clerks the process they follow for obtaining authorisation of overtime sheets, in particular during periods of annual leave. Compare this to the process which they should adopt to identify any control exceptions. |
| The finance director reviews the total list of bank transfers with the total to be paid per the payroll records.

Employees could be omitted and fictitious employees added to the payment listing, so although the payment listing total agrees to payroll totals, fraudulent payments could be made. | The finance director when authorising the payments should on a sample basis perform checks from payroll records to payment list and vice versa to confirm that payments are complete and only made to *bona fide* employees.

The finance director should sign the payments list as evidence that he has undertaken these checks. | Obtain a sample of payments list and review for signature by the finance director as evidence that the control is operating correctly. |

(b) **Differences between an interim and a final audit**

Interim audit

The interim audit is that part of the audit which takes place before the year end. The auditor uses the interim audit to carry out procedures which would be difficult to perform at the year end because of time pressure. There is no requirement to undertake an interim audit; factors to consider when deciding upon whether to have one include the size and complexity of the company along with the effectiveness of internal controls.

Typical procedures undertaken during the interim audit include consideration of inherent risks, documenting and testing of internal controls, testing of profit and loss transactions for the year to date and identification of potential problems which may affect the final audit work.

Final audit

The final audit will take place after the year end and concludes with the auditor forming and expressing an opinion on the financial statements for the whole year subject to audit. It is important to note that the final opinion takes account of conclusions formed at both the interim and final audit.

Typical work carried out at the final audit includes follow up of items noted at the inventory count, obtaining confirmations from third parties, analytical reviews of figures in the financial statements, substantive procedures of account balances and transactions, review of events after the reporting period and going concern review.

(c) **Payroll substantive procedures**

- Agree the total wages and salaries expense per the payroll system to the trial balance, investigate any differences.

- Cast a sample of payroll records to confirm completeness and accuracy of the payroll expense.

- For a sample of employees, recalculate the gross and net pay and agree to the payroll records to confirm accuracy.

- Re-perform the calculation of statutory deductions to confirm whether correct deductions for this year have been made in the payroll.

- Compare the total payroll expense to the prior year and investigate any significant differences.

- Review monthly payroll charges, compare this to the prior year and budgets and discuss with management for any significant variances.

- Perform a proof in total of total wages and salaries, incorporating joiners and leavers and the annual pay increase. Compare this to the actual wages and salaries in the financial statements and investigate any significant differences.

- Select a sample of joiners and leavers, agree their start/leaving date to supporting documentation, recalculate that their first/last pay packet was accurately calculated and recorded.

- Agree the total net pay per the payroll records to the bank transfer listing of payments and to the cashbook.

■ Agree the individual wages and salaries per the payroll to the personnel records for a sample to confirm bona fide employees.

■ Select a sample of weekly overtime sheets and trace to overtime payment in payroll records to confirm completeness of overtime paid.

(d) **Accrual for income tax payable on employment income**

Procedures the auditor should adopt in respect of auditing this accrual include:

■ Agree the year-end income tax payable accrual to the payroll records to confirm accuracy.

■ Re-perform the calculation of the accrual to confirm accuracy.

■ Agree the subsequent payment to the post year-end cash book and bank statements to confirm completeness.

■ Review any correspondence with tax authorities to assess whether there are any additional outstanding payments due; if so, agree they are included in the year-end accrual.

■ Review any disclosures made of the income tax accrual and assess whether these are in compliance with accounting standards and legislation.

Answer 38 GARCIA INTERNATIONAL

(a)   Garcia International's (Garcia) internal control

Deficiency	Control	Test of control
Currently the website is not integrated into inventory system. This can result in Garcia accepting customer orders when they do not have the goods in inventory. This can cause them to lose sales and customer goodwill.	The website should be updated to include an interface into the inventory system; this should check inventory levels and only process orders if adequate inventory is held. If inventory is out of stock, this should appear on the website with an approximate waiting time.	Test data could be used to attempt to process orders via the website for items which are not currently held in inventory. The orders should be flagged as being out of stock and indicate an approximate waiting time.
For goods despatched by local couriers, customer signatures are not always obtained. This can lead to customers falsely claiming that they have not received their goods. Garcia would not be able to prove that they had in fact despatched the goods and may result in goods being despatched twice.	Garcia should remind all local couriers that customer signatures must be obtained as proof of delivery and payment will not be made for any despatches with missing signatures.	Select a sample of despatches by couriers and ask Garcia for proof of delivery by viewing customer signatures.
There have been a number of situations where the sales orders have not been fulfilled in a timely manner. This can lead to a loss of customer goodwill and if it persists will damage the reputation of Garcia as a reliable supplier.	Once goods are despatched they should be matched to sales orders and flagged as fulfilled. The system should automatically flag any outstanding sales orders past a predetermined period, such as five days. This report should be reviewed by a responsible official.	Review the report of outstanding sales orders. If significant, discuss with a responsible official to understand why there is still a significant time period between sales order and despatch date. Select a sample of sales orders and compare the date of order to the goods despatch date to ascertain whether this is within the acceptable predetermined period.
Customer credit limits are set by sales ledger clerks. Sales ledger clerks are not sufficiently senior and so may set limits too high, leading to irrecoverable debts, or too low, leading to a loss of sales.	Credit limits should be set by a senior member of the sales ledger department and not by sales ledger clerks. These limits should be regularly reviewed by a responsible official.	For a sample of new customers accepted in the year, review the authorisation of the credit limit, and ensure that this was performed by a responsible official. Enquire of sales ledger clerks as to who can set credit limits.

AUDIT AND ASSURANCE (F8) – REVISION QUESTION BANK

Deficiency	Control	Test of control
Sales discounts are set by Garcia's sales team. In order to boost their sales, members of the sales team may set the discounts too high, leading to a loss of revenue.	All members of the sales team should be given authority to grant sales discounts up to a set limit. Any sales discounts above these limits should be authorised by sales area managers or the sales director. Regular review of sales discount levels should be undertaken by the sales director, and this review should be evidenced.	Discuss with members of the sales team the process for setting sales discounts. Review the sales discount report for evidence of review by the sales director.
Supplier statement reconciliations are no longer performed. This may result in errors in the recording of purchases and payables not being identified in a timely manner.	Supplier statement reconciliations should be performed on a monthly basis for all suppliers and these should be reviewed by a responsible official.	Review the file of reconciliations to ensure that they are being performed on a regular basis and that they have been reviewed by a responsible official
Changes to supplier details in the purchase ledger master file can be undertaken by purchase ledger clerks.	Only purchase ledger supervisors should have the authority to make changes to master file data. This should be controlled via passwords.	Request a purchase ledger clerk to attempt to access the master file and to make an amendment, the system should not allow this.
This could lead to key supplier data being accidently amended or fictitious suppliers being set up, which can increase the risk of fraud.	Regular review of any changes to master file data by a responsible official and this review should be evidenced.	Review a report of master data changes and review the authority of those making amendments.
Garcia has considerable levels of surplus plant and equipment. Surplus unused plant is at risk of theft. In addition, if the surplus plant is not disposed of then the company could lose sundry income.	Regular review of the plant and equipment on the factory floor by senior factory personnel to identify any old or surplus equipment. As part of the capital expenditure process there should be a requirement to confirm the treatment of the equipment being replaced.	Observe the review process by senior factory personnel, identifying the treatment of any old equipment. Review processed capital expenditure forms to ascertain if the treatment of replaced equipment is stated.
Purchase requisitions are authorised by production supervisors. Production supervisors are not sufficiently independent or senior to authorise capital expenditure.	Capital expenditure authorisation levels to be established. Production supervisors should only be able to authorise low value items, any high value items should be authorised by the board.	Review a sample of authorised capital expenditure forms and identify if the correct signatory has authorised them.

1088

(b) **Substantive procedures additions**

- Obtain a breakdown of additions, cast the list and agree to the non-current asset register to confirm completeness of plant and equipment (P&E).

- Select a sample of additions and agree cost to supplier invoice to confirm valuation.

- Verify rights and obligations by agreeing the addition of plant and equipment to a supplier invoice in the name of Garcia.

- Review the list of additions and confirm that they relate to capital expenditure items rather than repairs and maintenance.

- Review board minutes to ensure that significant capital expenditure purchases have been authorised by the board.

- For a sample of additions recorded in P&E, physically verify them on the factory floor to confirm existence.

Answer 39 HUMMINGBIRD SCENTS

(a)   **Board of directors**
Hummingbird Co
23 Buzzard Lane
Peregrine City
Hawk Country

4 December 2016

Dear Sirs,

Audit of Hummingbird Scents Co for the year ended 30 September 2016

Please find enclosed the report to management on deficiencies in internal controls identified during the audit for the year ended 30 September 2016. The appendix to this report considers deficiencies in the sales system and recommendations to address those deficiencies.

Please note that this report only addresses the deficiencies identified during the audit and if further testing had been performed, then more deficiencies may have been reported.

This report is solely for the use of management and if you have any further questions, then please do not hesitate to contact us.

Yours faithfully

An audit firm

APPENDIX

Deficiency	Control
Brenda the sales clerk receives customer orders, raises sales invoices and processes payments for hotel customers. This is a lack of segregation of duties and could lead to a risk of fraudulent transactions or errors, as no one checks the work undertaken by this clerk.	Another sales ledger clerk should be involved in the processing of hotel customer transactions so that no one individual undertakes all elements of the sales cycle. The work could be split so that one clerk raises orders and invoices but a second clerk processes the payments.
Hotel customers have contracted sales prices; however, as online trade prices are automatically loaded into the sales invoices, Brenda has to manually amend the invoices.	As hotel customers account for 40% of revenue, consideration should be given to amending the sales system so that each customer's agreed prices are pre-loaded, therefore no manual amendment of invoices would be required.
This significantly increases the risk of error, as if Brenda incorrectly increases the sales prices, then this can lead to a loss of customer goodwill and if they are too low, this results in a loss of revenue for Hummingbird.	If this is not feasible, then all sales invoices for hotel customers should be double checked by another member of the finance department prior to being sent out.
Credit limits are determined by the finance director when a new trade customer is set up in the system. However, these limits could be out of date, resulting in limits being too high and sales being made to poor credit risks or too low and Hummingbird losing potential revenue.	Customer credit limits should be regularly reviewed by the finance director and updated based on the level of sales transactions and credit risk.
Customer orders and goods despatched notes (GDN) are given a number based on the customer account number and order number. These numbers are not sequential. Without sequential numbers, it is difficult for Hummingbird to identify missing orders and to monitor if all orders are being despatched in a timely manner, leading to a loss of customer goodwill.	Sales orders and goods despatched notes should be sequentially numbered. On a regular basis, a sequence check of orders should be undertaken to identify any missing orders. Upon despatch, the GDN should be matched to the order; a regular review of unmatched orders should be undertaken to identify any unfulfilled orders.
Hummingbird has changed from a reliable national courier company to a cheaper local courier; as a result some orders have been delivered late. There is a risk that orders may be lost resulting in a loss of revenue for Hummingbird or orders arriving later than normal which would lead to a loss of customer goodwill.	The courier company should be set targets with regards to timeliness of despatches. A review should be undertaken of target despatch times and actual times taken by the new courier company. If late delays continue, then consideration should be given to changing back to the original courier company.
Trade customers' sales invoices are automatically generated by the system at the same time that the online order is placed. However, if goods are not despatched straight away, then customers could be invoiced in advance of receipt of their goods. This is likely to lead to a loss of customer goodwill and the early recognition of revenue in the accounting records.	The system should be amended so that it links into the despatch system. Sales invoices should not be raised until after goods have been despatched.

Deficiency	Control
If Hummingbird makes special offers or discounts sales, the master file data for sales prices is amended by a senior sales ledger clerk. There is a risk that these amendments could be made incorrectly resulting in a loss of sales revenue or overcharging of customers. In addition, the sales ledger clerk, although senior, is not senior enough to be given access to changing master file data as this could increase the risk of fraud.	When special offers or discounted sales occur, the changes to master file data should be made by a supervisor and each change checked by a responsible official to reduce the risk of errors occurring. Amendments to master file data should be restricted so that only supervisors and above can make changes.
Monthly statements are not sent to trade customers. If statements are not sent regularly, this increases the likelihood of errors and any disputed invoices not being quickly identified and resolved by Hummingbird.	Hummingbird should produce monthly customer statements for both hotel and trade customers and send them out promptly.
The sales ledger control account is only reconciled at the end of September in order to verify the year-end balance. If the sales ledger is only reconciled annually, there is a risk that errors will not be spotted promptly.	The sales ledger control account should be reconciled on a monthly basis to identify any errors. The reconciliations should be reviewed by a responsible official and they should evidence their review.

(b)   Substantive procedures for revenue

- Compare the overall level of revenue against prior years and budget and investigate any significant fluctuations.

- Obtain a schedule of sales for the year broken down into the two categories of hotel and trade customers and compare this to the prior year breakdown and for any unusual movements discuss with management.

- Calculate the gross profit margin for Hummingbird and compare this to the prior year and investigate any significant fluctuations.

- Select a sample of sales invoices for hotel customers and agree the sales prices back to the contracted rates to ensure the accuracy of invoices.

- Select a sample of credit notes raised, trace through to the original invoice and ensure invoice correctly removed from sales.

- Select a sample of trade customer orders placed online and agree these to the despatch notes and sales invoices through to inclusion in the sales ledger to ensure completeness of revenue.

- Select a sample of despatch notes both pre and post year end; follow these through to sales invoices in the correct accounting period to ensure that cut-off has been correctly applied.

Answer 40 BOULDER

(a)   Six financial statement assertions

- Existence – assets, liabilities or equity interests exist.

- Cut off – transactions and events have been recorded in the correct accounting period.

- Occurrence – transactions or events that have been recorded or disclosed have occurred and pertain to the entity.

- Accuracy, valuation and allocation – assets, liabilities and equity interests have been included in the financial statements at appropriate amounts and any resulting valuation or allocation adjustments have been appropriately recorded, and related disclosures have been appropriately measured and described. Amounts and other data related to recorded transactions and events have been recorded appropriately and related disclosures have been appropriately measured and described.

- Rights and obligations – the entity holds or controls the rights to assets, and liabilities or obligations of the entity.

- Classification – assets, liabilities, equity interests, transactions and events have been recorded in the proper accounts.

- Presentation – assets, liabilities, equity, transactions and events are appropriately grouped and clearly described and related disclosures are relevant and understandable.

(b)   Substantive audit procedures

In relation to both the payroll balances in the statement of financial position and the payroll transactions in the statement of profit or loss, ensure that appropriate disclosures had been made in the financial statements in accordance with accounting standards and the statutory framework. The disclosure of amounts paid to directors is particularly important.

(i)   Payroll balances in statement of financial position

(1)   Balances that are likely to appear in the statement of financial position of Boulder are dealt with in items 5–7 below. In all cases, ensure that the amounts appearing in the financial statements can be traced through to supporting schedules (existence) and ensure that the schedules are arithmetically accurate (accuracy).

(2)   Compare the payable balances at the year end to any payments made after the year end, to documentation supporting and authorising the bank transfer, and to the bank statement.

(3)   In all cases, the extent of testing noted below will depend on the results of tests of controls over payroll.

(4)   Perform analytical procedures on the amounts payable at the period end by reference to the number of employees, the amounts payable at the end of each week, month, quarter or year (as appropriate) during the period (and in prior periods) and with reference to profits, production or sales levels, and/or tax and social insurance rates, as appropriate.

(5)   Unpaid amounts due to the agency:

■   Confirm with the agency the amount payable to the agency at the year end or compare the payment made to the agency after the year end to the amount reported as payable at the year end.

■   Recalculate the amount payable and compare to documentation supporting the amount reported at the year end.

■   Compare the amounts payable (particularly the rates payable) to correspondence with the agency and check such correspondence for evidence of any disputes.

(6)   Unpaid wages and salaries due to permanent factory staff, administrative and sales staff and directors, and unpaid bonuses due to sales staff and directors:

■   Recalculate the amounts payable and compare to appropriately authorised clock cards or contracts, as appropriate.

(7)   Unpaid amounts due to tax authorities for tax and social insurance:

■   Review correspondence with the tax authorities for evidence of any disputes or underpayment.

(ii)   Payroll transactions in the statement of profit or loss

(1)   Trace the amounts appearing in the statement of profit or loss to supporting schedules and recalculate the amounts in the schedules to ensure accuracy.

(2)   Select a sample of payroll transactions and trace them through the ledgers and daybooks to source documentation such as clock cards for permanent factory staff, documentation showing the amounts produced or processed (agency staff) or contracts (administrative and sales staff and directors).

(3)   Trace a sample of payroll transactions in the opposite direction, through the daybooks and ledgers to the schedules supporting the financial statements and to the statement of profit or loss.

(4)   Perform analytical procedures on the amounts appearing in the ledgers for each period, for each category of employee with reference to production and sales levels as appropriate, the number of employees, and by comparison with prior periods, for example.

Answer 41 DONALD

(a)   Procedures for obtaining evidence

Inspection

Inspection involves examining records or documents, whether internal or external, in paper form, electronic form, or other media, or a physical examination of an asset.

■   Inspect a sample of purchase invoices and agree the amount is included correctly within the purchase ledger.

■   Inspect purchase orders for evidence of authorisation by a responsible official.

Observation

Observation consists of looking at a process or procedure being performed by others.

■ Observe the process for logging purchase invoices into the system to ensure that all invoices are entered completely and accurately.

■ Observe the goods received department to assess whether goods received are checked against purchase orders and reviewed for adequate quality.

Analytical procedures

Analytical procedures consist of evaluations of financial information through analysis of plausible relationships among both financial and non-financial data. Analytical procedures also encompass such investigation as is necessary of identified fluctuations or relationships that are inconsistent with other relevant information or that differ from expected values by a significant amount.

■ Calculate the operating profit margin/overhead ratio and compare it to last year and budget and investigate any significant differences.

■ Review monthly other expenses to identify any significant fluctuations and discuss with management.

Inquiry

Inquiry consists of seeking information of knowledgeable persons, both financial and non-financial, within the entity or outside the entity.

■ Discuss with management whether there have been any changes in the key suppliers used and compare this to the purchase ledger to assess completeness and accuracy of purchases.

■ Inquire of department heads the process they follow in authorising orders to ensure that it follows the specified company authorisation process.

Recalculation

Recalculation consists of checking the mathematical accuracy of documents or records. Recalculation may be performed manually or electronically.

■ Recalculate the accuracy of a sample of purchase invoices.

■ Recalculate the prepayments and accruals charged at the year end to ensure the accuracy of the other expenses.

Reperformance

Reperformance involves the auditor's independent execution of procedures or controls that were originally performed as part of the entity's internal control.

■ Reperform the purchase ledger control account reconciliation to ensure accuracy.

■ Select a sample of purchase orders and match them to the goods received notes and purchase invoices to ensure completeness of the purchase cycle.

Tutorial note: *The requirement specifically precluded consideration of external confirmation. Marks would be awarded for other examples relevant to purchases and other expenses (only one example required for each procedure).*

(b)

Audit risk	Audit response
Donald has ordered six planes which may not have been received by the year end. Only assets which physically exist at the year end should be included in property, plant and equipment.	Discuss with management whether the planes have arrived. If so then physically verify a sample to ensure existence.
The existing planes have been refurbished at a cost of $15m. This expenditure needs to be reviewed to assess whether it is of a capital nature and should be included within assets or expensed as repairs.	Review a breakdown of the costs and agree to invoices to assess the nature of the expenditure and if capital agree to inclusion within the asset register and if repairs agree to the income statement.
Donald has applied for a loan of $25m. It has not received this loan yet, but it has already ordered the planes and if it does not receive the money in time then it may struggle to pay for the planes ordered and this could result in going concern difficulties.	Discuss with management the status of the loan application and if still outstanding whether any other banks have been approached for the loan. Perform a detailed going concern review.
The travel agents who sell tickets on behalf of the airline are struggling to pay their outstanding balances to Donald. This could result in an increase in irrecoverable debts and receivables being overvalued.	Extended post year-end cash receipts testing and a review of the aged receivables ledger to be performed to assess valuation. An allowance for receivables to be discussed with management.
Donald's website has encountered difficulties with recording sales, this could lead to errors in relation to completeness of income.	Extended controls testing to be performed over the sales cycle to assess the extent of the errors. Detailed testing to be performed over completeness of income.
Due to the website errors tickets have been sold twice, therefore some customers will require refunds. At the year end there is a risk that the tickets to be refunded have not been removed from sales.	Review the cut-off of customer refunds around the year end to ensure that sales are complete and accurate.
Donald is closing its call centre and making the workforce redundant; as it has announced this to the staff then under IAS 37 *Provisions, Contingent Liabilities and Contingent Assets* a redundancy provision will be required for any staff not yet paid at the year end.	Discuss with management the status of the redundancy programme and review and recalculate the redundancy provision.

Answer 42 ANALYTICAL PROCEDURES

(a) **Factors that influence the reliability of audit evidence**

The following five factors are taken from ISA 500 *Audit Evidence*:

- Audit evidence is more reliable when it is obtained from independent sources outside the entity.

- Audit evidence that is generated internally is more reliable when the related controls imposed by the entity are effective.

- Audit evidence obtained directly by the auditor (e.g. observation of the application of a control) is more reliable than audit evidence obtained indirectly or by inference (e.g. inquiry about the application of a control).

- Audit evidence is more reliable when it exists in documentary form, whether paper, electronic, or other medium. For example, a contemporaneously written record of a meeting is more reliable than a subsequent oral representation of the matters discussed.

- Audit evidence provided by original documents is more reliable than audit evidence provided by photocopies or facsimiles.

Other examples are:

- Evidence created in the normal course of business is better than evidence specially created to satisfy the auditor.

- The best-informed source of audit evidence will normally be management of the company (although management's lack of independence may reduce its value as a source of such evidence).

- Evidence about the future is particularly difficult to obtain and is less reliable than evidence about past events.

(b) **Nature and purpose of analytical procedures**

- Analytical procedures involve:

    - the analysis of significant ratios and trends;
    - the investigation of fluctuations and relationships that are inconsistent with other relevant information (or which deviate from predicted amounts).

- Analytical procedures include the consideration of:

    - comparisons of the entities financial information with, for example, similar industry information;

    - relationships between financial and non-financial information.

- Procedures may involve simple comparison of current with prior years or a review of variance accounting.

- ■ They are used:

  - ❏ to assist in audit planning the nature, timing and extent of other audit procedures;

  - ❏ as substantive procedures (when more effective or efficient than tests of detail);

  - ❏ as an overall review.

Answer 43 NEWTHORPE ENGINEERING

Item	Answer	Justification
1	B	(2) and (3) are both procedures for verifying the recoverable amount of plant and equipment. Inspecting the unsold plant and equipment (1) is a test of the existence assertion. Inspecting evidence of ownership (4) is a test of the rights assertion.
2	D	Sampling goods received notes and goods despatch notes (1) is not necessary because other audit tests have confirmed that there are no purchases or sales cut-off errors. (2), (3) and (4) are all procedures that would be performed to verify the net realisable value estimate for inventory.
3	C	
4	D	Even if estimates were discussed during board and/or shareholder meetings it is unlikely that review of such discussions would provide evidence that the estimate is reasonable.
5	A	Management is responsible for determining the estimation. The factors used by management may, or may not, be subject to estimation uncertainty (the inherent lack of precision). (1), (2) and (3) are factors that influence lack of precision. The auditor must, using professional judgement, identify and assess the risk of material misstatement in estimates with particular reference to estimation uncertainty. But the auditor's professional judgement has no bearing on that estimation uncertainty.

Answer 44 TAM

Sample selection methods

The audit manager suggests checking all invoices, effectively ignoring any statistical sampling; in other words this is not statistical sampling. Audit tests will be applied to all of the sales invoices. This approach may be appropriate for the audit of Tam because:

- ■ The population is relatively small and it is likely to be quicker to test all the items than spend time constructing a sample.

- ■ All the transactions are not large but could be considered material in their own right, (e.g. compared to project). As all the transactions are material, then they all need to be tested.

The audit senior suggests using statistical sampling. This will mean selecting a limited number of sales invoices from the population using probability theory ensuring a random selection of the sample and then applying audit tests to those invoices only. This approach may be appropriate because:

- ■ The population consists of similar items (i.e. it is homogeneous) and there are no indications of the control system failing or changing during the year. There is the query about how long it will take to determine and produce a sample, which may make statistical sampling inappropriate in this situation.

The audit junior suggests using "random" sampling, which the junior auditor appears to understand as manually choosing which invoices to look at. The approach therefore involves an element of bias and is not statistical or true "random" sampling. While this approach appears to save time, it is not appropriate because:

- The sample selected will not be chosen "randomly" but on the whim of the auditor. Human nature will tend to avoid difficult items for testing.

- Also, as invoices will not have been chosen using statistical sampling, no valid conclusion can be drawn from the results of the test. If an error is found it will be difficult extrapolating that error on to the population.

Answer 45 CRIGHTON-WARD

Item	Answer	Justification
1	B	One of the primary purposes of the written representations from management is to reduce the possibility of a misunderstanding regarding management's responsibility for the financial statements. The first written representation states, "We have fulfilled our responsibilities ... for the preparation of the financial statements in accordance with ..."
2	A	The amount of the Lion's Roar claim is clearly material (more than 50% of profit before taxation). There is also a lack of definitive supporting evidence for the claim. The two main pieces of evidence available are the claim from Lion's Roar itself and the legal advice from Crighton-Ward's solicitors. However, the outcome cannot be accurately determined because the dispute has not been settled. The directors' argument suggests that the claim may not be justified, which is one possible outcome of the dispute. However, in order to obtain sufficient evidence to show how the treatment of the potential claim was decided for the financial statements, the auditor must obtain this opinion in writing. Reference must therefore be made to the claim in the written representations from management. The depreciation matter is unlikely to be included in the written representations from management because the auditor appears to have obtained sufficient evidence to confirm the accounting treatment.
3	C	(1), (2) and (4) would all be included in the written representation from management. (3) is incorrect because the statement would refer to material misstatements, not immaterial misstatement. (5) is incorrect as management's response to internal control deficiencies are generally detailed in the communication on internal control.
4	A	A) would be the basis for seeking written representations, in addition to the objective of obtaining written confirmation of these matters (which is not given as an option) on the basis that (B), (C) and (D) are clearly inappropriate.
5	D	ISA 580 *Written Representations*. The auditor should discuss the matter with management and the directors; re-evaluate the integrity of management and the directors and evaluate the effect that this may have on the reliability of representations (oral or written) and audit evidence in general; and take appropriate actions, including determining the possible effect on the opinion in the auditor's report in accordance with ISA 705 *Modifications to the Opinion in the Independent Auditor's Report*. The scenario implies that the auditors have asked for a representation that the management are not aware of any further reasons why an asset may be impaired.

Answer 46 RIGHTS AND REPRESENTATIONS

(a) **Auditor rights**

- Right of access to the company's books and records at any reasonable time to collect the evidence necessary to support the audit opinion.

- Right to require from the company's officers the information and explanations the auditor considers necessary to perform their duties as auditors.

- Right to receive notice of and attend meetings of the company in the same way as any member of the company.

- Right to speak at general meetings on any matter affecting the auditor or previous auditor.

- Where the company uses written resolutions, a right to receive a copy of those resolutions.

(b) **Written representations from management**

- No irregularities involving management or employees that could have a material effect on the financial statements.

- All books of account and supporting documentation have been made available to the auditors.

- Information and disclosures with reference to related parties is complete.

- Financial statements are free from material misstatements including omissions.

- No non-compliance with any statute or regulatory authority.

- No plans that will materially alter the carrying value or classification of assets or liabilities in the financial statements.

- No plans to abandon any product lines that will result in any excess or obsolete inventory.

- No events, unless already disclosed, after the end of the reporting period require disclosure in the financial statements.

(c) **Additional audit procedures**

- The auditor could expand the amount of test of controls in that audit area. This may indicate that the control weakness was not as bad as initially thought.

- The problem could be raised with the directors, either verbally or in the written representations from management, to ensure that they are aware of the problem.

- The auditor could perform additional substantive procedures on the audit area. This action will help to quantify the extent of the error and makes the implicit assumption that the control system is not operating correctly.

- If the matter is not resolved, then the auditor will also need to consider a qualification in the audit report; the exact wording depending on the materiality of the errors found.

Answer 47 GREENFIELDS

(a)   **Audit procedures for accounting estimates**

- Enquire of management how the accounting estimate is made and the data on which it is based.

- Determine whether events occurring up to the date of the auditor's report (after the reporting period) provide audit evidence regarding the accounting estimate.

- Review the method of measurement used and assess the reasonableness of assumptions made.

- Test the operating effectiveness of the controls over how management made the accounting estimate.

- Develop an expectation of the possible estimate (point estimate) or a range of amounts to evaluate management's estimate.

- Review the judgments and decisions made by management in the making of accounting estimates to identify whether there are indicators of possible management bias.

- Evaluate overall whether the accounting estimates in the financial statements are either reasonable or misstated.

- Obtain sufficient appropriate audit evidence about whether the disclosures in the financial statements related to accounting estimates and estimation uncertainty are reasonable.

- Obtain written representations from management and, where appropriate, those charged with governance whether they believe significant assumptions used in making accounting estimates are reasonable.

(b)   **Receivables balance owing from Yellowmix**

   (i)   Appropriateness of written representation

The written representation proposed by management is intended to verify valuation, existence and rights and obligations of a material receivables balance. As management has refused to allow the auditor to request direct confirmation of the balance and there has been little activity on the account for the past six months , very little evidence has been obtained by the auditor.

This representation would constitute entity generated evidence and this is less reliable than auditor generated evidence or evidence from an external source. If related control systems operate effectively then this evidence becomes more reliable. In addition if the representation is written as opposed to oral then this will increase the reliability as an evidence source.

Overall this representation is a weak form of evidence, as more reliable evidence was available (e.g. through direct confirmation).

(ii)   Additional procedures to reach a conclusion

In order to reach a conclusion on the balance the following procedures should be performed:

■   Discuss with management the reasons as to why a confirmation request was refused.

■   Review the post year-end period to identify whether any cash has now been received from Yellowmix.

■   Review correspondence with Yellowmix to assess reasons for the continued non-payment.

■   Review board minutes and legal correspondence to assess whether any legal action is being taken to recover the amounts due.

■   Discuss with management whether a provision or write down is now required.

■   Consider impact on audit opinion if balance is considered to be materially misstated.

Warranty provision

(i)   Appropriateness of written representation

In this case the auditor has performed some testing of the provision in order to obtain auditor generated evidence. The team has tested the calculations and assumptions. None of this is evidence from an external source.

The very nature of this provision means that it is difficult for the auditor to obtain a significant amount of reliable evidence as to the level of future warranty claims. Hence the written representation, whilst being an entity generated source of evidence, would still be useful as there are few other alternatives.

(ii)   Additional procedures to reach a conclusion

In order to reach a conclusion on the balance the following procedures should be performed:

■   Review the post year-end period to compare the level of claims actually made against the amounts provided.

■   Review the level of prior year provisions with the amounts claimed to assess the reasonableness of management's forecasting.

■   Review board minutes to assess whether any changes are required to the level of the provision as a result of an increased or decreased level of claims by customers.

(c)   Refusal to provide written representation on warranty provision

Steps to be taken

ISA 580 *Written Representations* provides guidance to the auditor in the case where written representations are requested from management but they refuse to provide.

If management does not provide the requested written representation on the warranty provision the auditor of Greenfields should discuss the matter with management to understand why they are refusing.

In addition the auditor should re-evaluate the integrity of Greenfields' management and consider the effect that this may have on the reliability of other representations (oral or written) and audit evidence in general.

The auditor should then take appropriate actions, including determining the possible effect on the audit opinion.

Impact on audit report

As the auditor is unable to obtain sufficient appropriate evidence to conclude that the warranty provision is free from material misstatement then a modified audit opinion will be required.

The warranty provision is material but not pervasive and therefore a qualified "except for" opinion would be appropriate.

The basis for opinion section of the audit report will describe the reason for the modification; namely that management refused to provide a written representation in relation to the warranty provision and hence we are unable to form an opinion on this balance. The opinion section will be amended to state "except for".

Answer 48 WALSH

(a)   **Use of Computer-Assisted Audit Techniques (CAATs)**

Testing programmed controls

Reliance on CAATs will force the auditor to rely on programmed controls during an audit; in fact using CAATs may be the only way to test controls within a computer system. Use of the CAAT enables the auditor to meet the auditing standard requirement of obtaining appropriate audit evidence.

For example, in Walsh, an overtime report is generated by the computer, although this can also be overridden by the accountant. Test data can be used to check that the overtime report is being created correctly and audit software can monitor that only the accountant's password can be used to override the overtime payment.

Test larger number of items

Using CAATs enables the auditor to test a larger number of items quickly and accurately, meeting the auditing standard requirement of obtaining sufficient audit evidence.

Using audit software, the auditor can check the deduction and net pay calculations of a significant proportion of wages calculations – or all of them if necessary. Checking each calculation manually would take a long time.

Test actual accounting records

Using CAATs enables the auditor to test the actual accounting records (the electronic version) rather than relying on printouts or other copies of the data. It is always appropriate for the auditor to test original documentation where possible.

In the case of Walsh, the actual wages will be tested rather than any paper copies.

Cost

After initial set-up costs, using CAATs is likely to be cost effective; the same audit software programs can be run each year as long as the client does not change the accounting systems.

In Walsh, the system has just been implemented. Hopefully the wages system will be used for a number of years, making the use of CAATs cost-effective for the audit firm.

(b) **Examples of the use of audit software**

Calculation checks. For example, re-calculation of net pay for a number of employees to ensure the mathematical calculation is correct.

Reviewing the list of employees paid each week/month and printing a list of employees, who have not be been paid, for further investigation.

Detecting unreasonable items. For example, reviewing the list of net wages for large or negative payments.

Detecting violation of system rules. For example, where other people besides the accountant have been overriding overtime payments or employees amending their own gross wages.

Conducting new analysis as part of the analytical review of wages. For example, calculating total wages for the year from the number of employees and average wages paid.

Completeness checks. For example ensuring there is an electronic record of all employees who "clocked in" for a day's work and "clocked out" again.

(c) **Use of test data**

Audit test data consists of data submitted by the auditor for processing on the client's computer-based accounting systems. The data can be processed during a normal processing run (a "live" testing situation) or in a special run outside of the normal processing cycle (a "dead" testing situation).

In Walsh, the auditor can create a "dummy employee" record on the wages master file, and then use a magnetic card to mimic that employee working a certain number of hours in the company over the course of, for example, one week.

Knowing how many hours has been input into the wages system; the auditor can calculate the expected net pay and then compare this to the actual net pay produced by the computer system.

If the amounts agree then this provides appropriate audit evidence of the accuracy of recording and processing of the wages software.

The problems of using this audit technique include:

- The possibility that the client's computer system will be damaged by the testing being undertaken by the auditor. For example, by errors being caused by entering data that the client's software cannot process.

- The need to reverse or remove any transactions input by the auditor. The transactions may be incorrectly or incompletely removed leaving dummy data in the client's live computer system.

- Use of test data can be expensive – the auditor needs to ensure that the benefit gained from the test outweighs the expense. In this situation, it will take a long time to input employee details and there may be more efficient audit tests available.

Answer 49 DELPHIC

(a)   **Audit procedures using audit software**

Procedure	*Reason for procedure*
Cast the receivables ledger to ensure it agrees with the total on the receivables control account.	To ensure the completeness and accuracy of recording of items in the receivables ledger and control account.
Compare the balance on each receivable account with its credit limit to ensure this has not been exceeded.	To check for violation of system rules.
Review the balances in the receivables ledger to ensure no balance exceeds total sales to that customer.	To check for unreasonable items in the ledger.
Calculate receivables days for each month end to monitor control of receivables over the year.	To obtaining new/relevant statistical information.
Stratify receivables balances to show all material items and select appropriate sample for testing.	To select items for audit testing.
Produce an aged receivables analysis to assist with the identification of irrecoverable receivables.	To assist with receivables valuation testing.

(b)   **Problems of using audit software**

Cost

There may be substantial setup costs to use the software, especially where the computer systems of the client have not been fully documented, as is the situation in Delphic. A cost benefit analysis from the audit point-of-view should be carried out prior to deciding to use audit software.

Lack of software documentation

The computer audit department at Delphic cannot confirm that all system documentation is available, especially for the older "legacy" systems currently in use. This again confirms the view that use of audit software should be deferred until next year to avoid extensive setup costs which cannot be recouped due to system changes.

Change to clients' systems

Changes to clients' computer systems can result in costly amendments to the audit software. Given that Delphic's systems will change next year, this is almost certain to result in amendments to the software. Starting to use audit software this year is therefore not advisable.

Outputs obtained

The audit manager needs to be clear exactly what audit assertions are to be tested with the audit software and what outputs are expected. Starting testing just to obtain knowledge of the system is inappropriate as testing may be too detailed and output produced that is not required, increasing the cost for the client.

Use of copy files

The use of copy files means that the auditor will not be certain that these are the actual files being used within Delphic's computer systems, especially as the provenance of those files will not be checked. To ensure that the files are genuine either the auditor should supervise the copying or the "live" files on Delphic's computer systems should be used.

Answer 50 WEAR WRAITH

(a)   **Audit work on railway trucks**

■   Examine board minutes authorising the purchase of the trucks (authorisation).

■   Cast the non-current asset ledger; agree total of railway trucks to the general ledger and financial statements (completeness).

■   Ensure that railway trucks are actually stated as such in the non-current asset note. As a material item, separate disclosure of this category is allowed (disclosure).

■   Cast the non-current asset note in the financial statements. Ensure the note agrees to the amount disclosed in the statement of financial position (disclosure).

■   For a sample of assets from the ledger, confirm existence by physically seeing the trucks or see other corroborative evidence of their use (existence).

■   Identify the supplier of railway trucks from a purchase invoice. Obtain all invoices from this supplier and confirm all are recorded in the non-current asset register (completeness). Also, during non-current asset inspection, record details of some railway trucks and ensure those trucks are recorded in the non-current asset register.

■   Examine a sample of purchase invoices to confirm ownership of the trucks (rights and obligations).

■   Review company policy for depreciation as this is a new category of non-current asset. Confirm with amount charged in similar companies that the depreciation percentage appears to be reasonable (accuracy, valuation and allocation).

■   Agree depreciation charged in the non-current asset note to the amount on the statement of comprehensive income (accuracy, valuation and allocation).

■   Check a sample of depreciation calculations to ensure that they are accurate and that they conform to company policy or check overall calculation (accuracy, valuation and allocation).

■   Ensure that any delivery, testing, asset preparation costs have been correctly treated (i.e. capitalised) where this is appropriate) – (accuracy, valuation and allocation).

■   Current value may also be confirmed using a specialist or appropriate trade journal and compared to the carrying amount shown in the non-current asset register (accuracy, valuation and allocation).

(b) **Issues to raise with management**

Land and buildings

The depreciation rate has been correctly applied at 2% – given an estimated life for the land and buildings category of 50 years. However, the rate has been applied to the whole balance – that is land and buildings. Depreciation of land is incorrect.

To allocate depreciation accurately, a split is required between the land and buildings amounts in the financial statements. Buildings will then be depreciated, but not the land.

Plant and machinery

Depreciation has been charged in full in the year of acquisition, but not charged at all in the year of disposal. This appears to be an appropriate accounting policy – charging depreciation in the year of disposal would only amend the profit or loss on sale in that year and so have a neutral effect on the financial statements.

There appears to be an error in the disposals calculation as the depreciation amount exceeds the cost being eliminated There does not appear to be any logical reason for this and it should be discussed with the directors to identify the reason, if any, for this treatment.

When reason for the error is found, then the depreciation amount must be decreased (or cost eliminated increased) and the profit or loss on sale amended accordingly.

Motor vehicles – point 1

The depreciation percentage stated in the financial statements is 33%. However, the calculation is either 25% on the year-end balance or about 21% on cost brought forward and additions for the year. To be consistent, the non-current asset disclosure note must agree to the actual calculation in the non-current asset note.

The reason for the difference must be found and either the disclosure note or the depreciation calculation amended. If there has been a change in the depreciation rate, then this must also be disclosed in the financial statements.

It is apparent that the low charge arises from the fact that the company has fully-depreciated assets. The overall charge can be verified taking into account values of assets that are fully depreciated.

Motor vehicles – point 2

The cost and depreciation eliminated on sale are the same amount; this is not surprising given that the assets were fully depreciated. However, the depreciation policy for motor vehicles is to depreciate the category over three years. If those vehicles are now being kept for five years, then the depreciation rate is excessive and needs revising to show the actual useful life of the vehicles.

The depreciation rate needs to be discussed with company management, and if necessary the rate amended to reflect the actual life of the vehicles.

Answer 51 GALARTHA

Item	Answer	Justification
1	C	(1), (2) and (3) are all procedures and actions that the auditor should take. (4) is not appropriate as management is responsible for the financial statements and for making any necessary financial statement adjustments.
2	B	(2) and (3) are procedures regarding the existence of the containers. (1) is not practicable. (4) provides evidence of the completeness of the container records.
3	C	Cannot be (4) as the documents only relate to the original purchase. Inspection (or obtaining confirmation) of the statutory records relating to the investment will prove the entity has the right to the investment through continued ownership.
4	D	Qualified ("except for") opinion due to material misstatement on the grounds of non-compliance with *IAS 38 Intangible Assets* – only development costs can be capitalised.
5	C	If the new auditor cannot verify the existence of the inventory by any other means (e.g. a post year-end count and roll back) there will be uncertainty about the existence, and consequently valuation, of inventory. As all necessary evidence required has not been obtained an except for opinion will be issued noting that adjustments may be necessary to the inventory value.

Answer 52 TRENT TEXTILES

(a)   Prior to the commencement of the inventory count

■   Review last year's audit working papers and note the company's system for carrying out the inventory count and any problems experienced last year.

■   Ask the company's management the date the inventory is to be counted.

■   Ask for a copy of the company's instructions for physically counting the inventory and checking that it will ensure the inventory is counted accurately.

■   Check that the staff counting the inventory have been provided with the instructions before the inventory count.

■   Establish if any inventory is being held by third parties. If the value of this inventory is not material obtain written confirmation from the third party and reconcile balances to Trent's inventory records. If it is material, discuss with client to organise (and observe) a physical inventory count at the third party.

■   If there were problems with the inventory count last year, inform the company's management of these problems and ask that staff carrying out the physical count are aware of them so that they will not recur this year.

(b) **Procedures to ensure accurate recording of inventory**

- Ensure that the staff have been briefed by the company's management prior to the physical count, and that they are aware of the inventory they are required to count.

- Inventory sheets should be sequentially numbered, and an employee should be responsible for recording the issue and return of inventory sheets. At the end of the count this employee should ensure that all the inventory sheets have been returned by the counters, and that there is a record of the inventory sheet numbers used.

- Inventory quantities and descriptions should be recorded on the sheets with a pen, and any changes should be initialled by either the staff counting the inventory or the manager in charge of the inventory count. The staff counting the inventory should sign the bottom of the inventory sheets, and any incomplete inventory sheets should be ruled off so that no more items can be added (after the inventory count).

- Ideally, staff should not count inventory which they are responsible for, as this represents a weakness in the system of internal control. However, staff who are responsible for the inventory are likely to describe and count it more accurately than other staff. If staff count their own inventory, there should be more supervision and checks by management to ensure it is counted accurately.

- Staff should count the inventory systematically; by, for instance, going from left to right along shelves. Inventory should be marked when counted to ensure it is counted once and once only. Staff should count the inventory in pairs, with one employee counting the inventory and the other recording the descriptions and quantities on the inventory sheets.

- As Trent Textiles is a manufacturer, it is important that the inventory sheets accurately record the description of the inventory and its state in work in progress. If any employee has difficulty in identifying the inventory, he should consult the manager in charge of the inventory count. For inventory like balls of wool; it is important the weight of the inventory is correctly determined.

- Staff should record the condition of slow-moving, damaged or obsolete inventory on the inventory sheets. This is important, as it indicates inventory which may be worth less than cost.

- There should be no movement of inventory during the physical count, as this could result in the inventory not being counted or being counted twice.

- Management should perform test counts, and check these counts to those counted by the staff counting the inventory. Any significant differences should be investigated.

- At the end of the count, management should ensure that all inventory has been counted, including work-in-progress and goods in the production area.

- In order to determine correct cut-off, management should record the last numbers of documents prior to the inventory count of:

  - goods dispatched (i.e. last shipping note number);
  - goods received (i.e. last receiving report number) returns to suppliers; and
  - returns from customers.

(c) **At the inventory count**

■ To confirm that the inventory count is being carried out in accordance with the client's procedures the auditor must ensure that:

❑ Inventory is counted systematically;

❑ The inventory is marked when counted;

❑ The counting is performed carefully;

❑ There is a proper description of the items on the inventory sheets, including their description and state of completion;

❑ Inventory which is slow moving, damaged, obsolete and seconds is properly recorded on the inventory sheets;

❑ There is no movement of inventory during the physical count.

■ Perform a sample of test counts, concentrating on large value items. These checks will be performed:

❑ From the inventory sheets to the physical inventory, to ensure that inventory on the inventory sheets exists;

❑ From the physical inventory to the inventory sheets; to ensure that all inventory which exists appears on the inventory sheets.

Record details of the test counts in the audit working papers. These details will include a description of the item, its part number and quantity, and the inventory sheet number on which the count is recorded. Mark the inventory sheet so that the item can be identified at the final audit.

■ Any errors found in these counts will be discussed with the staff counting the inventory, the inventory will be counted again, and the correct quantity will be recorded on the inventory sheets and in working papers.

■ Where inventory is recorded by weight, check that the company's procedures correctly determine this weight, and test check the weight of a sample of these items.

■ If there is any inventory in sealed boxes, ask for a sample of these boxes to be opened to ensure that they contain the garments (or other items) stated on the note on the box. For a further sample of boxes, check their weight to ensure they are likely to contain the quantity stated on the note on the box.

■ Record:

❑ The inventory sheet numbers used. Copy all inventory sheets at the end of the count. This will highlight any additions or amendments to the inventory sheets and any inventory sheets which have been added after the end of the count.

❑ Details of the last numbers before the inventory count recording (to assist in cut-off testing):

– dispatch of goods;
– receipt of goods;
– returns from customers;
– returns to suppliers.

■   At the end of the inventory count, check that all the inventory has been counted, by test checking that items in the factory are recorded on the inventory sheets.

■   Complete the audit firm's checklist relating to the inventory count, complete working papers and reach a conclusion on the reliability of the inventory count process.

■   Note any errors and weaknesses found during the inventory count, so that they can be followed up at the final audit.

Answer 53 SMOOTHBRUSH

Tutorial note: *This question is not current exam style for a 30-mark question as it does not predominantly cover just one topic area drawn from syllabus areas B, D or D.*

(a)   Audit risks

Identification	*Explanation*
Smoothbrush supplies 60% of its goods to Homewares at a significantly reduced selling price, hence inventory may be overvalued.	Per IAS 2 *Inventories*, inventory should be stated at the lower of cost and net realisable value (NRV). Therefore, as selling prices are much lower for goods sold to Homewares, there is a risk that the NRV of some inventory items may be lower than cost and hence that inventory could be overvalued.
Recoverability of receivable balances as receivables may be overstated.	Smoothbrush has extended its credit terms to Homewares from one month to four months. Hence there is an increased risk as balances outstanding become older, that they may become irrecoverable.
Valuation of plant and equipment.	The production facility has a large amount of unused plant and equipment. As per IAS 16 *Property, Plant and Equipment* and IAS 36 *Impairment of Assets*, this plant and equipment should be stated at the lower of its carrying value and recoverable amount, which may be at scrap value depending on its age and condition.
Cut-off of purchases and inventory may not be accurate.	Smoothbrush imports goods from South Asia and the paint can be in transit for up to two months. The company accounts for goods when they receive them. Therefore at the year end only goods that have been received into the warehouse should be included in the inventory balance and a respective payables balance recognised.
New inventory system introduced in the year. This could result in inventory balances being misstated.	Smoothbrush has introduced a continuous/perpetual inventory counting system in the year. These records will be used for recording inventory at the year end. If the records and new system have not initially been set up correctly there is a risk that the year end balances may not be fairly stated.
Inventory may be overstated as Smoothbrush no longer has an allowance for slow-moving items.	Unless all slow-moving/obsolete items are identified at the year end and their value written down, there is a risk that the overall value of inventory may be overstated.

Identification	*Explanation*
Provisions/contingent liability disclosures may not be complete.	The company's finance director (FD) has left and is intending to sue Smoothbrush for unfair dismissal. However, the company does not intend to make any provision/disclosures for sums due to the FD.
	Under IAS 37 *Provisions, Contingent Liabilities and Contingent Assets*, if there is a present obligation, a probable outflow of resources to settle the obligation and a reliable estimate can be made of the obligation then a provision should be recognised.
	If the obligation is only possible, or if there is a present obligation but it is not recognised as there is not a probable outflow of resources, or the amount of the obligation cannot be measured with sufficient reliability then a contingent liability should be disclosed, unless the likelihood of payment is remote.
Detection risk is higher due to the changes in the finance department.	The financial controller has been appointed as temporary FD and this lack of experience could result in an increased risk of errors arising in the financial statements. In addition the previous FD is not available to help the finance or audit team.
Inventory may be over or understated if the perpetual inventory counts are not complete and accurate.	The inventory counts are to cover all of the inventory lines. If any areas of the warehouse are not counted then this will need to be done at the year end.
	In addition inventory adjustments arising from the counts must be verified and updated by an appropriate member of the finance team to ensure that the records are accurate.

(b)   **Assessing risks**

ISA 315 *Identifying and Assessing the Risks of Material Misstatement through Understanding the Entity and Its Environment*, requires auditors "to identify and assess the risks of material misstatement, whether due to fraud or error, at the financial statement and assertion levels".

It is vitally important for auditors to assess engagement risks at the planning stage, this will ensure that attention is focused early on the areas most likely to cause material misstatements.

A thorough risk assessment will also help the auditor to fully understand the entity, which is vital for an effective audit.

Any unusual transactions or balances would also be identified early, so that these could be addressed in a timely manner.

In addition, as most auditors adopt a risks based audit approach then these risks need to be assessed early in order for the audit strategy and detailed work programmes to be developed.

Assessing risks early should also result in an efficient audit. The team will only focus their time and effort on key areas as opposed to balances or transactions that might be immaterial or unlikely to contain errors.

In addition assessing risk early should ensure that the most appropriate team is selected with more experienced staff allocated to higher risk audits and high risk balances.

A thorough risk analysis should ultimately reduce the risk of an inappropriate audit opinion being given. The audit would have focused on the main risk areas and hence all material misstatements should have been identified, resulting in the correct opinion being given.

It should enable the auditor to have a good understanding of the risks of fraud, money laundering, etc.

Assessing risk should enable the auditor to assess whether the client is a going concern.

(c)

Suitable controls	Explanation
The inventory count team should be independent of the warehouse team.	Currently the team includes a warehouse staff member and an internal auditor. There should be segregation of roles between those who have day-to-day responsibility for inventory and those who are checking it. If the same team are responsible for maintaining and checking inventory, then errors and fraud could be hidden.
Timetable of counts should be regularly reviewed to ensure that all areas are counted.	The warehouse has been divided into 12 areas that are each due to be counted once over the year. All inventory is required to be counted once a year, hence if the timetable is not monitored then some areas could be missed out.
Movements of inventory should be stopped from the designated areas during continuous/ perpetual inventory counts.	Goods will continue to move in and out of the warehouse during the counts. Inventory records could be under/over stated if product lines are missed or double counted due to movements in the warehouse.
Inventory counting sheets should be pre-printed with a description or item code of the goods, but the quantities per the records should not be pre-recorded.	The inventory sheets produced for the count have the quantities pre-printed, therefore a risk arises that the counting team could just agree with the record quantities, making under counting more likely, rather than counting the inventory lines correctly.
A second independent team should check the counts performed by the inventory count team.	By counting the lines twice this should help to ensure completeness and accuracy of the counts, and hence that any inventory adjustments are appropriate.
Inventory checks should be performed in two ways; from records to inventory physically present in the warehouse and from the warehouse to the records.	Currently the team is comparing the records to the inventory in the warehouse. Two way counting ensures that inventory lines are not over or understated. If the count is only performed from the records to the warehouse then this will only ensure existence or overstatement of the records. To ensure completeness is addressed then the inventory in the warehouse must be compared to the records as well.
Any damaged or obsolete goods should be moved to a designated area, where a responsible official then inspects it, it should not be removed from the sheets.	Damaged or obsolete goods should be written down or provided against to ensure that they are stated at the lower of cost and net realisable value. This may not involve fully writing off the inventory item as is currently occurring. This is an assessment that should only be performed by a suitably trained member of the finance team, as opposed to the inventory count team.

Suitable controls	Explanation
After the count, the inventory count sheets should be compared to the inventory records, any adjustments should be investigated and if appropriate the records updated in a prompt manner by an authorised person.	At the year end the inventory of Smoothbrush will be based on the records maintained. Hence the records must be complete, accurate and valid. It is important that only individuals authorised to do so can amend records. Senior members of the finance team should regularly review the types and levels of adjustments, as recurring inventory adjustments could indicate possible fraud.

(d)   Substantive procedures

(i)   To confirm valuation of inventory

■   Select a representative sample of goods in inventory at the year end, agree the cost per the records to a recent purchase invoice and ensure that the cost is correctly stated.

■   Select a sample of year end goods and review post year end sales invoices to ascertain if net realisable value is above cost or if an adjustment is required.

■   For a sample of manufactured items obtain cost sheets and confirm:

❑   raw material costs to recent purchase invoices;
❑   labour costs to time sheets or wage records;
❑   overheads allocated are of a production nature.

■   Review aged inventory reports and identify any slow moving goods, discuss with management why these items have not been written down.

■   Compare the level/value of aged product lines to the total inventory value to assess whether the allowance for slow-moving goods of 1% should be reinstated.

■   Review the inventory records to identify the level of adjustments made throughout the year for damaged/obsolete items. If significant consider whether the year-end records require further adjustments and discuss with management whether any further write downs/allowance may be required.

■   Follow up any damaged/obsolete items noted by the auditor at the inventory counts attended, to ensure that the inventory records have been updated correctly.

(ii)   To confirm completeness of provisions or contingent liability

■   Discuss with management the nature of the dispute between Smoothbrush and the former finance director (FD), to ensure that a full understanding of the issue is obtained and to assess whether an obligation exists.

■   Review any correspondence with the former FD to assess if a reliable estimate of any potential payments can be made.

■   Write to the company's lawyers to obtain their views as to the probability of the FD's claim being successful.

■   Review board minutes and any company correspondence to assess whether there is any evidence to support the former FD's claims of unfair dismissal.

- Obtain a written representation from the directors of Smoothbrush confirming their view that the former FD's chances of a successful claim are remote, and hence no provision or contingent liability is required.

Answer 54 MISTIREAD

(a)   **Advantages of perpetual inventory systems**

- There is no disruption caused by an annual inventory count.

- There is more accurate and regular inventory counting, which enables errors and slow moving or damaged inventory to be identified earlier.

- Actual inventory balances are known at any time, allowing re-ordering of best-selling books to take place on a timely basis. There will also be fewer causes of inventory reaching zero causing stock outs with orders not being fulfilled.

- Increased control over storekeepers because inventory is being reviewed regularly; this should decrease any pilferage.

- Auditors can rely on the computerised inventory system, reducing substantive audit tests of inventory during the year and at the year end.

(b)   **Audit procedures**

Physical count	*Reason for*
Arrange a meeting with the internal audit department.	Determine the extent to which reliance can be placed on the work of the internal audit department.
Discuss the procedures carried out and review working papers produced during the continuous inventory checks.	
For any errors identified, ensure that appropriate adjustments were made to the perpetual inventory system.	
Visit the warehouse and obtain a sample of inventory items already recorded on the perpetual inventory system and agree to the book inventory.	To ensure that the inventory recorded on the computer system actually exists.

Physical count	*Reason for*
For a sample of books in the warehouse, obtain details and agree perpetual computer system records.	To ensure that all inventory is recorded on the inventory computer system – and there is completeness of recording.
Review the condition of the books, taking details of any which appear to be old or damaged.	To confirm that any inventory which is damaged or unsaleable is correctly valued.
Form an opinion regarding the overall accuracy of the perpetual inventory system.	To confirm that inventory quantities have been correctly recorded.
Ensure all inventory lines are counted at least once per year in discussion with the internal audit department.	To confirm that all inventory is counted regularly.

(c) **Engagement letter**

■ Discuss the matter again with the directors in an attempt to reach a suitable compromise.

■ Remind the directors that statutory audits require the directors to make all the necessary information and explanations available to the auditor.

■ Explain that lack of information on the website will result in a limitation in scope of the audit work.

■ Further explain that because the lack of evidence appears to relate to a material amount that the auditor's report will have to be modified with an "except for" qualification due to the lack of information and the possibility of misstatement of non-current assets.

■ Finally note that auditor may have to decline to continue to act for MistiRead unless suitable terms of engagement can be agreed.

Answer 55 PINEAPPLE BEACH HOTEL

(a) **Financial statement assertions and year-end inventory substantive procedures**

(i) *Existence*

Assets, liabilities and equity interests exist.

Substantive procedures

During the inventory count select a sample of assets recorded in the inventory records and agree to the warehouse to confirm the assets exist.

Obtain a sample of pre year-end goods despatch notes and agree that these finished goods are excluded from the inventory records.

(ii) *Rights and obligations*

The entity holds or controls the rights to assets, and liabilities are the obligations of the entity.

Substantive procedures

Confirm during the inventory count that any goods belonging to third parties are excluded from the inventory records and count.

For year-end raw materials and finished goods confirm title belongs to the company by agreeing goods to a recent purchase invoice in the company name.

(iii) *Completeness*

All assets, liabilities and equity interests that should have been recorded have been recorded, and all related disclosures that should have been included in the financial statements have been included.

Substantive procedures

Obtain a copy of the inventory listing and agree the total to the general ledger and the financial statements.

During the inventory count select a sample of goods physically present in the warehouse and confirm recorded in the inventory records.

Review all inventory disclosures for completeness and correctness.

(iv)   Accuracy, valuation and allocation

Assets, liabilities and equity interests are included in the financial statements at appropriate amounts and any resulting accuracy, valuation or allocation adjustments are appropriately recorded, and related disclosures have been appropriately measured and described.

Substantive procedures

Select a sample of goods in inventory at the year end, agree the cost per the records to a recent purchase invoice and ensure that the cost is correctly stated.

Select a sample of year-end goods and review post year-end sales invoices to ascertain if net realisable value is above cost or if an adjustment is required.

(v)   Classification

Assets, liabilities and equity interests have been recorded in the proper accounts.

Substantive procedures

Select a sample of sales invoices and trace the cost to cost of sales to ensure that the cost has been expensed.

(vi)   Presentation

Assets, liabilities and equity interests are appropriately aggregated and disaggregated and clearly described, and disclosures are relevant and understandable.

Substantive procedures

Review the financial statements to verify that inventory is properly presented as a current asset and that the footnotes include all required inventory disclosures.

(b) **Substantive procedures**

Depreciation

- ■ Review the reasonableness of the depreciation rates applied to the new leisure facilities and compare to industry averages.

- ■ Review the capital expenditure budgets for the next few years to assess whether there are any plans to replace any of the new leisure equipment, as this would indicate that the useful life is less than 10 years.

- ■ Review profits and losses on disposal of assets disposed of in the year, to assess the reasonableness of the depreciation policies.

- ■ Select a sample of leisure equipment and recalculate the depreciation charge to ensure that the non-current asset register is correct.

- ■ Perform a proof in total calculation for the depreciation charged on the equipment, discuss with management if significant fluctuations arise.

- ■ Review the disclosure of the depreciation charges and policies in the draft financial statements.

Food poisoning

- ■ Review the correspondence from the customers claiming food poisoning to assess whether Pineapple has a present obligation as a result of a past event.

- ■ Send an enquiry letter to the lawyers of Pineapple to obtain their view as to the probability of the claim being successful.

- ■ Review board minutes to understand whether the directors believe that the claim will be successful or not.

- ■ Review the post year-end period to assess whether any payments have been made to any of the claimants.

- ■ Discuss with management as to whether they propose to include a contingent liability disclosure or not, consider the reasonableness of this.

- ■ Obtain a written management representation confirming management's view that the lawsuit is unlikely to be successful and hence no provision is required.

- ■ Review the adequacy of any disclosures made in the financial statements.

(c) **Working papers**

- ■ Name of client – identifies the client being audited.

- ■ Year-end date – identifies the year end to which the audit working papers relate.

- ■ Subject – identifies the area of the financial statements that is being audited, the topic area of the working paper, such as receivables confirmation procedures.

- ■ Working paper reference – provides a clear reference to identify the number of the working paper, for example, R12 being the 12th working paper in the audit of receivables.

- ■ Preparer – identifies the name of the audit team member who prepared the working paper, so any queries can be directed to the relevant person.

- Date prepared – the date that the audit work was performed by the team member; this helps to identify what was known at the time and what issues may have occurred subsequently.

- Reviewer – the name of the audit team member who reviewed the working paper; this provides evidence that the audit work was reviewed by an appropriate member of the team.

- Date of review – the date the audit work was reviewed by the senior member of the team; this should be prior to the date that the audit report was signed.

- Objective of work/test – the aim of the work being performed, could be the related financial statement assertion; this provides the context for why the audit procedure is being performed.

- Details of work performed – the audit tests performed along with sufficient detail of items selected for testing.

- Results of work performed – whether any exceptions arose in the audit work and if any further work is required.

- Conclusion – the overall conclusion on the audit work performed, whether the area is true and fair.

Answer 56 LILY WINDOW GLASS

(a) **Inventory count arrangements**

(i) *Deficiencies*	*(ii)* *Recommendations*
The warehouse manager is planning to supervise the inventory count. Whilst he is familiar with the inventory, he has overall responsibility for the inventory and so is not independent. He may want to hide inefficiencies and any issues that arise so that his department is not criticised.	An alternative supervisor who is not normally involved with the inventory, such as an internal audit manager, should supervise the inventory count. The warehouse manager and his team should not be involved in the count at all.
There are ten teams of counters, each team having two members of staff. However, there is no clear division of responsibilities within the team. Therefore, both members of staff could count together rather than checking each other's count; and errors in their count may not be identified.	Each team should be informed that both members are required to count their assigned inventory separately. Therefore, one counts and the second member checks that the inventory has been counted correctly.
The internal audit teams are undertaking inventory counts rather than reviewing the controls and performing sample test counts. Their role should be focused on confirming the accuracy of the inventory counting procedures.	The internal audit counters should sample check the counting undertaken by the ten teams to provide an extra control over the completeness and accuracy of the count.
Once areas are counted, the teams are not flagging the aisles as completed. Therefore there is the risk that some areas of the warehouse could be double counted or missed out.	All aisles should be flagged as completed, once the inventory has been counted. In addition, internal audit or the count supervisor should check at the end of the count that all 20 aisles have been flagged as completed.

(i) *Deficiencies*	*(ii)* *Recommendations*
Inventory not listed on the sheets is to be entered onto separate sheets, which are not sequentially numbered. Therefore the supervisor will be unable to ensure the completeness of all inventory sheets.	Each team should be given a blank sheet for entering any inventory count which is not on their sheets. Blank sheets should be sequentially numbered; unused sheets should be returned to the supervisor to check the sequence of all sheets at the end of the count.
Although the sheets are completed in ink and sequentially numbered there is no indication that they are signed by the counting team. Therefore if any issues arise with the counting in an aisle, it will be difficult to follow up as the identity of the counting team will not be known.	All inventory sheets should be signed by the relevant team upon completion of an aisle. When the sheets are returned, the supervisor should check that they have been signed.
Damaged goods are not being stored in a central area, and instead the counter is just noting on the inventory sheets the level of damage. However, it will be difficult for the finance team to decide on an appropriate level of write down if they are not able to see the damaged goods. In addition, if these goods are left in the aisles, they could be inadvertently sold to customers or moved to another aisle.	Damaged goods should be clearly flagged by the counting teams and at the end of the count appropriate machinery should be used to move all damaged windows to a central location. This will avoid the risk of selling these goods. A senior member of the finance team should then inspect these goods to assess the level of any write down or allowance.
Lily Window Glass (Lily) undertakes continuous production and so there will be movements of goods during the count. Inventory records could be under/overstated if goods are missed or double counted due to movements in the warehouse.	It is not practical to stop all inventory movements as production needs to continue. Any raw materials required for 31 December should be estimated and put to one side. These will not be included as raw materials and instead will be work-in-progress. The goods which are manufactured on 31 December should be stored to one side, and at the end of the count should be counted once and included within finished goods. Any goods received from suppliers should be stored in one location and counted once at the end and included as part of raw materials. Goods to be despatched to customers should be kept to a minimum for the day of the count.
The warehouse manager is to assess the level of work-in-progress and raw materials. In the past, a specialist has undertaken this role. It is unlikely that the warehouse manager has the experience to assess the level of work-in-progress as this is something that the factory manager would be more familiar with.	A specialist should be utilised to assess both work-in-progress and the quantities of raw materials.
In addition, whilst the warehouse manager is familiar with the raw materials, if he makes a mistake in assessing the quantities then inventory could be materially misstated.	The warehouse manager could estimate the raw materials and the specialist could check it. This would give an indication as to whether he is able to accurately assess the quantities for subsequent inventory counts.

(b)   **Procedures during the inventory count**

- Observe the counting teams of Lily to confirm whether the inventory count instructions are being followed correctly.

- Select a sample and perform test counts from inventory sheets to warehouse aisle and from warehouse aisle to inventory sheets.

- Confirm the procedures for identifying and segregating damaged goods are operating correctly.

- Select a sample of damaged items as noted on the inventory sheets and inspect these windows to confirm whether the level of damage is correctly noted.

- Observe the procedures for movements of inventory during the count, to confirm that no raw materials or finished goods have been omitted or counted twice.

- Obtain a photocopy of the completed sequentially numbered inventory sheets for follow up testing on the final audit.

- Identify and make a note of the last goods received notes (GRNs) and goods despatched notes (GDNs) for 31 December in order to perform cut-off procedures.

- Observe the procedures carried out by the warehouse manager in assessing the level of work-in-progress and consider the reasonableness of any assumptions used.

- Discuss with the warehouse manager how he has estimated the raw materials quantities. To the extent that it is possible, re-perform the procedures adopted by the warehouse manager.

- Identify and record any inventory held for third parties (if any) and confirm that it is excluded from the count.

(c)   **Computer-assisted audit techniques (CAATs)**

(i)   *Audit procedures using CAATs*

The audit team can use audit software to calculate inventory days for the year-to-date to compare against the prior year to identify whether inventory is turning over slower, as this may be an indication that it is overvalued.

Audit software can be utilised to produce an aged inventory analysis to identify any slow moving goods, which may require write down (e.g. if broken) or an allowance (e.g. if not a popular design).

Cast the inventory listing to confirm the completeness and accuracy of inventory.

Audit software can be used to select a representative sample of items for testing to confirm net realisable value and/or cost.

Audit software can be utilised to recalculate cost and net realisable value for a sample of inventory.

CAATs can be used to verify cut-off by testing whether the dates of the last GRNs and GDNs recorded relate to pre year end; and that any with a date of 1 January 2017 onwards have been excluded from the inventory records.

CAATs can be used to confirm whether any inventory adjustments noted during the count have been correctly updated into final inventory records.

(ii) *Potential advantages of using CAATs*

■ CAATs enable the audit team to test a large volume of inventory data accurately and quickly.

■ If CAATs are utilised on the audit of Lily, then as long as they do not change their inventory systems, they can be cost effective after setup.

■ CAATs can test program controls within the inventory system as well as general IT controls, such as passwords.

■ Allows the team to test the actual inventory system and records rather than printouts from the system which could be incorrect.

■ CAATs reduce the level of human error in testing and hence provide a better quality of audit evidence.

■ CAATs results can be compared with traditional audit testing; if these two sources agree, then overall audit confidence will increase.

■ The use of CAATs frees up audit team members to focus on judgemental and high risk areas, rather than number crunching.

(iii) *Potential disadvantages of using CAATs*

■ The cost of using CAATs in this first year will be high as there will be significant set up costs, it will also be a time-consuming process which increases costs.

■ As this is the first time that CAATs will be used on Lily's audit, then the team may require training on the specific CAATs to be utilised.

■ If Lily's inventory system is likely to change in the foreseeable future, then costly revisions may be required to the designed CAATs.

■ The inventory system may not be compatible with the audit firm's CAATs, in which case bespoke CAATs may be required, which will increase the audit costs.

■ If testing is performed over the live inventory system, there is a risk that the data could be corrupted or lost.

■ If testing is performed using copy files rather than live data, there is the risk that these files are not genuine copies of the actual files.

■ In order to perform CAATs, there must be adequate systems documentation available. If this is not the case for Lily, then it will be more difficult to devise appropriate CAATs due to a lack of understanding of the inventory system.

Answer 57 WESTERN INDUSTRIES

(a) **Relevant assertions**

Tutorial note: *Accounts receivable is an account balance. The relevant assertions for account balances are completeness, existence, accuracy, valuation and allocation, rights and obligations, classification and presentation.*

Completeness – All accounts receivable that should have been recorded have been recorded and all related disclosures that should have been included in the financial statements have been included.

Existence – Accounts receivable that have been recorded exist, meaning they represent actual amounts owed by real customers.

Accuracy, valuation and allocation – Accounts receivable are included in the financial statements at the correct amount, an appropriate valuation allowance for uncollectible/irrecoverable amounts has been appropriately recorded, and related disclosures have been appropriately measured and described.

Rights and obligations – The entity holds or controls the right to receive the payments on the accounts receivable.

Classification – Accounts receivable have been recorded in the proper accounts.

Presentation – Accounts receivable are appropriately aggregated and clearly described and related disclosures are relevant and understandable.

(b) **Confirmation responses**

Ames

(i)   Audit procedure – Verify the date of recording the cash receipt (in the cash book) and date of bank deposit (paying-in slip and bank statement).

(ii)   Conclusion – If the cash receipt and deposit occurred before 31 December, $25,000 is not a receivable at the year end; it should be included in the bank and cash balance. If the cash receipt and deposit occurred after 31 December, then this is a valid receivable at year end.

Brown

(i)   Audit procedure – Review the terms of the consignment agreement between Brown and Western and any correspondence between the entities that substantiates Brown's claim that the goods have not been sold.

(ii)   Conclusion – If there is a valid consignment arrangement and the goods have not been sold, there is no trade receivable at the year end. The cost of the consigned goods ($35,000) should be included in inventory.

     Tutorial note: *Under IFRS 15 revenue will not be recognised in respect of the consigned goods until they are sold by Brown (i.e. when control passes from Western to Brown).*

Copper

(i)   Audit procedure – Examine the sales invoice, despatch note and other shipping documentation to determine when the goods were shipped to the customer.

(ii)   Conclusion – If the goods received by the customer on 4 January 2017 were despatched before the year end $35,000 is a receivable at the year end. If despatched after the year end there is no receivable; the cost of the goods should be included in inventory.

Devon

(i)   Audit procedure – Verify the date on which Devon signed for the receipt of the goods to delivery confirmation notices (or similar) which the courier provides to Western (e.g. in support of invoices).

(ii)   Conclusion – Since control of the goods did not pass to Devon until the goods were received there is no trade receivable at the year end.

Epoch

(i)   Audit procedure – Inspect the cancelled sales order and examine any correspondence between Brown and Western that confirms that the order was cancelled. Inspect any credit note raised after the year end to cancel the sales invoice.

(ii)   Conclusion – This is not a trade receivable at the year end. If the goods were despatched before the year end they should not have been delivered but returned to inventory.

Fynes

(i)   Audit procedure – Inspect the goods return (inwards) note to confirm that Western received back the duplicated shipment. Inspect the credit note raised after the year to cancel the second invoice.

(ii)   Conclusion – $20,000 of the $40,000 is not a receivable at the year end even though Fynes took control of the duplicate shipment and did not return the goods until after the year end. Western cannot recognise revenue for goods sent in error.

(c)   Valuation of trade receivables

Accounts receivable are reported in the financial statements net of the allowance for uncollectible accounts (credit losses). The valuation risk for trade receivables is the risk that the allowance will be understated and thus the net amount will be overstated. In order to address this risk, the auditor should perform the following procedures:

- Understand the terms of payment and management's policy on ageing debts;

- Compare the amounts of the gross receivables balance and the allowance to prior years and to expectations based on current year sales and collection policies;

- Test the allowance for uncollectible accounts (an accounting estimate) using one or a combination of the following procedures:

    ❏   Review and test management's process used to develop the allowance;

    ❏   Make an independent estimate of the allowance and compare to the recorded allowance;

    ❏   Review subsequent events to confirm the allowance, including subsequent collection of cash for material accounts receivable and any material write-offs after the year end.

Answer 58 SHERWOOD MACHINES

Item	Answer	Justification
1	C	Positive confirmations should be sent to Sherwood's customers because the risk of material misstatement is high due to misstatements revealed by prior year confirmations, the number of customers with high balances and the internal control weaknesses. There is nothing to suggest that Sherwood's customers will ignore confirmation requests.
2	B	When the balance is not agreed by the customer, the auditor should reconcile the difference. The majority of items making up any difference should be due to timing (i.e. cash and goods in transit). Invoices not included by the customer should agree to despatch notes raised before the year end. Payments included by the customer should agree to cash received shortly after (not before) the year end. There is no point in sending a second confirmation request. The auditor should not ask Sherwood to adjust the customer's receivable balance unless a misstatement has been confirmed.
3	B	If the customer is unable to confirm the balance, the auditor should perform alternative procedures, such as agreeing subsequent cash receipts (not cash receipts from before the year end) and supporting documentation (e.g. invoice and despatch note). The auditor would not send a second confirmation request.
4	B	To test for understatement the direction of the test should be from a source document to the accounting records or financial statements. Both A and B do this but only B covers receivables at the year end. Combined, both A and B are elements of cut-off testing.
5	D	If the client refuses permission for a customer to be sent a confirmation request, the auditor's scepticism must ask why. Normally the auditor should search for alternative evidence on that receivable balance but with increased scepticism as the customer is a friend of the client.

Answer 59 ALTERNATIVE PROCEDURES

(a)   Direct confirmation of receivables

Evidence

- Auditors often seek direct confirmation of receivables to ensure that the amounts stated in the entity's accounts receivable ledger are not overstated. Confirmation also provides evidence in relation to certain frauds and the quality of internal controls.

- Confirmation that an amount is owed is not confirmation that the amount will be paid and auditors need additional evidence on the recoverability of receivables.

- There are two types of confirmation, positive and negative. In the former case, the customer is requested to reply in any case, and the auditor can either insert the balance to be confirmed or the customer can be requested to do so. In the latter case, a reply is only requested if the customer disagrees. This method is only suitable where receivables are well-controlled.

Alternative procedures

■   Where no reply is received it is important that alternative evidence is obtained on the same balance (and not to test another balance). Where there is a discrepancy between the client's records and the customer's records, the matter should be investigated and resolved.

■   Sometimes the customer can provide a reconciliation particularly if the matter only relates to timing differences. On other occasions there may be a dispute and an allowance for non-recoverability may be necessary.

■   Alternative evidence for receivables includes payment of the amount after the period-end, a review of contracts and signed delivery notes, and analytical procedures on the ageing of receivables.

(b)   Confirmation of inventory held by third parties

Evidence

■   It is often not possible for auditors to confirm inventory held by third parties by attendance at an inventory count and therefore the only evidence available is confirmation from the third party.

■   It is particularly important to ensure that the confirmation is genuine because of the possibility of fraudulent collusion between the third party and the client to inflate inventory and profit figures.

■   The reliability of service from the third party and the quality of documentation and correspondence are all taken account of as part of the auditor's risk assessment in this area.

Alternative procedures

■   If the inventory held by the third party is likely to be material, the auditor must consider the possibility of visiting the third party and attending the inventory count.

■   The auditor may review and test the controls over the movement of inventory to and from the third party and the related records, in order to reduce the level of substantive evidence needed at the period-end.

■   Records that show "negative" inventory (more "outs" than "ins") at either the client or the third party may be indicative of misclassifications, for example.

Answer 60 TORRES LEISURE CLUB

Item	Answer	Justification
1	C	In any accounting system there are inherent limitations of the internal controls, the risk of collusion being one. However, all other factors in the scenario indicate that the internal controls over sales and accounts receivable can be relied upon if audit tests do not indicate otherwise.
2	B	Occurrence, classification and presentation are assertions relevant to subscription income. Existence (1) and rights and obligations (5) are not relevant because they are assertions related to account balances rather than transactions.

| 3 | D | Statement 2 is not appropriate because the confirmation needs to be received in writing. (A verbal confirmation is not sufficient.) Statement 3 is not appropriate because not all differences will be errors. (The senior should first identify whether the differences relate to timing differences or whether there are possible errors in the accounting records.) |

| 4 | B | Interim testing is appropriate because most of the sales are made in the first nine months of the year. As revenue is a material balance, interim testing should be tests of details, followed by analytical procedures performed on transactions occurring from the interim date to the year-end date. The auditor is unlikely to perform tests of controls at an interim date. |

Tutorial note: *The low volume of transactions means that it is more efficient and effective to adopt a substantive approach.*

| 5 | A | To test for understatement the direction of the test should go from a source document up to the accounting records or financial statements. Only A and D go in this direction but in D the goods should only be recorded as a sale if they have been despatched. |

Answer 61 CHESTNUT & CO

Item	Answer	Justification
1	D	Statements (2), (3) and (4) are all audit procedures that could be used to gather evidence related to Palm's disputed receivable. Statement (1) is not an appropriate audit procedure as the Palm, not the auditor, is responsible for making any necessary adjusting entries.
2	B	Any adjustment to allow for the irrecoverability of a trade receivable will have the effect of reducing amounts receivable (which reduces total assets) and increasing expense (which reduces profit before tax). Therefore, only these benchmarks are relevant.
3	B	If management refuses to provide against this receivable, the audit report will need to be modified. As receivables are overstated and the error is material but not pervasive a qualified opinion would be necessary.
4	C	Statements (3) and (4) are both audit procedures that would provide the auditor with evidence related to the completeness and existence of inventory. An analytical review to assess inventory turnover (Statement (1)) provides evidence related to valuation. Recalculation of a sample of inventory value calculations and count sheet castings (Statement (2)) provides evidence related to accuracy.
5	D	It is perfectly acceptable for the external auditor to use the systems documentation prepared by the internal auditors as part of obtaining an understanding of internal controls provided the external auditor carries out walk-through checks to confirm the accuracy of this documentation.

Answer 62 HAWTHORN ENTERPRISES

(a)   **Assertions for classes of transactions and events**

Occurrence

The transactions and events that have been recorded or disclosed have actually occurred and such transactions and events pertain to the entity.

Substantive procedures

Select a sample of sales transactions recorded in the sales day book; agree the details back to a goods despatched note (GDN) and customer order.

Review the monthly breakdown of sales per key product, compare to the prior year and budget and investigate any significant differences.

Completeness

All transactions and events that should have been recorded have been recorded, and all related disclosures that should have been included in the financial statements have been included.

Substantive procedures

Select a sample of GDNs raised during the year; agree to the sales invoice and that they are recorded in the sales day book.

Review the total amount of sales, compare to the prior year and budget and investigate any significant differences.

Accuracy

The amounts and other data relating to recorded transactions and events have been recorded appropriately, and related disclosures have been appropriately measured and described.

Substantive procedures

Select a sample of sales invoices and recalculate that the totals and calculation of sales tax are correct.

For a sample of sales invoices, confirm the sales price stated agrees to the authorised price list.

Cut-off

Transactions and events have been recorded in the correct accounting period.

Substantive procedures

Select a sample of pre and post year-end GDNs and agree that the sale is recorded in the correct period's sales day books.

Review the post year-end sales returns and agree if they relate to pre year-end sales that the revenue has been correctly removed from the sales day book.

Classification

Transactions and events have been recorded in the proper accounts.

Substantive procedures

Agree for a sample of sales invoices that they have been correctly recorded within revenue nominal account codes and included within revenue in the financial statements.

Presentation

Transactions and events are appropriately aggregated or disaggregated and clearly described and related disclosures are relevant and understandable in the context of the requirements of the applicable financial reporting framework.

Substantive procedures

Review the presentation of revenue on the statement of profit or loss and other comprehensive income and the relevant footnotes.

(b)   **Substantive procedures**

    (i)   *Supplier statement reconciliations*

- Select a representative sample of year-end supplier statements and agree the balance to the purchase ledger of Hawthorn. If the balance agrees, then no further work is required.

- Where differences occur due to invoices in transit, confirm from goods received notes (GRN) whether the receipt of goods was pre year end, if so confirm that this receipt is included in year-end accruals.

- Where differences occur due to cash in transit from Hawthorn to the supplier, confirm from the cashbook and bank statements that the cash was sent pre year end.

- Discuss any further adjusting items with the purchase ledger supervisor to understand the nature of the reconciling item, and whether it has been correctly accounted for.

    (ii)   *Bank reconciliation*

- Obtain Hawthorn's bank account reconciliation and cast to check the additions to ensure arithmetical accuracy.

- Agree the balance per the bank reconciliation to an original year-end bank statement and to the bank confirmation letter.

- Agree the reconciliation's balance per the cash book to the year-end cash book.

- Trace all the outstanding lodgements to the pre year-end cash book, post year-end bank statement and also to paying-in-book pre year end.

- Trace all unpresented cheques through to a pre year-end cash book and post year-end statement. For any unusual amounts or significant delays, obtain explanations from management.

- Examine any old unpresented cheques to assess if they need to be written back into the purchase ledger as they are no longer valid to be presented.

(iii)   Receivables

- Review the aged receivable ledger to identify any slow moving or old receivable balances, discuss the status of these balances with the credit controller to assess whether they are likely to pay.

- Select a significant sample of receivables and review whether there are any after date cash receipts, ensure that a sample of slow moving/old receivable balances is also selected.

- Review customer correspondence to identify any balances which are in dispute or unlikely to be paid.

- Review board minutes to identify whether there are any significant concerns in relation to payments by customers.

- Calculate average receivable days and compare this to prior year, investigate any significant differences.

- Inspect post year-end sales returns/credit notes and consider whether an additional loss allowance against receivables is required.

- Select a sample of goods despatched notes (GDN) before and just after the year end and follow through to the sales ledger to ensure they are recorded in the correct accounting period.

- Select a sample of year-end receivable balances and agree back to valid supporting documentation of GDN and sales order to ensure existence.

Answer 63 BANK AND CASH

(a)   Errors and misappropriations – cash

(i)   Receipts

- Money paid into the bank may be stolen. If cash is not properly controlled it is possible to falsify documentation in relation to receivables, and to pay company receipts into private bank accounts. This is sometimes known as "teeming and lading".

- Money paid into the bank may be incorrectly accounted for, either by the bank or by the company, if there are no controls to check the accuracy of the company's records or the bank statements. This could mean that the internal records and the financial statements are incorrect.

(ii)   Payments

- Money paid out of the bank may be paid to incorrect suppliers, or may be paid for incorrect amounts resulting in operational difficulties with cash and supplier management.

- Money paid out of bank accounts may also be misappropriated by payments for goods and services that are not received, or simply by payments into private bank accounts if there are no controls to prevent this.

(b) **Principal audit objectives of cash audit and related audit evidence**

- *Existence* – to ensure that the cash actually exists at a given date (i.e. it is not overstated). The related evidence will include cash counts. Cash counts need not necessarily be conducted at each location (unless the amounts are material), the firm might consider conducting counts on a rotational basis, year on year. If it is necessary to conduct counts at all locations, it may be possible to use the offices of another firm of auditors (with the permission of the client). The decision as to which sites to visit might be determined on the basis of materiality and analytical procedures. Cash balances should be reconciled to records held at the shop and records held at head office. Any shortfalls in cash, or "IOUs"[1] should be thoroughly investigated.

- *Completeness* – to ensure that there is no unrecorded cash. This means reconciling cash balances to records held at the shop and records held at head office, as above, ensuring that proper sales cut-off has been achieved.

- *Rights and obligations* – to ensure that the company has a right to the cash (i.e. it is an asset). This primarily means checking to ensure that credit card vouchers are correctly made payable to the company, and not to third parties. Reconciliation to the month (year) end of each credit card company statement.

- *Accuracy, valuation and allocation* – Valuation is generally not an issue for cash unless and entity enters into material foreign currency transactions.

- *Classification* – to ensure that cash is presented in the proper account. Classification is generally not an issue for cash as all cash accounts are generally accumulated and reported as a single cash balance.

- *Presentation* – to ensure that cash is appropriately aggregated and disclosed. If any of the shops had overdrafts against deposits that are reported as an offset to cash, it is necessary to check the bank contract for agreement to a right of offset. If there is no agreement or the company is not legally entitled to offset the overdraft against deposits, the overdraft should be presented and disclosed as a liability.

(c) **Why auditors seek bank confirmations – matters confirmed**

This matter is noted in ISA 505 *External Confirmations.*

Auditors seek bank confirmations in order to provide third party, written evidence in relation to the statement of financial position disclosure of cash, liabilities and related items.

The matters typically confirmed by the bank include:

- Details of all bank balances, overdrafts and loans held at all branches.
- The charges or restrictions over any such accounts.
- The terms and repayment conditions of loans and overdrafts.
- Any right of set-off between accounts in credit and other balances.
- Any securities held by the bank (such as mortgage documentation).
- Any relationships with other banks the bank is aware of.
- Additional information such as details of trade finance and derivative instruments (such as foreign exchange contracts, options, futures and swaps).

---

[1] "I Owe You" – where cash has been taken without proper authorisation.

Answer 64 NEWTHORPE, TOUREX AND PUDCO

Item	Answer	Justification
1	C	It is not necessary to ask the audit firm's lawyers about the likely outcome of the case. (The auditor would rather obtain a confirmation from Newthorpe's lawyers about the likely outcome, but this was not one of the options.) The other three procedures are likely to be performed.
2	C	Assigning different audit teams and engagement partners to each audit can help manage the conflict of interest. It is not necessary to resign from either audit (A) because both companies are aware of the situation and do not object. Although having the audits performed by separate offices (B) would mitigate the conflict of interest, this is not required. It is not the auditor's responsibility to facilitate negotiations between the two companies (D).
3	B	The auditor is most likely to issue a qualified opinion on Pudco's financial statements due to lack of evidence because the lawyers refuse to provide a confirmation related to the legal negotiations. In this case, a disclaimer of opinion would be unsuitable because the lack of evidence is material but not pervasive.
4	B	The auditor is most likely to issue a qualified opinion for Tourex because the lack of any recognition of the contingent liability is a material but not pervasive misstatement.
5	D	A receivables confirmation has nothing to do with contingent liabilities; the other options may reveal the existence of one.

Answer 65 METCALF

(a)   **Factors affecting sufficiency**

■   Assessment of inherent risk – as inherent risk increases, then more audit evidence will be required to reduce detection risk.

■   Materiality of the item – a decrease in materiality means that more audit evidence will be required to ensure that no material error has occurred.

■   Nature of the accounting and control systems – where the accounting and control systems are poor then more audit evidence is necessary as less reliance can be placed on those systems.

■   Control risk – determine the extent to which the directors have implemented a sound system of internal control; poor internal controls increase control risk, decreasing reliance that can be placed on those controls.

■   Experience from previous audits – good experience from previous audits will decrease the amount of evidence required as the auditor can place reliance on previous review of clients' systems.

■   Result of audit procedures – if the results of different audit procedures agree with each other less evidence is needed (overall the evidence is more persuasive). However, where results are in conflict then more evidence is required.

■   Quality of information available – some sources of audit evidence are more reliable than others, meaning less evidence is needed when relying on those sources. For example, documentary evidence is more reliable than oral evidence.

(b)   (i)   Trade payables

Audit procedure	*Reason for procedure*
Cast the list of trade payables and agree the total to the payables ledger and then to the general ledger.	To confirm that the list is complete, is accurately stated in the general ledger and contains no unusual or reconciling items which must be investigated.
Test, on a sample basis that payables on the list agree to the individual ledger balance and from the ledger to the list.	To confirm that the list agrees to the payables ledger.
Compare trade payables individually and in total to prior year balances and explain any unusual changes.	To explain changes in the balances (e.g. the increase in payables could indicate cash flow problems and Metcalf is delaying payment to suppliers in response to this). Comparison may also indicate lack of completeness of the list where payables balances have been omitted.
Select a sample of individual payables accounts for testing, focusing on material balances, zero balances and a sample of other items.	Material balances should always be tested to ensure correctness and test a large value of payables. Some zero balances are tested to ensure that invoices have not been omitted from one supplier.
Select population from purchase invoices received after the year end. Trace to evidence of goods receipt and where goods received prior to the year end; ensure invoice amount included in purchase accrual.	To confirm completeness of recording of purchase.
Obtain year-end supplier statements (from Metcalf or direct from suppliers via a confirmation request letter). Agree the balance on the statement to the individual account in Metcalf's payables ledger. Where necessary, reconcile the balances taking into account cash and invoices in transit.	Agree the payables balance to independent third party evidence to confirm accuracy, completeness and existence of the ledger balance.
Trace a sample of purchase invoices recorded in the purchase day book (PDB) just prior to the year end to goods received note (GRN), ensuring that the goods were received prior to the end of the year.	To ensure that liabilities recorded in the PDB are represented by goods received during that year, and recorded in the correct period (cut-off testing).
Trace a sample of GRNs prior to the year end to purchase invoice or the "goods received not invoiced" accrual .	To ensure completeness of recording of amounts payable.
Trace a sample of GRNs just after the year end to purchase invoice. Ensure that invoices are recorded in the PDB after the year end.	To ensure that the purchases figure is not overstated in this year's financial statements.
List all debit balances and obtain an explanation from the client.	To confirm why the balance arose and consider re-classification as receivables. Debit balances may indicate control weaknesses with further implications for audit testing.

(ii)   **Accruals**

Audit procedure	*Reason for procedure*
Cast the list of accruals and agree individual amounts to the general ledger accounts.	Confirm that the list is complete, the balances are accurately stated in the general ledger and contains no unusual or reconciling items which must be investigated.
Compare individual accruals with amount in the prior year accounts.	To account for unusual differences and identify omissions from the list this year.
Agree accruals to payments made after the end of the year for example, amounts payable for tax deducted from wages payments to remittance to the tax authority.	To help ensure the accuracy of the amounts paid and confirm that the accruals are genuine.
Review payments after the year end to determine whether any accruals are required. Where the need for an accrual is identified, ensure this is included in the accruals list.	To confirm completeness of the accruals listing.
Check calculations of individual accruals to supporting documentation for example, tax deductions from wages to the amount shown on the payroll as deducted from wages for the last month of the year.	To check that the accrual has been calculated correctly and therefore testing for over or understatement of each accrual.

(iii)   **Provision for legal action**

Audit procedure	*Reason for procedure*
Discuss the provision with the directors.	To attempt to confirm whether the company is liable for the payment and confirm that an out-of-court settlement is appropriate.
Obtain a letter from Metcalf's lawyers.	To provide evidence on whether Metcalf may be liable for payment and check the amount provided is approximately correct.
Review any correspondence with the customer.	To help determine Metcalf's liability and determine whether the customer may accept the out-of-court settlement.
Obtain a letter of representation from the directors.	To confirm that the directors are considering settlement out of court.
If possible, trace the payment made after the end of the year to receipt from the customer stating that the payment is accepted in "full and final settlement" (i.e. no other payments are expected to be made).	To confirm the accuracy of the amount stated in accruals.

Answer 66 ROSE LEISURE CLUB

(a)   **Fundamental principles**

Integrity – to be straightforward and honest in all professional and business relationships.

Objectivity – to not allow bias, conflict of interest or undue influence of others to override professional or business judgements.

Professional Competence and Due Care – to maintain professional knowledge and skill at the level required to ensure that a client receives competent professional services, and to act diligently and in accordance with applicable technical and professional standards.

Confidentiality – to respect the confidentiality of information acquired as a result of professional and business relationships and, therefore, not to disclose any such information to third parties without proper authority, nor use the information for personal advantage.

Professional Behaviour – to comply with relevant laws and regulations and avoid any action that discredits the profession.

(b)   **Substantive procedures**

      (i)   *Trade payables and accruals*

- Calculate the trade payable days for Rose Leisure Clubs (Rose) and compare to prior years, investigate any significant difference, in particular any decrease for this year.

- Compare the total trade payables and list of accruals against prior year and investigate any significant differences.

- Discuss with management the process they have undertaken to quantify the understatement of trade payables due to the cut-off error and consider the materiality of the error.

- Discuss with management whether any correcting journal entry has been included for the understatement.

- Select a sample of purchase invoices received between the period of 25 October and the year end and follow them through to inclusion within accruals or as part of the trade payables journal adjustment.

- Review after date payments; if they relate to the current year, then follow through to the purchase ledger or accrual listing to ensure they are recorded in the correct period.

- Obtain supplier statements and reconcile these to the purchase ledger balances, and investigate any reconciling items.

- Select a sample of payable balances and perform trade payables' external confirmation procedures. Follow up any non-replies and any reconciling items between the balance confirmed and the trade payables' balance.

- Select a sample of goods received notes before the year end and after the year end and follow through to inclusion in the correct period's payables balance, to ensure correct cut-off.

1134

(ii)   *Receivables*

- For non-responses, with the client's permission, the team should arrange to send a follow-up confirmation request.

- If the receivable does not respond to the follow up, then with the client's permission, the senior should telephone the customer and ask whether they are able to respond in writing to the confirmation request.

- If there are still non-responses, then the senior should undertake alternative procedures to confirm receivables.

- For responses with differences, the senior should identify any disputed amounts, and identify whether these relate to timing differences or whether there are possible errors in the records of Rose.

- Any differences due to timing, such as cash in transit, should be agreed to post year-end cash receipts in the cash book.

- The receivables ledger should be reviewed to identify any possible mispostings as this could be a reason for a response with a difference.

- If any balances have been flagged as disputed by the receivable, then these should be discussed with management to identify whether a write down is necessary.

(iii)   *Reorganisation*

- Review the board minutes where the decision to reorganise the business was taken, ascertain if this decision was made pre year end.

- Review the announcement to shareholders in late October, to confirm that this was announced before the year end.

- Obtain a breakdown of the reorganisation provision and confirm that only direct expenditure from restructuring is included.

- Review the expenditure to confirm that there are no retraining costs included.

- Cast the breakdown of the reorganisation provision to ensure correctly calculated.

- For the costs included within the provision, agree to supporting documentation to confirm validity of items included.

- Obtain a written representation confirming management discussions in relation to the announcement of the reorganisation.

- Review the adequacy of the disclosures of the reorganisation in the financial statements to ensure they are in accordance with IAS 37 *Provisions, Contingent Liabilities and Contingent Assets*.

Answer 67 FIREFLY TENNIS CLUB

(a)   **Audit tests for completeness of income**

All income

For a sample of paying-in slips during the year, trace amount banked to the bank statements agreeing the total banked.

Agree the total per the paying-in slip to the cash book to confirm that the total has been correctly recorded in the cash book.

Confirm that the analysis on the bank paying-in slips is correctly recorded between membership fees and court hire in the cash book.

Cast the cash book to confirm total income for the year.

Agree total income received and the analysis of membership fees and court hire to the financial statements.

Membership fees

Compare the list of members at the beginning of the year with the membership at the end of the year to determine how many members did not renew their membership during the year. This is normally approximately 10%.

Confirm total membership fees are correct by analytical review. Membership income should be:

430 members less 10% = 387
387 × $200 = $77,400
50 new members at 50% fee = 50 × $100 = $5,000
Total fee income $82,400

Agree the membership fee income to the financial statements. If the amount is materially different enquire of the treasurer why this is the case.

Court hire fees

Obtain the list of court hires from the clubhouse.

For a number of weeks, determine how many hours courts were hired for. Agree this time to the bank paying-in slip (hours × $5 should equal the amount banked).

Ask the secretary to explain any differences in amounts banked.

(b)   Audit tests on expenditure

Perform analytical review on expenditure this year compared to last year. Obtain reasons for any unusual amounts (e.g. increased expenditure on tennis balls due to increased number of matches).

For a sample of purchase invoices, ensure recorded in the cash book and that the amount and analysis of expenditure (e.g. lighting, tennis balls, etc) is correct.

Obtain the statements from the debit card used by the club official – trace items from the statements to the cash book to ensure all expenditure has been recorded.

For a sample of entries in the cash book, agree to the bank statements to ensure they represent actual expenditure.

Cast and cross cast the cash book to ensure the book is arithmetically correct.

For totals in the cash book, agree to the trial balance and financial accounts, ensuring that the presentation in the accounts is correct (e.g. stated as tennis balls, line painting, etc).

(c)   Limitation of internal control testing

Internal control testing is limited in relatively small audits such as FireFly Tennis Club for the following reasons:

■   There is a lack of segregation of duties. The club has only a limited number of staff in responsible positions. This means segregation of duties between, for example, authorising of purchase invoices and paying them, is not possible.

■   Lack of authorisation controls. In small organisations, the senior officials tend to be the people "authorising" transactions and also carrying them out. For example, the treasurer effectively authorises purchase invoices by paying for them rather than a senior official signing the invoice and a more junior clerk paying the invoice.

■   Cost. Establishing an internal control system can be expensive. It may therefore not be cost effective for a small entity to establish a detailed internal control system.

■   Management override. Even if there was an internal control system in place, senior officials are in a position to override that system. For example, the club treasurer could pay for his own expenses using the club debit card.

Answer 68 BLUESBERRY HOSPITAL

(a)   Purpose of value for money audit

A value for money (VFM) audit focuses on whether the best combination of services has been obtained for the lowest level of resources.

In performing a VFM audit an auditor will commonly focus on three areas; economy, efficiency and effectiveness (the "3Es").

Economy – Keeping the cost of resources used to a minimum.
Efficiency – The relationship between the output from goods and services and the resources used to produce them.
Effectiveness – How well the organisation's objectives have been achieved.

(b) **Operating environment to provide best value for money**

Existing strengths	*Further improvements*
Bluesberry has an internal audit department to monitor the internal control environment. This will help to provide advice over value for money.	The internal audit department could provide advice to departments on initial implementation of procedures rather than just reviewing them afterwards.
The centralised buying department purchases all medical supplies after researching for the lowest costs. This ensures that the hospital is being economical as the least amount of resources is being used.	However, care must be taken to ensure that the quality of the goods purchased is considered as well as the cost.
	To improve the process the buying department could consider establishing an approved supplier listing. In order to be placed on the list both the cost and quality of goods has to be of an adequate level, hence improving the efficiency of the goods purchased.
All orders are authorised by a purchasing director. This will ensure that only valid expenditure is incurred.	The purchasing director is a senior individual and it is not necessarily an efficient use of his time for him to authorise every purchase order, especially as there is a considerable number of them. The buying team receive in excess of 200 forms a day.
	Instead a purchasing supervisor should be designated to authorise orders up to a pre-set level with only orders above this level going to the director for authorisation. This should free the director to focus on other areas where costs can be reduced within the hospital.
Bluesberry has introduced an overtime scheme which has seen a reduction in the use of temporary staff, which was expensive. This has resulted in an overall reduction in labour costs and possibly improved care levels with permanent rather than temporary staff working, who may better understand the patients' needs.	Although overall costs may have been reduced, a smaller number of staff now has to cover all of the required staffing hours. Their efficiency levels must have reduced as they are working normal shifts and then overtime.
	To improve this further the human resources department should embark on a recruitment drive to find permanent staff members to fill gaps and reduce overall overtime and temporary staff usage.
The hospital has implemented a new procedure of time clocking in and out cards to record the hours staff members have worked. This ensures that staff are only paid for the hours they have worked, as opposed to being paid with no record of whether they have actually worked for the required hours.	This system is also used to determine overtime payments; however, there does not appear to be any authorisation of this overtime and employees could be being paid simply for staying longer hours as opposed to filling a staffing gap.
	This could be further improved in that a report of overtime hours per staff member should be sent on a weekly basis to the department head for authorisation. This should ensure that the hospital keeps its labour costs to a minimum.

Existing strengths

Further improvements

Bluesberry has heavily invested in new surgical equipment, which has improved patient recovery rates and will lead to more operations being performed. With improving recovery rates and utilisation of equipment the overall effectiveness of the hospital will improve.

This equipment is not being utilised efficiently as there is a shortage of trained medical staff. In order to maximise the efficiency and effectiveness of this equipment it would be advisable to look at ways to address these staff shortages.

For example, there may be medical staff at other hospitals who wish to be seconded to Bluesberry to gain experience on this new type of surgical equipment.

A capital expenditure committee has been established to plan and authorise the purchase of significant capital items.

This should ensure that significant cash flow expenditure is budgeted for, and that the expenditure will be for valid items only.

The committee is made up of senior managers, however, due to some capital expenditure being very significant in value, it would be improved further if board approval was required for any orders above a designated level. The board would have an overriding requirement to consider whether this expenditure would deliver value for money for the hospital.

(c)   **Substantive procedures for property, plant and equipment**

(i)   Accuracy, valuation and allocation

■   Review depreciation policies for reasonableness by comparison to prior year, industry practices, the entity's replacement policy and the profits/losses arising on disposal of assets.

■   For a sample of assets recalculate the depreciation charge for the year and agree to the entity asset register.

■   Perform a proof in total calculation of depreciation, considering the timing of additions and disposals and compare this expectation to the actual charge, and investigate any significant differences.

■   If any assets have been revalued during the year then assess the reasonableness of the valuer. In particular consider their experience, independence, scope of work and assumptions used.

■   Agree the revalued amounts to a valuation report, for a sample recalculate the revaluation surplus and agree to the revaluation reserve.

■   For a sample of the new surgical equipment additions vouch the cost to a recent purchase invoice.

(ii) *Completeness*

- Reconcile the schedule of non-current assets with the general ledger.

- Select a sample of assets physically present at the entity's premises and inspect the asset register to ensure that these are included.

- Re-perform the reconciliation of the non-current asset register to the general ledger, investigate any differences.

- Review the repairs and maintenance expense account in the statement of comprehensive income for items of a capital nature.

(iii) *Rights and obligations*

- Verify ownership of property via inspection of title deeds and land registration documents.

- For a sample of additions agree to purchase invoices to verify invoice relates to the entity.

- Review any new lease agreements to ensure assets are correctly treated as finance or operating leases.

- Inspect vehicle registration documents to confirm ownership of motor vehicles.

Answer 69 DYLAN

Item	Answer	Justification
1	D	Subsequent events include both events occurring after the period end but before the date of the auditor's report as well as facts that become known after the date of the auditor's report.
2	D	The auditor does not have an active responsibility to make continuing inquiries between the date of the auditor's report and the date on which the financial statements are issued.
3	B	(1) and (2) are both actions the auditor should take. (3) is not correct because a subsequent event that is material can affect this year's financial statements. (4) is not correct because subsequent events can occur any time after the period end date.
4	B	(4) is not a suitable action. As subsequent events may require amendment to, or disclosure in, the financial statements, they also require additional audit procedures on the affected transaction and account balances. However, assuming the entity correctly handles the subsequent events to the auditor's satisfaction, the auditor may still issue an unmodified report. The existence of a subsequent event is not reason alone for a issuing a qualified report.
5	C	After signing the auditor' report, but before the AGM, the auditor should consult with the directors on any subsequent events *of which they are aware* (i.e. a "passive" review). There is no requirement in this period for an "active" review.

Tutorial note: *Representations are only relevant to the audit if obtained prior to signing the auditor's report.*

Answer 70 SHARP

Tutorial note: *This 20-mark question relates mainly to syllabus area E and is therefore non-exam style. Also, part (b) has been provided to illustrate how errors may be considered in financial terms. The F8 exam would not include such an "accounting focussed" question.*

(a)   **Significance of findings**

     (1)   *Payments to suppliers $10,172*

     ■   If this was deliberate "window-dressing" an adjustment might be appropriate. The amount is material, being 14% of cash at bank.

     ■   However, the payments were processed and cleared the bank soon after the year end. Though cash and payables may be understated there is no effect on net current assets. If an adjustment was made the reduction in liquidity ratios would be negligible.

     ■   The clerical error should be noted in the draft report to management to avoid repetition. As the error could be considered as not being significant, an adjustment appears not to be necessary.

     (2)   *Credit notes not recognised $7,542*

     ■   Receivables, net current assets, revenue and profit before tax are overstated by $7,542. The error represents 7% of profit before tax and is therefore considered material.

     ■   Stricter controls over the introduction of price increases should be recommended in the draft report to management.

     ■   An adjustment for further allowance is proposed.

     (3)   *Additions to plant and machinery $52,000*

     ■   Though the errors detected amounting to $2,500 were not material (to total assets, net assets and profit), it is possible that a material error may exist in the $39,000 not tested. A simple extrapolation suggests a potential error of $7,500 (1.2 % of total assets, 3.75% net assets and 7% of profit).

     ■   If a material error is found to have occurred it would usually be appropriate to reconsider the depreciation charge for the year. However, the depreciation error would need to be greater than $5,300 (5% × $106,000) to be considered material. It is also highly unlikely that any adjustment would be made based on performance materiality (e.g. if performance materiality was set at 50% of planning materiality, this would mean the depreciation error would need to be at least $2,650, representing a depreciation rate of 35% on plant and equipment – a rate of 10% could be considered the norm).

     ■   The systems weakness in the classification of expenditure should be noted in the draft report to management.

(4)   Warranty provision $25,000

■   Detailed tests suggest a maximum potential understatement of $5,000 which is 5% of profit before tax and 17% of net current assets and may be considered material.

■   IAS 37 *Provisions, Contingent Liabilities and Contingent Assets* states that in providing for a contingency a prudent estimate of the amount involved should be included in the accounts. Since the estimate requires a certain degree of judgement an adjustment would only be appropriate if it can be certain that management's estimate is not sufficiently prudent.

■   On balance, accepting that the estimate is not highly subjective and that professional scepticism has been appropriately applied, it appears that the client's estimate should be accepted.

(5)   "Uninsured risk" provision $20,000

■   This should only be carried forward if the provision meets the requirements of IAS 37 (past event, present obligation, unavoidable, future economic outflow).

■   As no amounts have ever been charged against it, and there is no indication of an applicable event, the $20,000 should be written back to profit or loss. The write back should be disclosed separately since it represents 19% of profit and is clearly material.

(b)   Financial effect on the draft accounts

			Profit or loss		Statement of financial position	
			DR	CR	DR	CR
			$000	$000	$000	$000
		Profit per draft accounts		106		
(1)	DR	Cash			10	
	CR	Payables				10
(2)	DR	Revenue	8			
	CR	Receivables				8
(3)	DR	Repairs	7			
	CR	Non-current assets				7
(4)	DR	Warranty claims	5			
	CR	Payables				5
(5)	DR	Payables			20	
	CR	Profit or loss		20		

Overall effect on profit and total assets less current liabilities $Nil.

Of these, item 1 (payments to suppliers) and item 4 (warranty provision) would be classified as unadjusted errors. The payment to suppliers was a simple clerical error and the warranty provision is acceptable as a reasonable estimate. The overall impact on the financial statements of these items, separately and cumulatively is not material.

Item 3 (repairs) should be discussed further with management. If management accepts the extrapolation, the financial statements should be adjusted. If not, further audit tests to clarify the potential error must be carried out. If no further errors are found, the initial error of $2,500 may be left as an unadjusted error. Given the nature of warranty claims, the cumulative impact of unadjusted errors would remain immaterial.

Answer 71 ZEEDIEM

Item	Answer	Justification
1	A	Event 1 is adjusting because it provides further evidence of conditions existing at the end of the reporting period. Because it is material, ZeeDiem should adjust its financial statements by writing down inventory to $225,000 to reflect the net realisable value of the defective mattresses.
2	C	In response to Event 1, the auditor should obtain documentation from the insurers confirming their estimate of the value of the mattresses (1), confirm with the spring supplier's liquidator that no refund can be expected for the defective springs (2), and review production and inventory records to confirm that the defective springs were not used in other mattresses (4). Performing an additional inventory count as a surprise audit procedure (3) would not help determine the adequacy of the adjustment for the defective inventory.
3	B	In response to Event 2, relevant documents include board minutes (1), the environmental legislation (3) and interim reports from the Environmental Agency (4) to determine the extent of the damage. The personnel file for the truck driver involved (2) is irrelevant to the assessment of the implications for the financial statements.
4	D	Strong direction, supervision and review of the work of the audit team are essential to ensure effective and efficient audit finalisation. Monitoring time and costs is a practice management element. Preparation of adequate working papers is a subset of supervision and review.
5	B	Inquiry about any material adjustments made after year-end could provide evidence regarding transactions that could require adjustment to and/or disclosure in the year-end financial statements.

Answer 72 HUMPHRIES

Tutorial note: *This 20-mark question relates mainly to syllabus area E and is therefore non-exam style.*

(a)   **ISA 560 "Subsequent Events" responsibilities**

   (i)   *Between the year-end date and the date the auditor's report is signed*

The auditor shall perform audit procedures designed to obtain sufficient appropriate audit evidence that all events occurring between the date of the financial statements and the date of the auditor's report that require adjustment of, or disclosure in, the financial statements have been identified.

The auditor is not, however, expected to perform additional audit procedures on matters to which previously applied audit procedures have provided satisfactory conclusions.

(ii)   *Between the dates of the auditor's report and when the financial statements are issued*

The auditor has no obligation to perform any audit procedures regarding the financial statements after the date of the auditor's report.

However, if a fact becomes known to the auditor that, had it been known to the auditor at the date of the auditor's report, may have caused him to amend the auditor's report, the auditor shall: discuss the matter with management, determine whether the financial statements need amendment and, if so, inquire how management intends to address the matter in the financial statements.

If management amends the financial statements, the auditor shall carry out the necessary audit procedures, extend the subsequent events testing to the date of the new auditor's report, and provide a new auditor's report on the amended financial statements.

(b)   Receivable

(i)   *Amendment to the financial statements*

A customer, owing $0·3 million at the year end, is experiencing significant going concern difficulties. This information was received after the year end but provides further evidence of the recoverability of the receivable balance at the year end. Under IAS 10 *Events after the Reporting Period*, if the customer is experiencing cash flow difficulties just a few months after the year end, then it is highly unlikely that the $0·3m was recoverable as at 30 September.

The receivables balance is overstated and consideration should be given to adjusting this balance, if material, through the use of an allowance for receivables or by being written off.

(ii)   *Audit procedures to form a conclusion on the amendment*

■   Review of the correspondence with the customer to assess whether there is any likelihood of payment.

■   Discuss with management why they feel an adjustment is not required.

■   Review the post year-end period to see if any payments have been received from the customer.

(iii)   *Impact on the auditor's report if unresolved*

The receivable of $0·3 million is not material as it represents 4% of profit ($0·3 ÷ $7·5) and 0·4% of revenue ($0·3 ÷ $78) and therefore, although overstated, it does not require adjustment. However, the $0·3m should be noted in the summary of unadjusted errors.

As the error is immaterial then no amendment is required to the audit opinion.

Lawsuit

(i)   *Amendment to the financial statements*

A key supplier is suing Humphries for $1 million; the company has made contingent liability disclosures. However, subsequent to the year end the supplier agreed to settle at $0·6 million and it is likely the company will agree. Although the settlement was agreed after the year end, it provides further evidence that the company had a present obligation as at 30 September.

The financial statements should be adjusted with the contingent liability disclosures being removed and instead a provision of $0·6 million being recorded.

(ii)   Audit procedures to form a conclusion on the amendment

■   The auditor should contact the company's lawyers to ask their view on whether the settlement is probable and whether $0·6 million is the likely amount.

■   Review the correspondence with the supplier to confirm that the amount they are willing to accept is in fact $0·6 million.

■   Discuss with management whether it is probable that they will pay this sum and obtain a written representation confirming this.

(iii)   Impact on the auditor's report if unresolved

The sum being claimed is $1 million but the probable payment is $0·6 million, this is material as it represents 8% of profit ($0·6 ÷ $7·5) and hence management should provide for this amount.

If management refuse to provide then the auditor's report will need to be modified. As management has not complied with IAS 37 *Provisions, Contingent Liabilities and Contingent Assets* and the error is material but not pervasive then a qualified "except for" opinion would be necessary.

The opinion section would be qualified "except for". The basis for qualified opinion section would explain the material misstatement in relation to the lack of a provision and the effect on the financial statements.

Warehouse

(i)   Amendment to the financial statements

The warehouse in Bass has been subject to a flood in late November, the entire inventory has been disposed of and the company has insurance in place. This event occurred after the year end and the flood would not have been in existence at 30 September, and hence this event indicates a non-adjusting event.

The financial statements should not be adjusted; however, if the effect of any uninsured losses is material, then disclosure of the nature of the event and any estimates of the financial effects may be required. If the amount is not material it may not be necessary to include any disclosures.

(ii)   Audit procedures to form a conclusion on the amendment

■   Discuss the matter with the directors, checking whether the company has sufficient inventory to continue trading in the short term.

■   Obtain a written representation confirming that the company's going concern status is not affected.

■   Obtain a schedule showing the inventory destroyed and compare this to the average inventory in the other two warehouses to see if the amount claimed to be damaged is reasonable.

■   Review any correspondence from the insurers, confirming the amount of the insurance claim to assess the extent of any uninsured amounts.

(iii)   *Impact on the auditor's report if unresolved*

The amount of damaged inventory is likely to be material; however, Humphries has insurance and so it is only the uninsured level of inventory which should possibly be disclosed.

If disclosures are not required, because the uninsured loss is immaterial, there will be no reporting implications for the auditor's report.

If disclosure of this subsequent event is required and management refuse to make these disclosures, then the auditor's report will need to be modified with a qualified "except for" opinion.

If the effect of the uninsured level of inventory is such that it creates doubts about the company's going concern status, consideration should be given to modifying the audit opinion. This would involve including a section titled "Material Uncertainly Related to Going Concern" drawing attention to a note to the financial statements that fully explains the possible risk in relation to going concern (i.e. disclosure in the financial statement **must** be adequate).

Answer 73 VIOLET & CO

Item	Answer	Justification

1   D

Tutorial note: *The audit team will seek to confirm revenue (and receivables) by other means. If unable to do this, then two significant balances in the financial statements will not have been confirmed.*

Alternative procedures would likely include examining alternative records (e.g. invoice listings, despatch notes, cash book receipts) (1) and performing analytical procedures (2). The individual customer' balances are not known, so direct confirmation with customers is not possible (3). The auditors would not be able to confirm reported revenue by relying on the internal audit (since they have no more information than is available to the auditor) (4).

Tutorial note: *The auditor would always review after-date cash receipts from customers in settlement of amounts they owed at the reporting date.*

2   D

If the audit is unable to obtain sufficient appropriate evidence about the revenue and receivables balances, the auditor cannot form an opinion on these amounts in the financial statements. But, however material, the matter is not pervasive as, for example, expense, liability, equity and other asset balances are not affected.

Tutorial note: *Also, the auditor should expect to obtain some audit evidence through the use of analytical procedures.*

3   C

Fuchsia is facing going concern problems as it has experienced difficult trading conditions and it has a negative cash outflow. However, the financial statements have been prepared on a going concern basis, even though it is possible that the company is not a going concern. The prior year financial statements showed a profit of $1·2m and the current financial statements show a loss before tax of $4·4m, the net cash outflow of $3·2m represents 73% of this loss ($3·2 \div 4·4$m) and hence is a material issue.

4	C	Whether Fuchsia has been making timely payments on its debts (3) does not necessarily affect its ability to obtain future credit. Even if the company has not yet defaulted, loan providers may be unwilling to extend further credit due to the company's decline in profits and gloomy outlook. The reasonableness of the assumptions used to create the cash flow forecasts (4) also does not affect Fushia's ability to obtain future credit.

Tutorial note: *Also, there is no need for the auditor to ask the lenders for confirmation since cash book payments against payment schedules will confirm this.*

5	A	If a company is not a going concern, an adverse opinion should be expressed if the financial statements are prepared on a going concern basis. No emphasis of matter paragraph or key audit matters section would be included.

Answer 74 PANDA

Item Answer   *Justification*

1	B	Panda's quality control procedures have identified that inventory costing $850,000 has a scrap value of $100,000. This information was obtained after the year end but provides further evidence of the net realisable value of inventory at the reporting date end and hence is an adjusting event.

2	B	(1), (4), and (5) are all procedures that should be performed by the auditor. (1) because there could potentially be other inventory which requires writing down. (4) because the adjustment will only be required if the defective inventory was produced prior to year end. (5) because the auditor needs to assess the amount of the potential adjustment. (2) and (3) are both irrelevant to the accounting treatment.

3	C	IAS 2 *Inventories* requires inventory to be valued at the lower of cost and net realisable value. Thus the defective inventory must be written down to its net realisable value. The write down of $750,000 ($850 – $100) is material as it represents 13.4% ($0.75m ÷ $5.6m) of profit before tax. Hence, the directors should amend the financial statements by writing down the inventory to $0.1 million.

4	D	Of the procedures suggested only the recalculation of cost is relevant to the value of damaged inventory.

Tutorial note: *As the event is non-adjusting the inventory will be included at cost (or net realisable value if lower) as at the reporting date. This value will also be relevant to the amount of loss disclosed in the note of events after the reporting date.*

5	A	As a non-adjusting event, the assets should not be written off; their carrying amounts were not affected *as at the reporting date*. However, as the uninsured loss is material ($0.9m ÷ $5.6m = 16% of profit before tax), the event should be disclosed in a note and include the financial effect (i.e. carrying amount of assets to be written off).

Answer 75 SAVAGE & CO

Item	*Answer*	*Justification*
1	B	Statements (2) and (3) are correct. Statement (1) is incorrect because the auditor has a responsibility to accumulate *all* misstatements which arise over the course of the audit, both material and immaterial, unless they are very small amounts. Statement (4) is incorrect because misstatements should be communicated to those charged with governance on a timely basis, which means that there it will often be the case that misstatements are communicated with those charged with governance during the course of the audit, rather than at the end of the audit.
2	B	Only the Dawson issue should be considered material. Czech has capitalised research expenditure of $0.5m and development expenditure of $3.2m. ISA 38 *Intangible Assets* requires capitalisation of development expenditures (subject to criteria being met) but research expenditures must be expensed to profit or loss. Therefore, the error is $0.5m, which is 1.9% of profit before tax. An error of less than 5% is not generally considered to be material. Dawson is unable to provide audit evidence regarding wages and salaries for a two-month period which amount to 11% of profit before tax. An amount greater than 10% of profit before tax should be considered material.
3	A	If Czech Co management refuses to correct the material error, a qualified opinion would be appropriate because the error is material but not pervasive. If Dawson Co management refuses to correct the issue, a qualified opinion would be appropriate because the auditor is unable to obtain sufficient appropriate evidence in relation to a material, but not pervasive, issue.
4	C	Procedures A, B and D would be undertaken as part of the overall review of the financial statements. However, procedure C is undertaken when reviewing subsequent events occurring between the date of the financial statements and the date of the auditor's report.
5	C	Savage & Co's next course of action would be to discuss management's refusal to amend the financial statements with those charged with governance.

Answer 76 BULLFINCH.COM

Item	*Answer*	*Justification*
1	B	(1), (2) and (4) are audit procedures that should be performed to form a conclusion about the need for adjustment of the 2016 financial statements. Recalculating the allowance (3) will not provide any evidence regarding the need to write down or write off the receivable.
2	D	The auditor should not include a disclaimer of opinion in the new auditor's report (4). Since Bullfinch made the required amendment, the auditor may issue an unmodified opinion in the new auditor's report.
3	C	Only an event that provides further evidence of conditions existing at the end of the period is considered an adjusting event. In this case, only (3) and (4) are adjusting events. (1), (2) and (5) are all non-adjusting events as they are indicative of conditions that arose after the end of the reporting period.

> **Tutorial note:** *According to IAS 16 revaluations should be made sufficiently regularly so that carrying amount is not materially different from fair value at the reporting date. So the sale at a significant loss shortly after the reporting date provides evidence that as at the reporting date the land is overstated.*

4   A   Statement 2 is not correct. If an event occurs after the financial statements are issued, the auditor has already signed the auditor's report and so is not able to now include a qualified opinion.

5   A   The final stage of an audit would likely include analytical procedures to assess the reasonableness of figures presented (A). The rest of the procedures listed would occur during the planning and risk assessment phase (D) or during the substantive procedures phase (B and C).

Answer 77 CREMORNE

Item   Answer   *Justification*

1   C   The finance director's view that the write down should be reflected after the end of the reporting period is incorrect. As at the end of the reporting period the material could not be used in Highways Agency contracts and the lower of its cost and net realisable value was $2 million. The carrying amount of inventory and profit should be reduced by $5 million.

2   B   The traditional benchmarks from which to choose are ½–1% of revenue, 5–10% of profit and 1-2% of total assets. However, the valuation of inventory affects profit; revenue is irrelevant and so not appropriate. The inventory valuation also affects total assets (and total net assets) but the percentage applied to just *one* class of assets would need to be *more* than 1–2%.

> **Tutorial note:** *1% of $7m inventory is only $70,000. This is not appropriate (too low) as 5% of profit is $2m.*

3   A   IAS 16 *Property, Plant and Equipment* requires that useful lives of assets (accounting estimates) be reviewed regularly and that depreciation be adjusted where there is a change in useful life. The finance director's argument is irrelevant as the new earthmovers have a useful life of only five years and the useful lives of the two as yet unsold older items is also five years (as evidenced by the sale of the five year items during the year). Depreciation has already been allowed at 10% so should be increased by $2 million additional expense.

4   A   If there were no other uncorrected errors the auditor might consider the amount to be insufficiently material to justify issuing a modified audit opinion if the financial statements were not adjusted. It is only just material (5% of profit). It might be argued that as depreciation is based on an estimate (of the useful economic lives of the assets) it is not something that can be precise amount and, on a qualitative basis, the financial statements are not materially misstated. However, this analysis considers only the current year effect, but depreciation is accumulated. So considering the effect of depreciating at only 10% rather than 20%, the assets would be in the books at half their cost in five years' time – when they should have been written down completely.

5   D   Statements (2) and (4) would appear in a typical unmodified auditor's report.

> **Tutorial note:** *There is no longer a statement of responsibility "to express an opinion ...". According to ISA 700 (Revised) the statement is "Our objectives are to obtain reasonable assurance about whether the financial statements as a whole are free from material misstatement ". The auditor's report would also state that the audit was conducted in accordance with International Auditing Standards, not International Financial Reporting Standards.*

Answer 78   MINNIE

Tutorial note: *This 20-mark question relates mainly to syllabus area E and is therefore non-exam style.*

(a)   **Misstatements**

ISA 450 *Evaluation of Misstatements Identified During the Audit* considers what a misstatement is and deals with the auditor's responsibility in relation to misstatements.

It identifies a misstatement as being "A difference between the amount, classification, presentation, or disclosure of a reported financial statement item and the amount, classification, presentation, or disclosure that is required for the item to be in accordance with the applicable financial reporting framework. Misstatements can arise from error or fraud."

It also then defines uncorrected misstatements as "Misstatements that the auditor has accumulated during the audit and that have not been corrected".

There are three categories of misstatements:

(1)   Factual misstatements are misstatements about which there is no doubt.

(2)   Judgemental misstatements are differences arising from the judgements of management concerning accounting estimates that the auditor considers unreasonable, or the selection or application of accounting policies that the auditor considers inappropriate.

(3)   Projected misstatements are the auditor's best estimate of misstatements in populations, involving the projection of misstatements identified in audit samples to the entire populations from which the samples were drawn.

The auditor has a responsibility to accumulate misstatements which arise over the course of the audit unless they are very small amounts. Identified misstatements should be considered during the course of the audit to assess whether the audit strategy and plan should be revised. The auditor should determine whether uncorrected misstatements are material in aggregate or individually.

All misstatements should be communicated to those charged with governance on a timely basis and request that they make necessary amendments. If this request is refused then the auditor should consider the potential effect on the auditor's report.

A written representation should be requested from management to confirm that unadjusted misstatements are immaterial.

> **Tutorial note:** *ISA 450 was a relatively new auditing standard when this question was set. The model answer is more comprehensive than would normally be expected for 4 marks and is provided for the benefit of future candidates.*

(b) **Reliance on the work of an independent valuer**

ISA 500 *Audit Evidence* requires auditors to evaluate the competence, capabilities including expertise and objectivity of a management expert.

This would include consideration of the qualifications of the valuer and assessment of whether they were members of any professional body or industry association.

In addition, the auditor should meet with the expert and discuss with them their relevant expertise; in particular whether they have valued similar properties to Minnie in the past. Also consider whether they understand the accounting requirements of IAS 16 *Property, Plant and Equipment* in relation to valuations.

The expert's independence should be ascertained, with potential threats such as undue reliance on Minnie or a self-interest threat such as share ownership considered.

The valuation should then be evaluated. The assumptions used should be carefully reviewed and compared to previous revaluations at Minnie. These assumptions should be discussed with both management and the valuer to understand where the misstatement has arisen.

In order to correct the misstatement, it might be necessary for the valuer to undertake further work and this should be agreed.

Daffy & Co would not be able to state in the auditor's report that they had relied on an expert for the property valuation.

(c) **Additional issues**

(i) *Depreciation on land and buildings*

Depreciation has been provided on the land element of property, plant and equipment which is contrary to IAS 16.

The error is material as it represents 7% of profit before tax ($0·7m ÷ $10m) and hence management should remove this from the financial statements.

If management refuse to amend this error then the auditor's report will need to be modified. As management has not complied with IAS 16 and the error is material but not pervasive then a qualified "except for" opinion would be necessary.

The opinion section would be qualified "except for" – due to material misstatement. The basis for qualified opinion section would need to include an explanation of the material misstatement in relation to the provision of depreciation on land and the effect on the financial statements.

(ii) *Wages program*

Minnie's wages program has been corrupted leading to a loss of payroll data for a period of two months. The auditors should attempt to verify payroll in an alternative manner. If they are unable to do this then payroll for the whole year would not have been verified.

Wages and salaries for the two month period represents 11% of profit before tax ($1·1m ÷ $10m) and therefore is a material balance for which audit evidence has not been available.

The auditors will need to modify the auditor's report as they are unable to obtain sufficient appropriate evidence in relation to a material, but not pervasive, element of wages and salaries and therefore a qualified "except for" opinion will be required.

The opinion section will be qualified "except for" – due to insufficient appropriate audit evidence. The basis for qualified opinion section will include an explanation of the limitation in relation to the lack of evidence over two months of payroll records.

(iii)   Lawsuit

The company is being sued by a competitor for breach of copyright. This matter has been correctly disclosed in accordance with IAS 37 *Provisions, Contingent Liabilities and Contingent Assets*.

The lawsuit is for $5m which represents 50% of profit before tax ($5m ÷ $10m) and hence is a material matter. This is an important matter which needs to be brought to the attention of the users.

An emphasis of matter paragraph would need to be included in the auditor's report, in that the matter is appropriately disclosed but is fundamental to the users' understanding of the financial statements; this will not affect the audit opinion which will be unmodified in relation to this matter.

An emphasis of matter paragraph would explain clearly about the lawsuit and cross references to where in the financial statements the disclosure of this contingent liability can be found.

Answer 79 PAPRIKA

Item	Answer	Justification
1	D	(1), (3) and (4) are all factors that Brown & Co should consider prior to placing reliance on the work of the independent expert. Brown & Co should not consider whether using the expert's work will increase efficiency in completing the audit.

Tutorial note: *Whether or not it improves efficiency, if the expert's work is not competent, reliable, or independent, the auditor cannot rely on it.*

Item	Answer	Justification
2	D	The opinion paragraph should include the identity of the entity, Paprika & Co (1), reference to the notes to the financial statements, including significant accounting policies (4), and identify the financial reporting framework (3). This paragraph does not need to identify the auditor.
3	C	The auditor is not able to obtain absolute assurance and cannot confirm that the financial statements contain no errors. This is because the auditor does not test every transaction or balance as it is not practical. The auditor tests only a sample of transactions and may only consider material balances. Hence the auditor's responsibility is to provide only reasonable assurance that financial statements are free from material misstatements, whether due to fraud or error.
4	C	Management is responsible for the preparation and fair presentation of financial statements and for internal control.

Tutorial note: *Although management is responsible for assessing the company's ability to continue as a going concern (as an aspect of "preparation and fair presentation") it is the auditor's responsibility to conclude whether that basis of accounting is appropriate.*

| 5 | B | (2) and (3) are correct. (2) is correct because the auditor is required to obtain sufficient and appropriate evidence and therefore should carry out any necessary procedures. Availability and experience of team members should not dictate the level of testing performed. (3) is correct because the auditor's report only provides an opinion on the financial statements. Brown & Co will review the effectiveness of the internal controls and they will report on any key deficiencies identified during the course of the audit to management. |

Answer 80 CORSCO

Item	Answer	*Justification*
1	C	Although there are some indicators of going concern problems, the company has net assets and the fact that it has been approached by take-over bidders does not necessarily indicate going concern problem (possibly quite the opposite). The current year' audit opinion issued is not likely to make reference to the going concern basis of accounting, as in previous years. The situation has not deteriorated significantly in the current year.
2	B	(1) and (3) are both difficulties that could be faced by Corsco if its auditor's report draws attention to the use of the going concern basis of accounting (i.e. other than in standard wording of auditor's responsibilities). If Harris & Johnson's auditor's report has drawn attention to the matter it has been issued and it is therefore too late to ask another auditor for a second opinion. An audit committee's responsibility is to oversee the integrity of financial reporting controls, risk management and other procedures rather than remedy going concern issues. Responsibility for the latter lies with management.
3	C	The auditor should enquire of management if it knows of indicators of significant doubt beyond the period of assessment (i.e. at least 12 months from the end of the reporting period). (A) and (D) are not true because the auditor must obtain evidence to conclude on the basis of preparation in all cases. B is incorrect as ISA 570 specifies that it is not the auditor's responsibility to undertake a responsibility which is management's.
4	D	(1) and (2) each describe accurately management's responsibility with respect to going concern assessments. (3) is inaccurate because when making the going concern assessment, management should take into account all available information about the future, even though there is inherent uncertainty related to future events or conditions. (4) is inaccurate because there is no expectation for management to provide auditors with cash forecasts to support its going concern assessment.
5	B	(2), (4) and (5) are all matters that would be considered by Harris & Johnson during the planning of the audit as indicators of potential going concern difficulties. A retiring CEO is a common occurrence and Key West will have a succession plan to appoint a new CEO. Absence of a cash flow forecast is not an indicator of a going concern problem; the auditor must consider other sources from which to obtain appropriate evidence.

> **Tutorial note:** *A "healthy" cash flow statement should show net cash from operations (i.e. positive) not used in (i.e. negative). If the CEO had suddenly died, this would be considered an indicator of a potential going concern problem.*

Answer 81 MEDIMADE

Tutorial note: *This 20-mark question relates mainly to syllabus area E and is therefore non-exam style.*

(a)   **Going concern**

The going concern assumption means that management believes the company will continue in business for the foreseeable future.

IAS 1 *Presentation of Financial Statements* requires that management automatically prepare financial statements on a going concern basis unless they believe that the company will soon cease trading.

(b)

Indicators	Why could impact going concern
Medimade has seen a significant decline in demand for its products.	If the company is not able to increase demand for its products then it will struggle to generate sufficient operating cash flows leading to going concern difficulties.
Medimade generates 90% of its revenue through sales of just two products, and this market has now become very competitive.	As the market is very competitive and Medimade has only two products then it is very dependent on these and must ensure that it makes sufficient sales as otherwise it may face difficulties in meeting all expenses.
Lack of investment in future product development	As current products reach the end of their life-cycle they will bring in diminishing cash flows. Without new products to generate future income operating cash flows will be strained.
The company is struggling to recruit suitably trained scientific staff to develop new products.	The company has decided that it needs to develop new products, however, this is a highly specialised area and therefore it needs sufficiently trained staff. If it cannot recruit enough staff it could hold up product development and stop the company from increasing revenue.
Medimade was unable to obtain suitable funding for its $2m investment in plant and machinery.	If Medimade was unable to obtain finance for its investment, then this could indicate that the banks deem the company to be too risky to lend money to. They may be concerned that Medimade is unable to meet its loan payments, suggesting cash flow problems.
Some trade payables have been paid much later than their due dates.	Failing to make payments to suppliers on time could ultimately lead to some of them refusing to supply Medimade. Therefore the company may need to find alternative suppliers and they could be more expensive which will decrease operating cash flows and profits.
Some suppliers have withdrawn credit terms from Medimade resulting in cash on delivery payments.	As Medimade must now make cash on delivery payments, then it puts additional pressure on the company's overdraft, which has already grown substantially. This is because the company has to pay for goods in advance but it may not receive cash from its receivables for some time later.
The overdraft facility has increased substantially and is due for renewal next month.	Medimade's overdraft has grown significantly and it is heavily dependent on it to pay its expenses. If the bank does not renew the overdraft and the company is unable to obtain alternative finance then it may not be able to continue to trade.

(c)   Procedures

Obtain the company's cash flow forecast and review the cash in and out flows. Assess the assumptions for reasonableness and discuss the findings with management to understand if the company will have sufficient cash flows.

Review any current agreements with the bank to determine whether any key ratios have been breached.

Review any bank correspondence to assess the likelihood of the bank renewing the overdraft facility.

Discuss with the directors whether they have contacted any alternative banks for finance or whether they have any other means of repaying the bank overdraft.

Review the company's post year end sales and order book to assess if the levels of trade are likely to increase and if the revenue figures in the cash flow forecast are reasonable.

Review post year end correspondence with suppliers to identify if any further restrictions in credit have arisen, and if so ensure that the cash flow forecast reflects an immediate payment for trade payables.

Inquire of the lawyers of Medimade as to the existence of litigation and claims; if any exist then consider their materiality and impact on the going concern basis.

Perform audit tests in relation to subsequent events to identify any items that might indicate or mitigate the risk of going concern not being appropriate.

Review the post year end board minutes to identify any other issues that might indicate financial difficulties for the company.

Review post year end management accounts to assess if in line with cash flow forecast.

Consider whether any additional disclosures as required by IAS 1 *Presentation of Financial Statements* in relation to material uncertainties over going concern should be made in the financial statements.

Obtain a written representation confirming the director's view that Medimade is a going concern.

(d)   Impact on report

The directors of Medimade have agreed to make going concern disclosures. The implications for the auditor's report depend on the adequacy of these disclosures. If adequate, the auditor's opinion will be unmodified. However, a Material Uncertainty Related to Going Concern section would be required. This will state that the auditor's opinion is not modified, identify that there is a material uncertainty and will cross reference to the disclosure note made by management. This section would be included after the basis for opinion section.

If the disclosures made by management are not adequate the auditor's opinion will need to be modified. A disagreement modification will be required. This will usually be a qualified "except for" opinion but could be an adverse opinion if the matter is pervasive.

A basis for opinion section describing the matter giving rise to the modification will be included after the opinion section and this will clearly identify the going concern uncertainty. The opinion section will be amended to state "except for" or the financial statements are not fairly presented.

Answer 82 STRAWBERRY KITCHEN DESIGNS

Item	Answer	Justification
1	C	(2), (3) and (4) are indications that Strawberry may not be a going concern. Having a major customer cease trading will result in a significant loss of future revenues and profit. Future cash flows will decrease if the customer cannot be replaced. If Strawberry continues to have monthly net cash outflows its overdraft will further increase and the company may run out of available cash. Unless Strawberry can raise alternative finance or sell non-current assets, it is difficult to see how they will be able to raise $4.8 million to repay the loan. (1) is not an indication because the fact that Strawberry is in an industry with many competitors and seasonal sales has no bearing on potential financial or cash flow issues.
2	B	(1) and (3) are audit procedures that should be performed in order to assess whether the company is a going concern. (2) is not correct because confirmations are generally sent for asset accounts such as accounts receivables, rather than accounts payable. Confirming the existence of accounts payable would not help with the assessment of going concern. (4) is not correct because general inquiries about fraud do not specifically help with the assessment of going concern.
3	C	Under IFRS the period of assessment should be at least, but not limited to, 12 months after the end of the reporting period. So expected future losses (2) and the loan repayment (3) should be included in consideration of the foreseeable future. Management's plans to dispose of assets to maintain adequate cash flows (1) and guarantees of other financial support (4) are mitigating factors (i.e. against modification).
4	B	Postponement of significant expenditures is a mitigating factor. Plans to discuss with lenders about the terms of all debt and loan agreements are not sufficient to be a mitigating factor; an actual agreement must be in place. Plans to hire a new sales director are also not a mitigating factor. A strong relationship with its supplier is not a mitigating factor and Strawberry currently has poor relationships with suppliers due to slow payments and threatened legal action.
5	D	The audit opinion may be unmodified, qualified, or adverse, depending on the adequacy of disclosure made by management. If there is adequate disclosure, the auditors should express an unmodified opinion and include a Material Uncertainty Related to Going Concern section. If there is inadequate disclosure, auditors should express a qualified or adverse opinion, depending on the level of disclosure made.

Answer 83 CLARINET

Tutorial note: *This 20-mark question relates mainly to syllabus area E and is therefore non-exam style.*

(a) **Procedures to undertake in relation to the uncorrected misstatement**

- The extent of the potential misstatement should be considered and therefore a large sample of inventory items should be tested to identify the possible size of the misstatement.

- The potential misstatement should be discussed with Clarinet's management in order to understand why these inventory differences are occurring.

- The misstatement should be compared to materiality to assess if the error is material individually.

■   If not, then it should be added to other errors noted during the audit to assess if in aggregate the uncorrected errors are now material.

■   If material, the auditors should ask the directors to adjust the inventory balances to correct the misstatements identified in the 2016 year end.

■   Request a written representation from the directors about the uncorrected misstatements including the inventory errors.

■   Consider the implication for the auditor's report if the inventory errors are material and the directors refuses to make adjustments.

(b)   **Going concern indicators**

A new competitor, Drums, has entered the market and gained considerable market share from Clarinet through competitive pricing. There is a risk that if Clarinet continues to lose market share this will impact on future cash flows.

In addition, there may be pressure on Clarinet to drop their prices in order to compete, which will impact profits and cash flows.

A significant customer has stopped trading with Clarinet and moved its business to Drums. This could result in a significant loss of future revenues and profit, and unless this customer can be replaced, there will be a reduction of future cash flows.

A number of Clarinet's specialist developers have left the company and joined Drums and the company has found it difficult to replace these employees due to their experience and skills. The company is looking to develop new products and in order to do this, it needs sufficiently trained staff. If it cannot recruit enough staff, then it could hold up the product development and stop the company from increasing revenue.

Clarinet's main supplier who provides specialist equipment has just stopped trading. If the equipment is highly specialised, there is a risk that Clarinet may not be able to obtain these products from other suppliers which would impact on their ability to trade. More likely, there are other suppliers available but they may be more expensive which will increase the outflows of Clarinet and worsen the cash flow forecast.

Clarinet needs to raise finance to develop new products in order to gain market share; they approached their shareholders for further finance but they declined to invest further. If Clarinet is unable to obtain suitable finance, then it may be that the shareholders deem Clarinet to be too risky to invest in further. They may be concerned that Clarinet will not be able to offer them a suitable return on their investment, suggesting cash flow problems. In addition, if Clarinet cannot obtain alternative finance, then it will not be able to develop the products it needs to.

Clarinet's overdraft has grown significantly during the year. If the bank does not renew the overdraft and the company is unable to obtain alternative finance, then it may not be able to continue to trade.

Clarinet's cash flow forecast shows a significantly worsening position for the coming 12 months. If the company continues to have cash outflows, then it will increase its overdraft further and will start to run out of available cash.

One of Clarinet's customers is planning to sue the company for loss of revenue due to hardware being installed by Clarinet in the customer's online ordering system not operating correctly. If the customer is successful, then Clarinet may have to pay a significant settlement which will put further pressure on cash flows. In addition, it is unlikely that this customer will continue to trade with Clarinet and if the problems become known to other customers, this may lead to a further loss of revenue and cash flows as well as impact on Clarinet's reputation.

(c)   **Going concern procedures**

■ Obtain the company's cash flow forecast and review the cash in and outflows. Assess the assumptions for reasonableness and discuss the findings with management to understand if the company will have sufficient cash flows.

■ Perform a sensitivity analysis on the cash flows to understand the margin of safety the company has in terms of its net cash in/outflow.

■ Discuss with the finance director whether any new customers have been obtained to replace the one lost.

■ Review the company's post year-end sales and order book to assess if the levels of trade are likely to increase in light of the increased competition from Drum and if the revenue figures in the cash flow forecast are reasonable.

■ Discuss with the directors whether replacement specialist developers have been recruited to replace those lost to Drum.

■ Review any agreements with the bank to determine whether any covenants have been breached, especially in relation to the overdraft.

■ Review any bank correspondence to assess the likelihood of the bank renewing the overdraft facility.

■ Review the correspondence with shareholders to assess whether any of these are likely to reconsider increasing their investment in the company.

■ Discuss with the directors whether they have contacted any banks for finance to help with the new product development.

■ Enquire of the lawyers of Clarinet as to the existence of any additional litigation and request their assessment of the likelihood of Clarinet having to make payment to their customer who intends to sue for loss of revenue.

■ Perform audit tests in relation to subsequent events to identify any items which might indicate or mitigate the risk of going concern not being appropriate.

■ Review the post year-end board minutes to identify any other issues which might indicate further financial difficulties for the company.

■ Review post year-end management accounts to assess if in line with cash flow forecast.

■ Consider whether any additional disclosures as required by IAS 1 *Presentation of Financial Statements* in relation to material uncertainties over going concern should be made in the financial statements.

■ Consider whether the going concern basis is appropriate for the preparation of the financial statements.

■ Obtain a written representation confirming the directors' view that Clarinet is a going concern.

(d) **Auditor's report**

The directors of Clarinet have agreed to make going concern disclosures; however, the impact on the auditor's report will be dependent on the adequacy of these disclosures. If the disclosures are adequate, then the auditor's report will be modified as a Material Uncertainty Related to Going Concern section would be required.

The section will state that the audit opinion is not modified, indicate that there is a material uncertainty and will cross reference to the disclosure note made by management. It would be included immediately after the basis for opinion section.

If the disclosures made by management are not adequate, the audit opinion will need to be modified as there is a material misstatement. Depending on the materiality of the issue, this will be either qualified or an adverse opinion.

A basis for opinion section describing the matter giving rise to the modification will be included after the opinion section and this will clearly identify the lack of disclosure over the going concern uncertainty. The opinion section will be amended to state "except for" or the financial statements are not fairly presented.

Answer 84 OCTBALL

Tutorial note: *This 20-mark question relates mainly to syllabus area E and is therefore non-exam style.*

(a) **Advantages of appointing NFA**

Expertise available

The NFA partnership will be able to provide the necessary expertise for internal audit work. They may be able to provide a broader range of expertise as they serve many different clients therefore staff may be available for specialist work that Octball could not afford to employ.

Buy-in skills as necessary

If internal audit is only required for specific functions or particular jobs each year then the expertise can be purchased as required. Taking this approach will minimise in-house costs.

Independence/Qualifications

No information is provided on the qualification of staff in NFA, although as an independent firm it is likely that care will be taken that staff do remain independent and have the appropriate qualifications in order that they can provide an appropriate high level of service.

Audit techniques – training

Outsourcing will remove the need for training internal staff. Effectively training will be provided for "free" as the outsourcing firm will be responsible for keeping staff up-to-date with new auditing techniques and processes.

Disadvantages of appointing NFA

Fee pressure

NFA may experience some fee pressure, but only in respect of maintaining cost effectiveness of the internal audit department. The relationship needs to be managed carefully to ensure that NFA do not decrease the quality of their work due to insufficient fees.

Knowledge

The NFA partnership will not have any prior knowledge of Octball. This will be a disadvantage as this will mean the partnership will need time to ascertain the accounting systems and controls etc in Octball before commencing work. However, providing an independent view may identify control weaknesses that the current internal audit department have missed.

Location

The NFA partnership may not be able to provide this service to Octball as they are a local firm and therefore the issue of travel and working away from home would remain.

Continuity of service – staffing

As provision of audit services is the NFA partnership's main activity, they should also be able to budget for client requirements although this cannot be guaranteed as staff may still leave. However, as a larger internal auditing firm, they will be able to offer staff better career progression which should assist staff retention.

(b) **Issues to be considered by the external auditor**

Objectivity and independence

Objectivity in carrying out the external audit would be threatened if reviewing systems and working papers that were recommended or prepared by the firm in its capacity as the internal auditor. Although recommending systems and preparing working papers may be tasks carried out as internal auditor, the firm must ensure that separate staff are assigned to the tasks associated with each of the roles of internal and external audit.

Staff of the external audit firm appointed to the internal audit of Octball will work "day in, day out" with other employees of the company. Safeguards will be needed to reduce the threat of familiarisation to an acceptable level.

Training

A firm of auditors will automatically provide training for its audit staff to comply with professional regulations (e.g. compulsory continuing professional development). Any staff provided to serve the internal audit function will need appropriate training and experience in internal audit.

Resources

The external auditor will need staff with the necessary skills for what will be effectively full-time work in undertaking the internal audit work in Octball. Skills may not be an issue because external audit staff will already understand audit procedures. However, assigning staff full-time to Octball to overcome the company's staffing issues may result in the audit firm facing staffing issues in meeting other client commitments.

Fee pressure

There may be fee pressure on an external audit firm; either to maintain the cost effectiveness of the internal audit department or to maintain the competitiveness of the audit fee itself in order to keep the internal audit work.

Knowledge

The external auditor will already have knowledge of Octball. This will assist in establishing the internal audit department as systems documentation will already be available and the audit firm will already be aware of potential weaknesses in the control systems.

(c) **Controls to maintain the standard of the internal audit department**

- If T&M are appointed, ensure that the internal and external audit is managed by different departments in the firm.

- Setting and review of performance measures such as cost, areas reviewed, etc with explanations obtained for any significant variances.

- Use of appropriate audit methodology, including clear documentation of audit work carried out, adequate review, and appropriate conclusions drawn.

- Review of working papers by myself, ensuring adherence to International Standards on Auditing where appropriate and any in-house standards on auditing.

- The work plan for internal audit is agreed prior to work commencing and this is followed by the outsourcing company.

Answer 85 SAXOPHONE

Tutorial note: *This 20-mark question relates mainly to syllabus area A and is therefore non-exam style.*

(a) **Advantages/disadvantages of outsourcing internal audit department**

Saxophone

Advantages

Staffing: Saxophone wishes to expand its internal audit department in terms of size and specialist skills. If they outsource, there will be no need to spend money in recruiting further staff as Cello & Co (Cello) will provide the staff members.

Immediate solution: As the current internal audit department is small, then outsourcing can provide the number of staff needed straight away.

Skills and experience: Cello is likely to have a large pool of staff available to provide the internal audit service to Saxophone.

In addition, the audit firm is likely to have staff with specialist skills already available.

Cost savings: Outsourcing can be an efficient means to control the costs of internal audit as any associated costs such as training will be eliminated as Cello will train its own employees. In addition, the costs for the internal audit service will be agreed in advance. This will ensure that Saxophone can budget accordingly.

Flexibility: If the internal audit department is outsourced, Saxophone will have total flexibility in its internal audit service. Staff can be requested from Cello to suit the company's workloads and requirements. This will ensure that, when required, extra staff is readily available for as long or short a period as needed.

Disadvantages

Existing internal audit department: Saxophone has an existing internal audit department; if they cannot be redeployed elsewhere in the company, then they may need to be made redundant and this could be costly for Saxophone. Staff may oppose the outsourcing if it results in redundancies.

Increased costs: As well as the cost of potential redundancies, the internal audit fee charged by Cello may over a period of time increase, proving to be very expensive.

Knowledge of company: Cello will allocate available staff members to work on the internal audit assignment; this may mean that each visit the staff members are different and hence they may not fully understand the systems of Saxophone. This will decrease the quality of the services provided and increase the time spent by Saxophone's employees in explaining the system to the auditors.

Loss of in-house skills: If the current internal audit team is not deployed elsewhere in the company, valuable internal audit knowledge and experience may be lost. If Saxophone then decided at a future date to bring the service back in-house, this might prove to be too difficult.

Confidentiality: Knowledge of company systems and confidential data will be available to Cello. Although the engagement letter would provide confidentiality clauses, this may not stop breaches of confidentiality.

Control: Saxophone currently has more control over the activities of its internal audit department; however, once outsourced it will need to discuss areas of work and timings well in advance with Cello.

Cello

Advantages

Additional fees for Cello: The audit firm will benefit from the internal audit service being outsourced as this will generate additional fee income. However, the firm will need to monitor the fees to ensure that they do not represent too high a percentage of their total fee income. As a public interest company, fee income should not represent more than 15% of gross practice income for two consecutive years.

Disadvantages

Independence: If Cello provides both external audit and internal audit services, there may be a self-review threat especially where the internal audit work is relied upon by the external auditor team. The firm would need to take steps to ensure that separate teams are put in place as well as additional safeguards.

(b)   Corporate governance

(i) Weaknesses	*(ii) Recommendations*
Bill Bassoon is now the chairman; however, until last year he was the chief executive. The chairman is supposed to be an independent non-executive director and hence cannot have previously been the chief executive.	Bill Bassoon should return to his role as chief executive as this will fill the current vacancy and an independent non-executive director should be recruited to fill the role of chairman.
The roles of chairman and chief executive are both very important and carry significant responsibilities; hence this prevents too much power residing in the hands of one individual.	
The board is comprised of five executives and only three non-executive directors.	At least half of the board should be comprised of non-executive directors. Hence the board of Saxophone should consider recruiting and appointing an additional one to two non-executive directors.
There should be an appropriate balance of executives and non-executives, to ensure that the board makes the correct objective decisions, which are in the best interest of the stakeholders of the company, and no individual or group of individuals dominates the board's decision-making.	
Bill Bassoon is considering appointing his close friend as a non-executive director; the friend has experience of running a manufacturing company.	Only independent non-executives with relevant experience and skills should be appointed to the board of Saxophone. The close friend of Bill Bassoon is unlikely to meet these criteria, as he has no experience in the insurance industry, and so should not be appointed.
Non-executives bring valuable experience to a company, but they must also exercise their independent judgement over the whole board. If this director is a close friend of Bill Bassoon, then it is possible that he will not be independent. In addition, other than being a former chief executive, he does not have any relevant experience of the insurance industry and so it is questionable what value he will add to Saxophone.	
The remuneration for directors is set by Jessie Oboe, the finance director. However, no director should be involved in setting their own remuneration as this may result in excessive levels of pay being set.	There should be a fair and transparent policy in place for setting remuneration levels. The non-executive directors should decide on the remuneration of the executives. The finance director or chairman should decide on the pay of the non-executives.
All directors' remuneration is in the form of an annual bonus. However, the pay should motivate the directors to focus on the long-term growth of the business. Annual targets can encourage short-term strategies rather than maximising shareholder wealth.	The remuneration of executives should be restructured to include a significant proportion aimed at long-term company performance. Perhaps they could be granted share options, as this would help to move the focus to the longer term.

1163

(i)	*Weaknesses*	*(ii)*	*Recommendations*
	In addition, non-executive directors' pay should not be based on meeting company targets as their pay should be independent of how the company performs.		Non-executives should be paid an annual fee for their services, which is unrelated to how Saxophone performs.
	Saxophone does not currently have an audit committee. Audit committees undertake an important role in that they help the directors to satisfy their responsibility of accountability with regards to maintaining an appropriate relationship with the company's auditor.		Saxophone should appoint an audit committee as soon as possible. The committee should be comprised of at least three independent non-executives, one of whom should have relevant financial experience. The three current non-executives should be appointed to the audit committee, assuming they meet the requirements of independence.
	A new sales director was appointed nine months ago, however, he has not undergone any board training. All directors should receive induction training when they first join the board so that they are fully aware of their responsibilities.		The new sales director should immediately receive relevant training from Bill Bassoon to ensure that he has a full understanding of his role and responsibilities.
	Saxophone is not planning to hold an annual general meeting (AGM) as the number of shareholders are such that it would be too costly and impractical. However, the AGM is an important meeting in that it gives the shareholders an opportunity to raise any concerns, receive an answer and vote on important resolutions. The proposal to send the financial statements and resolutions by email is not appropriate as it does not allow shareholders an opportunity to raise relevant questions.		The company should continue to hold the AGM. Sending information by email in advance of the meeting may be practical and save some costs; however, this should not be seen as a replacement for the AGM.

(i)	*Weaknesses*	*(ii)*	*Recommendations*

Answer 86 BUSH-BABY HOTELS

Item	Answer	Justification

1   C

(1), (3), and (4) each describe how a new internal audit department could assist BBH's directors in preventing and/or detecting fraud and/or error. (2) is not correct because it is not the role of internal audit to judge the company's objectives or the board's strategies to achieve those objectives.

Tutorial note: *Also, the appropriateness of such objectives and strategies would not assist in preventing and detecting fraud and error.*

2   B

(1), (2), and (3) each describe limitations of BH establishing and maintaining an internal audit department. (4) is not correct, because an internal audit department is not required to be independent. Although the internal audit function can be outsourced, it is often in-house and therefore never truly independent.

3   B

Value for money (VFM) is defined as the evaluation of management's achievements in terms of economy, efficiency, and effectiveness of operations. VFM is the correct response as only this would deal with "relevant benchmarks", "indicators" and "performance" for a company with a primary objective of making a profit.

Tutorial note: *Best value audits apply to public sector and other entities that have a duty to deliver services.*

4   A

(2) and (3) could be valid conclusions. (1) is not valid, because holding obsolete inventory would not necessarily result in any difference and could result in higher physical quantities (e.g. if obsolete inventory is identified and adjusted on the records but not physically removed). (4) is not valid, because even if there is no difference there could still be inventory issues, such as obsolescence or fraud (involving falsification of the records as well as theft of inventory).

5   C

(1), (2) and (3) are additional functions that could be undertaken by the internal audit department. (4) is not because the role of internal audit is to evaluate and improve the effectiveness of risk management, control and governance processes. Reviews of employees' eligibility for promotion would be undertaken by the human resources department.

Answer 87 ZPM

(a)   Factors to consider when evaluating and testing the work of the internal auditor

- Check to ensure that the work is performed by persons having adequate technical training and proficiency as internal auditors, by ensuring appropriate training programmes are in place and the auditor has appropriate qualifications.

- Ensuring that the work of assistants is properly supervised, reviewed and documented by reviewing the procedure manuals of internal audit and the audit working papers produced.

- Determining that sufficient and appropriate audit evidence is obtained to afford a reasonable basis for the conclusions reached, again by reviewing the internal auditor's working papers.

- Checking that the conclusions reached are appropriate in the circumstances and that any reports prepared are consistent with the results of the work performed by reviewing the work performed and the reports produced.

- Ensuring any exceptions or unusual matters disclosed by internal audit are properly resolved by the external auditor and management.

(b)(i)   Objectives of internal audit

Year-end inventory count

The main aim of the year-end inventory count is to ensure that the figure for inventory in the financial statements is accurate. The objective of the internal audit department is to check the accuracy of the inventory count to ensure that the physical goods inventory is correctly stated on the inventory sheets. This objective is achieved by checking the control system over counting inventory. Internal audit work will involve ensuring that all inventory is counted, teams of two people are counting inventory, and then performing test counts to determine the accuracy of the test counts.

Internal controls over procurement systems

The internal auditor will be ensuring that the procurement system is achieving its key objectives and operating according to company guidelines. Specific aims will include:

- ensuring purchases are authorised;
- quantity discounts are obtained; and
- inventory received is recorded on goods received notes or similar.

Reviewing operations of the marketing department

The internal auditor will review the work of the marketing department with aims such as ensuring that the process is being managed effectively and information is available to the marketing manager as required. Where deficiencies in the information provided are noted, then an internal audit report will highlight those deficiencies and make recommendations for improvement to the information systems. The objectives of internal audit in this case are more to ensuring the efficiency of operations rather than any specific financial objective.

(ii)   Objectives of the external auditor

Year-end inventory count

The external auditor also needs to ensure that the figure for inventory is materially correct for the financial statements. Part of the work of the external auditor is to attend the physical inventory count to ensure that the quantities and condition of inventory is correctly recorded. Given that ZPM does not appear to have any perishable inventory, the main objective will be to ensure correct recording of inventory quantity.

Internal controls over procurement systems

The external auditor will test the procurement system with the overall objective of determining that the purchases and payables figures in the financial statements are correct. The objectives of testing will be to ensure that the control system over procurement is operating efficiently, and ensure complete and accurate recording of purchases and payables liabilities. If errors are found then this implies that the financial statements could also contain errors.

Reviewing operations of the marketing department

As the operations of the marketing department do not normally impact on the financial statements, the external auditor may not actually review this function.

(iii)   Reliance by the external auditor

Year-end inventory count

ZPM has 103 stores – which is likely to mean that the external auditor will not be able to attend the inventory count in all stores, simply due to lack of staff. However, if inventory count procedures are the same at all stores, then reliance can be placed on the internal auditor to attend some stores and check that the internal control systems are being correctly applied in those stores. This reliance does not mean that the external auditor does not carry out any work; the external auditor will compare results from stores tested with those of the internal auditor. Results should be about the same; any differences in terms of errors found will be investigated, and reasons for those differences obtained.

Internal controls over procurement systems

The external auditor may rely on the work of the internal auditor regarding the procurement systems, where the work of the internal auditor is relevant to the financial statements. Some areas such as ensuring quantity discounts are obtained are less important than ensuring completeness of recording of liabilities. Again, the external auditor must perform some work on the procurement systems; the presence of an internal auditor simply means that the work can be reduced.

Reviewing operations of the marketing department

Given that the external auditor does not need to review the operations of the marketing department then no formal reliance is needed on the work of the internal auditor. However, internal audit reports may be reviewed to determine, for example, the effectiveness of advertising spend, etc to help determine the going concern situation of the company. In the case of ZPM, the effectiveness of advertising new stores could be reviewed.

Item   Answer   Justification

MCQs 1 AUDIT AND OTHER ASSURANCE ENGAGEMENTS

1.1   D   There are two types of conclusion which can be given: a conclusion expressed in positive terms and a conclusion expressed in negative terms. A conclusion expressed in negative terms is indicated by the phrase "nothing has come to our attention" which indicates the restricted work carried out and hence the fact that the assurance is limited, as opposed to reasonable. Hence this type of assurance is limited level of assurance expressed negatively.

1.2   D   A statutory audit provides reasonable assurance, which reflects the comprehensiveness of the audit procedures carried out. No assurance engagement, not even a statutory audit can give absolute assurance. A review of a set of financial statements is carried out under ISRE 2400 which requires a limited level of assurance because procedures are limited to enquiry and analytical review.

1.3   C   Apply a questioning mind to the information and evidence he obtains would indicate professional scepticism. The alternative options offered are all a step too far.

1.4   D   Statement 1 is incorrect as ISAs are issued by the International Auditing and Assurance Standards Board rather than the IASB who issue accounting standards. Statement 2 is incorrect as ISAs do not override local legislation.

MCQs 2 EXTERNAL AUDIT

2.1   D   The objective of the external audit of a limited company is to provide assurance on the credibility of the financial statements by reporting in "true and fair" terms.

2.2   C   Under many jurisdictions the auditors are appointed by, and report to, the shareholders. In some cases, the procedure is delegated to the directors but would be approved by the shareholders at the next general meeting. The key point here is that the shareholders' *approval* must be obtained.

2.3   B   Under most jurisdictions' legal requirements, the directors of a company have a duty to prepare financial statements which give a true and fair view and are in accordance with the relevant legislation.

2.4   C   The International Federation of Accountants (IFAC) oversees the IAASB as well as the International Ethics Standards Board for Accountants (IESBA), the International Accounting Education Standards Board (IAESB) and the International Public Sector Accounting Standards Board.

2.5   B   (3) and (6) are true statements.

(1) Only applicable ISAs need be applied during the course of an audit. Any ISA that is not relevant to the circumstances of the audit can be ignored.

(2) ISAs do not override local regulations. Local regulations take precedent where there is a conflict.

(4) ISAs require auditors to use their professional judgement when applying them rather than just blindly following rules.

(5) An appropriately qualified auditor not only has to pass examinations, they must also have a minimum period of practical experience and must continue to keep technically up to date (continuing professional development/education).

2.6   A   Access to books, accounts and records is generally included in company legislation relating to auditors. Information required from company officials is usually limited to the purpose of the audit; unlimited information on any matter would not be appropriate or required. Reporting any matter to any legal authority would be a breach of confidentiality unless the matter was specifically required to be reported on by regulation, contract or law (e.g. suspicion of money laundering). Board meetings generally deal with matters of business confidentiality and as for any non-board member, auditors can only attend if invited to do so by the board.

MCQs 3 CORPORATE GOVERNANCE

3.1   C   Accountability and remuneration are corporate governance principles related to directors, not the auditors. All the other elements are taken from the OECD and UK codes.

3.2   D   The committee is effectively the link between the Board of Directors and the external auditors. The committee also deals with many internal audit matters rather than the directors.

MCQs 4 PROFESSIONAL CODES OF ETHICS AND CONDUCT

4.1   D   When the total fees from an audit client represent a large proportion of the total fees of the firm expressing the audit opinion, the dependence on that client and concern about losing it create a self-interest or intimidation threat. Exit Co is not a listed entity but it may still be considered a public interest client because of its size ("large"). The 15% fee level is a benchmark when considering potential self-interest or intimidation threat with public interest entities. The fact that the total fees will be just below 15%, indicates the potential for them to exceed 15%. For listed companies, the first step when the fee level exceeds 15% for two consecutive years is to discuss what action to take with the audit committee. Stu & Co are taking appropriate action before the size of the fees becomes an independence issue. Steps A and B may be considered at a later stage. Step C is not relevant in relation to the size of the fees.

4.2   D   In the case of situations 1 and 4, the auditor has an obligation to disclose details of their clients' affairs to third parties. Situations 2 and 3 are ones where voluntary disclosure should be made.

MCQs 5 AUDITOR APPOINTMENT

5.1   C   The ACCA *Code of Ethics and Conduct* states that "a professional accountant in public practice will need to obtain the client's permission, preferably in writing, to initiate discussion with an existing accountant".

5.2   B   Results of previous audits and the need to maintain professional scepticism should be included in an audit strategy as opposed to an audit engagement letter.

MCQs 6 DOCUMENTATION

6.1   D   When standardised working papers are used properly, they help to instruct staff and facilitate the delegation of work while providing a means to control its quality.

6.2   C   The letter of engagement is more likely to be on the permanent file than the current file because it is of relevance to more than just the current audit. The other documents all relate to a particular year's audit.

MCQs 7 AUDIT PLANNING

7.1   D   A describes an ICQ/ICEQ, B an IFRS/disclosure checklist, C an audit manual.

7.2   C   Audit planning benefits an audit of financial statements in various ways. Three of which are listed at A, B and D. Adequate audit planning would not provide any assurance concerning the risk of the existence of material misstatement in a set of financial statements.

7.3   D   The audit strategy sets the scope, timing and direction of the audit. A, B and C relate to audit risk (e.g. responses). Materiality, audit risk and internal control all relate to the direction of the audit.

MCQs 8 UNDERSTANDING THE ENTITY

8.1   A   Whilst the prior year audit file will be useful, the system may have changed in the intervening period. The company's website is very unlikely to contain details on the internal control system.

8.2   D   *All* of the factors listed would be indicative of increased audit risk.

MCQs 9 INTERNAL CONTROL

9.1   B   Review by management of the monthly bank reconciliation would be a control activity. If internal audit were then to check to see if this had happened, this would be monitoring of controls.

9.2   A   An advantage of using systems flowcharts to document internal controls is that flowcharts provide a visual depiction of a client's activities.

9.3   C   An ICQ is used by the auditor to document the auditor's understanding of internal controls. Tests of controls are required to assess control risk (A) and the effectiveness of the control environment (B).

         Tutorial note: *General controls and application controls are classifications of controls in a computer environment. ICQs are applicable to understanding internal controls in manual as well as computerised systems.*

9.4   C   An effective system of internal control can enhance profitability, allow a company to better manage its resources and demonstrate compliance with laws and regulations. However, an effective system of internal control does not cut down the time needed for the audit because tests of controls must be performed when the auditor wants to place reliance on controls.

MCQs 10 AUDIT MATERIALITY

10.1   B   The director's loan from the company (an asset), although less than the performance materiality level should be tested as it is a statutory requirement to disclose the exact amount. Disclosure of transactions with directors is considered to be material by nature. Sundry income being greater than the performance materiality level must also be tested.

10.2   B   A conclusion cannot yet be drawn as the reason for the error has not been established. Although each error is less than performance materiality, cumulatively the error may be material. In addition, as the CFO authorised the payments, suspicion of potential fraud must be considered. Discussion with the CFO would not be appropriate as he is a prime suspect. At this stage, extending the sample would not be appropriate as it is clear errors (or a possible fraud) have occurred. Because of the potential fraudulent authorisation, a senior member of the audit team should be involved to provide guidance for the next step.

10.3   A   ISA 320 *Materiality in Planning and Performing an Audit*.

MCQs 11 FRAUD, LAW AND REGULATIONS

11.1   B   Reviewing internal control questionnaires provides information about control policies and procedures, but is not likely to provide information about actual transactions or events and is therefore unlikely to uncover non-compliance with laws and regulations.

11.2   A   The auditor has a primary duty to report the fraud to those charged with governance. As the company is a listed company, this would initially be to the audit committee as the fraud was carried out by a director. It would only be reported in the audit report if it affected the true and fair view.

MCQs 12 TESTS OF CONTROL

12.1   B   A and C are only appropriate to (1) and (2). D is an application control.

12.2   D   A general control relates to the environment within which a computer based system is developed, maintained and operated. It is independent of the applications that are run on the system. 4 meets this definition. 1, 2 and 3 deal with the completeness and accuracy of the records and the validity of the entries made and are application controls.

12.3   A   If a control is to ensure liabilities are not understated it must involve validating that all goods received have been invoiced. Only A does this. B goes in the wrong direction (testing for overstatement); in C the goods may not have been received (therefore liabilities will be overstated); D is a control but not for this objective.

12.4   C   If a control is to meet this objective it must involve checking that all goods despatched have been recorded as sales (testing for understatement). Only C does this. A goes in the wrong direction (testing overstatement) and in B there is no check on despatch. D is a control but not with this objective.

12.5   D   Preparation of system flowcharts aids the auditor in understanding the client's internal controls, but provides no evidence of the operating effectiveness of controls. Tests of controls, which include inquiry and observation of client personnel and inspection of documents and records, provide evidence of operating effectiveness.

12.6   D   Because the auditor is independently performing certain procedures that are part of the client's internal control (and were previously performed by the client), the procedure used by the auditor is reperformance.

12.7   A   When a client's IT system is extensively integrated throughout the company's accounting system, evidence for a substantive audit test may not be available and the auditor will need to place greater reliance on tests of internal controls related to the IT system.

12.8   D   Sequential numbering of invoices confirms the completeness of sales invoices, however, it does not give assurance that all goods despatched are invoiced. Agreeing invoices back to orders does not confirm that the goods have actually been despatched yet.

MCQs 13 COMMUNICATION ON INTERNAL CONTROL

13.1   A   All significant deficiencies and other matters that are deemed of sufficient importance, should be reported to those charged with governance (as well as separately to relevant management). Those matters considered significant should be at the forefront of the report.

13.2   A   As the determination of the estimate is based on objective criteria, there will be no need for a sensitivity analysis. With B, any fraud carried out by management is significant. Similarly with C as directors are involved, independent scrutiny is essential.

13.3   A   The detail of the audit work carried out would never be revealed to the client. If the client were to require a more detailed review of the systems beyond that required for audit, this entails additional assurance services to be agreed with the client. ISA 265 suggests that items 1 and 2 may be included within the report to management to enhance the audit service provided.

MCQs 14 SERVICE ORGANISATIONS

14.1   B   Payroll processing is usually a fairly straight forward operation. The scenario indicates that appropriate controls are in operation at Alhare to ensure completeness and accuracy of the payroll. Provided the auditor's assessment of the design and implementation of the controls at Alhare are satisfactory there will be no need to consider the processing system at the service provider.

14.2   D   Where a client uses a service provider and the processing of those transactions are considered to be complex (e.g. involving a complex integrated system) the auditor will need to perform procedures (understanding the design and implementation of controls plus compliance testing of key controls) at the service provider or request a Type 2 report from the service provider's auditor. Where access to the system is denied, the auditor will not be able to obtain sufficient appropriate audit evidence.

14.3   D   When determining whether to place reliance on the assurance report issued by a service provider's auditor, an auditor should consider the competence and independence of the service provider's auditor. A, B, and C are not required.

14.4   D   A Type I report provides assurance on the design and implementation of internal controls for a service organisation based on its management's description of the service organisation's function provided to its clients. This will not be the same as the controls over the service organisation's accounting and finance function. A Type 2 report will include the same detail as a Type 1 report plus detailed testing (and results) of those controls carried out by the auditor of the service provider.

MCQs 15 AUDIT EVIDENCE

15.1   D   A, B and C are all factors relating to the auditor – only D relates to the client and hence the risk of misstatement. With a tight deadline, errors are more likely to be made by the client requiring an appropriate response from the auditor (nature, timing and EXTENT).

| 15.2 | B | ISAs make it very clear that the auditor will be unable, when auditing a sophisticated computer based system, to obtain sufficient audit assurance from substantive testing alone. The scenario states that a sophisticated system has been installed implying an increased reliance on computer based (CAATs) testing of controls. |

| 15.3 | C | Sales orders documenting credit approval would be a relevant item for an auditor to examine when determining if internal controls over revenue are operating as designed. A, B and D are all evidence used in substantive procedures and not tests of controls. |

| 15.4 | B | Examining a sample of sale invoices for recording in the correct revenue accounts is testing the classification assertion. |

| 15.5 | C | Comparing the date of purchase transactions to the dates they were recorded is a cut-off test. |

| 15.6 | D | The relevant assertions when testing account balances are completeness, accuracy, allocation and valuation, rights and obligations, existence, presentation and classification. The cut-off assertion is relevant when testing transactions, not account balances. |

| 15.7 | D | Audit procedure A describes reperformance, B is describing inquiry rather than confirmation and procedure C is describing recalculation. |

MCQs 16 ANALYTICAL PROCEDURES

| 16.1 | B | The analytical procedures should reveal a misallocation of distribution costs as advertising expenses. It is unlikely to reveal A, C or D as this year's and last year's figures would be comparable. |

| 16.2 | B | A, C and D would all have the reverse effect. Note that this question compares mark up with gross profit. They must first be put onto the same basis to decide if there is an increase or decrease. |

| 16.3 | B | A, C and D would have the reverse effect or the errors cancel out. |

MCQs 17 ACCOUNTING ESTIMATES

| 17.1 | C | When evaluating accounting estimates for reasonableness, the auditor may develop an independent expectation of the estimates or test the calculation of the estimates. The auditor is not required to gather evidence to restate prior year estimates. |

| 17.2 | B | The auditor should pay most attention to what is unexpected. |

| 17.3 | C | Complexity, not simplicity, would increase the risk. Assumptions that are sensitive, rather than not sensitive, would also increase the risk. |

MCQs 18 USING THE WORK OF AN EXPERT

| 18.1 | B | The auditor may choose to perform substantive procedures to verify the specialist's findings if the specialist is related to the client, but the auditor is not required to do so. A, C, and D are correct statements concerning the use of the work of a specialist. |

18.2	D	The work of an expert who has a relationship with a client may be acceptable under certain circumstances. If the expert has a relationship with the client (e.g. employee), the auditor should assess the risk that the expert's objectivity might be impaired. If the auditor believes that the relationship might impair the expert's objectivity, the auditor should perform additional procedures with respect to the expert's assumptions, methods, or findings to determine that the findings are not unreasonable or should engage another independent expert for that purpose.

18.3	B	When expressing an unmodified opinion, the auditor generally will not refer to the work or findings of an expert. The auditor may, however, make reference to the expert in a modified opinion to explain the nature of the modification. The auditor may need the permission of the expert before referencing the expert in the report.

MCQs 19 AUDIT SAMPLING

19.1	D	The stated objective is to test receivables for overstatement therefore the sample may be selected from the list of customers' year end balances – a bias towards large balances would be more likely to detect material overstatement. This will be achieved by using professional judgement to determine what is large (e.g. all balances greater than performance materiality or through the use of monetary unit sampling.

19.2	D	(1), (4) and (6) are true.

		(2)	Population size affects the decision to sample rather than the size of the sample.
		(3)	In order to minimise the risk of an error going undetected by the auditor a large sample size must be tested.
		(5)	The more likely an error the more effort must be directed to that area. Therefore the size of the sample should be larger.

19.3	C	The question describes monetary unit sampling (MUS).

		(A) Value weighted selection is unlikely to detect understatement. An item which is understated will be lower in value and therefore less likely to be selected. (B) Value weighted selection can detect systematic errors but only those leading to overstatement. (C) MUS will select the higher values rather than the lower. (D) Only errors of overstatement would be detected.

19.4	C	A deviation concealed by a forged document deserves broader consideration than a deviation of the same size caused by an error.

MCQs 20 WRITTEN REPRESENTATIONS

20.1	C	When the accounting records are unavailable, it is not acceptable to obtain a written representation as this represents an inability to obtain sufficient and appropriate audit evidence and if material would result in a modified auditor's report.

MCQs 21 COMPUTER-ASSISTED AUDIT TECHNIQUES

21.1	A	Only A deals with data that would be stored on the master file. B, C and D are incorrect as they do not refer to the customer master file. Also, a computer enquiry can only select and make comparisons, not verify data.

21.2   A   The problem has arisen because of "programming inadequacies". Programming is controlled by general controls so these need reviewing.

21.3   C   The use of audit software involves an audit program being used against the client's data (i.e. the data being audited). Test data is the auditor's data being processed by the client's system (i.e. B).

21.4   D   Entering dummy data into the company's own computer system is a test data technique as it involves the use of the company's system rather than the auditor's own computer programs.

MCQs 22 NON-CURRENT ASSETS

22.1   C   To test for existence the auditor should work from the financial statements to the physical item. However, the financial statements do not itemise the individual items that make up non-current assets so the auditor will need to select a sample from the non-current asset register (having checked that this record agrees to the financial statements). A sample from the register should include both assets held at the beginning of the year and purchases during the year.

       Tutorial note: *Options A and B are testing in the wrong direction (for understatement). The requisition would evidence that a purchase was bona fide (for the benefit of the company) but an asset would not exist until the purchase occurred.*

22.2   A   Checking depreciation rates and calculations would be the most relevant to verify carrying amount (provided that the opening carrying amount is verified). The other options are relevant to the assertions of existence/ownership.

       Tutorial note: *Physical inspection will provide some evidence relevant to the carrying amount (e.g. if they are not road-worthy and should be written down). However, the main determinants of carrying amount are cost and depreciation.*

MCQs 23 INVENTORY

23.1   B   Analysis of inventory turnover provides evidence about accuracy, valuation and allocation (i.e. if inventory turns over slowly, there is a possibility of the inventory becoming obsolete and of no value), existence and completeness (an increase or decrease in inventory turnover could indicate that inventory is over or understated. However, analysis of inventory turnover provides no evidence about rights and obligations.

23.2   C   Testing to determine whether all inventory on hand is reflected in closing inventory is a test of completeness, generally done as part of the physical observation of the inventory count.

23.3   A   All items should be counted at least once during the year, not necessarily at the same time. A standard approach could be to count all material items on a regular basis (e.g. once every quarter – 8% of material items in one month then the same again in 3 months later, etc) and all other items only once during the year. In jewellery shops, for example, the inventory is counted and checked every day. The auditor should attend at least one of the counts to observe the procedures (as in a standard year end observation).

MCQs 24 EXTERNAL CONFIRMATIONS, RECEIVABLES AND SALES

24.1   C   A positive confirmation always asks respondents to reply to the auditor indicating whether or not they agree with the information provided. A negative confirmation also asks the customer to agree with the information provided but respond only if they do not agree (i.e. there is a problem),

24.2   D   A shipping document with no sales invoice is evidence of understatement of sales because goods have been shipped but no sale has been recorded.

MCQs 25 SHARE CAPITAL, RESERVES AND DIRECTORS' REMUNERATION

25.1   C   In most jurisdictions, directors loans are illegal. In all cases they must be disclosed, regardless of the level of the transaction. The auditor may also have a statutory duty to give relevant information in his audit report.

25.2   B   When a client company does not maintain its own statutory records, the auditor should request the agent and registrar to confirm in writing the number of shares issued and outstanding.

25.3   C   This procedure can be used by the auditor to provide evidence of the existence and occurrence assertion. Inspecting the board minutes would also provide evidence of authorisation. Additional tests of the existence and occurrence assertions include inspecting the share certificate book and reviewing the share transfer confirmation.

MCQs 26 LOANS, BANK AND CASH

26.1   C   Setting up the bank mandate would be on the client's letterhead, but after that each year the bank confirmation letter would be sent on the auditor's letterhead (the detail would refer to the original mandate from the client). Receivable (as well as payable) confirmations will always be on the client's letterhead because of confidentiality – the client asking the customer to correspond confidential information to the auditor.

26.2   C   When an auditor performs tests on year-end bank reconciliations and sends standard bank confirmations to all banks where the client has transacted business during the year, the auditor is testing the existence assertion.

   Tutorial note: *The completeness assertion is also tested using these procedures.*

26.3   A   Off-setting assets and liabilities under IFRS is generally prohibited unless it is allowed under a specific IFRS or there is a legal right of set-off. Any other treatment would impair the fact that right of off-set exists and so is within the overall borrowing limit.

26.4   C   This constitutes window dressing and an adjusting event under criteria laid down in IAS 10 *Events After the Reporting Period*. Cheques should be accounted for at the date they are sent out.

MCQs 27 LIABILITIES, PROVISIONS AND CONTINGENCIES

27.1   C   The problem, as described in the scenario, is one of goods received before the year end not being accrued for, because an invoice has not been received. C is the only action that directly addresses this problem. Other tests would include after date review of invoices and cash payments (to identify items that relate to pre-year end transactions).

B – Addresses the wrong problem.

A/D – Goods not invoiced before the year end will not be on the suppliers' records.

C – Should pick up additional accruals needed.

27.2   D   When testing accounts payable for completeness through confirmation, the sample should be selected from the population of all known suppliers.

27.3   D   Although all the procedures are appropriate to the audit of trade payables only (2) and (3) are directed towards *completeness* (testing to the purchase ledger). (1) and (4) are relevant to the assertion of *existence* (testing from the purchase ledger).

MCQs 28 SMALL BUSINESS AND NOT-FOR-PROFIT ORGANISATIONS

28.1   A   Estimating the remaining useful lives of non-current assets (and hence the depreciation charge) is a management decision and cannot be undertaken by the auditor when preparing the financial statements.

28.2   A   In many not for profit organisations, cash transactions are a major element and a high risk area. Controls over the receipt, banking, payment and authorisation of cash must be strong.

28.3   D   The further removed from the day to day operation of a business, the greater the need for internal controls to be implemented. The more "hands on" directors are in a small business, the more they are able to directly control the processes. This will of course mean a potentially higher risk of a director being able to manipulate the business records.

MCQs 29 AUDIT FINALISATION

29.1   A   Statement 2 is not correct as if an event occurs after the financial statements are issued, the auditor has already signed the audit report and so is not able to now include a qualified opinion.

MCQs 30 THE AUDITOR'S REPORT ON FINANCIAL STATEMENTS

30.1   A   The financial statements give a true and fair view, except for the lack of full disclosure concerning the divergence from the requirements of the financial reporting standard. If the auditor did not agree with the departure, then the opinion would have been qualified "except for" on the basis of material misstatement of the financial statements. If the auditor considered it to also be pervasive, then an adverse opinion would be given. In D, as no disclosure had been made, the Emphasis of Matter paragraph would be irrelevant.

30.2   C   Inherent uncertainties such as these do not give rise to modified opinions. As the situation is fully explained in a note to the financial statements, an Emphasis of Matter paragraph would be used. This does not affect the opinion, but does mean that the report is modified.

MCQs 31 GOING CONCERN

31.1   A   There appears to be significant concern over the company's status as a going concern. The auditor should draw attention to this in a Material Uncertainty Related to Going Concern section because the matter is properly disclosed.

Tutorial note: *If adequate disclosures were not made, then an adverse opinion would be given.*

31.2   D   If management are unwilling to make their assessment of going concern this would result in a modified opinion with a qualified or disclaimer opinion. If the going concern basis is not appropriate, then an adverse opinion should be provided rather than a qualified opinion as the matter is material and pervasive.

MCQs 32 INTERNAL AUDIT

32.1   B   Statement 1 is not correct as internal audit (IA) should not report to the finance director as this would impact on their independence. Some of the internal controls and functions IA review are the responsibility of the finance director and they may not act on any recommendations which appear to criticise their department. Statement 2 is correct as companies are not required to implement and maintain an IA function. Corporate governance principles recommend that listed companies maintain an IA function and annually consider the need for such a function; however, they do not require it.

MCQs 33 USING THE WORK OF INTERNAL AUDIT

33.1   D   The internal auditors' work may affect the nature, timing, and extent of the audit, including procedures the auditor performs when obtaining an understanding of the entity's internal control, when assessing risk, and when performing substantive procedures.

33.2   C   Because the auditor has the ultimate responsibility to express an opinion on the financial statements, judgments about assessments of risk, the materiality of misstatements, the sufficiency of tests performed, the evaluation of significant accounting estimates, and other matters affecting the auditor's report should always be those of the auditor.

33.3   B   A is incorrect as internal auditors are not required to be members of any professional body. C is incorrect as external auditors report to shareholders rather than those charged with governance. D is incorrect as internal auditors can be independent of the company, if, for example, the internal audit function has been outsourced.

Fundamentals Level – Skills Module

Audit and Assurance

Specimen Exam applicable from
September 2016

Time allowed: 3 hours 15 minutes

This question paper is divided into two sections:

Section A – ALL 15 questions are compulsory and MUST be attempted

Section B – ALL THREE questions are compulsory and MUST be
attempted

Do NOT open this question paper until instructed by the supervisor.

Do NOT record any of your answers on the question paper.

This question paper must not be removed from the examination hall.

The Association of Chartered Certified Accountants

Section A – ALL 15 questions are compulsory and MUST be attempted

Please use the grid provided on page two of the Candidate Answer Booklet to record your answers to each multiple choice question. Do not write out the answers to the MCQs on the lined pages of the answer booklet.

Each question is worth 2 marks.

The following scenario relates to questions 1–5

You are an audit manager of Buffon & Co, and you have just been assigned the audit of Maldini Co (Maldini). The audit engagement partner who is responsible for the audit of Maldini, a listed company, has been in place for approximately eight years and her son has just been offered a role with Maldini as a sales manager. This role would entitle him to shares in Maldini as part of his remuneration package.

Maldini's board of directors is considering establishing an internal audit function, and the finance director has asked Buffon & Co about the differences in the role of internal audit and external audit. If the internal audit function is established, the directors have suggested that they may wish to outsource this to Buffon & Co.

The finance director has suggested to the board that if Buffon & Co is appointed as internal as well as external auditors, then fees should be renegotiated with at least 20% of all internal and external audit fees being based on the profit after tax of the company as this will align the interests of Buffon & Co and Maldini.

1   From a review of the information above, your audit assistant has highlighted some of the potential risks to independence in respect of the audit of Maldini.

    (1) Audit partner has been in the position for eight years
    (2) Maldini has asked for advice regarding role of internal audit
    (3) Maldini has asked Buffon & Co to carry out internal audit work
    (4) Fees will be based on 20% of profit after tax

    Which of the following options correctly identifies the valid threats to independence and allocates the threat to the appropriate category?

	Self-interest	Self-review	Familiarity
A	1 only	2 and 3	4 only
B	1 only	2 only	4 only
C	2 only	3 and 4	1 only
D	4 only	3 only	1 only

2   In relation to the audit engagement partner holding the role for eight years and her son's offer of employment with Maldini:

    Which of the following safeguards should be implemented in order to comply with ACCA's *Code of Ethics and Conduct*?

    A   The audit partner should be removed from the audit team
    B   An independent review partner should be appointed
    C   The audit partner should be removed if her son accepts the position
    D   Buffon & Co should resign from the audit

3 In line with ACCA's *Code of Ethics and Conduct*, which of the following factors must be considered before the internal audit engagement should be accepted?

(1) Whether the external audit team have the expertise to carry out the internal audit work
(2) If the assignments will relate to the internal controls over financial reporting
(3) If management will accept responsibility for implementing appropriate recommendations
(4) The probable timescale for the outsourcing of the internal audit function

A 1, 2 and 3
B 2 and 3 only
C 1 and 4 only
D 1, 3 and 4

4 Following management's request for information regarding the different roles of internal and external audit, you have collated a list of key characteristics.

(1) Appointed by audit committee
(2) Reports are publicly available to shareholders
(3) Review efficiency and effectiveness of operations to improve operations
(4) Express an opinion on the truth and fairness of the financial statements

Which of the following options correctly allocates the above statements to the relevant auditor?

	External	Internal
A	2, 3 and 4	1 only
B	1 and 4	2 and 3
C	2 and 4	1 and 3
D	2 only	1, 3 and 4

5 If the internal and external audit assignments are accepted, what safeguards, if any, are needed in relation to the basis for the fee?

A As long as the total fee received from Maldini is less than 15% of the firm's total fee income, no safeguards are needed
B The client should be informed that only the internal audit fee can be based on profit after tax
C The fees should be based on Maldini's profit before tax
D No safeguards can be applied and this basis for fee determination should be rejected

The following scenario relates to questions 6–10

Balotelli Beach Hotel Co (Balotelli) operates a number of hotels providing accommodation, leisure facilities and restaurants. You are an audit senior of Mario & Co and are currently conducting the audit of Balotelli for the year ended 31 December 20X4. During the course of the audit a number of events and issues have been brought to your attention:

Non-current assets and depreciation
Balotelli incurred significant capital expenditure during the year updating the leisure facilities at several of the company's hotels. Depreciation is charged monthly on all assets on a straight line basis (SL) and it is company policy to charge a full month's depreciation in the month of acquisition and none in the month of disposal.

6   During the audit of non-current assets, the audit team has obtained the following extract of the non-current assets register detailing some of the new leisure equipment acquired during the year.

Extract from Balotelli's non-current assets register

Date	Description	Original cost $	Depreciation policy	Accumulated depreciation $	Charge for the year $	Carrying value $
1 May 20X4	15 treadmills	18,000	36 months SL	0	4,000	14,000
15 May 20X4	20 exercise bikes	17,000	3 years SL	0	5,667	11,333
17 August 20X4	15 rowing machines	9,750	36 months SL	0	2,167	7,583
19 August 20X4	10 cross trainers	11,000	36 months SL	0	1,528	9,472
		55,750		0	13,362	42,388

In order to verify the depreciation expense for the year, you have been asked to perform a proof in total. This will involve developing an expectation of the depreciation expense for the year and comparing this to the actual expense to assess if the client has calculated the depreciation charge for the year correctly.

What is the expected depreciation expense for the above assets for the year ended 31 December 20X4 and the resultant impact on non-current assets?

A   Depreciation should be $10,660, assets are understated
B   Depreciation should be $18,583, assets are understated
C   Depreciation should be $9,111, assets are overstated
D   Depreciation should be $12,549, assets are overstated

7   The audit assistant who has been assigned to help you with the audit work on non-current assets has expressed some uncertainty over why certain audit procedures are carried out and specifically is unsure what procedures relate to the valuation and allocation assertion.

Which of the following audit procedures are appropriate to test the VALUATION assertion for non-current assets?

(1)   Ensure disposals are correctly accounted for and recalculate gain/loss on disposal
(2)   Recalculate the depreciation charge for a sample of assets ensuring that it is being applied consistently and in accordance with IAS 16 *Property, Plant and Equipment*
(3)   Review the repairs and maintenance expense accounts for evidence of items of a capital nature
(4)   Review board minutes for evidence of disposals during the year and verify that these are appropriately reflected in the non-current assets register

A   1 and 2
B   1, 3 and 4
C   2, 3 and 4
D   2 and 3 only

Food poisoning

Balotelli's directors received correspondence in November 20X4 from a group of customers who attended a wedding at one of the company's hotels. They have alleged that they suffered severe food poisoning from food eaten at the hotel and are claiming substantial damages. Management has stated that based on discussions with their lawyers, the claim is unlikely to be successful.

8   **In relation to the claim regarding the alleged food poisoning, which of the following audit procedures would provide the auditor with the MOST reliable audit evidence regarding the likely outcome of the litigation?**

    A   Request a written representation from management supporting their assertion that the claim will not be successful

    B   Send an enquiry letter to the lawyers of Balotelli to obtain their view as to the probability of the claim being successful

    C   Review the correspondence from the customers claiming food poisoning to assess whether Balotelli has a present obligation as a result of a past event

    D   Review board minutes to understand why the directors believe that the claim will not be successful

Trade receivables

Balotelli's trade receivables have historically been low as most customers are required to pay in advance or at the time of visiting the hotel. However, during the year a number of companies opened corporate accounts which are payable monthly in arrears. As such, the trade receivables balance has risen significantly and is now a material balance.

9   As trade receivables is a material balance, the audit partner has asked that the audit team carry out a trade receivables circularisation.

    Which of the following are benefits of carrying out a trade receivables circularisation?

    (1)   It provides evidence from an independent external source

    (2)   It provides sufficient appropriate audit evidence over all relevant balance assertions

    (3)   It improves audit efficiency as all customers are required to respond

    (4)   It improves the reliability of audit evidence as the process is under the control of the auditor

    A   1 and 2

    B   1, 2 and 4

    C   2 and 3

    D   1 and 4 only

10 The results of the trade receivables circularisation carried out by the audit team on balances as at 31 December 20X4 are detailed below. You have been asked to consider the results and determine if additional audit procedures are required.

Customer	Balance per sales ledger $	Balance per customer confirmation $	Comment
Willow Co	42,500	42,500	
Cedar Co	35,000	25,000	Invoice raised 28 December
Maple Co	60,000	45,000	Payment made 30 December
Laurel Co	55,000	55,000	A balance of $20,000 is currently being disputed by Laurel Co
Oak Co	15,000		No reply

Which of the following statements in relation to the results of the trade receivables circularisation is TRUE?

A   No further audit procedures need to be carried out in relation to the outstanding balances with Willow Co and Laurel Co

B   The difference in relation to Cedar Co represents a timing difference and should be agreed to a pre year-end invoice

C   The difference in relation to Maple Co represents a timing difference and should be agreed to pre year-end bank statements

D   Due to the non-reply, the balance with Oak Co cannot be verified and a different customer balance should be selected and circularised

The following scenario relates to questions 11–15

Cannavaro.com is a website design company whose year end was 31 December 20X4. The audit is almost complete and the financial statements are due to be signed shortly. Profit before tax for the year is $3·8 million and revenue is $11·2 million.

The company has only required an audit for the last two years and the board of directors has asked your firm to provide more detail in relation to the form and content of the auditor's report.

During the audit it has come to light that a key customer, Pirlo Co, with a receivables balance at the year end of $285,000, has just notified Cannavaro.com that they are experiencing cash flow difficulties and so are unable to make any payments for the foreseeable future. The finance director has notified the audit team that he will write this balance off as an irrecoverable debt in the 20X5 financial statements.

11 To explain to the board the content of the audit report, the audit partner has asked you to provide details as to why certain elements are included within an unmodified report.

   Which of the following explains the purpose of the ADDRESSEE element of the unmodified audit report in line with ISA 700 *Forming an Opinion and Reporting on Financial Statements*?

   A It demonstrates the point at which sufficient appropriate evidence has been obtained
   B It clarifies who may rely on the opinion included within the report
   C It explains the role and remit of the audit
   D It sets out the location where the auditor practises

12 The audit assistant assigned to the audit of Cannavaro.com wants a better understanding of the effect subsequent events have on the audit and has made the following statements:

   (1) All material subsequent events require the numbers in the financial statements to be adjusted
   (2) A non-adjusting event is a subsequent event for which NO amendments to the current year financial statements are required
   (3) The auditor's responsibilities for subsequent events which occur prior to the audit report being signed are different from their responsibilities after the audit report has been issued
   (4) The auditor should request a written representation confirming that all relevant subsequent events have been disclosed

   Which of the statements above in relation to subsequent events are true?

   A 1 and 3
   B 2, 3 and 4
   C 1, 2 and 4
   D 3 and 4 only

13 The audit engagement partner has asked you to make an initial assessment of the materiality of the issue with the outstanding receivables balance with Pirlo Co and to consider the overall impact on the financial statements.

   Which of the following correctly summarises the effect of the outstanding balance with Pirlo Co?

	Material	Financial statement impact
A	No	Revenue is overstated
B	No	Gross profit is understated
C	Yes	Profit is overstated
D	Yes	Going concern principle is in doubt

8

14 The audit engagement partner requires you to perform additional procedures in order to conclude on the level of any adjustment needed in relation to the outstanding balance with Pirlo Co.

Which TWO of the following audit procedures should be performed to form a conclusion as to whether the financial statements require amendment?

(1) Discuss with management the reasons for not amending the financial statements
(2) Review the cash book post year end for receipts from Pirlo Co
(3) Send a request to Pirlo Co to confirm the outstanding balance
(4) Agree the outstanding balance to invoices and sales orders

A 1 and 2
B 1 and 4
C 2 and 3
D 2 and 4

15 The finance director has asked you to outline the appropriate audit opinions which will be provided depending on whether the company decides to amend or not amend the 20X4 financial statements for the issue identified regarding the recoverability of the balance with Pirlo Co.

Which of the following options correctly summarises the audit opinions which will be issued depending on whether or not the 20X4 financial statements are amended?

	Financial statements amended	Financial statements not amended
A	Unmodified	Unmodified with emphasis of matter
B	Unmodified with emphasis of matter	Qualified 'except for'
C	Unmodified	Adverse
D	Unmodified	Qualified 'except for'

(30 marks)

[P.T.O.

Section B – ALL THREE questions are compulsory and MUST be attempted

Please write your answers to all parts of these questions on the lined pages within the Candidate Answer Booklet.

16 Milla Cola Co (Milla) manufactures fizzy drinks such as cola and lemonade as well as other soft drinks and its year end is 30 September 20X5. You are an audit manager of Totti & Co and are currently planning the audit of Milla. You attended the planning meeting with the audit engagement partner and finance director last week and the minutes from the meeting are shown below. You are reviewing these as part of the process of preparing the audit strategy document.

Minutes of planning meeting for Milla
Milla's trading results have been strong this year and the company is forecasting revenue of $85 million, which is an increase from the previous year. The company has invested significantly in the cola and fizzy drinks production process at the factory. This resulted in expenditure of $5 million on updating, repairing and replacing a significant amount of the machinery used in the production process.

As the level of production has increased, the company has expanded the number of warehouses it uses to store inventory. It now utilises 15 warehouses; some are owned by Milla and some are rented from third parties. There will be inventory counts taking place at all 15 of these sites at the year end.

A new accounting general ledger has been introduced at the beginning of the year, with the old and new systems being run in parallel for a period of two months. In addition, Milla has incurred expenditure of $4·5 million on developing a new brand of fizzy soft drinks. The company started this process in July 20X4 and is close to launching their new product into the market place.

As a result of the increase in revenue, Milla has recently recruited a new credit controller to chase outstanding receivables. The finance director thinks it is not necessary to continue to maintain an allowance for receivables and so has released the opening allowance of $1·5 million.

The finance director stated that there was a problem in April in the mixing of raw materials within the production process which resulted in a large batch of cola products tasting different. A number of these products were sold; however, due to complaints by customers about the flavour, no further sales of these goods have been made. No adjustment has been made to the valuation of the damaged inventory, which will still be held at cost of $1 million at the year end.

As in previous years, the management of Milla is due to be paid a significant annual bonus based on the value of year-end total assets.

Required:

(a) **Explain audit risk and the components of audit risk.** (5 marks)

(b) **Using the minutes provided, identify and describe SEVEN audit risks, and explain the auditor's response to each risk, in planning the audit of Milla Cola Co.** (14 marks)

(c) **Identify the main areas, other than audit risks, which should be included within the audit strategy document for Milla Cola Co; and for each area provide an example relevant to the audit.** (4 marks)

The finance director has requested that the deadline for the 20X6 audit be shortened by a month and has asked the audit engagement partner to consider if this will be possible. The partner has suggested that in order to meet this new tighter deadline the firm may carry out both an interim and final audit for the audit of Milla to 30 September 20X6.

Required:

(d) **Explain the difference between an interim and a final audit.** (3 marks)

(e) **Explain the procedures which are likely to be performed during an interim audit of Milla and the impact which it would have on the final audit.** (4 marks)

(30 marks)

10

17 Baggio International Co (Baggio) is a manufacturer of electrical equipment. It has factories across the country and its customer base includes retailers as well as individuals, to whom direct sales are made through their website. The company's year end is 30 September 20X5. You are an audit supervisor of Suarez & Co and are currently reviewing documentation of Baggio's internal control in preparation for the interim audit.

Baggio's website allows individuals to order goods directly, and full payment is taken in advance. Currently the website is not integrated into the inventory system and inventory levels are not checked at the time when orders are placed. Inventory is valued at the lower of cost and net realisable value.

Goods are despatched via local couriers; however, they do not always record customer signatures as proof that the customer has received the goods. Over the past 12 months there have been customer complaints about the delay between sales orders and receipt of goods. Baggio has investigated these and found that, in each case, the sales order had been entered into the sales system correctly but was not forwarded to the despatch department for fulfilling.

Baggio's retail customers undergo credit checks prior to being accepted and credit limits are set accordingly by sales ledger clerks. These customers place their orders through one of the sales team, who decides on sales discount levels.

Raw materials used in the manufacturing process are purchased from a wide range of suppliers. As a result of staff changes in the purchase ledger department, supplier statement reconciliations are no longer performed. Additionally, changes to supplier details in the purchase ledger master file can be undertaken by purchase ledger clerks as well as supervisors.

In the past six months, Baggio has changed part of its manufacturing process and as a result some new equipment has been purchased, however, there are considerable levels of plant and equipment which are now surplus to requirement. Purchase requisitions for all new equipment have been authorised by production supervisors and little has been done to reduce the surplus of old equipment.

Required:

(a) In respect of the internal control of Baggio International Co:

   (i)   Identify and explain SIX deficiencies;
   (ii)   Recommend a control to address each of these deficiencies; and
   (iii) Describe a test of control Suarez & Co would perform to assess whether each of these controls, if implemented, is operating effectively.

   Note: The total marks will be split equally between each part.   (18 marks)

(b) Describe substantive procedures Suarez & Co should perform at the year end to confirm plant and equipment additions.   (2 marks)

(20 marks)

18 Vieri Motor Cars Co (Vieri) manufactures a range of motor cars and its year end is 30 June 20X5. You are the audit supervisor of Rossi & Co and are currently preparing the audit programmes for the year-end audit of Vieri. You have had a meeting with your audit manager and he has notified you of the following issues identified during the audit risk assessment process:

Land and buildings

Vieri has a policy of revaluing land and buildings, this is undertaken on a rolling basis over a five-year period. During the year Vieri requested an external independent valuer to revalue a number of properties, including a warehouse purchased in January 20X5. Depreciation is charged on a pro rata basis.

Work in progress

Vieri undertakes continuous production of cars, 24 hours a day, seven days a week. An inventory count is to be undertaken at the year end and Rossi & Co will attend. You are responsible for the audit of work in progress (WIP) and will be part of the team attending the count as well as the final audit. WIP constitutes the partly assembled cars at the year end and this balance is likely to be material. Vieri values WIP according to percentage of completion, and standard costs are then applied to these percentages.

Required:

(a) **Explain the factors Rossi & Co should consider when placing reliance on the work of the independent valuer.**

(5 marks)

(b) **Describe the substantive procedures the auditor should perform to obtain sufficient and appropriate audit evidence in relation to:**

(i) **The revaluation of land and buildings and the recently purchased warehouse; and** (6 marks)

(ii) **The valuation of work in progress.** (4 marks)

(c) During the audit, the team has identified an error in the valuation of work in progress, as a number of the assumptions contain out of date information. The directors of Vieri have indicated that they do not wish to amend the financial statements.

Required:

Explain the steps Rossi & Co should now take and the impact on the audit report in relation to the directors' refusal to amend the financial statements. (5 marks)

(20 marks)

End of Question Paper

Section A

1	D
2	A
3	B
4	C
5	D
6	A
7	A
8	B
9	D
10	B
11	B
12	D
13	C
14	A
15	D

Rationale

1   Statement 1 – Partner has been in role for eight years, contravenes ACCA's *Code of Ethics and Conduct* and represents a familiarity threat.

Statement 3 – Providing internal audit services raises a self-review threat as it is likely that the audit team will be looking to place reliance on the internal control system reviewed by internal audit.

Statement 4 – This represents fees on a contingent basis and raises a self-interest threat as the audit firm's fee will rise if the company's profit after tax increases.

Statement 2 – Is not a threat to independence and therefore D is the correct answer.

2   If the engagement partner's son accepts the role and obtains shares in the company, it would constitute a self-interest threat but as the partner has already exceeded the seven-year relationship rule in line with ACCA's *Code of Ethics and Conduct*, the partner should be rotated off the audit irrespective of the decision made by her son. As Maldini is a listed company, an independent review partner should already be in place. It is unlikely that the firm needs to resign from the audit (due to stated circumstances) as the threats to objectivity can be mitigated.

Therefore option A is correct.

3   Statement 1 is inappropriate as the external and internal audit team should be separate and therefore consideration of the skills of the external audit team is not appropriate in the circumstances.

Statement 4 does not apply in that the timescale of the work is not relevant to consider the threats to objectivity.

Statement 2 and 3 are valid considerations – as per ACCA's *Code of Ethics and Conduct* providing internal audit services can result in the audit firm assuming a management role. To mitigate this, it is appropriate for the firm to assess whether management will take responsibility for implementing recommendations. Further, for a listed company the *Code* prohibits the provision of internal audit services which review a significant proportion of the internal controls over financial reporting as these may be relied upon by the external audit team and the self-review threat is too great.

Therefore option B is correct.

4   Internal audit are appointed by the audit committee (external audit usually by the shareholders) and it is the role of internal audit to review the effectiveness and efficiency of internal controls to improve operations. External audit looks at the operating effectiveness of internal controls on which they may rely for audit evidence and a by-product may be to comment on any deficiencies they have found but this is not a key function of the role.

Therefore statements 1 and 3 relate to internal audit.

The external auditor's report is publicly available to the shareholders of the company (internal audit reports are addressed to management/TCWG) and the external auditor provides an opinion on the truth and fairness of the financial statements.

Therefore statements 2 and 4 relate to external audit.

C is therefore the correct answer.

5   The proposal in relation to the fees is a contingent fee basis which is expressly prohibited by ACCA's *Code of Ethics and Conduct* and therefore the only viable option here is to reject the fee basis – D is therefore correct.

6   Depreciation should be calculated as:

Treadmills/exercise bikes = (18,000 + 17,000)/36 x 8 months =   7,778
Rowing machines/cross trainers = (9,750 + 11,000)/36 x 5 months =   2,882

Total   10,660

Therefore the correct answer is A and assets are currently understated as too much depreciation has currently been charged.

Option B is based on depreciation being applied for a full year instead of for the relevant months.

Option C is based on depreciation not being charged in the month of acquisition (i.e. seven and four months).

Option D is based on depreciation for the exercise bikes being divided by the three years instead of allocated on a monthly basis.

7   Test 4 is a test for existence and test 3 is for completeness. All other tests are relevant for valuation. Option A is correct.

8   While all procedures would be valid in the circumstances, only the written confirmation from the company's lawyers would allow the auditor to obtain an expert, third party confirmation on the likelihood of the case being successful. This would provide the auditor with the most reliable evidence in the circumstances. Therefore B is the correct answer.

9   As per ISA 505 *External Confirmations*, the evidence obtained from the trade receivables circularisation should be reliable as it is from an external source and the risk of management bias and influence is restricted due to the process being under the control of the auditor. Therefore 1 and 4 are benefits and option D is therefore correct.

Customers are not obliged to answer and often circularisations have a very low response rate. A circularisation will not provide evidence over the valuation assertion for receivables and therefore 2 and 3 are drawbacks of a circularisation.

10   A is incorrect as the balance with Laurel Co would need to be followed up due to the dispute.

C is incorrect as this represents a payment in transit and the payment would need to be agreed to post year-end bank statements – if the cash was received pre year end this would represent a cut-off issue as this should no longer be included in receivables.

D is incorrect as the sample chosen should be verified even if there is no response. As per ISA 505, the auditor should adopt alternative procedures.

Therefore B is the only statement which is true as this does represent a timing difference (invoice in transit) and should be agreed to a pre year-end invoice.

11   Addressee – sets out who the report is addressed to – usually the shareholders – and is there to clarify who can place reliance on the audit opinion. B is therefore the correct option.

12   Statement 1 is false as not all subsequent events will require an adjustment to the numbers within the financial statements. IAS 10 *Events after the Reporting Period* makes a distinction between an adjusting and non-adjusting event. Only material adjusting events would require an amendment to the figures within the financial statements.

Statement 2 is false as while a non-adjusting event would not require a change to the numbers within the financial statements, IAS 10 may require a disclosure to be made. If the non-adjusting event is material, non-disclosure could still result in a modification to the audit report.

Statement 3 is true as the auditor is required to carry out procedures up to the date of the audit report to gain sufficient appropriate audit evidence that all relevant subsequent events have been identified and dealt with appropriately. After the audit report is issued, the auditor does not need to actively look for subsequent events but is only required to respond to subsequent events which they become aware of.

Statement 4 is true as ISA 560 *Subsequent Events* requires the auditor to obtain written confirmation from management/those charged with governance that all subsequent events have been identified and dealt with in accordance with the appropriate reporting framework.

D is therefore correct.

13   The outstanding balance with Pirlo Co is likely to be irrecoverable as the customer is experiencing financial difficulties.

The balance is material at 7·4% of profit before tax and 2·5% of revenue.

Currently profit and assets are overstated by $285,000. Therefore the correct option is C.

14   Writing to the customer/agreeing to invoices, while valid procedures during the audit to verify the existence of an outstanding balance, would not allow the auditor to assess the recoverability of the balance which is the key issue in determining whether an adjustment is required. Therefore options 3 and 4 are incorrect.

Post year-end cash testing is the best way for the auditor to assess if the balance is recoverable wholly or in part and therefore the cash book should be reviewed for any receipts which will change the assessment of the debt after the year end. The issue should also be discussed with management to understand their reasons for not wanting to amend the financial statements as this may be due to a change in circumstances.

15 The debt with Pirlo Co should be provided for and is material to the financial statements at 7·4% of profit before tax and 2·5% of revenue. This represents a material misstatement which is material but not pervasive. As such, if no adjustment is made the auditor will be required to provide a qualified 'except for' opinion. If the required change is made, then no material misstatement exists and therefore the auditor will be able to issue an unmodified opinion.

Section B

16 (a) Audit risk and its components

Audit risk is the risk that the auditor expresses an inappropriate audit opinion when the financial statements are materially misstated. Audit risk is a function of two main components being the risks of material misstatement and detection risk. Risk of material misstatement is made up of two components, inherent risk and control risk.

Inherent risk is the susceptibility of an assertion about a class of transaction, account balance or disclosure to a misstatement which could be material, either individually or when aggregated with other misstatements, before consideration of any related controls.

Control risk is the risk that a misstatement which could occur in an assertion about a class of transaction, account balance or disclosure and which could be material, either individually or when aggregated with other misstatements, will not be prevented, or detected and corrected, on a timely basis by the entity's internal control.

Detection risk is the risk that the procedures performed by the auditor to reduce audit risk to an acceptably low level will not detect a misstatement which exists and which could be material, either individually or when aggregated with other misstatements. Detection risk is affected by sampling and non-sampling risk.

(b) Audit risks and responses

Audit risk	Auditor response
Milla has incurred $5m on updating, repairing and replacing a significant amount of the production process machinery.	The auditor should review a breakdown of these costs to ascertain the split of capital and revenue expenditure, and further testing should be undertaken to ensure that the classification in the financial statements is correct.
If this expenditure is of a capital nature, it should be capitalised as part of property, plant and equipment (PPE) in line with IAS 16 *Property, Plant and Equipment*. However, if it relates more to repairs, then it should be expensed to the statement of profit or loss	
If the expenditure is not correctly classified, profit and PPE could be under or overstated.	
At the year end there will be inventory counts undertaken in all 15 warehouses.	The auditor should assess which of the inventory sites they will attend the counts for. This will be any with material inventory or which have a history of significant errors.
It is unlikely that the auditor will be able to attend all 15 inventory counts and therefore they need to ensure that they obtain sufficient appropriate audit evidence over the inventory counting controls, and completeness and existence of inventory for any warehouses not visited.	For those not visited, the auditor will need to review the level of exceptions noted during the count and discuss with management any issues which arose during the count.
Inventory is stored within 15 warehouses; some are owned by Milla and some rented from third parties. Only warehouses owned by Milla should be included within PPE. There is a risk of overstatement of PPE and understatement of rental expenses if Milla has capitalised all 15 warehouses.	The auditor should review supporting documentation for all warehouses included within PPE to confirm ownership by Milla and to ensure non-current assets are not overstated.
A new accounting general ledger system has been introduced at the beginning of the year and the old system was run in parallel for two months. There is a risk of opening balances being misstated and loss of data if they have not been transferred from the old system correctly.	The auditor should undertake detailed testing to confirm that all opening balances have been correctly recorded in the new accounting general ledger system.
In addition, the new accounting general ledger system will require documenting and the controls over this will need to be tested.	They should document and test the new system. They should review any management reports run comparing the old and new system during the parallel run to identify any issues with the processing of accounting information.

Audit risk	Auditor response
Milla has incurred expenditure of $4·5 million on developing a new brand of fizzy drink. This expenditure is research and development under IAS 38 *Intangible Assets*. The standard requires research costs to be expensed and development costs to be capitalised as an intangible asset.	Obtain a breakdown of the expenditure and undertake testing to determine whether the costs relate to the research or development stage. Discuss the accounting treatment with the finance director and ensure it is in accordance with IAS 38.
If Milla has incorrectly classified research costs as development expenditure, there is a risk the intangible asset could be overstated and expenses understated.	
The finance director of Milla has decided to release the opening balance of $1·5 million for allowance for receivables as he feels it is unnecessary. There is a risk that receivables will be overvalued, as despite having a credit controller, some balances will be irrecoverable and so will be overstated if not provided against.	Extended post year-end cash receipts testing and a review of the aged receivables ledger to be performed to assess valuation and the need for an allowance for receivables. Discuss with the director the rationale for releasing the $1·5m opening allowance for receivables.
In addition, due to the damaged inventory there is an increased risk of customers refusing to make payments in full.	
A large batch of cola products has been damaged in the production process and will be in inventory at the year end. No adjustment has been made by management.	Detailed cost and net realisable value testing to be performed to assess how much the inventory requires writing down by.
The valuation of inventory as per IAS 2 *Inventories* should be at the lower of cost and net realisable value. Hence it is likely that this inventory is overvalued.	
Due to the damaged cola products, a number of customers have complained. It is likely that for any of the damaged goods sold, Milla will need to refund these customers.	Review the breakdown of sales of damaged goods, and ensure that they have been accurately removed from revenue.
Revenue is possibly overstated if the sales returns are not completely and accurately recorded.	
The management of Milla receives a significant annual bonus based on the value of year-end total assets. There is a risk that management might feel under pressure to overstate the value of assets through the judgements taken or through the use of releasing provisions.	Throughout the audit, the team will need to be alert to this risk. They will need to maintain professional scepticism and carefully review judgemental decisions and compare treatment against prior years.

(c) **Audit strategy document**

The audit strategy sets out the scope, timing and direction of the audit and helps the development of the audit plan. It should consider the following main areas:

It should identify the main characteristics of the engagement which define its scope. For Milla it should consider the following:

- Whether the financial information to be audited has been prepared in accordance with IFRS.

- To what extent audit evidence obtained in previous audits for Milla will be utilised.

- Whether computer-assisted audit techniques will be used and the effect of IT on audit procedures.

- The availability of key personnel at Milla.

It should ascertain the reporting objectives of the engagement to plan the timing of the audit and the nature of the communications required, such as:

- The audit timetable for reporting and whether there will be an interim as well as final audit.

- Organisation of meetings with Milla's management to discuss any audit issues arising.

- Location of the 15 inventory counts.

- Any discussions with management regarding the reports to be issued.

- The timings of the audit team meetings and review of work performed.

- If there are any expected communications with third parties.

The strategy should consider the factors which, in the auditor's professional judgement, are significant in directing Milla's audit team's efforts, such as:

- The determination of materiality for the audit.

- The need to maintain a questioning mind and to exercise professional scepticism in gathering and evaluating audit evidence.

It should consider the results of preliminary audit planning activities and, where applicable, whether knowledge gained on other engagements for Milla is relevant, such as:

–   Results of previous audits and the results of any tests over the effectiveness of internal controls.

–   Evidence of management's commitment to the design, implementation and maintenance of sound internal control.

–   Volume of transactions, which may determine whether it is more efficient for the audit team to rely on internal control.

–   Significant business developments affecting Milla, such as the change in the accounting system and the significant expenditure on an overhaul of the factory.

The audit strategy should ascertain the nature, timing and extent of resources necessary to perform the audit, such as:

–   The selection of the audit team with experience of this type of industry.

–   Assignment of audit work to the team members.

–   Setting the audit budget.

Tutorial note: *The answer is longer than required for four marks but represents a teaching aid.*

(d)   Differences between an interim and a final audit

Interim audit

The interim audit is that part of the audit which takes place before the year end. The auditor uses the interim audit to carry out procedures which would be difficult to perform at the year end because of time pressure. There is no requirement to undertake an interim audit; factors to consider when deciding upon whether to have one include the size and complexity of the company along with the effectiveness of internal controls.

Final audit

The final audit will take place after the year end and concludes with the auditor forming and expressing an opinion on the financial statements for the whole year subject to audit. It is important to note that the final opinion takes account of conclusions formed at both the interim and final audit.

(e)   Procedures which could be undertaken during the interim audit include:

–   Review and updating of the documentation of accounting systems at Milla.

–   Discussions with management on the recent growth and any other changes within the business which have occurred during the year to date at Milla to update the auditor's understanding of the company.

–   Assessment of risks which will impact the final audit of Milla.

–   Undertake tests of controls on Milla's key transaction cycles of sales, purchases and inventory, and credit control.

–   Perform substantive procedures on profit and loss transactions for the year to date and any other completed material transactions.

Impact of interim audit on final

If an interim audit is undertaken at Milla, then it will have an impact on the final audit and the extent of work undertaken after the year end. First, as some testing has already been undertaken, there will be less work to be performed at the final audit, which may result in a shorter audit and audited financial statements possibly being available earlier. The outcome of the controls testing undertaken during the interim audit will impact the level of substantive testing to be undertaken. If the controls tested have proven to be operating effectively, then the auditor may be able to reduce the level of detailed substantive testing required as they will be able to place reliance on the controls. In addition, if substantive procedures were undertaken at the interim audit, then only the period from the interim audit to the year end will require to be tested.

17 (a)   Baggio International's (Baggio) internal control

Deficiency	Control recommendations	Test of control
Currently the website is not integrated into the inventory system.	The website should be updated to include an interface into the inventory system; this should check inventory levels and only process orders if adequate inventory is held.	Test data could be used to attempt to process orders via the website for items which are not currently held in inventory.
This can result in Baggio accepting customer orders when they do not have the goods in inventory. This can cause them to lose sales and customer goodwill	If inventory is out of stock, this should appear on the website with an approximate waiting time.	The orders should be flagged as being out of stock and indicate an approximate waiting time.
For goods despatched by local couriers, customer signatures are not always obtained. This can lead to customers falsely claiming that they have not received their goods. Baggio would not be able to prove that they had in fact despatched the goods and may result in goods being despatched twice.	Baggio should remind all local couriers that customer signatures must be obtained as proof of delivery and payment will not be made for any despatches with missing signatures.	Select a sample of despatches by couriers and ask Baggio for proof of delivery by viewing customer signatures.
There have been a number of situations where the sales orders have not been fulfilled in a timely manner. This can lead to a loss of customer goodwill and if it persists will damage the reputation of Baggio as a reliable supplier.	Once goods are despatched, they should be matched to sales orders and flagged as fulfilled. The system should automatically flag any outstanding sales orders past a predetermined period, such as five days. This report should be reviewed by a responsible official.	Review the report of outstanding sales orders. If significant, discuss with a responsible official to understand why there is still a significant time period between sales order and despatch date. Select a sample of sales orders and compare the date of order to the goods despatch date to ascertain whether this is within the acceptable predetermined period.
Customer credit limits are set by sales ledger clerks. Sales ledger clerks are not sufficiently senior and so may set limits too high, leading to irrecoverable debts, or too low, leading to a loss of revenue.	Credit limits should be set by a senior member of the sales ledger department and not by sales ledger clerks. These limits should be regularly reviewed by a responsible official.	For a sample of new customers accepted in the year, review the authorisation of the credit limit, and ensure that this was performed by a responsible official. Enquire of sales ledger clerks as to who can set credit limits.
Sales discounts are set by Baggio's sales team. In order to boost their sales, members of the sales team may set the discounts too high, leading to a loss of revenue.	All members of the sales team should be given authority to grant sales discounts up to a set limit. Any sales discounts above these limits should be authorised by sales area managers or the sales director. Regular review of sales discount levels should be undertaken by the sales director, and this review should be evidenced.	Discuss with members of the sales team the process for setting sales discounts. Review the sales discount report for evidence of review by the sales director.
Supplier statement reconciliations are no longer performed. This may result in errors in the recording of purchases and payables not being identified in a timely manner.	Supplier statement reconciliations should be performed on a monthly basis for all suppliers and these should be reviewed by a responsible official.	Review the file of reconciliations to ensure that they are being performed on a regular basis and that they have been reviewed by a responsible official.
Changes to supplier details in the purchase ledger master file can be undertaken by purchase ledger clerks. This could lead to key supplier data being accidently amended or fictitious suppliers being set up, which can increase the risk of fraud.	Only purchase ledger supervisors should have the authority to make changes to master file data. This should be controlled via passwords. Regular review of any changes to master file data by a responsible official and this review should be evidenced.	Request a purchase ledger clerk to attempt to access the master file and to make an amendment; the system should not allow this. Review a report of master data changes and review the authority of those making amendments.

Deficiency	Control recommendations	Test of control
Baggio has considerable levels of surplus plant and equipment. Surplus unused plant is at risk of theft.

In addition, if the surplus plant is not disposed of, then the company could lose sundry income. | Regular review of the plant and equipment on the factory floor by senior factory personnel to identify any old or surplus equipment.

As part of the capital expenditure process, there should be a requirement to confirm the treatment of the equipment being replaced. | Observe the review process by senior factory personnel, identifying the treatment of any old equipment.

Review processed capital expenditure forms to ascertain if the treatment of replaced equipment is as stated. |
| Purchase requisitions are authorised by production supervisors.

Production supervisors are not sufficiently independent or senior to authorise capital expenditure. | Capital expenditure authorisation levels to be established. Production supervisors should only be able to authorise low value items, any high value items should be authorised by the board. | Review a sample of authorised capital expenditure forms and identify if the correct signatory has authorised them. |

(b) Substantive procedures – additions

- Obtain a breakdown of additions, cast the list and agree to the non-current asset register to confirm completeness of plant and equipment (P&E).

- Select a sample of additions and agree cost to supplier invoice to confirm valuation.

- Verify rights and obligations by agreeing the addition of plant and equipment to a supplier invoice in the name of Baggio.

- Review the list of additions and confirm that they relate to capital expenditure items rather than repairs and maintenance.

- Review board minutes to ensure that significant capital expenditure purchases have been authorised by the board.

- For a sample of additions recorded in P&E, physically verify them on the factory floor to confirm existence.

18 (a) Reliance on the work of an independent valuer

ISA 500 *Audit Evidence* requires auditors to evaluate the competence, capabilities including expertise and objectivity of a management expert. This would include consideration of the qualifications of the valuer and assessment of whether they were members of any professional body or industry association.

The expert's independence should be ascertained, with potential threats such as undue reliance on Vieri Motor Cars Co (Vieri) or a self-interest threat such as share ownership considered.

In addition, Rossi & Co should meet with the expert and discuss with them their relevant expertise, in particular whether they have valued similar land and buildings to those of Vieri in the past. Rossi & Co should also consider whether the valuer understands the accounting requirements of IAS 16 *Property, Plant and Equipment* in relation to valuations.

The valuation should then be evaluated. The assumptions used should be carefully reviewed and compared to previous revaluations at Vieri. These assumptions should be discussed with both management and the valuer to understand the basis of any valuations.

(b) (i) Substantive procedures for land and buildings

- Obtain a schedule of land and buildings revalued this year and cast to confirm completeness and accuracy of the revaluation adjustment.

- On a sample basis, agree the revalued amounts to the valuation statement provided by the valuer.

- Agree the revalued amounts for these assets are included correctly in the non-current assets register.

- Recalculate the total revaluation adjustment and agree correctly recorded in the revaluation surplus.

- Agree the initial cost for the warehouse addition to supporting documentation such as invoices to confirm cost.

- Confirm through a review of the title deeds that the warehouse is owned by Vieri.

- Recalculate the depreciation charge for the year to ensure that for assets revalued during the year, the depreciation was based on the correct valuation and for the warehouse addition that the charge was for six months only.

- Review the financial statements disclosures of the revaluation to ensure they comply with IAS 16 *Property, Plant and Equipment.*

(ii) Substantive procedures for work in progress (WIP)

- Prior to attending the inventory count, discuss with management how the percentage completions are attributed to the WIP, for example, is this based on motor cars passing certain points in the production process?

- During the count, observe the procedures carried out by Vieri staff in assessing the level of WIP and consider the reasonableness of the assumptions used.

- Agree for a sample that the percentage completions assessed during the count are in accordance with Vieri's policies communicated prior to the count.

- Discuss with management the basis of the standard costs applied to the percentage completion of WIP, and how often these are reviewed and updated.

- Review the level of variances between standard and actual costs and discuss with management how these are treated.

- Obtain a breakdown of the standard costs and agree a sample of these costs to actual invoices or payroll records to assess their reasonableness.

- Cast the schedule of total WIP and agree to the trial balance and financial statements.

- Agree sample of WIP assessed during the count to the WIP schedule, agree percentage completion is correct and recalculate the inventory valuation.

(c) Audit report

Discuss with the management of Vieri why they are refusing to make the amendment to WIP.

Assess the materiality of the error; if immaterial, it should be added to the schedule of unadjusted differences. The auditor should then assess whether this error results in the total of unadjusted differences becoming material; if so, this should be discussed with management; if not, there would be no impact on the audit report.

If the error is material and management refuses to amend the financial statements, then the audit report will need to be modified. It is unlikely that any error would be pervasive as although WIP in total is material, it would not have a pervasive effect on the financial statements as a whole. As management has not complied with IAS 2 *Inventories* and if the error is material but not pervasive, then a qualified opinion would be necessary.

A basis for qualified opinion paragraph would need to be included before the opinion paragraph. This would explain the material misstatement in relation to the valuation of WIP and the effect on the financial statements. The opinion paragraph would be qualified 'except for'.

Marks

Section A

Questions 1–15 multiple choice (each question is worth 2 marks)   **30**

Section B   *Marks available   Marks awarded*

16 Milla Cola Co

(a)	**Component of audit risk**		
	Explanation of audit risk	2	
	Explanation of components of audit risk: Inherent, control and detection risk	3	
		5	

(b)	**Audit risks and responses** (only 7 risks required)		
	$5 million expenditure on production process	2	
	Inventory counts at 15 warehouses at year end	2	
	Treatment of owned v third party warehouses	2	
	New general ledger system introduced at the beginning of the year	2	
	Release of opening provision for allowance for receivables	2	
	Research and development expenditure	2	
	Damaged inventory	2	
	Sales returns	2	
	Management bonus based on asset values	2	
	Max 7 issues, 2 marks each	14	

(c)	**Audit strategy document**		
	Main characteristics of the audit	1	
	Reporting objectives of the audit and nature of communications required	1	
	Factors which are significant in directing the audit team's efforts	1	
	Results of preliminary engagement activities and whether knowledge gained on other engagements is relevant	1	
	Nature, timing and extent of resources necessary to perform the audit	1	
	Restricted to	4	

(d)	**Difference between interim and final audit**		
	Interim audit	2	
	Final audit	2	
	Restricted to	3	

(e)	**Procedures/impact of interim audit on final audit**		
	Example procedures	3	
	Impact on final audit	3	
	Restricted to	4	
Total marks		30	

23

17 Baggio International Co

(a) **Control deficiencies, recommendations and tests of controls** (only 6 issues required)

Website not integrated into inventory system	3
Customer signatures	3
Unfulfilled sales orders	3
Customer credit limits	3
Sales discounts	3
Supplier statement reconciliations	3
Purchase ledger master file	3
Surplus plant and equipment	3
Authorisation of capital expenditure	3
Max 6 issues, 3 marks each	18

(b) Substantive procedures for PPE

Cast list of additions and agree to non-current asset register	1
Vouch cost to recent supplier invoice	1
Agree addition to a supplier invoice in the name of Baggio to confirm rights and obligations	1
Review additions and confirm capital expenditure items rather than repairs and maintenance	1
Review board minutes to ensure authorised by the board	1
Physically verify them on the factory floor to confirm existence	1
Other	
Restricted to	2
Total marks	20

18 Vieri Motor Cars Co

(a) Reliance on independent valuer

ISA 500 requires consideration of competence and capabilities of expert	1
Consider if member of professional body or industry association	1
Assess independence	1
Assess whether relevant expertise of type of properties as Vieri Motor Cars	1
Evaluate assumptions	1
	5

(b) (i) Substantive procedures for revaluation of land and buildings

Cast schedule of land and buildings revalued this year	1
Agree the revalued amounts to the valuation statement provided by the valuer	1
Agree the revalued amounts included correctly in the non-current assets register	1
Recalculate the total revaluation adjustment and agree recorded in the revaluation surplus	1
Agree the initial cost for the warehouse to invoices to confirm cost	1
Confirm through title deeds that the warehouse is owned by Vieri	1
Recalculate the depreciation charge for the year	1
Review the financial statements disclosures for compliance with IAS 16 *Property, Plant and Equipment*	1
Other	
Restricted to	6

(ii) Substantive procedures for work in progress (WIP)

Discuss with management how the percentage completions are attributed to WIP	1
Observe the procedures carried out in the count in assessing the level of WIP; consider reasonableness of the assumptions used	1
During the count, agree a sample of percentage completions are in accordance with Vieri's policies	1
Discuss with management the basis of the standard costs	1
Review the level of variances between standard and actual costs	1
Obtain a breakdown of the standard costs and agree a sample of these costs to actual invoices	1
Cast the schedule of total WIP and agree to the trial balance and financial statements	1
Agree sample of WIP assessed during the count to the WIP schedule, agree percentage completion is correct and recalculate the inventory valuation	1
Other	
Restricted to	4

(c) Impact on audit report

Discuss with management reasons for non-amendment	1
Assess materiality	1
Immaterial – schedule of uncorrected adjustments	1
Material not pervasive – qualified opinion	1
Basis for qualified opinion paragraph	1
Opinion paragraph – qualified 'except for'	1
Restricted to	5
Total marks	20

ACCA

PAPER F8

AUDIT AND ASSURANCE

REVISION QUESTION BANK SUPPLEMENT

For Computer Based Examinations to June 2017

This training material has been prepared and published by Becker Professional Development International Limited:

Parkshot House
5 Kew Road
Richmond
Surrey
TW9 2PR
United Kingdom

Acknowledgement

Past ACCA examination questions are the copyright of the Association of Chartered Certified Accountants and have been reproduced by kind permission.

CONTENTS

This supplement includes OT question types that will appear **only** in a computer-based exam, but provides valuable practice for all students whichever version of the exam they are sitting.

ACCA's CBE Specimen will be accessible from the exam resource finder
http://www.accaglobal.com/uk/en/student/exam-support-resources.html

INTRODUCTION

"Multiple choice – single answer" – is the standard OT type in paper-based examinations. In CBE this type is presented with radio bullets instead of A B, C, D options.

Illustration

ISA 580 *Written Representations* require auditors to obtain written representations to support other evidence.

For which of the following matters would a written representation NOT be suitable as audit evidence?

○ That all deficiencies in internal control known to management have been communicated to the auditor

○ That subsequent events requiring adjustment or disclosure in the financial statements have been dealt with appropriately

○ That the payroll charge for three months of the year is correctly stated when the accounting records were unavailable for that period

○ That management has fulfilled its responsibility for the preparation and presentation of the financial statements

How to answer?

✓ Click on a radio button to select an answer from the choices provided.

✓ You can select only one.

✓ If you want to change your answer, click on your new choice and the original choice will be removed automatically.

Answer

● That the payroll charge for three months of the year is correctly stated when the accounting records were unavailable for that period

Tutorial note: *When the accounting records are unavailable, it is not acceptable to obtain a written representation as this represents an inability to obtain sufficient and appropriate audit evidence and, if material would result in a modified auditor's report.*

OTHER OT TYPES

The following OT types appear **only** in CBE:

(1)   Multiple response
(2)   Pull down list
(3)   Number entry
(4)   Hot area
(5)   Enhanced matching

These are illustrated below.

(1)   Multiple response

Description – candidates are required to select more than one response from the options provided by clicking the appropriate tick boxes.

Illustration 1

To understand an entity, auditors use various sources of information.

Which THREE of the following would be the best sources of information about a company's financial systems?

   ☐   The company's systems procedure manuals

   ☐   The internal audit function's system notes

   ☐   The prior year audit file

   ☐   Inquiries made of company staff

   ☐   The company's website

How to answer?

✓   Three is the maximum you are permitted to select.

✓   You can deselect a chosen answer by clicking on it to clear it.

✓   When you have chosen the required number, deselecting an answer will allow you to select another answer.

Answer

   ☑   The company's systems procedure manuals

   ☑   The internal audit function's system notes

   ☑   Inquiries made of company staff

(2)   Pull down list

Description – candidates are required to select one answer from a list of choices within a drop down list.

Illustration 2

The following timetable relates to your audit of Crighton-Ward:

31 January	–	All audit field work completed
28 February	–	Financial statements approved by board of directors
5 March	–	Auditor's report signed
25 April	–	Annual general meeting held

Which of the following is the most appropriate date on which to obtain the signed written representation from management?

Select... ▼
31 January
28 February
4 March
24 April

Answer

4 March The date of the written representations shall be as near as practicable to, but not after, the date of the auditor's report on the financial statements.

(3)   Number entry

Description – candidates are required to key in a numerical response.

Illustration 3

Beckstead & Co is the auditor of Granite Co, a furniture manufacturer for the year ended 31 December 2016. As part of the audit of property, plant and equipment the audit senior must recalculate the carrying amount of machinery as at 31 December 2016.

At the beginning of the year, the carrying amount of machinery was $2.85 million after accumulated depreciation of $1.05 million. During the year, Granite charged $413,000 depreciation expense. There were no additions but a machine with an original cost of $279,000 and accumulated depreciation of $249,000 was sold.

What is the carrying amount of machinery at 31 December 2016.

$ [   ]

How to answer?

✓ Enter a numerical value in the answer box.

✓ The **only** permitted characters for numerical answer are:

  ❑ One full stop as a decimal point (if required);

  ❑ One minus symbol at the front of the figure if the answer is negative.

    For example: -10234.35

✘ No other characters, including commas, are accepted.

✓ You can change your answer by adding permitted characters or deleting one or more highlighted characters.

Answer

$ 2407000

(4)   Hot area

Description – candidates are required to select one or more areas in an image as their answer(s).

Illustration 4

Identify, by clicking on the relevant box in the table below, whether each of the following statements about a sample size is true or false.

The higher the inherent risk the greater the sample size	TRUE	FALSE
The bigger the population the bigger the sample size	TRUE	FALSE
The lower the acceptable detection risk the lower the sample size	TRUE	FALSE
The higher the tolerable misstatement the lower the sample size	TRUE	FALSE
The higher the expected error the lower the sample size	TRUE	FALSE
The more the population is stratified the lower the sample size	TRUE	FALSE

How to answer?

✓   Click on a hotspot area to select an answer from the hotspot choices provided.

✓   You can select only one per line.

✓   The selected area will be highlighted.

✓   If you want to choose a different answer on a particular line click on the alternative area.

Answer

The higher the inherent risk the greater the sample size	**TRUE**	
The bigger the population the bigger the sample size		**FALSE**
The lower the acceptable detection risk the lower the sample size		**FALSE**
The higher the tolerable misstatement the lower the sample size	**TRUE**	
The higher the expected error the lower the sample size		**FALSE**
The more the population is stratified the lower the sample size	**TRUE**	

(5) Enhanced matching

Description – candidates are required to select and drag their chosen answers to other ("hot") areas of the screen.

Illustration 5

During the current year audit, the auditor performs tests of controls over the revenue cycle.

Indicate which type of evidence gathering method is being used in each procedure.

Observation	Inspection	Reperformance

Procedures	
The auditor carries out the same procedures that were initially done by the client to ensure numerical sequencing of sales orders.	
The auditor examines a sample of sales orders for evidence of credit approval.	
The auditor watches as the client's employees perform a periodic review of the open sales order file.	

Answer

Procedures	
The auditor carries out the same procedures that were initially done by the client to ensure numerical sequencing of sales orders.	Reperformance
The auditor examines a sample of sales orders for evidence of credit approval.	Inspection
The auditor watches as the client's employees perform a periodic review of the open sales order file.	Observation

Illustration 6

Different audit tests can provide cumulative evidence to support specific management assertions.

Match the following audit tests to the relevant assertion.

Audit test
Recalculating the amortisation of intangible assets to determine whether the amortisation period is reasonable
Gathering evidence to detect sales made after the end of the year that have been recorded before year end
Gathering evidence related to an entity's control of obtaining credit approval before shipping goods to customers
Tracing share-related transactions recorded during the year to the board minutes
Sending standard bank confirmations and performing tests on the client's year-end bank reconciliations
Selecting a sample of payment vouchers and comparing the dates on the vouchers to the dates the transactions were recorded in the purchase journal

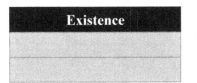 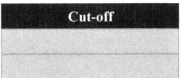 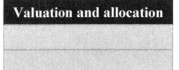

Existence	Cut-off	Valuation and allocation

Answer

Existence	Cut-off	Valuation and allocation
Tracing share-related transactions recorded during the year to the board minutes	Gathering evidence to detect sales made after the end of the year that have been recorded before year end	Recalculating the amortisation of intangible assets to determine whether the amortisation period is reasonable
Sending standard bank confirmations and performing tests on the client's year-end bank reconciliations	Selecting a sample of payment vouchers and comparing the dates on the vouchers to the dates the transactions were recorded in the purchase journal	Gathering evidence related to an entity's control of obtaining credit approval before shipping goods to customers

Illustration 7

Match each of the definitions to the correct risk.

Definitions		**Risks**
The risk that the auditor's substantive procedures will not detect and correct material errors in the financial statements		Inherent risk
The risk that a misstatement could occur that could be material, either individually or when aggregated with other misstatements		Control risk
The risk that a misstatement will not be prevented, or detected and corrected, on a timely basis by the entity's internal control		Detection risk

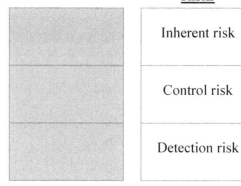

Answer

Definitions	
The risk that the auditor's substantive procedures will not detect and correct material errors in the financial statements	Detection risk
The risk that a misstatement could occur that could be material, either individually or when aggregated with other misstatements	Inherent risk
The risk that a misstatement will not be prevented, or detected and corrected, on a timely basis by the entity's internal control	Control risk

Question 1 SERENA

The following scenario relates to questions 1–5

Serena Co has been trading for over 20 years and obtained a listing on a stock exchange five years ago. It provides specialist training in accounting and finance. The directors recently received an email from a significant shareholder who is concerned that Serena Co does not comply with corporate governance principles.

Serena Co's board is comprised of six directors: four executives who originally set up the company and two non-executive directors who joined Serena Co just prior to the listing. The board has not established an audit committee and no internal audit function has been set up to monitor internal controls.

The chief executive officer, Daniel Brown, has recently taken on the role of chairman of the board. The finance director and the chairman make decisions on the appointment and remuneration of the external auditors. The executive directors' remuneration is proposed by the finance director and approved by the chairman. They are paid an annual salary and share options. Since the company listed, the directors have remained unchanged continuing the practice of automatic annual reappointment.

1 **Which TWO of the following describes the benefits to Serena of forming an audit committee?**

    ☐   The audit committee will provide a formal link between the auditors, the non-executive directors and the shareholders

    ☐   The audit committee will assume responsibility for making decisions regarding the appointment and remuneration of the external auditors and executive directors

    ☐   The audit committee will assume responsibility for the company's financial statements and budgets

    ☐   An audit committee can monitor and review the company's internal controls

2 **Identify, by clicking on the relevant box in the table below, whether each individual (or group of individuals) should be included on the audit committee of Serena.**

CEO, Daniel Brown	INCLUDED	EXCLUDED
Two non-executive directors	INCLUDED	EXCLUDED
Finance director	INCLUDED	EXCLUDED
Three of the executive directors	INCLUDED	EXCLUDED

3   The board has compiled the following responses to the email from the shareholder:

    (1)   The composition of our board, with four executive directors and two non-executive directors, allows for strong governance because the executive directors understand the company's decision making and operations

    (2)   Our CEO, Daniel Brown, is a strong chairman of the board because of the perspective he brings as the day-to-day leader of Serena

    (3)   The inclusion of share options in the directors' remuneration package helps to keep them focused on the long-term results of Serena

    (4)   One of the strengths of our board is the many years we continue to serve as directors, which gives us a deep understanding of the company's history

Which of these responses reflects a correct understanding of the principles of corporate governance?

A	3 only
B	1 and 2 only
C	3 and 4
D	1, 2 and 4

4   In a recent board meeting, Daniel Brown suggested that an internal audit department be created that reports directly to the board.

Which THREE of the following functions could internal audit perform and be considered independent of management?

☐   Examination of financial and operational information for management

☐   Authorisation of transactions in excess of limits set by management

☐   Review of accounting systems and related controls

☐   Advising management on cost effective controls for systems and activities

☐   Routinely preparing bank reconciliations

5   In response to Daniel Brown's suggestion, the finance director suggested that they hire Serena's external auditors to carry out the internal audit function, rather than create an internal audit department.

Under what circumstances could an internal audit function be carried out by the entity's external auditor?

Select... ▼
When any threats to the external auditor's objectivity have been reduced to an acceptable level
When requested to do so by those charged with governance
When combining the two functions would result in lower costs
When the internal audit functions have no direct impact on the financial statements

(10 marks)

Question 2 STARK

The following scenario relates to questions 1–5

You are a manager in the audit firm of Ali & Co, and this is the first time you have been assigned the audit of one of the firm's established clients, Stark Co (Stark). The main activity of Stark is providing investment advice to individuals on retirement planning, purchase of shares and securities and investing in tax-efficient savings schemes. Stark is regulated by the relevant financial services authority and is considered to be a public interest entity.

Mr Son has been the audit engagement partner for Stark for the previous nine years and so has excellent knowledge of the client. Mr Son has informed you that he would like his daughter Zoe to be part of the audit team this year; Zoe is currently studying for her first set of fundamentals papers for her ACCA qualification. Mr Son also informs you that Mr Far, an audit junior, received investment advice as a regular client of Stark during the year and intends to do the same next year.

In an initial meeting with Stark's finance director, you learn that the audit team will not be entertained on Stark's yacht this year. Instead, he has arranged a balloon flight costing less than one-tenth of the expense of using the yacht and hopes this will be acceptable. The director also states that the fee for tax advisory services this year should be based on a percentage of tax saved.

1   From a review of the information above, your audit assistant has highlighted some of the potential risks to independence in respect of the audit of Stark.

     Identify, by clicking on the relevant boxes in the table below, the categories of threat, if any, that are presented by each potential threat to independence.

Potential threat	Category of threat		
Engagement partner has been in the position for nine years	Familiarity	Self-interest	Self-review
The audit junior receives investment advice	Familiarity	Self-interest	Self-review
The audit team has been offered a balloon flight	Familiarity	Self-interest	Self-review
The fee for tax advisory services will be based on a percentage of tax saved	Familiarity	Self-interest	Self-review

2   **In relation to Mr Son holding the role for nine years and his request that his daughter be part of the audit team, which of the following safeguards should be implemented in order to comply with ACCA's *Code of Ethics and Conduct*?**

Select...   ▼
Ali & Co should resign from the audit
An independent review partner should be appointed
Mr Son should be removed from the audit team
Mr Son should be removed if his daughter is part of the team

3   **In line with ACCA's *Code of Ethics and Conduct*, which TWO of the following factors must be considered before the tax advisory services engagement can be accepted?**

☐   The level of tax expertise in the audit engagement team

☐   The period of time over which the advice is expected to be provided

☐   The extent to which the advice will be supported by tax law or regulation

☐   The extent to which the outcome of the tax advice will have a material effect on the financial statements

4   **What safeguards, if any, are required in relation to the basis for the fees for taxation services and the external audit assignment?**

A   As long as the total fee received from Stark is less than 15% of Ali & Co's total fee income, no safeguards are required

B   Stark Co should be informed that the taxation services must be based on time spent and experience of staff involved

C   As long as the audit fee is based on time spent and experience of staff involved, no safeguards are required

D   Taxation services cannot be accepted as there are no safeguards to reduce the threat to objectivity in the conduct of the external audit

5   The finance director further suggests that Ali & Co be paid a fixed fee for representing Stark in a dispute regarding the amount of sales tax payable to the taxation authorities.

In line with ACCA's *Code of Ethics and Conduct*, which of the following factors must be considered by Ali & Co?

A   Fixed fees are prohibited
B   The audit firm cannot perform this service
C   The fee may be contingent depending on the outcome of the dispute
D   The client's management must provide written representation that the basis of the dispute is not unlawful

(10 marks)

Question 3 LV FONES

The following scenario relates to questions 1–5

You are the audit manager of Jones & Co and you are planning the audit of LV Fones Co, which has been an audit client for four years and specialises in manufacturing luxury mobile phones.

During the planning of the audit you have ascertained the following:

The employees of LV Fones Co are entitled to purchase mobile phones at a discount of 10%. The audit team has in previous years been offered the same level of staff discount.

During the year the financial controller of LV Fones was ill and unable to work. The company had no spare staff able to fulfil the role and a qualified audit senior of Jones & Co was seconded to the client for three months. The audit partner has recommended that the audit senior work on the audit as he has good knowledge of the client. The fee income from LV Fones was boosted by this engagement and, along with the audit and tax fee, now accounts for 16% of the firm's total fees.From a review of the correspondence files you note that the audit partner and finance director have known each other socially for many years and took a family holiday together last summer. As a result of this friendship the partner has not yet spoken to the client about the fee for last year's audit, 20% of which is still outstanding.

1   From a review of the information above, your audit assistant has highlighted some of the potential risks to independence in respect of the audit of LV Fones.

Identify, by clicking on the relevant boxes in the table below, which categories of threat, if any, are presented by each potential threat to independence.

Potential threat	Category of threat		
The audit team in previous years was offered a staff discount of 10% on luxury mobile phones	Familiarity	Self-interest	Self-review
An audit senior of Jones & Co has been on secondment as the financial controller of LV Fones and is part of the current audit team	Familiarity	Self-interest	Self-review
Total fee income from LV Fones is 16% of the total fees for the audit firm	Familiarity	Self-interest	Self-review
The partner and finance director know each other socially and have holidayed together	Familiarity	Self-interest	Self-review

2   **In relation to the audit senior's work on secondment and his current position as an audit senior, which of the following safeguards should be implemented in order to comply with ACCA's *Code of Ethics and Conduct*?**

A   Jones & Co should determine what areas the audit senior assisted the client on and make sure that the senior does not audit those areas

B   An independent review partner should be appointed to oversee the work of the audit senior

C   The audit senior should be removed from the engagement

D   No safeguards are necessary as the audit senior was only on secondment to LV Fones for three months

3   **In relation to the unpaid fee still outstanding for last year's audit, what safeguard should Jones & Co implement in order to comply with ACCA's *Code of Ethics and Conduct*?**

A   Resign from the current year audit

B   Regard the outstanding fee to be a loan to the client and continue with the current year audit

C   Cease work on the current year audit until the fee is paid in full

D   Agree a payment schedule with LV Fones that results in the fees being paid before much more work is done on the current year audit

4   The finance director of LV Fones has asked the partner if Jones & Co can take on a consultancy project to evaluate several possible new sales systems, advise on which system should be selected, and oversee the installation of the new system.

Which of the following threats would arise, if the consultancy project is accepted by Jones & Co?

Select... ▼
Advocacy
Familiarity
Self-review
Intimidation

5   Jones & Co has been asked to accept nomination to take on three new statutory audit clients:

(1)   Titania Co, a listed company, will also require Jones & Co to prepare the financial statements

(2)   The finance director of Puck Co, an unlisted company, is the brother of one of the partners of Jones & Co

(3)   ArchRise Co which plans to go public in the next two years

In line with ACCA's *Code of Ethics and Conduct*, identify how Jones & Co should respond to each nomination.

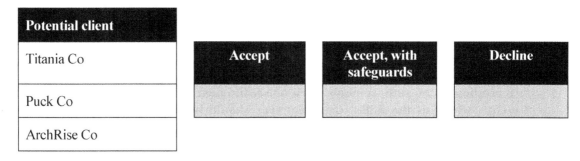

Potential client	Accept	Accept, with safeguards	Decline
Titania Co			
Puck Co			
ArchRise Co			

(10 marks)

Question 4 WILLOW WANDS

The following scenario relates to questions 1–5

You are an audit senior of Beech & Co and have been allocated to the audit of Willow Wands Co (Willow), a listed company which has been an audit client for eight years and specialises in manufacturing musical instruments.

Having completed seven years as the audit engagement partner for Willow, Bethan Oak has recently been rotated off the audit engagement. The current audit partner, Sandeep Pine, has suggested that in order to maintain a close relationship with Willow, Bethan should be the independent review partner this year. In addition, Willow has requested that Bethan assists them by attending their audit committee meetings, as a non-executive director has recently left the company.

Willow has also asked Sandeep and the other partners at Beech & Co to help them in recruiting a new non-executive director.

The total fees received by Beech & Co for last year equated to 16% of the firm's total fee income. This year's fees could be greater.

1 From a review of the information above, you have determined that there are four potential threats to independence in respect of the audit of Willow.

Indicate whether each of these potential treats is a self-interest threat or a familiarity threat.

Potential threat	Self-interest threat	Familiarity threat
The proposal that the former engagement partner be independent review partner		
The request that the former engagement partner attends audit committee meetings		
The request for help in recruiting a new non-executive director		
Total fees for the year could be greater than 16%		

2 Sandeep has been informed that the father of a new trainee assigned to the Willow audit team owns a 10% interest in Willow.

Which of the following safeguards are appropriate in this situation?

(1) Beech & Co should resign from the current period audit engagement
(2) Disposal of the interest by the team member's father
(3) Independent reviews of the audit work performed by the team member
(4) Removal of the team member from the willow engagement

A 1, 2 and 4
B 2, 3 and 4
C 1, 2 and 3
D 1, 3 and 4

3 The audit manager for Willow has just announced that he is leaving Beech & Co to join Willow as the financial controller. He will leave Beech before the commencement of the current period audit of Willow.

Which TWO of the following procedures should be implemented to ensure quality control over engagement performance?

☐ A new audit manager should be appointed

☐ Beech & Co should resign from the current period audit engagement

☐ Any work performed by the former audit manager should be independently reviewed

☐ The audit plan should be modified so that the former manager is not overly familiar with the audit approach

4 **Identify, by clicking on the relevant box in the table below, whether each statement regarding the principles of the UK Corporate Governance Code is true or false.**

There should be a rigorous and transparent procedure for the appointment of new directors to the board	TRUE	FALSE
The board should use the annual general meeting (AGM) to communicate with investors	TRUE	FALSE
The non-executive chairman should decide on the remuneration of all directors	TRUE	FALSE
All directors should receive induction training on joining the board	TRUE	FALSE

5 **Which of the following statements best expresses Beech & Co's duty of confidentiality to Willow and its other clients in respect of information acquired in the course of professional work?**

A   The auditor should only reveal confidential client data after having received consent from the client's board of directors to do so

B   The auditor must supply any client data requested of him by a shareholder at the annual general meeting

C   The auditor should never reveal client confidential data unless it is essential to the understanding of a modified auditor's report

D   The auditor should reveal certain client confidential data if there is a legal right or duty to do so

(10 marks)

Question 5 TORRES LEISURE CLUB

The following scenario relates to questions 1–5

Torres Leisure Club Co (Torres) operates a chain of health and fitness clubs. Its year end was 31 October 2016. You are the audit manager and the year-end audit is due to commence shortly. The following matter has been brought to your attention:

Torres's trade receivables have historically been low as most members pay monthly subscriptions in advance. However during the year a number of companies have taken up group memberships at Torres and hence the receivables balance is now material. The audit senior has undertaken a direct confirmation of accounts receivable balances at the year end; however, a number of customers have not responded and a number of responses show differences.

Your preliminary evaluation of Torres' internal controls over sales and accounts receivable is that they are effective in ensuring the completeness and accuracy of the accounting records because the company has implemented multiple controls, including good segregation of duties. However, the auditor is aware that the effectiveness of the company's internal controls is limited by the possibility of collusion.

1   The auditor must determine the level of reliance on internal controls and what types and extent of testing are to be performed in the audit of Torres' sales and receivables.

Indicate the proper auditor assessment for each of the categories listed below.

Reduced	High	Extensive

Auditor assessment categories	
Level of reliance on controls	
Extent of tests of controls	
Extent of substantive procedures	

2   Subscription income is material to the financial statements of Torres.

Identify, by clicking on the relevant box in the table below, whether each assertion is relevant to subscription income.

Existence	RELEVANT	NOT RELEVANT
Occurrence	RELEVANT	NOT RELEVANT
Classification	RELEVANT	NOT RELEVANT
Presentation	RELEVANT	NOT RELEVANT
Rights and obligations	RELEVANT	NOT RELEVANT

3   **Which TWO of the following audit procedures and actions are appropriate to obtain sufficient and appropriate audit evidence in relation to Torres's trade receivables?**

   ⌐   For non-responses, the audit senior should arrange to send a follow-up request for confirmation

   ⌐   If the customer does not respond to the follow up, the senior should telephone the customer and obtain verbal confirmation of the receivable balance

   ⌐   For each response with differences, the audit senior should propose adjustments for the errors in Torres's accounting records

   ⌐   Any balances that have been flagged as disputed should be discussed with management to determine whether a loss allowance is necessary

4 Another audit client, Blackmoore Co, sells around 30 units of product each year. The majority of sales are made in the first nine months of the year. Annual sales have not changed significantly in the past five years.

Which of the following approaches to the audit of revenue would be most effective in the audit of Blackmoore?

A Perform all audit procedures after the year end because the volume of transactions is low

B Perform tests of details at the end of nine months followed by analytical procedures from that interim date to the year end

C Perform analytical procedures at the end of nine months and additional analytical procedures after the year end

D Perform tests of controls at the end of nine months and tests of details at the year end

5 **In order to detect an understatement of sales, which of the following procedures would be most effective?**

A Select sales delivery notes and check the details with the related sales invoices
B Select sales invoices and check the details with the related sales orders
C Select sales invoices and check the details with the related sales delivery notes
D Select sales orders and check the details with the related sales invoices

(10 marks)

Question 6 DYLAN

The following scenario relates to questions 1–5

You are currently completing the audit of Dylan Co for the year ended 31 August. It is proposed that the financial statements will be approved on 17 November and that the auditor's report will be signed on that date. The financial statements will be issued on 5 December.

1 **Which of the following are subsequent events in line with ISA 560 *Subsequent Events*?**

(1) Events occurring after a sale is made to a customer
(2) Events occurring after any cash transaction
(3) Events occurring after the period end, but before the date of the auditor's report
(4) Facts that become known after the date of the auditor's report

A 1 and 2
B 1 and 4
C 2 and 3
D 3 and 4

2 **Identify, by clicking on the relevant box in the table below, whether each of the following statements in relation to the auditor's responsibility for subsequent events is true or false.**

The auditor has an active responsibility to make continuing inquiries between the date of the auditor's report and the date the financial statements are issued	TRUE	FALSE
The auditor has no active responsibility to make continuing inquiries after the date of the auditor's report	TRUE	FALSE
The auditor has an active responsibility to make continuing inquiries between the date of the financial statements and the date of the auditor's report	TRUE	FALSE
The auditor has an active responsibility to make continuing inquiries between the date of the financial statements and the date on which sufficient appropriate evidence has been obtained	TRUE	FALSE

3 **Which TWO actions should the auditor take if a material event occurs between 31 August and 17 November that may require amendment to, or disclosure in, Dylan's financial statements?**

☐ Advise management how to properly account for and adequately disclose the event in the financial statements

☐ If not amended or disclosed in the financial statements, qualify the auditor's report because the matter is material

☐ Write a memo for the audit file because subsequent events will affect next year's financial statements but not this year's

☐ Require management to sign a management representation letter taking responsibility for the subsequent event and its effect on future financial statements

4 Between 17 November and 5 December, the auditor becomes aware of an event that is material and may require amendment to, or disclosure in, the financial statements of Dylan.

Which of the following are actions the auditor would most likely take?

(1) Request that the financial statements as they currently stand and the auditor's report thereon should not be issued

(2) Extend the subsequent event review procedures

(3) If the financial statements are amended, provided a new auditor's report dated not earlier than the date the amended financial statements are approved

(4) Issue a qualified auditor's report because the subsequent events were not found until after the date of the initial auditor's report

A   1 and 2 only
B   1, 2 and 3
C   2 and 3 only
D   1, 3 and 4

5   ISA 560 *Subsequent Events* sets out the auditor's responsibilities for the period between the year end and the annual general meeting (AGM).

What action is the auditor required to take after signing the auditor's report and before the AGM?

Select...
Obtain a representation from the directors that no material events after the reporting period have occurred in that period of time
Search for evidence of events after the reporting period that may change the audit opinion
Consult with the directors on any events after the reporting period that might change the audit opinion
None, because the auditor's responsibilities cease after the auditor's report is signed

(10 marks)

Question 7 VIOLET & CO

The following scenario relates to questions 1–5

You are the audit manager of Violet & Co and you are currently reviewing the audit files for two of your clients for which the audit fieldwork has been completed. The audit seniors have raised the following issues:

Daisy Designs Co (Daisy)

Daisy's year end is 30 September, however, subsequent to the year end the sales ledger has been corrupted by a computer virus attack. Although Daisy's finance director was able to produce the financial statements before the attack, the audit team has been unable to access the sales ledger to undertake detailed testing of revenue or year-end receivables.

Daisy's internal auditors performed tests of control on the revenue cycle throughout the year and found them to be well-designed and working effectively. The internal auditor has confirmed that there are no backup files for the sales ledger.

All other accounting records were unaffected. Daisy's revenue is $15.6 million, its receivables are $3.4 million and profit before tax is $2 million.

Fuchsia Enterprises Co (Fuchsia)

Fuchsia has experienced difficult trading conditions and has lost significant market share. The cash flow forecast reviewed during the audit fieldwork shows a significant net cash outflow. Management is confident that further funding can be obtained and so has prepared the financial statements on the going concern basis with no additional disclosures. The audit senior is highly sceptical about this. The prior year financial statements showed a profit before tax of $1.2m; however, the current year loss before tax is $4.4 million and the forecast net cash outflow for the next 12 months is $3.2 million.

1   **Which THREE of the following audit procedures are appropriate to confirm the revenue of Daisy Designs?**

☐   Examine any alternative records which detail revenue for the year

☐   Perform analytical procedures such as monthly comparison of revenue to the prior year

☐   Agree trade receivables balances with customers through direct confirmation requests

☐   Make inquiries of the internal auditors and rely on their evaluation of the accuracy of the reported revenue

☐   Review cash receipts after year end in settlement of amounts owed at the reporting date

2   **What would be the effect on the auditor's opinion for Daisy if the auditor is unable to obtain sufficient appropriate evidence in relation to the revenue and receivables balances?**

A   Disclaimer, because the auditor is unable to form an opinion on the financial statements as a whole

B   Adverse, because the auditor cannot agree that the financial statements are fairly presented

C   Disclaimer, because the corrupted records give rise to the suspicion of fraud

D   Qualified to the effect that except for the revenue and receivables balances the financial statements are fairly presented

3   **Which of the following best describes the audit risk associated with Fuschia's cash flow forecast and whether or not it is material to the audit?**

A   The cash flow forecast is inaccurate and the amount of the forecasted cash outflow is material

B   The cash flow forecast is inaccurate, but because it is a forecast it is not material

C   Fuchsia faces going concern problems and the large decline in profits is material

D   Fuchsia is facing going concern problems but since management is confident it can obtain further funding it is not material

4 **Identify, by clicking on the relevant box in the table below, whether each of the following audit procedures is appropriate to evaluate Fuschia's ability to obtain further funding.**

Discuss with management whether any new source of finance has now been secured	APPROPRIATE	NOT APPROPRIATE
Review the most recent board minutes to see if management's view on Fuchsia's future as a going concern has changed	APPROPRIATE	NOT APPROPRIATE
Confirm with providers of loan finance that Fuchsia has been making timely payments on its debts	APPROPRIATE	NOT APPROPRIATE
Review the cash flow forecast for the next 12 months and assess the reasonableness of the assumptions used	APPROPRIATE	NOT APPROPRIATE

5 There are several dates significant in the finalisation of an audit.

Rank the following dates in chronological order from earliest to latest.

Auditor's report issued
Financial statements authorised
End of the reporting period
Financial statements issued

EARLIEST	
LATEST	

(10 marks)

Question 8 CREMORNE

The following scenario relates to questions 1–5

Cremorne is a construction company with annual sales of $350 million. Its draft financial statements shows a profit for the year ended 30 June 2016 of $40 million. This is your audit firm's first audit of Cremorne. On completing audit work at the company's premises, the following two matters are outstanding:

Inventory valuation

Inventories include $7 million, at cost, of scrap rubber which is widely used for road surfacing in many countries. The Highways Agency, which is the state authority for road construction, currently bans the use of this material. However, as this ban was known to be under review and, on being offered a special price, Cremorne speculated on a favourable outcome of the review and purchased the material. In August 2016, shortly before Cremorne's financial statements were approved, the Highways Agency reported that the ban would continue. If Cremorne uses it on non-Highways Agency contracts its net realisable value would not exceed $2 million. The finance director maintains that, as the Highways Agency' report was issued after the end of the reporting period, any write down of the inventory should be reflected only in next year's financial statements.

Depreciation

Five years ago, Cremorne purchased two earthmovers and a further two for $2.5 million each in July 2012. Depreciation has been allowed at 10% straight line. For the year just ended, Cremorne decided to scrap the first two earthmovers and replace them with the latest model at a cost of $4 million each. Cremorne's chief engineer tells you that technology is developing so rapidly that he expects such machines to be replaced every five years. The finance director claims that 10% depreciation is standard in the industry and reflects the physical life of the machines. He argues that as continued improvements in technology cannot be assumed there is no justification for increasing depreciation to 20%. If these assets are depreciated at 20% instead of 10% the additional expense would be $2 million.

1 **By what amount should inventory of scrap rubber be written down in Cremorne's financial statements for the year ended 30 June 2016?**

   [ ] $000

2 **Which of the following benchmarks are appropriate to evaluating any identified misstatement in the valuation of inventories?**

   (1)   ½% of revenue, $350 million
   (2)   5% profit, $40 million
   (3)   1% inventory, $7 million

   A   1 and 2 only
   B   2 only
   C   1, 2 and 3 only
   D   1, 2 and 3

3 **What adjustment for depreciation of the earthmovers, if any, should be made in the financial statements for the year ended 30 June 2016?**

A   Increase depreciation expense by $2 million to recognise the change in depreciation from 10% to 20% on all earthmovers

B   Increase depreciation expense by $800,000 to recognise the change in depreciation from 10% to 20% on the two new earthmovers only

C   Make no adjustment for the current year, but disclose the effect of using 20% as the depreciation rate for all new earthmovers in the notes

D   Recognise $2 million additional depreciation expense as a prior period adjustment as it is a change in accounting policy

4   The directors have decided not to make any changes to the draft financial statements in relation to the depreciation of earthmovers.

Assuming that there are no other uncorrected errors, what audit opinion will be issued?

Select... ▼
Qualified, as the matter is material when considering its cumulative effect over time
Unmodified, as the matter alone is neither material nor pervasive
Adverse, as the matter affects both total assets and profit or loss for the year
Disclaimer, as the matter is disputed with management, regardless of its materiality

5   **Identify, by clicking on the relevant box in the table below, whether each statement is a correct statement that should be included in a typical unmodified auditor's report.**

Our responsibility is to express an opinion on these financial statements based on our audit	CORRECT	INCORRECT
We believe that the audit evidence we have obtained is sufficient and appropriate to provide a basis for our audit opinion	CORRECT	INCORRECT
We conducted our audit in accordance with International Financial Reporting Standards	CORRECT	INCORRECT
From the matters communicated with those charged with governance, we determine those matters that were of most significance in the audit of the financial statements of the current period	CORRECT	INCORRECT

(10 marks)

Answer 1 SERENA

Item Answer   Justification

1

    ☑ The audit committee will provide a formal link between the auditors, the non-executive directors and the shareholders

    ☑ An audit committee can monitor and review the company's internal controls.

2

CEO, Daniel Brown		NOT INCLUDED
Two non-executive directors	INCLUDED	
Finance director		NOT INCLUDED
Three of the executive directors		NOT INCLUDED

3   A   The inclusion of share options in the directors' remuneration is an element of good corporate governance because it keeps the directors focused on the long-term. (1) does not reflect the principles of corporate governance because at least half of the board should be NEDs. (2) does not reflect the principles of corporate governance because there should be a clear division of responsibility between the CEO and the chairman of the board. (4) does not reflect the principles of corporate governance because board members should submit themselves regularly to re-election by the shareholders.

4

    ☑ Examination of financial and operational information for management

    ☑ Review of accounting systems and related controls

    ☑ Advising management on cost effective controls for systems and activities

Tutorial note: *Internal audit should not have operational responsibilities so should not authorise transactions or routinely prepare bank reconciliations.*

5   Subject to specific regulatory requirements (e.g. specific banning of the external auditor providing other services) the internal audit function may be carried out by the external auditor **when any threats to the external auditor's objectivity have been reduced to an acceptable level**.

Tutorial note: *The potential threats are self-interest and self-review. These can be reduced to an acceptable level where the work carried out by the external auditor does not involve any accounting and financial statement systems and members of the internal audit function are not involved in the external audit.*

Answer 2 STARK

Item Answer   Justification

1

Potential threat	Category of threat		
Engagement partner has been in the position for nine years	Familiarity		
The audit junior receives investment advice			
The audit team has been offered a balloon flight	Familiarity	Self-interest	
The fee for tax advisory services will be based on a percentage of tax saved		Self-interest	Self-review

That the engagement partner has been in role for nine years contravenes ACCA's *Code of Ethics and Conduct* and represents a *familiarity* threat.

That the audit junior receives investment advice is not yet a threat to independence. "As a regular client" Mr Far will have paid for the advice (i.e. a normal commercial transaction). Also, his position is not one of seniority (so is unlikely to influence the audit) and his work will be reviewed (as a normal quality control procedure).

Acceptance of gifts from a client, unless of an insignificant amount, is not allowed. The balloon flight poses *familiarity* and *self-interest* risks.

Tutorial note: *The fact that the flight costs less than the yacht expense is irrelevant.*

The fee for tax advisory is proposed on a contingency basis and raises a *self-interest* threat as Ali & Co's fee will rise if tax savings are found. There would also be a *self-review* threat since tax advice should have a bearing on calculations of current and deferred tax.

Tutorial note: *Pressure to gain the highest tax refund for the client could tempt the audit firm to suggest illegal tax avoidance schemes.*

2   **Mr Son should be removed from the audit team** as he has been a key audit partner for longer than the permitted seven-year period.

Tutorial note: *To show complete independence, Zoe should not be part of the audit team. However, if Mr Son is no longer the engagement partner then this removes the ethical threat and Zoe could be included in the audit team.*

3

☑   The extent to which the advice will be supported by tax law or regulation

☑   The extent to which the outcome of the tax advice will have a material effect on the financial statements

4   B   The contingent fee basis for the taxation services must be rejected.

5   B   Where taxation services involve acting as an advocate for an audit client before a court in the resolution of a tax matter that is material to the financial statements the advocacy threat created would be so significant that no safeguards could eliminate or reduce the threat to an acceptable level. Therefore, Ali & Co cannot perform this type of service for Stark.

Tutorial note: As the dispute concerns sales tax it will almost certainly be material (e.g. since ½ – 1% revenue is generally considered material).

Answer 3 LV FONES

Item Answer   Justification

1

Potential threat	Category of threat		
The audit team in previous years was offered a staff discount of 10% on luxury mobile phones	Familiarity	Self-interest	
An audit senior of Jones & Co has been on secondment as the financial controller of LV Fones and is part of the current audit team	Familiarity		Self-review
Total fee income from LV Fones is 16% of the total fees for the audit firm		Self-interest	
The partner and finance director know each other socially and have holidayed together	Familiarity	Self-interest	

Tutorial notes:

The audit team receiving the staff discount on the luxury phone represents a self-interest threat and a familiarity threat.

The audit senior's secondment as the financial controller of LV Fones represents a self-interest threat if he prepared records or schedules that support the year-end financial statements and then audits those documents. There is also a familiarity threat as the management and directors of LV Fones may still treat him as part of their management team.

The total fee income from LV Fones is 16% of the total fees for the audit firm. If the fees for audit and recurring work exceed 15% then there is a self-interest threat.

Personal relationships between the client and members of the audit team can create a familiarity or self-interest threat.

2   C   In relation to the self-review threat, the firm should clarify exactly what areas the senior assisted the client on. If he worked on areas not related to the financial statements then he may be able to remain in the audit team. However, it is likely that he has worked on some related schedules and therefore he should be removed from the audit team to ensure that independence is not threatened. In relation to the familiarity threat, there is no safeguard that could reduce this threat to an acceptable level. The senior should not be a member of the audit team.

3   D   Jones & Co should chase the outstanding fees. If they remain outstanding, the firm should discuss with those charged with governance the reasons for the continued non-payment, and ideally agree a payment schedule which will result in the fees being settled before much more work is performed for the current year audit.

4   **Self-review** threat – the audit firm will audit the system it has implemented.

5

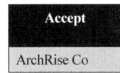 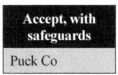 

Accept	Accept, with safeguards	Decline
ArchRise Co	Puck Co	Titania Co

Tutorial note: *Decline Titania Co as it is not acceptable to prepare and audit the financial statements of a listed company (because of self-review threat and the specific public interest of a listed company). Accept Puck Co with safeguards (e.g. not letting the FD's brother have any direct (e.g. team member) or indirect (e.g. unofficial advisor) part in the audit). The brother is a close family member (parent, child or sibling) as opposed to an immediate family member (spouse, partner or dependent). (The closer the key players are to influencing the audit or the financial decisions of the entity, the higher the probability that no safeguard would be adequate.) Accept ArchRise Co.*

Answer 4 WILLOW WANDS

Item   Answer   Justification

1

Self-interest threat	Familiarity threat
The request that the former engagement partner attends audit committee meetings	The proposal that the former engagement partner be independent review partner
The request for help in recruiting a new non-executive director	
Total fees for the year could be greater than 16%	

Tutorial note: *The proposal for the former engagement partner to undertake the role of independent review partner represents a familiarity threat as the partner will have been associated with Willow for a long period of time and so may not retain professional scepticism and objectivity. The other three potential risks represent self-interest threats.*

2   B   It is not necessary for Beech & Co to resign from the engagement because a close family member of an audit team member (and a very junior one at that) owns a financial interest in a client, although this would be an appropriate response if a family member of the *partner* owned the financial interest. The other three options listed are appropriate safeguards for this treat to independence.

3

☑ A new audit manager should be appointed

☑ The audit plan should be modified so that the manager is not overly familiar with the audit approach

Tutorial note: *Beech would not be required to resign from the engagement due to the audit manager leaving Beech to join Willow because the risks can be mitigated through quality control procedures. As the audit manager will leave before the current period audit begins there will be no work by him to be reviewed.*

4

There should be a rigorous and transparent procedure for the appointment of new directors to the board	**TRUE**	
The board should use the annual general meeting (AGM) to communicate with investors	**TRUE**	
The non-executive chairman should decide on the remuneration of all directors		**FALSE**
All directors should receive induction training on joining the board	**TRUE**	

Tutorial note: *The UK Corporate Governance Code states that no director should be involved in setting their own remuneration. Hence the non-executive chairman cannot set his own remuneration.*

5 D Under the confidentiality provisions of the ACCA's *Code of Ethics and Conduct*, disclosure should be made where there is a legal right or duty to do so. There may also be a professional duty or right to do so (e.g. to respond to an ACCA inquiry). This overrides option A.

Answer 5 TORRES LEISURE CLUB

Item   Answer   Justification

1

Auditor assessment categories	
Level of reliance on controls	High
Extent of tests of controls	Extensive
Extent of substantive procedures	Reduced

Tutorial note: *In any accounting system there are inherent limitations of the internal controls, the risk of collusion being one. However, all other factors in the scenario indicate that the internal controls over sales and accounts receivable can be relied upon if audit tests do not indicate otherwise.*

2

Existence		**NOT RELEVANT**
Occurrence	**RELEVANT**	
Classification	**RELEVANT**	
Presentation	**RELEVANT**	
Rights and obligations		**NOT RELEVANT**

Tutorial note: *Occurrence, classification and presentation are assertions relevant to subscription income. Existence and rights and obligations are not relevant because they are assertions related to account balances rather than transactions.*

3

☑ For non-responses, the audit senior should arrange to send a follow-up request for confirmation

☑ Any balances that have been flagged as disputed should be discussed with management to determine whether a loss allowance is necessary

Tutorial note: *If the customer does not respond to the follow up, alternative procedures are needed (e.g. obtaining evidence of existence, agreeing the make-up of the balance, confirming receipt of after-date cash). Just telephoning the customer is insufficient evidence.*

4   B   Interim testing is appropriate because most of the sales are made in the first nine months of the year. As revenue is a material balance, interim testing should be tests of details, followed by analytical procedures performed on transactions occurring from the interim date to the year-end date. The auditor is unlikely to perform tests of controls at an interim date.

Tutorial note: *The low volume of transactions means that it is more efficient and effective to adopt a substantive approach.*

5   A   To test for understatement the direction of the test should go from a source document up to the accounting records or financial statements. Only A and D go in this direction but in D the goods should only be recorded as a sale if they have been despatched.

Answer 6 DYLAN

Item	Answer	Justification
1	D	Subsequent events include both events occurring after the period end but before the date of the auditor's report as well as facts that become known after the date of the auditor's report.

2

The auditor has an active responsibility to make continuing inquiries between the date of the auditor's report and the date the financial statements are issued		**FALSE**
The auditor has no active responsibility to make continuing inquiries after the date of the auditor's report	**TRUE**	
The auditor has an active responsibility to make continuing inquiries between the date of the financial statements and the date of the auditor's report	**TRUE**	
The auditor has an active responsibility to make continuing inquiries between the date of the financial statements and the date on which sufficient appropriate evidence has been obtained	**TRUE**	

3

  ☑ Advise management how to properly account for and adequately disclose the event in the financial statements

  ☑ If not amended or disclosed in the financial statements, qualify the auditor's report because the matter is material

4	B	(4) is not a suitable action. As subsequent events may require amendment to, or disclosure in, the financial statements, they also require additional audit procedures on the affected transaction and account balances. However, assuming the entity correctly handles the subsequent events to the auditor's satisfaction, the auditor may still issue an unmodified report. The existence of a subsequent event is not reason alone for a issuing a qualified report.

5 **Consult with the directors on any events after the reporting period that might change the audit opinion.**

Tutorial note: *After signing the auditor' report, but before the AGM, the auditor should consult with the directors on any subsequent events of which they are aware (i.e. a "passive" review). There is no requirement in this period for an "active" review. Representations are only relevant to the audit if obtained prior to signing the auditor's report.*

Answer 7 VIOLET & CO

Item   Answer   Justification

1

☑   Examine any alternative records which detail revenue for the year

☑   Perform analytical procedures such as monthly comparison of revenue to the prior year

☑   Make inquiries of the internal auditors and rely on their evaluation of the accuracy of the reported revenue

Tutorial note: *The audit team will seek to confirm revenue (and receivables) by other means. If unable to do this, then two significant balances in the financial statements will not have been confirmed. Agreeing balances with customers and reviewing cash receipts after the year end are tests on balances and not transactions.*

2   D   If the auditor is unable to obtain sufficient appropriate evidence about the revenue and receivables balances, an opinion on these amounts in the financial statements cannot be formed. However material, the matter is unlikely to be pervasive as, for example, expense, liability, equity and other asset balances are not affected. Also, the auditor should expect to obtain some audit evidence through the use of analytical procedures.

3   C   Fuchsia is facing going concern problems as it has experienced difficult trading conditions and it has a negative cash outflow. However, the financial statements have been prepared on a going concern basis, even though it is possible that the company is not a going concern. The prior year financial statements showed a profit of $1·2m and the current financial statements show a loss before tax of $4·4m, the net cash outflow of $3·2m represents 73% of this loss (3·2 ÷ 4·4m) and hence is a material issue.

4

Discuss with management whether any new source of finance has now been secured	**APPROPRIATE**	
Review the most recent board minutes to see if management's view on Fuchsia's future as a going concern has changed	**APPROPRIATE**	
Confirm with providers of loan finance that Fuchsia has been making timely payments on its debts		**NOT APPROPRIATE**
Review the cash flow forecast for the next 12 months and assess the reasonableness of the assumptions used		**NOT APPROPRIATE**

Tutorial note: *Whether Fuchsia has been making timely payments on its debts does not necessarily affect its ability to obtain future credit. Even if the company has not yet defaulted, loan providers may be unwilling to extend further credit due to the company's decline in profits and gloomy outlook. Also, there is no need for the auditor to ask the lenders for confirmation since cash book payments against payment schedules will confirm this. The reasonableness of the assumptions used to create the cash flow forecasts also does not affect Fushia's ability to obtain future credit.*

5

EARLIEST	End of the reporting period
	Financial statements authorised
	Auditor's report issued
LATEST	Financial statements issued

Answer 8 CREMORNE

Item   Answer   Justification

1   **5000** $000

> **Tutorial note:** *The finance director's view that the write down should be reflected after the end of the reporting period is incorrect. As at the end of the reporting period the material could not be used in Highways Agency' contracts and the lower of its cost and net realisable value was $2 million. The carrying amount of inventory and profit should be reduced by $5 million.*

2   B   The traditional benchmarks from which to choose are ½–1% of revenue, 5–10% of profit and 1-2% of total assets. However, the valuation of inventory affects profit; revenue is irrelevant and so not appropriate. The inventory valuation also affects total assets (and total net assets) but the percentage applied to just *one* class of assets would need to be *more* than 1–2%.

> **Tutorial note:** *1% of $7m inventory is only $70,000. This is not appropriate (too low) as 5% of profit is $2m.*

3   A   IAS 16 *Property, Plant and Equipment* requires that useful lives of assets (accounting estimates) be reviewed regularly and that depreciation be adjusted where there is a change in useful life. The finance director's argument is irrelevant as the new earthmovers have a useful life of only five years and the useful lives of the two as yet unsold older items is also five years (as evidenced by the sale of the five year items during the year). Depreciation has already been allowed at 10% so should be increased by $2 million additional expense.

4   If Cremorne fails to adjust its financial statements, the auditor's report should be **qualified "except for"** as the matter affects is material when considering its cumulative effect over time.

> **Tutorial note:** *If there were no other uncorrected errors the auditor might consider the amount to be insufficiently material to justify issuing a modified audit opinion if the financial statements were not adjusted. It is only just material (5% of profit). It might be argued that as depreciation is based on an estimate (of the useful economic lives of the assets) it is not something that can be precise amount and, on a qualitative basis, the financial statements are not materially misstated. However, this analysis considers only the current year effect, but depreciation is accumulated. So considering the effect of depreciating at only 10% rather than 20%, the assets would be in the books at half their cost in five years' time – when they should have been written down completely.*

5

Our responsibility is to express an opinion on these financial statements based on our audit		**INCORRECT**
We believe that the audit evidence we have obtained is sufficient and appropriate to provide a basis for our audit opinion	**CORRECT**	
We conducted our audit in accordance with International Financial Reporting Standards		**INCORRECT**
From the matters communicated with those charged with governance, we determine those matters that were of most significance in the audit of the financial statements of the current period	**CORRECT**	

Tutorial note: *There is no longer a statement of responsibility "to express an opinion …". According to ISA 700 (Revised) the statement is "Our objectives are to obtain reasonable assurance about whether the financial statements as a whole are free from material misstatement ". The auditor's report would state that the audit was conducted in accordance with International Auditing Standards, not International Financial Reporting Standards.*

ABOUT BECKER PROFESSIONAL EDUCATION

Becker Professional Education provides a single destination for candidates and professionals looking to advance their careers and achieve success in:

- Accounting

- International Financial Reporting

- Project Management

- Continuing Professional Education

- Healthcare

For more information on how Becker Professional Education can support you in your career, visit www.becker.com.

Becker Professional Education
is an ACCA approved content provider

BECKER
PROFESSIONAL EDUCATION®